US-China Great Power Competition and The New World Order

Jiandong Ju

US-China Great Power Competition and The New World Order

palgrave
macmillan

Jiandong Ju
PBC School of Finance
Tsinghua University
Beijing, China

ISBN 978-981-95-3761-7 ISBN 978-981-95-3762-4 (eBook)
https://doi.org/10.1007/978-981-95-3762-4

Cover credit: Best View Stock

This Palgrave Macmillan imprint is published by the registered company Springer Nature Singapore Pte Ltd.
The registered company address is: 152 Beach Road, #21-01/04 Gateway East, Singapore 189721, Singapore

Preface

This is an English version of my Chinese book of the same title, updated to the most recent US-China tariff wars in 2025. Most of the content is translated from the Chinese version, which is based on my teaching materials from the past seven years at Tsinghua University.

The idea to publish an English version of the book is to let readers in the English-speaking world know exactly what students in one of China's top universities are taught about issues in US-China great power competition.

Following the outbreak of the US-China trade war in March 2018, I formed a "Great Power Competition" research team at the PBC School of Finance in Tsinghua University to delve into the topic.

In the spring of 2019, I introduced an undergraduate course on "US-China Trade Disputes and Reforms in Globalization" at Tsinghua University, the first undergraduate course on this topic in China (and perhaps in the world). Since then, I have been offering this course every spring semester. I always open the first class by saying: "This course is offered for the future of US-China competition, which will be on the shoulders of the students in the classroom now. My sincere hope is that young people from both countries can avoid a lose-lose competition, leading this world to a bright future!"

The course has received numerous accolades. It was recognized as an "Excellent Undergraduate Course" among Beijing universities in 2021, an "Excellent Course" by Tsinghua University in 2023, and a "National First-Class Undergraduate Course" by the Ministry of Education of the People's Republic of China, also in 2023. This book draws on my teaching materials from the course and simplifies the technical details for easier understanding.

I graduated from Tsinghua University's School of Economics and Management in 1987 and stayed on to teach. My first research topic was the opening up of Northeast Asia, which I published as an academic article, "A Proposal for Economic Cooperation in Northeast Asia," in 1989. I received my Ph.D. in economics from the Pennsylvania State University in 1995, specializing in international trade, industrial organization, and international finance. In the 1990s, the European Union, the North American Free Trade Agreement (NAFTA), and the World Trade Organization were established, leading to a wave of trade liberalization. My research focused on the tariff reforms of free trade agreements and the impact of rules of origin on welfare in affected countries. Back then, the relationship between multilateralism and regionalism and how many major regional trade agreements there should be in the world were hot topics for academic research. In the early 2000s, I proposed the idea of a tripod for global trade governance, with NAFTA, the European Union, and a hypothetical Asian Community as the three legs. Having been thinking the issue for more than 20 years, and colliding with the current practice of great power competition and the new Industrial Revolution, this idea of tripod global governance constitutes the main themes of this book. In fact, this book is the distillation of my 36 years of research on globalization.

The great Chinese historian Sima Qian (c.145–c.86 BC) once said the ideal state of scholarship is "to explore the relationship between heaven and human, to understand the changes from the past to the present, and to develop a school of thought." This book is my attempt to work along these three directions.

"To explore the relationship between heaven and human"—We reveal the core difference between the driving forces of development in the old (twentieth century) world and the new (twenty-first century) world, specifically, the shift from physical capital-driven development to human capital-driven development. Ideas, knowledge, and innovation have become the key drivers of social progress. We introduce the Innovative World Model to describe the process of Idea → Innovation → Technological Progress → Market Realization. It consists of two cycles: the cycle between the innovator (who can be compared to Sima Qian's "human") and the idea cloud (which can be compared to his "heaven") and the cycle between the innovator and the market (which can be compared to "earth"). Therefore, our Innovation World Model unifies "heaven, earth, and human." We also identify three conundrums in the innovation world: centralization versus decentralization, public versus private, and creation versus imitation.

"To understand the changes from the past to the present"—After reviewing the evolution of great power competitions and the world order going back to 1500, we posit that the world order is facing a paradigm shift from hegemonic succession to competitive coexistence. The root cause of contemporary world disorder is not the competition between China and the United States for the world hegemony, but the fundamental misalignment brought about by the mismatch between the world's economic fundamentals and its superstructure.

"To develop a school of thought"—We propose a rationalism framework for understanding great power competition and the world order. This framework is grounded in the tension among national overall, long-term, specific, and short-term interests. It integrates micro- and macroeconomics, theories of growth and crises, and constructs a theoretical model centered on long-term growth with multiple equilibria. Through this lens, we analyze the dynamics of "growth and crisis," "sharing and monopoly," and "peace and war."

This book covers hot issues, economic theory, and *weltanschauung* (worldview). Starting from the hot issues of great power competition and the new world order, we build a theoretical framework, running through our thinking on how the new world operates, with the following logical guide:

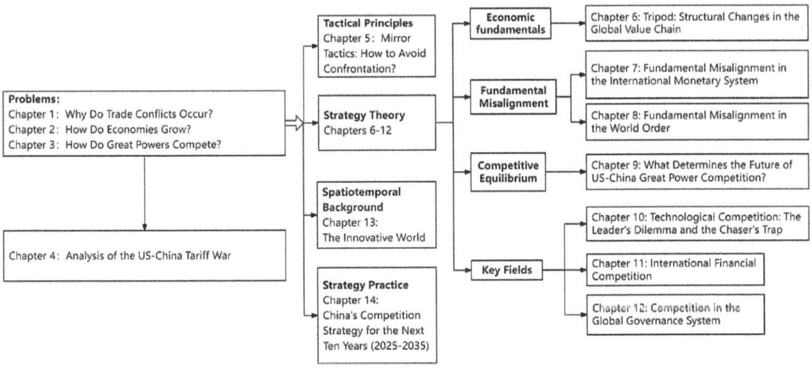

Chapters 1–3 raise questions: Why do international trade conflicts occur? How do economies grow? How do great powers compete? Chapter 4 analyzes the US-China trade dispute. The preceding four chapters present three principles and three theorems of international trade disputes, and establish a framework for analyzing conflicts in national overall, long-term, special, and short-term interests in trade disputes. Chapter 5 discusses tactics in great power competition. Chapter 6 describes structural changes in the global value chain (economic fundamentals). Chapters 7 and 8 explain fundamental misalignments in the international monetary system and the global governance system (the superstructure) vis-à-vis the economic fundamentals.

Chapter 9 builds a Growth-Crisis Model to analyze possible outcomes of US-China competition. Chapters 10–12 expand on the core areas of great power competition, namely technology, international finance, and global governance.

Chapter 13 presents the Innovative World Model and Chapter 14 draws from all the earlier chapters to lay out China's competition strategy in next ten years (2025–2035).

The compilation of this book took decades. First of all, I would like to thank my parents for raising me, for their love and care all the time. I thank my family for their support, love, and companionship; my teachers for their guidance; and my research partners for their helps

Every chapter in this book reflects the efforts of our "Great Power Competition" research team, which has held meetings almost every week for the past six years to discuss these issues, exchange ideas, review the literature, collect data, and organize the manuscript. I would like to thank the following team members: Lu Feng (Chapter 1); Bing Lu and La Wei (Chapter 2); Jianghuai Hou (Chapter 3); Xin Li and Yuankun Li (Chapter 4); Jie Ma (Chapter 5); Xinding Yu (Chapter 6); Guangtao Xia and Chen Huang (Chapter 7); Wan Peng (Chapters 8and 9); Xueyan Ma and Zhengwen Liu (Chapter 10); Yujia Yang (Chapter 11); Bin Liu and Xiaoyan Wang (Chapter 12); and Xiao Chen and Jialiang Zhang (Chapter 13). I would also like to thank Sijia Li for reading through the book and helping me organize the manuscript, and Zhiwei Xia for supporting the team administratively and logistically.

Throughout my seven years of teaching at Tsinghua University, I have been fortunate to have students who were enthusiastic in asking questions and participating in discussions. They have contributed to the continuous improvement of the course.

I am grateful to editors Meng Niu, Jiancheng Liang, and Ruimin Liu for helping me move my course from the university classroom to *Dedao* podcasts, "21 Lectures on International Trade Disputes," in 2021; and editors from Peking University Press, Junxiu Lin, Juan Li and Jingya Yan, for their hard work editing the Chinese version of the book. Finally, I would like to thank, without implicating, Dr. Ling Hui Tan for her help reviewing and editing the English version of the book.

US-China great power competition kicked off seven years ago in the last Trump administration and has entered the new stage in this Trump administration. This book is only the beginning of our exploration of it. As the world order changes, we will observe, reflect, and continuously improve our theories. Let's be a witness this history and welcome the bright future.

Beijing, China Jiandong Ju

Competing Interests The author has no competing interests to declare that are relevant to the content of this manuscript.

Contents

List of Figures

List of Tables

CHAPTER 1

Why Do Trade Conflicts Occur?

On December 25, 1991, Soviet President Mikhail Gorbachev announced his resignation, transferring state power to Russian President Boris Yeltsin. At 19:32 that day, the Soviet flag slowly descended over the Kremlin and was replaced by the Russian flag. The dissolution of the Soviet Union marked the end of the US-Soviet rivalry that started after World War II.

In January 1993, at a summit in Moscow, President Yeltsin and US President George H.W. Bush signed the second phase of the Strategic Arms Reduction Treaty, committing to reducing their stock of nuclear weapons by two-thirds. People around the world rejoiced, and the sunshine of peace seemed to finally dispel the nuclear cloud that had shrouded the world for half a century.

Almost 30 years later, on February 21, 2022, in a televised speech at the Kremlin, Russian President Vladimir Putin angrily asked the United States: "All right, you do not want to see us as friends or allies, but why make us an enemy?"[1] On February 24, Putin, unable to suppress his disappointment and anger toward the West, gave another televised speech where he said: "They deceived us, they lied."[2] He then announced the start of a "special military operation" involving more than a hundred thousand Russian soldiers

[1] President of Russia. "Address by the President of the Russian Federation," February 21, 2022. http://www.en.kremlin.ru/events/president/transcripts/67828, accessed on November 29, 2025

[2] President of Russia. "Address by the President of the Russian Federation," February 24, 2022. http://www.en.kremlin.ru/events/president/transcripts/67843, accessed on November 29, 2025.

J. Ju, *US-China Great Power Competition and The New World Order*, https://doi.org/10.1007/978-981-95-3762-4_1

in eastern Ukraine, sparking the largest scale war in Europe since World War II! On February 27, Putin ordered Russia's nuclear deterrent forces to be put on "combat alert," once again casting a nuclear shadow over the world.

The question asked by Putin to the United States—"Why do you want to be our enemy?"—raises a profound conundrum for great powers: even if they cannot be friends and allies, can't they coexist peacefully?

The exploration of competitive coexistence among major powers is the main theme of this book.

Competition between the world's dominant (hegemonic) nations and their challengers—referred to in this book as great power competition—has occurred several times in the past 500 years. For example: the struggle for maritime supremacy between Spain and Portugal at the end of the fifteenth century; the Anglo–Dutch Wars from the mid-seventeenth century to the late eighteenth century; the Anglo-French contest from the latter half of the seventeenth century to the mid-eighteenth century; the Anglo-German contest from 1885 to 1945; the Anglo-American competition from the 1880s to the 1940s; the Cold War between the United States and the Soviet Union from the 1940s to 1991; the US-Japan trade disputes from the 1960s to the 1990s; and the ongoing US-China competition that began in 2018.

Why do great powers compete? How do they compete? What defines winning or losing? Can great powers coexist? The answers to these questions determine the direction of the world order and affect the lives and welfare of the people in the world, especially those in the countries directly involved in great power competition. Investigating these questions is the main objective of this book.

In great power competition, war is the most brutal form. However, military competition is not the only form of competition; with today's nuclear deterrence, non-military forms of competition—such as trade, technology, finance, and global governance—have become more prevalent. When the Russia-Ukraine conflict broke out, US President Biden immediately promised that the United States would not send troops to Ukraine, but at the same time he announced comprehensive financial and economic sanctions against Russia. Thus, this book focuses on non-military competition between great powers, such as conflicts in trade, finance, technology, and global governance.

Let's start with the US-China trade conflict!

1.1 The Outbreak of the US-China Trade War

On March 23, 2018, US President Donald Trump signed a memorandum announcing plans to impose a 25% tariff on $50 billion worth of products imported from China under Section 301 of the 1974 Trade Act, triggering the US-China trade war.[3]

West of the Pacific in Beijing, people were shocked by this event. After all, just a few months earlier in November 2017, Trump had made a three-day visit to China, during which Chinese and American companies signed 34 cooperation projects with a total contract value of $253.5 billion—a new record in the history of US-China economic and trade cooperation. Relations between the two countries seemed to be at a peak. How could a trade war have erupted just a few months later?

Since the establishment of diplomatic relations between China and the United States in 1979, bilateral trade between the two countries has soared despite constant frictions. The United States launched Section 301 investigations into goods imported from China five times prior to 2018—in 1991, 1992, 1994, 1996, and 2010. Each time, the United States threatened to impose tariffs on Chinese imports, a resolution was reached at the last moment. Therefore, many assumed that, as in the past, Trump's tariff threat was just an expression of dissatisfaction and the two sides would eventually find a way to reconcile.

However, this time it was different. On June 15, 2018, the Office of the United States Trade Representative released a list of goods imported from China valued at $50 billion that would be subject to an additional 25% tariff. Subsequently, China announced a retaliatory list of goods imported from the United States, also valued at $50 billion, that would be subject to an additional 25% tariff. The tariff war had begun.

Contrary to China's initial perception of this event, people east of the Pacific in the United States did not perceive the US-China trade dispute as a sudden occurrence, but rather as an inevitable event that was 20 years late.

Even in the 1990s, when globalization was rapidly gaining ground, voices opposing trade liberalization were constantly heard within the United States. Ross Perot, a billionaire who ran for the US presidency in 1992 and 1996, primarily campaigned on a foreign policy platform opposing free trade with Mexico, arguing that it would lead to unemployment for manufacturing workers at home.

After the dissolution of the Soviet Union at the end of 1991, the United States' global leadership reached its peak. Thereafter, the United States began to view China as a potential competitor. From the 1990s onward, US-China relations became a significant issue in every US presidential election.

[3] 301 refers to Section 301 of the United States' "Trade Act of 1974," which stipulates that the Office of the United States Trade Representative can use this clause to investigate its trade partner countries. Investigations based on Section 301 are referred to as "301 investigations."

In the 2000 US presidential election, candidate George W. Bush criticized President Clinton's China policy and, for the first time, proposed shifting the US-China relationship from "strategic partnership" to "strategic competition." In 2001, Bush was sworn in as President of the United States, but before he could fulfill his campaign promise to change the position of US-China relations, the shocking 9/11 terrorist attack occurred and US foreign policy quickly turned to counter-terrorism. The United States needed China's support for its global counter-terrorism operations and postponed the plan to change the US-China relationship. In 2001, China joined the World Trade Organization (WTO)—direct investment by US multinational corporations in China flourished, and the global value chain presented a beautiful landscape of "American design, Chinese manufacture."

In the 2008 US presidential election, candidate Barack Obama criticized President Bush's China policy and once again proposed to change the US-China relationship. However, the global financial crisis broke out in September that year, and the US financial system was on the verge of collapse. The United States once again needed China to stand with it to jointly combat the economic recession brought about by the crisis. And once again, the United States had to postpone the plan to change the position of US-China relations.

When the US-China trade war broke out in 2018, it seemed to many in the United States that the long-awaited change in US-China relations had finally arrived!

From July 6, 2018, when China and the United States implemented the first round of additional tariffs, to January 15, 2020, when the first phase of an economic and trade agreement was signed in Washington, the two countries imposed five rounds of tariffs on each other. In 2020, the average tariff on US imports from China increased from 3% before the trade war to 19.3%, and the average tariff on China's imports from the United States increased from 8% before the trade war to 21.2%.[4]

On October 4, 2018, US Vice President Mike Pence delivered a speech at a US think tank, where he openly, comprehensively, and systematically criticized China from political, diplomatic, economic, military, and even historical perspectives.[5] From then on, the US-China conflict extended from the trade field to the ideological field, quickly expanding from a tariff war to technology disputes, investment disputes, and restrictions on personnel exchanges. The United States imposed sanctions on Chinese high-tech companies such as ZTE and Huawei. From 2018 to 2021, more than 500 Chinese entities and high-tech companies were added to the US government's sanctions list.

[4] "U.S.-China Trade War Tariffs: A Timeline," *Peterson Institute for International Economics*, last modified March 13, 2019. https://www.piie.com/research/piie-charts/2019/us-china-trade-war-tariffs-date-chart, accessed on November 29, 2025.

[5] Pence, Mike. "Remarks by Vice President Pence on the Administration's Policy Toward China." *The White House*, October 4, 2018. https://trumpwhitehouse.archives.gov/briefings-statements/remarks-vice-president-pence-administrations-policy-toward-china/, accessed on November 29, 2025.

Even after the COVID-19 pandemic broke out at the beginning of 2020, the Trump administration did not relax trade measures against China but instead, intensified them. On January 14, 2021, in the last week of the Trump administration's term, the US Department of Commerce added more than 10 Chinese high-tech companies to the sanctions list.

The escalating rhetoric and actions of the Trump administration even raised serious concerns within the US military. Mark Milley, Chairman of the US Joint Chiefs of Staff, made two separate calls to Li Zuocheng, Chief of the Joint Staff Department of the Central Military Commission of the Communist Party of China, in October 2020 and January 2021, respectively. Aiming to ease tensions between the two countries, Milley explicitly stated that the United States would not take proactive confrontational military actions. He even convened senior US military officials to review the nuclear weapon launch procedures and require that any launch orders from President Trump be approved by the Chairman of the Joint Chiefs of Staff.[6]

On January 20, 2021, Joe Biden was inaugurated as President of the United States, and the US-China trade war entered a new phase. Although the Biden administration has diverged from the Trump administration on domestic policies, it has continued the direction of US-China competition initiated during Trump's tenure. At the legislative level, the US Congress passed the "U.S. Innovation and Competition Act of 2021" and the "America COMPETES Act of 2022" to set the tone for competition with China.[7] At the executive level, President Biden signed the "Executive Order on Promoting American Economic Competition" and the "100-Day Supply Chain Review" to strengthen the domestic consensus on containing China. Biden considers China as "America's most serious competitor."[8] Unlike Trump's solo fight against China, Biden is uniting all possible forces globally to compete with China.

Donald Trump returned to the presidency on January 20, 2025; the US-China trade war entered the third stage. On February 4, 2025, President Trump raised tariffs on all imported goods from China by 10%, and on March 4, 2025, he raised tariffs on China by another 10%. On April 2, 2025, through a national emergency declaration, President Trump announced a "reciprocal tariff policy" in which he imposed an additional 34% tariff against China. China immediately responded with tariffs of the same amount on the United

[6] Collinson, Stephen. "Mark Milley Says He Took 'Oath to Constitution,' Not to Trump." *CNN*, September 28, 2021. https://edition.cnn.com/2021/09/28/politics/mark-milley-donald-trump-capitol-hill/index.html, accessed on November 29, 2025.

[7] "H.R. 4521, the America COMPETES Act of 2022." *U.S. House of Representatives*, 2023. https://adamsmith.house.gov/sites/evo-subsites/adamsmith.house.gov/files/2023-12/America-COMPETES-Act_Fact-Sheet.pdf, accessed on November 29, 2025.

[8] Biden, Joe. "Remarks by President Biden on America's Place in the World," *The White House*, February 5, 2021. https://www.whitehouse.gov/briefing-room/speeches-remarks/2021/02/04/remarks-by-president-biden-on-americas-place-in-the-world/, accessed on November 29, 2024.

States. The US-China trade war then escalated. By April 11, 2025, the tariff rates imposed by the United States and China on all imported goods from each other became prohibitive and reached 145% and 125%, respectively. After several rounds of negotiations, both nations reached agreement in which United States reduced its reciprocal tariff to 10% (excluding pre-negotiation average tariffs), and China dropped its high tariffs to 10%.

In China, people's understanding of the US-China trade war has evolved and deepened in recent years. As Ren Zhengfei, president of Huawei, said: "At first, we really thought we had made some mistakes and [we] were self-examining and self-correcting; then the second and third blows came, each harder than the last, and we realized they wanted to kill us."[9] Initially, the Chinese people thought the US-China trade conflict was just a trade dispute, but as the dispute expanded and US measures became increasingly severe, the core of the US-China trade war gradually became clear: this is actually a fight for the international order. The United States, in order to protect its own interests, aims to contain China's development and prevent China from challenging its world hegemony.

1.2 My Two Stories

Regarding the US-China great power competition, there seems to be a systematic cognitive bias among the people living on both sides of the Pacific. One of the purposes of this book is to bridge this cognitive gap through an objective, rational and systematic analysis.

I was born in Rugao City, Jiangsu Province, China, in 1963. In 1990, when I was 27 years old, I went to the United States to study and work. After living in the United States for 25 years, I resigned from my professorship at the University of Oklahoma in 2014 and returned to China. I have spent about half of my adult life in China and half in the United States. I have witnessed the changes in US-China relations and the changes in people's perceptions. My personal observations may help readers understand the evolution of US-China relations. Here, let me first share two stories about my departure from the United States.

Resignation

In July 2014, on a hot summer afternoon at the University of Oklahoma, sunlight filtered through the leaves, casting a mottled shadow on the ground. I walked into the office of Kelly R. Damphousse, the Dean of the College of Arts and Sciences.

[9] "Ren Zhengfei: The Past Strategy Was Skewed, and the Capability Did Not Meet the Real-Life Needs," *The Paper*, January 22, 2021. https://www.thepaper.cn/newsDetail_forward_10899453, accessed on November 29, 2025.

"Jiandong, congratulations on your appointment as the Dean of the School of International Business Administration at Shanghai University of Finance and Economics!" Kelly handed me a cup of coffee.

"Thank you, Kelly! This is my application for a year's leave, as always. Could you sign it for me?"

"No rush, no rush, I rarely see you. let's chat for a while." Kelly waved the application form in his hand.

Later, he looked up from his computer screen and said slowly, "In the past five years, you've been at the school for only four months each year."

"How could that be? I return to school every spring to teach!" I felt something was off.

"You return every New Year and leave for China in May," Kelly continued with a smile, though it seemed a bit forced. "Jiandong, we're old friends now. I can't approve your leave anymore."

I was silent for a while, then argued: "I'm doing research in international trade. As you know, China is now the largest goods trading country in the world...".

Kelly stopped me with a look, "Jiandong, I'm the Dean. Your colleagues and students in the department have been complaining about not seeing you."

"So what should I do?"

Kelly turned his head away from me, "You have two choices: either you return to school, no more leave; or you resign."

Twenty minutes later, as Kelly was signing my resignation letter, he suddenly looked up and asked skeptically, "How much salary does Shanghai University of Finance and Economics offer you?"

"The same as you offer."

That day was my birthday.

Handing in the Green Card

(Six months later).

In January 2015, at San Francisco International Airport, the immigration officer looked at me from behind his glasses and asked: "What brings you to the United States?"

"A conference."

"What conference?"

"The American Economic Association Annual Meeting."

He looked back at his computer screen, stood up, and said, "Come with me."

I followed him into a room next to the airport exit.

"Mr. Ju," he beckoned to me, "I've looked at your records. For the past four years, you've been in the United States for less than half a year each year."

I knew what he was going to say. "Sir, I work in China."

He nodded. "You're an economist?"

"Yes."

"I give you two choices: either return to work in the United States and live here at least half a year each year, or hand in your green card and cancel your permanent resident status."

"Sir," I looked at him, "Are there any other choices?"

He forced a smile: "No, Mr. Ju." He turned to look at his computer screen.

"Oh my God!" he suddenly exclaimed. "You've had your green card for 22 years! All these years, why didn't you become a US citizen? If you became a citizen, you could work in any country!"

I looked at him, not knowing what to say.

He was silent for a moment, expressionless; then he handed me the passport: "You can enter this time, but after returning to China, you need to hand in your green card at the US embassy. The next time you come to the US, you will need a visa."

He escorted me out of the room and suddenly patted my shoulder: "Mr. Ju, has China's economy surpassed the United States'?"

I looked at him and smiled, saying, "This is a bit complicated. According to the International Monetary Fund's purchasing power parity calculations, China has surpassed the United States. However, in terms of nominal GDP (Gross Domestic Product), it has not yet."

He shrugged: "I don't quite understand."

I extended my hand, shook hands with him and said goodbye: "You're welcome to visit China."

My two stories may help to illustrate that conflicts between great powers do not suddenly erupt. Long before we witness the symbolic events of great power competition, those who live and work in, and communicate between, the two countries year-round have more or less felt signs of a competitive streak. We can even argue that this competitive attitude has been long-standing and always simmering in the background.

1.3 How to Analyze International Trade Conflicts?

The US-China trade war and potential reform of the world order will profoundly affect the life of everyone in this world for the next decade, the century, or even the millennium. Establishing an analytical framework for international trade disputes and the evolution of the world order is the purpose of this book.

You might ask: Since this issue is so important, isn't there an existing theoretical framework that can be used to analyze it? This is the question we will answer in this section.

1.3.1 The Powerless Mainstream Economics: Arrow's Impossibility Theorem

Paul Samuelson, one of the most important founders of modern mainstream (neoclassical) economics, a Nobel laureate, and a professor at the

Massachusetts Institute of Technology, defined economics as "the study of how scarce resources are allocated." Among the ten principles of economics summarized by Harvard Professor Gregory Mankiw in his globally popular textbook, *Principles of Economics*, the fifth is: "Trade can benefit everyone." Neoclassical economics believes that the division of labor results in increased economic output, which allows for exchange and trade. Since the optimal division of labor is determined by a country's comparative advantage, exchange and trade realize the effective allocation of resources internationally. Hence, free trade benefits everyone in the trading countries.

So the question arises: If international trade benefits everyone, why are there international trade conflicts?

In fact, the division of labor and free trade creates winners and losers within a trading country, but everyone is better off only if the winners can find a way to compensate the losers. In other words, free trade makes the cake larger but it does not by itself guarantee that everyone gets a larger slice.

Neoclassical economics focuses on the aspect of effective allocation of scarce resources, but glosses over the distributional aspect. Modern mainstream economics, especially international trade theory, provides a good analytical framework for explaining the international specialization of production based on comparative advantage and demonstrating how this improves the efficiency of international resource allocation. However, it is silent when it comes to explaining the optimal distribution of economic output within and across countries.

Neoclassical economics is built upon strict mathematical models and statistical analysis. The most important foundation of the mathematical analysis framework in neoclassical economics is the theory of optimization under constraints, which is used to describe consumer behavior and producer behavior. Consumer behavior is analyzed with the utility maximization model (maximizing the consumer's utility subject to their budget constraint), and producer behavior is analyzed with the profit maximization model (maximizing the firm's profit subject to its cost of production). The optimization model is a good tool for analyzing individual behavior, but it encounters insurmountable obstacles when analyzing social behavior, especially in situations where individuals have conflicting interests. In order to apply the optimization method, social optimality must be defined. But does social optimality exist?

Nobel laureate Kenneth Arrow's "Impossibility Theorem" proves that when a group has three or more people and each person has three or more choices, the social preference of this group cannot be determined by voting. If the social preference cannot be determined, social optimality cannot be determined and it becomes very hard to use the optimization method to analyze distributional problems.

How to understand Arrow's impossibility theorem? Let's take an example of three people and three choices. Suppose Michael, Peter, and Robert are going out for breakfast together. They can go to the sandwich shop (Bread), the

Table 1.1 Individual rankings of three breakfast options

Ranking	*Michael*	*Peter*	*Robert*
Most preferred	Bread	Cereal	Noodle
Second preference	Cereal	Noodle	Bread
Third preference	Noodle	Bread	Cereal

porridge shop (Cereal), or the noodle shop (Noodle). The three individuals' preferences for these three options are shown in Table 1.1.

The three people have different preferences, so they decide where to go by voting.

First compare Bread and Cereal: both Michael and Robert prefer Bread and only Peter prefers Cereal. Majority rules, so Bread has more votes than Cereal.

Then compare Cereal and Noodle: both Michael and Peter prefer Cereal and only Robert prefers Noodle. Majority rules, so Cereal has more votes than Noodle.

Since the three people have decided that Bread is better than Cereal, and Cereal is better than Noodle, assuming that preferences are transitive, Bread ought to be better than Noodle. But both Peter and Robert prefer Noodle and only Michael prefers Bread, so Noodle has more votes than Bread.

Therefore, the group preferences decided by the three individuals voting are contradictory. According to the principle of transitive preferences, Bread is better than Noodle; but in direct voting, Noodle is better than Bread. As a result, the three individuals are unable to rank Bread, Cereal, and Noodle by the method of majority rule.

This example reflects the core of Arrow's Impossibility Theorem, that is, under general conditions, social preferences cannot be obtained by ranking different choices and voting by majority rule. If social preferences cannot be expressed as a social utility function, we cannot use the optimization method to solve social economic problems.

The core of social problems is income distribution. For example, suppose there is a total income of \$99 to be distributed among Michael, Peter, and Robert. Let (x, y, z) be the income distribution where x represents the amount to Michael; y, the amount to Peter; and z, the amount to Robert. Is it appropriate to distribute the aggregate income equally (33, 33, 33), or is it appropriate for Michael to get a larger share like (59, 20, 20) or even the vast majority like (95, 2, 2) and why? To analyze such questions, neoclassical economics is a bit at a loss. Conflicting interests between countries are essentially an international income distribution question. Neoclassical economics avoids discussing such a core issue of international trade, since there is no acceptable model of optimization with which to analyze it.

Although social preferences are hard to determine, economics often uses the principle of potential Pareto improvement: if the total benefits to society exceed the losses, then the government can implement a policy to make transfer payments from the beneficiaries to compensate the losers so that everyone's welfare improves.

However, the principle of potential Pareto improvement cannot be applied to international income distribution, because there does not exist such a world government to implement cross-national transfer payments by taking from the rich countries to supplement the poor countries.

1.3.2 Rational Analysis

Rational analysis in economics refers to the individual maximization of benefits: an action will be observed only if the benefit exceeds the cost to the action-taker. The inability to use optimization theory to solve the problem of optimal international income distribution does not mean that we cannot use rational analysis in economics to study international trade conflicts. In our analysis of trade conflicts, we still assume that each country, enterprise, and individual pursues the maximization of their own interests, and different individuals compete with one another in the process of maximizing their own interests to reach an equilibrium.

While we still use rational analysis, taking maximization of own interests (individual, group, national, global) as the core concept for analyzing international trade conflicts and the evolution of the world order, we are not constrained by optimization models and do not pursue the global social optimum. In other words, we seek reasonableness, not optimality; this book aims to explain "what is and why," not "what should be."

We will employ rational analysis to analyze not just economic issues and economic determinants. We try to incorporate our analytical framework into all important factors that affect international trade conflicts and the evolution of world order, such as international security, power, politics, culture, etc. Our analytical framework starts with national interests, focusing on long-term growth, and then analyzes international conflicts stemming from misalignments in countries' economic fundamentals, the international monetary system, and global governance.

Any international trade conflict is a conflict between national interests, so we start with national interests. Long-term growth not only represents the long-term and overall interests of a country, but also determines the country's strength, so we focus on long-term growth. The world order is the most important determinant of world peace and economic growth. Misalignments in country economic fundamentals, the international monetary system, and global governance lead to international conflicts that ultimately determine the evolution of the world order, so we analyze the conflicts resulting from these misalignments.

In this chapter, we first establish a framework for analyzing competing overall and long-term national interests of countries. In Chapter 4, we will establish a framework for analyzing competing specific and short-term interests of countries.

1.4 Three Principles in International Trade Conflicts

There are two aspects of any international trade activity: one is effective resource allocation across countries, determined by the classic principle of comparative advantage; the other is competing national interests of countries. In this section, we use the principle of international monopoly profits to illustrate competing overall national interests of countries, and the principle of the "growth trap of specialization solidification" to illustrate conflicting long-term national interests of countries.

In 1865, British economist William Jevons said with great passion: "The plains of North America and Russia are our corn fields; Chicago and Odessa our granaries; Canada and the Baltic are our timber forests; Australasia contains our sheep farms, and in Argentina and on the western prairies of North America are our herds of oxen; Peru sends her silver, and the gold of South Africa and Australia flows to London; the Hindus and the Chinese grow tea for us, and our coffee, sugar and spice plantations are in all the Indies. Spain and France are our vineyards and the Mediterranean our fruit garden; and our cotton grounds, which for long have occupied the Southern United States, are now being extended everywhere in the warm regions of the earth."[10]

We can explain Jevons' grandiose statement with three major principles. The first is international specialization driven by the comparative advantage. In his statement, he lists the products that each region will produce according to their comparative advantage (but he does not mention Britain, so what does Britain produce? Britain, of course, specializes in the production of "advanced" industrial goods, such as cloth and steel). The second is the principle of international monopoly profits: North America, Russia, South Africa, Australia, India, and China are all "ours." Who gets the gains from trade brought about by this international specialization? That, of course, is "ours"! Every penny of profit from these countries must be squeezed out by Britain's monopoly power and turned into shiny silver flowing to Britain. The third is the growth trap of specialization solidification. These "poor countries" can only specialize in agricultural and mineral products; they cannot "steal" the textile machinery and other industrial technologies of the British Empire, and they cannot compete with the "rich countries" in the production of industrial goods—they are stuck in the international specialization rut of agriculture and mining, and will not catch up with the British Empire or challenge its industry.

[10] Jevons, William Stanley, *The Coal Question: An Enquiry Concerning the Progress of the Nation, and the Probable Exhaustion of Our Coal-mines*, Pantianos Classics, 1866.

1.4.1 Comparative Advantage: Efficient International Resource Allocation

Comparative advantage is a fundamental principle in the theory of international trade. It is measured by the relative cost (or opportunity cost) of producing a good. The idea is that each country should produce and export those goods that have a lower opportunity cost for them. In other words, each country should specialize in those goods in which it has a comparative advantage.

For example, suppose Microsoft founder Bill Gates writes programs faster than his nanny and cooks better than his nanny. Then why doesn't Bill Gates write programs and cook his own food? Because if Bill Gates cooks on his own, then he has less time to write programs. In other words, relative to writing programs, the opportunity cost of cooking for Bill Gates is much higher than the opportunity cost of cooking for his nanny. Therefore, according to the principle of comparative advantage, Bill Gates should specialize in writing programs, and his nanny will specialize in cooking. The logic of specialization between countries is the same as in this example.

In international trade, we often use the example of two countries (Britain and India) and two goods (cloth and tea). If the cost of producing cloth relative to tea is lower in Britain than in India, then Britain has a comparative advantage in cloth production. Correspondingly, India has a comparative advantage in tea production. Therefore, Britain should produce more cloth while India should produce more tea, and the two countries should trade with each other, with Britain exporting cloth to and importing tea from India, and India exporting tea to and importing cloth from Britain. If each country specializes in doing what they are better at and the two countries trade with each other, resource allocation efficiency will be improved and they will each get more cloth and more tea than if they produced both goods on their own. Hence, international specialization and trade will improve welfare for both countries.

The determinants of comparative advantage are identified in two classic models: the technology-based model of David Ricardo and the factor endowment-based model of Eli Heckscher and Bertil Ohlin. In addition to these two classic models, Shang-Jin Wei and I proposed an institution-based comparative advantage model in 2005.[11]

The Ricardian model compares the relative labor productivity in producing two products. The Heckscher-Ohlin model compares the factor composition of the two products. In the above example, cloth is a capital-intensive product, while tea is a labor-intensive product. Britain is relatively capital-abundant, while India is relatively labor-abundant. Therefore, Britain has a comparative

[11] Ju, Jiandong and Shang-Jin Wei, "Endowment versus Finance: A Wooden Barrel Theory of International Trade," *CEPR Working Paper* 5109, 2005; Ju, Jiandong and Shang-Jin Wei, "When Is Quality of Financial System a Source of Comparative Advantage?" *Journal of International Economics*, 2011, 84, 178–187.

advantage in capital-intensive cloth production, while India has a comparative advantage in labor-intensive tea production.

Overall, the logic of comparative advantage is that each country participates in international specialization in the production of goods according to their relative costs, and trade between countries benefits all participating countries and improves their welfare.

Of course, these are all theories. What is international trade like in the real world?

Looking back through the history of international trade, we find that it is often paved by war and conquest, accompanied by blood and fire. For example, trade between Britain and India began in the seventeenth century, but the trade relationship between the two countries was not as simple as India exchanging tea for British cloth; the process was accompanied by conflict and war. The famous British East India Company established immigrant strongholds along the coast of India from 1609 and had absolute authority in India. In 1858, the British government officially took over India, making it one of Britain's most important colonies worldwide. If international specialization and trade can benefit both countries without any damage to them, why would Britain go to war to colonize India? Keep in mind that war and colonization come at a huge cost. If both countries involved in international trade always benefit from trade, why couldn't Britain simply trade with India?

These questions cannot be explained by the principle of comparative advantage, which only emphasizes the benefit of trade. We need to introduce two other principles to analyze competing national interests in international trade: the principle of international monopoly profits and the principle of the growth trap of specialization solidification.

1.4.2 *International Monopoly Profits: Competing Overall National Interests*

The principle of international monopoly profits refers to a country or its enterprises using their dominant position in the world market to obtain monopoly profits[12] from international trade. The struggle for market dominance can lead to international trade conflicts. We use the principle of international monopoly profits to analyze competing overall national interests between countries in international trade. Simply put, the principle of comparative advantage explains how to enlarge the pie through international specialization, while the principle of international monopoly profits explains how countries use their dominant position to divide the pie in their favor.

Let's return to the example of trade in tea and cloth between Britain and India. That example tells us that according to their comparative advantage, Britain will produce and export cloth, while India will produce and export

[12] In this book, monopoly refers to dominant firms charging price above the marginal cost, not necessarily a single producer in the market.

tea. But how are the international prices of tea and cloth determined? The classic comparative advantage model, whether it is the Ricardian model or the Heckscher-Ohlin model, assumes that the free trade prices of tea and cloth are determined in a perfectly competitive market where individual traders have no market power.

Suppose the relative (opportunity) cost of producing cloth to tea is 1 in Britain and 4 in India, that is, the resources used to produce one unit of cloth can otherwise be used to produce one unit of tea in Britain but four units of tea in India. For specialization and trade to take place, the free trade relative price of cloth to tea must fall between 1 and 4. For example, the free trade price of one unit of cloth can be $2 and the free trade price of one unit of tea, $1. Then the relative price of cloth to tea is 2—that is, one unit of cloth is worth two units of tea—and both countries will find it worthwhile to specialize and trade. But if the relative price is lower than 1, Britain would not find it worthwhile to export cloth (and import tea) and if the relative price is higher than 4, India would not find it worthwhile to import cloth (and export tea).

However, the assumption that free trade prices are determined by perfect competition does not always conform to reality.

We all know that international trade is driven by traders, and large multinational trading companies typically have significant monopoly and/or monopsony power. For instance, the British East India Company was not a small company in a competitive market. It had a vast organizational structure in India, even owning an army; it was essentially a powerful small empire. The free trade relative price of goods was not determined by perfect competition in the international market, but by the British East India Company thanks to its dominant market position, which determined how the gains from trade were shared between Britain and India.

Under this scenario, in the previous example, the relative price of cloth to tea under free trade depends on the relative strengths of the bargaining power held by Britain and India in the international market. If India's bargaining power is stronger, the pricing will favor the tea produced by India, and the relative price of cloth to tea will drop to the lowest value of 1. The historical fact is that Britain's conquest and colonization gave the British East India Company absolute dominance, so Britain could raise the relative price of cloth to tea to the highest level of 4. This way, Britain could obtain all the gains from trade while India would be no better off than it was before opening up to trade.

The painful experience of "free trade" between India and Britain has made the Indian people not so favorable toward international trade. Even now, India's domestic market is not very open. Of course, that is another story.

Looking back at the international trade conflicts between China and Britain, we can better understand the principle of international monopoly profits. After the Industrial Revolution, Britain needed a market to sell its goods. At the time, Chinese tea, silk, porcelain, and other luxury goods were very popular in the European market, while British exports of wool, tweed, and other industrial products were not very attractive to the Chinese. This caused a huge trade deficit for Britain vis-à-vis China. By the 1820s and 1830s, Britain's trade deficit with China was as high as two to three million taels of silver per year.

The capitalists of Britain could not accept such a situation. At first they protested strongly through diplomatic channels, but when this was ineffective, they resorted to a despicable method: smuggling a special commodity into China in large quantities—opium. As more and more Chinese people became addicted, the opium trade brought astonishing profits to the British bourgeoisie, the British government, the British East India Company, and opium dealers. It also broke China's trade advantage with Britain, turning China's trade surplus with Britain of more than two hundred years into a deficit. The opium trade caused serious harm to Chinese society. The Qing government took a series of measures to stop the opium trade, such as the famous Humen destruction of opium by Qing Governor General Lin Zexu. All of this eventually led to Britain launching the First Opium War against China in June 1840.

In Britain, the Opium War was termed the "Trade War." Essentially, it was a war triggered by Britain in order to gain control of trade with China, and thus obtain dominance, even by selling opium for exorbitant profits. This example highlights the essence of the principle of international monopoly profits: international trade is driven by international specialization, but it also brings about struggles between countries for market dominance. Struggles like these lead to international trade conflicts, which are not addressed by the principle of comparative advantage and classical international trade theory.

Britain seized international market dominance through conquest and colonization in the nineteenth century. How is the struggle for international market dominance realized today? Taking the United States as an example, its pursuit of market dominance is no longer through war and colonization, but through dominance in technology, finance, rulemaking, and the military.

Technological dominance. In the 1990s, China could not produce stored program control (SPC) telephone switching systems and had to import them at a price of 200,000 RMB per unit. Eventually, Huawei made technological breakthroughs, mastered the technology of SPC telephone exchanges, and began to produce them independently. The price dropped to 20,000 RMB per unit, showing the astonishing amount of profits realized by high-tech firms with technological dominance!

Financial dominance. The US dollar is the world's reserve currency. Many international transactions are denominated in dollars. The Federal Reserve not only can help American financial institutions and enterprises through the issuance of dollars to tide over crises and subsidize American household consumption, but also use the status of the dollar as an international currency in payment and pricing to impose sanctions on a country or some of its individuals and enterprises, for example, by freezing their bank accounts.

Rulemaking dominance. The United States typically exercises "long-arm jurisdiction," regulating and punishing other countries' multinational corporations according to US domestic laws and policies. In 2018, the United States accused ZTE Corporation of exporting goods to Iran in violation of US export control regulation, and fined ZTE $2.59 billion, equivalent to 80% of ZTE's profits over the past 30 years.

Military dominance. A strong military provides a strong backing for a great power. Even if the United States does not engage in large-scale wars, US military is a powerful complement to its technological, financial, and rulemaking dominance.

In general, a country can achieve a dominant position internationally through technology, finance, rulemaking, and the military. Taking advantage of its dominant position benefits the overall interests of this country, but damages the overall interests of other countries.

1.4.3 The Growth Trap of Specialization Solidification: Competing Long-Term National Interests

Economic issues are divided into static and dynamic problems. Static problems study the allocation of resources in the spatial dimension, while dynamic problems study the allocation of resources in the temporal dimension. The principles of comparative advantage and international monopoly profits are both studies of static problems, not dynamic problems. In this book, the most important dynamic problem is whether free trade can help countries grow faster. Our answer is: not necessarily! To explain, we need to introduce the third principle—the growth trap of specialization solidification.

Traditional economic growth models believe that if every country has the same technology, their per capita gross domestic product (GDP) will eventually converge. The main reason is due to the principle of diminishing returns to capital: the poorer the country, the scarcer the capital, the higher the return to capital, and the faster the economic growth. Thus, the economic growth of poor countries will be faster than that of rich countries, and eventually all countries will converge to the same per capita GDP. This holds true under a closed economy, that is, in the absence of international trade. But what would happen with free trade?

Free trade induces price convergence of tradable goods across nations. The capital-intensive products of rich countries are exported to poor countries, and the labor-intensive products of poor countries are exported to rich countries. Because products trade freely in the world market, the prices of these products will be equalized across all countries. Assuming perfectly competitive product markets, profit is zero, that is, the price of the product equals the cost of producing the product. Since product prices are equalized across all countries, their costs of production are also equalized across all countries. The cost of production is the sum of factor costs, that is, labor costs (or wages) plus capital costs (or returns to capital). Since free trade makes the prices of products equalized across all countries, their costs of production are equalized, and, assuming all countries share the same production technologies, factor costs are equalized. Assuming perfectly competitive factor markets, the factor cost equals the factor price, so factor prices are also equalized across all countries. Therefore, free trade will make wages and the returns to capital equalized across all—poor and rich—countries. This is the famous theorem of factor price equalization theorem in the theory of international trade.

Without trade, poor countries, due to their relative scarcity of capital, have a higher return to capital, which should lead to higher savings, higher investment, and higher growth than rich countries. With free trade, this is no longer the case. Poor countries, because of their comparative advantage, will be stuck forever producing and exporting labor-intensive products to, and importing capital-intensive products from, rich countries. Because the return to capital in poor countries will converge with that in rich countries, poor countries will lose the incentive to develop capital-intensive industries and catch up with the rich countries. In the long run, the rich countries are always rich and the poor countries are always poor. In this way, the international specialization brought about by free trade can become a growth trap for poor countries.

Is there any empirical data to support this principle? A large number of African and Latin American countries have long been trapped in poverty and low growth. The World Bank refers to these countries as "single-product countries." They have long been producing single resource-based products such as minerals or agricultural products, like coffee. These countries have not been able to industrialize, and their economies have been unable to escape the poverty trap of single resource-based production. If industrialization cannot be achieved and their product structure cannot be upgraded, free trade may have caused these countries to fall into the growth trap of specialization solidification.

An early illustration of the principle of the growth trap of specialization solidification was the so-called Great Divergence between the West (industrialized countries) and the East (agricultural countries) in history. After the Industrial Revolution in Britain, a significant divergence occurred in the development of the East and the West. The developed countries in the West moved toward industrialization and modernization, escaping the "Malthusian trap."[13] However, the East, represented by China and India, was trapped in the Malthusian trap for a long time.

China's industrialization mainly commenced with the establishment of the People's Republic of China in 1949; it developed rapidly after the reform and opening up in 1978, and its industrialization was basically completed by 2010.

Why didn't China fall into the growth trap of specialization solidification after opening up? Note that industrialization and industrial upgrading have

[13] The "Malthusian Trap" refers to the population growing faster than the food supply, so human society is always struggling on the edge of survival. There is a more detailed discussion later in the text.

always been central tasks of China's economic development. After the reform and opening up in 1978, attracting investment became the core assessment indicator for governments at all levels, especially at the grassroots level. Take Shenzhen as an example. Its development over the 40 years from 1978 to 2018 can be divided into four stages: processing trade in the 1980s and early 1990s, forming a "front shop and back factory" with Hong Kong; imitation and speedy production starting in the late 1990s; processing and manufacturing, or "Made in Shenzhen," starting in the early twenty-first century; and "Shenzhen Innovation" at the current stage. The people, enterprises, and government of Shenzhen did not rest on the comparative advantages of cheap land and labor in the 1980s, but seized opportunities to continuously achieve industrial upgrading in an open environment, driving high-speed economic growth.

Unlike China, developing countries in Africa, Latin America, and other regions of the world are even now still struggling to escape the growth trap and achieve industrialization. The income gap between the world's rich and poor countries is still huge, and it may even be getting bigger.

What deserves our attention is that the artificial intelligence revolution may bring about a second great divergence in the global economy, with the growth trap due to specialization solidification appearing in a new form. Some developed countries, led by the United States, focus on high-tech research and development, obtaining monopoly profits in high-tech industries, while most other countries, especially developing countries, focus on manufacturing and agriculture and can only obtain low returns as these jobs will increasingly be done by robots. Therefore, it is crucial for countries like China to strive for breakthroughs in technological innovation and continue industrial upgrading to maintain strong economic growth. However, China's breakthroughs in technological innovation will inevitably break the United States' dominant position in high-tech industries, leading to conflicts between China and the United States in trade, investment, and technology.

Free trade has indeed achieved better resource allocation across borders, improved global production efficiency, and also raised the consumption levels of people in most countries. However, in the long term, free trade may also solidify countries' specialization roles, causing developing countries to fall into a growth trap. Therefore, for developing countries, the significance of participating in free trade is not only to produce according to their comparative advantage, but more importantly, to absorb technology from developed countries through free trade, so as to be able to achieve industrial upgrading and jump out of the growth trap. However, the efforts of poor countries to escape the growth trap due to specialization will inevitably lead to competition and conflicts with rich countries.

1.5 Conclusion

Before ending this chapter, let me take you back to December 31, 1999, in Norman, Oklahoma, in the central United States.

After graduating with a doctorate from the Pennsylvania State University in 1995, I went to work at the University of Oklahoma in Norman, living in a half-century-old house—Madison 4006—only 300 meters from the campus. In front of the house was a row of towering ginkgo trees, and in the backyard were two sturdy walnut trees: one stout, its umbrella-like canopy covering the entire backyard; the other tall, its high branches full of walnuts.

1999 was the transition from the old to the new millennium, and even in the quiet university town, rumors about disasters and the end of the world were incessant. But on the last day of the twentieth century, the town was peaceful, and no disaster occurred. Celebrations were being held all over the world, waiting for the arrival of the new millennium. In the afternoon, cheers and festive sounds west of the Pacific could be heard on the TV as Beijing entered the new millennium 13 hours ahead of Central US time.

At that moment of transition from the old to the new millennium, I started to think about issues in trade conflicts and the new world order. How will the world change in the new millennium? What will the new world order look like?

Walking into the backyard, I heard the neighbor's dog's barking intermingled with the cheers on the TV. The afternoon sun shone on the walnuts on the tree and the golden leaves all over the ground. I couldn't help but write a five-character Chinese poem[14]:

Backyard
December 31, 1999, in the United States

Open the door at the dog's bark,
Sun shines on the walnuts dark.
White cloaks cover green stalks,
Red beans on green branches shake.
Fallen leaves keep warmth inside,
The west wind takes a long flight.
Time rushes on the other side,
Already comes the dawn light.

[14] The poem is translated from Chinese.

CHAPTER 2

How Do Economies Grow?

In Chapter 1, we discussed why international trade conflicts occur. The answer lies in competing national interests. So, what represents a country's long-run and overall interests? The answer is the long-run growth of the aggregate economy, specifically, the long-run growth of GDP. GDP equals per capita GDP multiplied by the population, so there are two ways for GDP to grow. One is through extensive growth, where per capita GDP remains constant, but the population grows; the other is through intensive growth, where the population remains constant, but per capita GDP rises. Extensive growth represents simple scale expansion, while intensive growth represents improvements in productivity and living standards. Aggregate growth is typically a combination of both extensive and intensive growth.

A country's aggregate growth can be achieved through peaceful means by improving productivity, or through war and plunder. For example, conquering the land and population of other countries through war will increase the aggregate economy of the victorious country relative to the defeated country.

The long-run growth of the aggregate economy represents both a country's strength and its fundamental interests. For example, the growth of the aggregate GDP of the British Empire (including colonies) includes both the extensive growth driven by the increase in population and resources of the colonies, and the improvement in productivity driven by the Industrial Revolution.

The rise and fall of great powers and the evolution of the world order can all be measured by long-term growth in GDP. To understand great power competition, one needs to be able to view the long-run and overall interests of various countries from the perspective of aggregate growth. Therefore, in this

J. Ju, *US-China Great Power Competition and The New World Order*,
https://doi.org/10.1007/978-981-95-3762-4_2

chapter, we first review the historical data of long-run growth in the world over the past two thousand years, that is, from the first year of the Common Era to the present. Next, we use the "dual-wheel drive" model and the "growth theorem" to explain how long-run growth occurs. Finally, we apply this model to various stages of globalization and analyze the main features of the current globalization.

2.1 Two Thousand Years of Economic Growth

Over the past forty years of reform and opening up, China's economic landscape has undergone earth-shaking changes. After more than forty years of rapid development, China's per capita GDP had surpassed the world average in 2022, reaching $12,720.2. But how significant is this change? In the historical dimension, what is China's current economic development level compared to the year 1949, or even compared to the first year of the Common Era over two thousand years ago?

To answer this question, we need to clarify one thing: that is, how to compare prices and currencies between different countries, or between different historical periods in the same country.

For example, in the famous work of Chinese fiction, "All Men Are Brothers," about 1000 years ago, before Wu Song went up to Jingyang Gang to fight the tiger, he drank 18 bowls of wine and paid one tael of silver. Today, a bottle of Maotai wine costs about 2000 RMB. So, which is more expensive: Wu Song's 18 bowls of wine 1000 years ago or a bottle of Maotai wine today? Without clarifying this issue first, it is impossible to accurately measure the current level of economic development relative to the past.

To give another example, in February 1990 I went from Tsinghua University to study at the Pennsylvania State University in the United States. Before going abroad, I had my hair cut in Beijing, which cost me 2 RMB. After going abroad, I had my hair cut at a barbershop in the town of State College, and the price of a haircut was $10, which was about 40 RMB according to the exchange rate at that time. How do we compare the standard of living in State College versus Beijing in 1990?

World-renowned economic historian Angus Maddison dedicated his career to quantifying the economic development history of various countries over the past two thousand years. Maddison used the concept of purchasing power parity (PPP), that is, converting the price level in different countries and different historical periods into the purchasing power of US dollars in 1990 (or "international dollars").

Why did Maddison choose this metric?

In order to make meaningful comparisons of different countries' GDP, it is necessary to convert their nominal GDP figures (measured in local currency units) into a common currency (such as the US dollar). One way to do this is to use the market (nominal) exchange rate. But the nominal exchange rate may not reflect the purchasing power of the currency, that is, the value of currency in terms of real goods and services that it can buy, like haircuts. In the above example, the nominal exchange rate in 1990 was about 4 RMB: $1, but in PPP terms, $10 could buy one haircut in the United States and 20 haircuts in China. Maddison used the purchasing power of the US dollar in 1990 as a common unit of measure to compare the level of economic development in various countries and periods. The so-called PPP exchange rates convert the GDP of different countries and periods in local currencies and current prices into PPP-adjusted international dollars, thereby facilitating comparison. Through Maddison's database of the growth history in various countries, we can get an intuitive feel for world economic growth over the past 2000 years.

Let's first examine the growth of GDP per capita over the past 2000 years. According to Maddison's calculations (see Table 2.1), from 1 to 1000 AD, the average annual growth rate of global GDP per capita was -0.002%, and the level of economic development was basically stagnant; from 1000 AD to the Age of Discovery in 1500 AD, the average annual growth rate increased to 0.052%; from the Industrial Revolution in 1820 to the eve of World War I in 1913, the average annual growth rate rose to 0.88%; and after two world wars, from 1950 to 2018, the average annual growth rate reached 2.94%.

We can broadly say: the annual per capita GDP growth in today's world is equivalent to 56 years of per capita GDP growth 1000 years ago.

So, what about China? According to Maddison's data, in 1 AD, China's per capita GDP was 450 international dollars (based on 1990 PPPs), and in 1949 it was 447 international dollars. These two numbers indicate that in the 1950 years from 1 AD to 1949, China's per capita GDP basically did not change. In 1978, China's per capita GDP reached 978 international dollars, more than double that of 1949. From 1978 to 2022, China's per capita GDP increased by about ten times. One can see that starting from the year AD 1, the growth of China's per capita GDP is all due to the development of the People's Republic of China in the past 70 years.

Every time I see these numbers, I am reminded of the countryside of my hometown, Rugao, in Jiangsu Province. The income gap between urban and

Table 2.1 Growth of the global economy and population over the past 2000 years

Period (AD)	*Average annual GDP per capita growth rate (%)*	*Total population at the end year of the period (in ten thousands)*	*Average annual population growth rate (%)*
1–1000	–0.002	26,848.27	0.015
1000–1500	0.052	43,737.34	0.098
1500–1820	0.052	104,114.24	0.27
1821–1913	0.88	179,124.64	0.59
1914–1950	0.91	252,417.27	0.93
1950–2018	2.94	746,956.80	1.61

Data source Maddison Project Database (2020) and author's calculations

rural areas in China is quite large. In 1978, although the national average per capita GDP was twice as high as it was 2000 years ago, the level of economic development in the countryside of Rugao was similar to what it was back in those times: people in my hometown were lighting oil lamps, most of the farmland was plowed by oxen, and about half of the people lived in thatched houses.

That is to say, I personally experienced concentrated changes in the level of economic development over 2000 years in China, the most impressive of which is in the area of transportation.

I was born in July 1963 in Daizhuang Commune, Rugao County (now Rugao City). My mother gave birth to me alone at Daizhuang Primary School. I was a premature baby, weighing less than 3.3 lbs at birth. After I was born, my father came to pick us up to return to my grandmother's house about 10 km away. Because my mother and I were both very weak, we couldn't ride on my father's bicycle, and, of course, there were no cars, so my father found a small boat to take us via the waterway. It took five hours to travel the 10 km of waterway from Daizhuang Primary School in the morning, and it was not until the afternoon that we arrived at my grandmother's house. The hot July weather, coupled with the long journey, caused me to suffer a life-threatening heatstroke.

As related to me by my father, 80 years ago, in the 1940s, my grandfather would travel by waterway to Shanghai to sell grain from Rugao, and the journey would take a full seven days by boat. Today, it takes 20 minutes to drive from Daizhuang Primary School to my grandmother's house, and with the high-speed railway, it just takes one hour to travel from Rugao to Shanghai. Therefore, compared with the past, the development speed of China now can be summed up with the old saying: "Just seven days in the present, but things change like a thousand years in the past."

2.2 The Dual-Wheel Drive Model

Over the past 2000 years, the main developments in human society and economic growth have occurred in the last 200 years; in China, they have occurred in the last 70 years. So, what happened in the last 200 years? What are the forces that drive the rapid development of modern civilization?

To understand economic growth, we first need to understand the concept of GDP. GDP refers to the total market value of all final goods and services produced by a country within a given period using the factors of production within its territory. GDP is both total output and the total income of factors within a country's territory, so there are three ways to measure it: from the production side, by adding up the value added at each stage of production of all the goods and services produced in the country; from the expenditure side, by adding up the value of all purchases made by final users in the country; and from the income side, by adding up all factor incomes generated by the production of goods and services in the country.

From the income side, the GDP growth comes from three forces: technological progress, capital accumulation, and population growth. Among them, the most critical is technological progress because without technological progress, neither population growth nor capital accumulation would be possible.

Why is this the case? Let's first look at the famous Malthusian Trap: the population grows exponentially, while the food supply and other resources for survival grow linearly. When population growth outpaces agricultural production, the excess population will always be eliminated in some way, such as through war and famine. Thus, the cycle repeats, and human society will always struggle on the edge of survival. As shown in Table 2.1, from 1 to 1000 AD, the world's total population hardly grew, and it remained almost constant until the Industrial Revolution.

Next, let's examine the impact of technological progress on capital accumulation. Capital accumulation results from savings. Without technological progress, the resources created by humans each year are just enough to maintain survival for that year. As a result, overall, from 1 AD until the Industrial Revolution, there was hardly any capital accumulation.

The Innovation-Market Cycle

Classic growth theory in economics textbooks, whether the exogenous growth model or the endogenous growth model, clearly identifies innovation as the most crucial driver of growth. However, classic growth theory often focuses on describing the relationship between technology growth and economic growth from a macro perspective, while neglecting the mechanism of achieving technology innovation. To use an analogy, classic growth theory explains changes in the forest but not the growth process of each tree from small to large.

So, how does a small tree grow? How is innovation and technological progress achieved by businesses and individuals?

Let's explore this question from the micro perspective of a business. A business must first invest in research and development (R&D) to generate innovations and make technological progress. When the innovative products can be sold at a sufficient scale in the market, they can earn enough profits to support subsequent R&D investment, promoting further technology innovation. This is the innovation-market cycle shown in Fig. 2.1.

This innovation-market cycle emphasizes the importance of market scale for profits: the larger the market scale, the larger the monopoly profits brought by innovation. This is precisely what classic growth theory overlooks: classic growth theory generally assumes that the profit rate brought by technology does not change with scale; it focuses on the average contribution of technological progress, capital accumulation, and population to total growth. This simplification is mainly for the convenience of handling the theoretical model mathematically, but it overlooks the key role of market scale in

Fig. 2.1
Innovation-market cycle

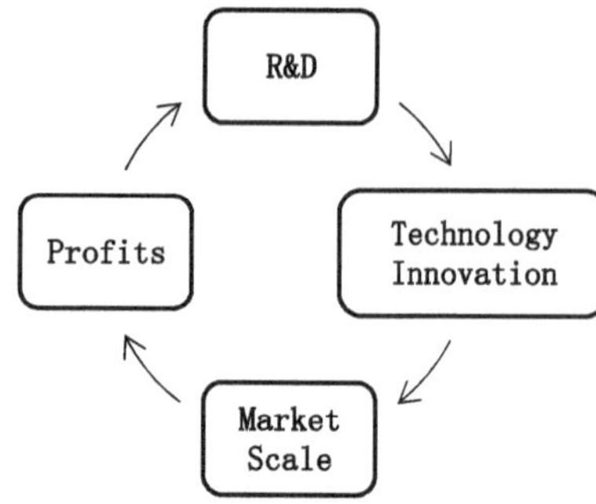

enlarging monopoly profits and incentivizing and promoting a virtuous cycle of innovation.

In this book, we emphasize the importance of monopoly profits brought by market scale through the innovation-market cycle. We extend the innovation-market cycle from the business level to the national level, establishing a Dual-Wheel Drive model to explain economic growth.

Imagine this scenario: a country's long-term economic growth is like a two-wheeled carriage in motion, where one wheel is "innovation" and the other is "market scale." Only when both wheels are strong and roll forward together can the carriage run fast and steady. However, if one wheel has a problem or can't keep up, not only will the carriage not be able to run, but there is also a risk of it overturning.

Using the Dual-Wheel Drive model to analyze the history of global GDP growth, the conclusion is clear: the world economy has experienced rapid development over the past two hundred years primarily due to two factors. First, the Industrial Revolution, which sparked technological innovation; and second, globalization, which expanded market size.

The First Industrial Revolution began in the mid-eighteenth century in central England, marked by the invention and large-scale use of steam engines and spinning machines. By the 1830s and 1840s, England's cotton textile industry had been mechanized, and mechanization began to spread to other industrial sectors. Mechanization allowed England and some European countries to transition from agricultural economies to industrial economies, greatly accelerating their economic growth.

The First Industrial Revolution ushered humanity into the mechanical age. The Second Industrial Revolution, which occurred from the second half of the nineteenth century to the early twentieth century, brought humanity into the electrical age. The Third Industrial Revolution, which began in the second half of the twentieth century after World War II, ushered humanity into the information age. The ongoing Fourth Industrial Revolution has initiated the era of artificial intelligence (AI) for humanity. The Industrial Revolution(s) caused the global economic growth rate to cross the 1% threshold around 1820 and to skyrocket to 4% after entering the twentieth century.

Of course, having just the wheel of technological innovation is not enough. The other wheel of the Dual-Wheel Drive model—the expansion of market scale—is equally crucial. If the market size is not large enough, who will buy the products produced through technological innovation? Where will the profits come from? Without profits, how can continuous investment in technology research and development be sustained? How can the wheel of technological innovation roll?

Two Examples

To better understand this Dual-Wheel Drive model, we present two examples. The first example is Zheng He's voyages to the Western Ocean during the Ming Dynasty in China. Zheng's first voyage took place in 1405, nearly a hundred years before Christopher Columbus discovered the so-called New World. At its peak, Zheng's fleet consisted of 63 large ships and over 27,000 people, reaching as far as the eastern part of Africa, the Red Sea, and the Middle East.

Zheng's voyages to the Western Ocean were not only great adventures but also great technological innovations. China's advanced shipbuilding industry, use of the compass, accumulated maritime knowledge and experience, and large number of trained sailors provided the necessary conditions for Zheng's voyages.

According to the "Zheng He Navigation Map," Zheng's fleet combined astronomical positioning with the use of the navigation compass, improving the accuracy of determining a ship's position and course. This technique, known as "star-leading," represented the most advanced level of astronomical navigation in the world at that time. Thanks to innovative technologies designed to ensure onboard freshwater storage, ship stability, and buoyancy, Zheng's fleet could sail under harsh conditions where "huge waves met the sky, and giant waves were like mountains," with "cloud sails high, day and night stars racing," and accidents were rare.

Why didn't such great adventures and innovations as Zheng's voyages strongly promote Ming Dynasty maritime trade and thereby stimulate economic growth and development, like Columbus' discovery of the New World did a hundred years later?

The nature of Zheng's voyages to the Western Seas was primarily diplomatic, with tribute activities as the main focus—akin to going to various places to "shake hands" and "cut ribbons." The emphasis on "politics leading the way" overlooked economic benefits, leading to a situation where more was given than received. These voyages did not serve as a vehicle for economic activity, nor did they significantly promote civilian trade. In the context of Fig. 2.1, Zheng's voyages only brought about innovations in navigation technology, but these innovations were not accompanied by expanded trade and economic activities, and therefore did not lead to market enlargement and an increase in profits. As a result, they could not feed further innovation and form a virtuous "Innovation-Market" cycle. Zheng only had one wheel of innovation and exploration, and not the other wheel of market scale to drive the carriage of economic growth. Therefore, this spectacular diplomatic activity came to an abrupt end after seven voyages to the Western Seas.

Of course, mere expansion of scale is also not enough. The second example is the expansion of the Mongol Empire in the early thirteenth century. At its peak, the Mongol Empire covered more than 33 million square km and surpassed one-fifth of the world's land area, extending its influence to West Asia and North Asia, and reaching as far as Eastern Europe and Egypt. It was the second-largest empire in human history after the British Empire. But why did it disintegrate in less than a century? The reasons are complex from different perspectives, but from an economic point of view, an important factor is that the Mongol Empire only conquered lands and peoples but did not achieve economic growth.

The expansion of the Mongol Empire's population and territory did not bring about market prosperity. In the context of the Dual-Wheel Drive model, the territorial expansion of the Mongol Empire lacked the support of technology innovation. The Mongol Empire's conquest of the Eurasian continent relied mainly on a powerful military force, manifested in the formidable combat power of the heavy cavalry corps and brutal slaughter in the occupied areas. However, its conquest was not accompanied by innovation and development in civilian technology. On the contrary, the war led to a sharp decline in the population of the occupied areas, causing civilian technology to regress, the economy to decline, and the people to suffer. Without the economic prosperity and development brought about by the innovation-market cycle, the rapid disintegration of the Mongol Empire in less than a century was inevitable.

The above two examples show that for long-term economic growth, both technological innovation and market scale expansion are indispensable. In contrast, the maritime explorations of Columbus and Ferdinand Magellan are typical examples of the Dual-Wheel Drive model. Columbus discovered the phenomenon of the compass needle deviating westward when he entered the Western Hemisphere. His first long-distance exploration lasted more than 220 days, covering a round trip of more than 8000 nautical miles, a one-way trip of more than 4000 nautical miles, and a transoceanic voyage of more than 30 days without sight of land. This pushed ocean navigation from near-shore to a new stage far from land. This was an innovation in navigation technology, laying an important foundation for Magellan's subsequent circumnavigation. In addition to technological innovation, what's more important is that the motivation for the maritime explorations by Columbus and Magellan was spices, gold, conquest, and colonization. Driven by profits, they discovered the New World, leading to the expansion of colonies and the development of international trade. Therefore, in the great voyages of Columbus and Magellan, the two wheels of technological innovation and market scale were turning together, directly promoting the process of globalization and the development of the world economy.

2.3 The Growth Theorem

The Dual-Wheel Drive model describes the micro-mechanism of economic growth, while the Growth Theorem describes the intermediate-mechanism of economic growth, establishing the relationship between long-run growth and sustained industrial structure upgrading.

> The Growth Theorem: A necessary and sufficient condition for an economy to maintain long-run growth is the continuous upgrading of its industrial structure.

The source of long-term growth is innovation. Innovation is necessary for the emergence of new products, technologies, and industries. Each product (or industry) has a life cycle, going through the process of entering the market, expanding sales, reaching its peak, shrinking, and exiting the market. Figure 2.2 illustrates a process of continuous upgrading of the industrial structure, where the horizontal axis represents per capita GDP, and the vertical axis represents the contribution of the product (or industry) to the economy (measured by the ratio of the output value of the product or industry to GDP). Moving along the horizontal axis, as per capita GDP increases with economic growth, the industrial structure is upgraded and new products constantly come on the market, first product 1, then product 2, then product 3, and so on. When per capita GDP is k_1, product 1 is the dominant product in the economy and its share in GDP is at a peak. However, product 1 gradually loses its importance, and product 2 is introduced. Eventually, product 2 surpasses product 1 in importance and by the time per capita GDP rises to k_2, the share of product 2 in GDP is at its peak. After that, product 2 begins to shrink in importance as product 3 is introduced, and so on. The share of each product (or industry) in GDP presents an inverted U shape as the economy (per capita GDP) grows.

Industrial structure upgrading can be divided into technology upgrading and product upgrading. Technology upgrading brings about an increase in labor productivity, such as through the extensive use of agricultural machinery in agricultural production, and the large-scale use of industrial robots in industrial production. Product upgrading is the production of more advanced products, whether in the same industry or in a new industry. The former is like upgrading from producing low value-added wheat to higher value-added bread; the latter is like upgrading from producing low value-added agricultural products to high value added industrial products.

Industrial structure upgrading, whether it is technology upgrading or product upgrading, generally implies an increase in the capital intensity of the production process, that is, a rise in the capital-labor ratio. Ju, Lin, and Wang (2015) analyzed manufacturing data in the United States from 1958 to 2005 and found that US manufacturing indeed experienced a continuous upgrading

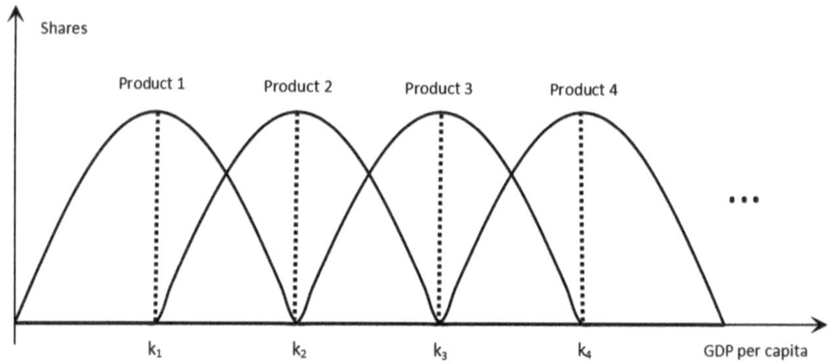

Fig. 2.2 Industrial structure upgrading

process from labor-intensive industries to capital-intensive industries. Each industry exhibited an inverted U-shaped life cycle, going through the process of entry, expansion, peaking, shrinking, and exiting the market, starting with more labor-intensive industries and moving on to more capital-intensive industries—the more capital-intensive the industry, the later it entered the market and reached its peak.[1]

The growth theorem can help us understand the "principle of the growth trap of specialization solidification" that was discussed in Chapter 1: without industrial structure upgrading, there is no economic growth. For example, the rapidly growing Shenzhen economy clearly shows the process of industrial structure upgrading, starting from the processing trade and moving on to product imitation, Shenzhen manufacturing, and now Shenzhen innovation. In contrast, some African "single-product" countries have been producing single resource-based products or agricultural products for a long time, without achieving industrial upgrading or economic growth.

2.4 The Four Stages of Globalization

Globalization has brought about the vitality of international trade and the expansion of the global market. The expansion of the global market has transformed technological innovations into tangible profits. The increase in profits feeds back to new innovations. The innovation-market cycle has driven the waves of globalization forward, each wave surpassing the last.

Figure 2.3 shows the four stages of economic activity: innovation, production, exchange (trade), and consumption (market).

In the early agricultural era, the four stages of innovation, production, exchange, and consumption are all bundled together within a country, a

[1] Ju, Jiandong, Justin Yifu Lin, and Yong Wang. "Endowment Structures, Industrial Dynamics, and Economic Growth," *Journal of Monetary Economics* 76 (October 5, 2015): 244–63. https://doi.org/10.1016/j.jmoneco.2015.09.006.

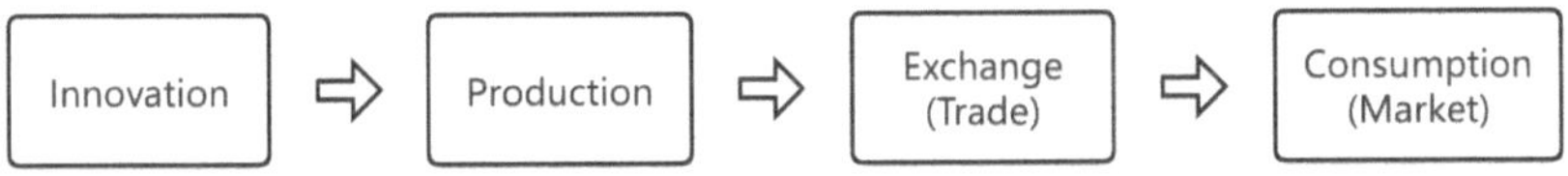

Fig. 2.3 Four stages of economic activity

village, or even a family. A housewife may start by sewing clothes for herself and her family, and then the expansion of market scale occurs when she "discovers the market," that is, when she finds that other families are also interested in the clothes she sews. Similarly, the clothes produced by a country for the local population may also turn out to be attractive to residents of other countries. Thus, the second stage of market scale expansion is the decoupling of production and consumption within a country: clothes can be produced in one country and sold to another country for consumption through international trade.

The third stage of market scale expansion is the decoupling of different stages of the production process: a car engine can be produced in Germany, tires made in Thailand, and the whole car assembled in China. The fourth stage of market scale expansion will be the decoupling of different stages of the innovation process.

The corresponding globalization process unfolds in reverse order of the four stages of economic activity. First is the globalization of the market, or the global discovery era; then the globalization of trade, or the global trade era; next is the globalization of production, or the global production era; and finally, the globalization of innovation, or the global innovation era.

In this section, we use the Dual-Wheel Drive model to analyze these four eras of globalization in turn.

2.4.1 Global Discovery Era: 1500–1819

Starting in the late 1400s, famous European navigators such as Columbus, Magellan, and Vasco Da Gama, with support from the monarchs in Spain and Portugal, set sail and ushered in the era of global discovery.

The most prominent feature of this era was the geographical discovery of the New World in the Americas. With the discovery of the New World, commodities such as cotton, spices, silk, and ivory began to be traded between Europe and the Americas. For the first time, European goods could be sold everywhere in the world, marking the discovery of the global market. In the Age of Great Navigation, countries such as Portugal, Spain, the Netherlands, and Britain opened the door to international trade through colonization, promoting their own economic development. The geographical discoveries of the Age of Great Navigation expanded the scale of the global market and increased the demand for European products.

The increase in demand increased the motivation for technological innovation. The invention of machinery technology during this period, such as textile-weaving machinery brought more profits to the Europeans. This innovation-market virtuous cycle was a key element in the First Industrial Revolution and the rolling forward of the wave of globalization.

2.4.2 *Global Trade Era: 1820–1978*

After the era of global discovery, globalization progressed in reverse order to that in Fig. 2.3, transitioning to the era of global trade. This was a time of rapid technological innovation, with the First and Second Industrial Revolutions occurring in succession. The development and widespread use of steam engines, textile machinery, railways, automobiles, and electricity greatly increased productivity.

This stage is called the era of global trade because the advent of transportation technology—especially maritime transportation technology—greatly reduced the cost of long-distance transportation, enabling the "decoupling" of production and consumption: most industrial goods were produced in industrialized countries in Europe and America but consumed globally through international trade. Global trade was driven by large multinational corporations, such as the famous British East India Company. With these multinational corporations as intermediaries, labor, resources, and markets around the world were activated, allowing global trade to develop and mature.

Products can be divided into two categories. The first category consists of products intended for final consumption, such as bread, clothes, cars, and so on—which we call "final goods." The second category consists of products intended for use in production, such as flour, cotton, car parts, and so on—which we call "intermediate goods" or "input goods." International trade in goods can also be divided into "final goods trade" and "intermediate goods trade." The era of global trade was dominated by final goods trade.

The first half of the global trade era, from 1820 to 1913, belonged to Britain. During this period, Britain actively developed overseas trade and engaged in colonization—it accumulated a wealth of capital, expanded its products to a vast overseas market, and obtained the cheapest sources of raw materials globally. At home, a large amount of cheap labor was created as wealthy landowners took over communally owned land under the Enclosure Movement, forcing displaced farmers to migrant to cities for work. But even so, its booming handicraft industry could not meet the growing market demand. A revolution in production technology was needed. Britain, as the birthplace of the First Industrial Revolution and the hegemon of global trade, also became the dominant world power of the time.

After 1870, new technologies and inventions emerged in an endless stream and were applied to various industrial fields, promoting further economic development and bringing about the rise of the Second Industrial Revolution. The world entered the electrical era. Between the First and Second Industrial Revolutions, the world order changed. After two world wars, Britain lost its hegemonic position to the United States.

The second half of the global trade era belonged to the United States. The global currency changed from the pound to the dollar. "Countries want independence, nations want liberation, and the people want revolution"—colonial rule of large parts of Africa, Asia, and Latin America by the British and Europeans largely came to an end after World War II. US hegemony turned to be characterized by technology hegemony, financial hegemony, rulemaking hegemony, and military hegemony.

2.4.3 *Global Production Era: 1978–2018*

After the era of global trade came the third stage of globalization: the era of global production. The technological innovations of this era, mainly represented by computers and the internet, characterized the Third Industrial Revolution: Digital Revolution. The development of information and communication technology greatly reduced the cost of remote information exchange in the production process, making long-distance production collaboration possible. This enabled a second decoupling in the production process, leading to the globalization of production.

The most notable feature of the global production era was the formation of the so-called global value chain, which pulled countries around the world into a network of international production and specialization. In this stage, global trade gradually shifted from being primarily final product trade to being primarily intermediate-product trade, that is, from trading consumption goods like bread, clothes, and cars to trading production inputs like flour, cotton, and car parts. The share of intermediate-product trade in global trade increased and exceeded 50% during this period.

2.4.4 *Global Innovation Era: 2018 to Present*

Following the era of global production, we have now entered the era of global innovation. Economic growth in this era is fundamentally different from economic growth in previous eras: in previous eras, economic growth was mainly driven by physical capital accumulation, but in the global innovation era, economic growth is mainly driven by human capital accumulation and technological innovation. The fundamental difference between these two modes of economic growth stems from the difference between physical capital and human capital, knowledge, and technology, which is manifested in three aspects.

First, the distribution of physical capital (financial capital) is more concentrated, while the distribution of human capital is relatively more dispersed. Financial capital (such as stocks, bonds, bank loans) represents the ownership of physical capital (such as machines, factories), and financial capital can be highly concentrated globally, resulting in great inequality between rich and poor countries, and between the rich and poor within a country. However, human capital—represented by the population with more than two years of tertiary education—can be more evenly distributed globally.

Second, physical capital is typically a private good, while scientific knowledge is typically considered a public good. The difference between private goods and public goods lies in two aspects: exclusion and rivalry. Exclusion means that the good has characteristics that can prevent others from using it, for example, Wi-Fi with password access (mobile hotspot) is excludable, while broadcasting is non-excludable. Rivalry means that one person's consumption of the good will affect others' consumption of it, for example, food and clothing are rival, while national defense and weather forecasts are non-rival. Private goods refer to products that are both excludable and rival, while public goods refer to products that are non-excludable and non-rival. Scientific knowledge, in its pure form, belongs to all mankind: no one can be stopped from learning, and one person's learning does not subtract from the learning of others.

Third, the production of physical products generally has the characteristic of diminishing returns to scale, while the production of virtual products such as scientific knowledge generally has the characteristic of increasing returns to scale. Diminishing returns to scale means that the larger the production scale, the lower the production efficiency, and thus the higher the average cost; increasing returns to scale means that the larger the production scale, the higher the production efficiency, and thus the lower the average cost. For example, with AI, doubling the data leads to more than doubling the results. This attribute of increasing returns to scale is one characteristic of a natural monopoly: the larger the enterprise, the lower its average cost of production, thus giving birth to super-large enterprises like Amazon, Google, Microsoft, Alibaba, and Tencent.

The main form of economic organization is gradually evolving from the production of physical private goods with decreasing returns to scale to the production of virtual public goods with increasing returns to scale in the global innovation era. The market economy model of perfect competition is no longer the most useful theoretical framework and capitalism and free markets governed by the "invisible hand" are no longer the most useful benchmark practices in the global innovation era. If markets in new innovative products like AI are left unchecked, they will not resemble perfect competition but will instead grow into global monopolies.

Monopolies tend to bring about extreme wealth disparities, especially when they abuse their monopoly power to obtain excessive profits, which can stifle innovation in the rest of society ("no grass grows under the big tree"). Therefore, the benchmark form of economic organization in the global innovation era must be a combination of an effective market and a facilitating government, that is, using the power of the government to balance the market power of monopolies so as to achieve more effective resource allocation and more equal income distribution. The standard model of perfect competition is no longer the benchmark theory in the global innovation era; our Dual-Wheel Drive model based on the innovation-market cycle is a more appropriate analytical framework now.

2.5 Evolution in Forms of Global Dominance

As globalization has progressed from the market discovery stage to the trade stage, production stage, and innovation stage, the form of global dominance by the hegemonic countries has also gradually evolved.

During the global discovery era and the first half of the global trade era, Britain and other hegemonic countries like the Netherlands, Portugal, and Spain dominated global economic activities. They dominated in innovation, technology, and industrial production; their multinational companies dominated international trade; and they even dominated global consumption through colonization.

By the second half of the global trade era, especially after World War II, as colonies gained independence one after another, the hegemonic countries' dominance over global consumption was broken.

Starting from 1978, as globalization entered the production era and trade liberalization swept the world, the hegemonic countries' domination of international trade was broken. From 1978 to 1991, the world's top three economies were the United States, the Soviet Union, and Japan. After the collapse of the Soviet Union, Russia's economy plummeted, and the United States, Japan, and Germany accounted for the largest share of the world's GDP.

After the 1990s, China's economy grew rapidly, rising from seventh in the world in the first decade of the twenty-first century to second. In 2021, the United States accounted for 24% of the world's GDP, while China accounted for 18%, and the 28 EU countries accounted for 17%. As globalization enters the innovation era, technological innovation is still dominated by developed countries such as the United States, but their domination of industrial production has been broken, replaced by a "tripod" global production pattern led by the United States, China, and Europe.

As the global innovation stage moves forward, should and will the developed countries' domination of technological innovation be broken?

CHAPTER 3

How Do Great Powers Compete?

Competition among great powers is one of the enduring themes in world politics. In the relationship between great powers, mysteries can hide beneath a calm surface. Disputes and conflicts may seem sudden, but in fact, there have been warning signs long ago.

In November 2017, US President Trump proudly showcased his granddaughter reciting the "Three Character Classic" in Chinese during his visit to China. A few months later, in March 2018, the Trump administration suddenly initiated a trade war against China. Why did this US-China trade war break out in 2018, and subsequently extend to become a comprehensive conflict covering investment, technology, people-to-people exchange, finance, and even military and ideological aspects? Why does US President Biden consider China to be the United States' most serious competitor? What are China and the United States competing in or for?

As described in Chapter 2, since the second half of the global trade era, the world order led by Britain and Western Europe and, subsequently, the United States, has changed. A new era—the Global Innovation Era—is upon us with an unstoppable momentum; a new world order is developing, like a sunrise bursting with light seen from the top of a mountain, like a baby growing in the womb. The dual wheels of innovation and market scale that drive global economic growth and world development have embarked on a new track since 2018. Globalization has entered the innovation era—the sky has changed, and the ways and the order on earth must change accordingly. After more than 20 years of rapid development in China, China and the United States have finally entered the stage of the great power competition, and the core of US-China competition is the transformation of the world order.

J. Ju, *US-China Great Power Competition and The New World Order*,
https://doi.org/10.1007/978-981-95-3762-4_3

How should we understand the evolution of US-China relations? In this chapter, we will use the framework of "Six fields, Three elements, Five stages" to analyze past, present, and future great power competitions, understand the evolution of US-China relations at various stages, identify the characteristics of current US-China competition, and predict the future of US-China competition.

3.1 Six Fields of Competition

Great power competition refers to competition between the world's leading great power (or the incumbent power) and the rising power that is striving to catch up. Since 1500, there have been a number of great power competitions, between Spain and Portugal, Britain and the Netherlands, Britain and France, Britain and Germany, Britain and the United States, the United States and the Soviet Union, and the United States and Japan, prior to the current US-China competition. Due to the data limitation, this section analyzes five great power competitions over the past few hundred years: Britain-Germany, Britain-US, US-Soviet Union, US-Japan, and US-China. We find that the competition mainly focuses on six areas, or fields—(1) manufacturing; (2) aggregate economy; (3) technology; (4) finance; (5) military; and (6) global governance—and proceeds roughly in that order.

Manufacturing represents a country's industrial level and is generally the first field where the rising power achieves significant breakthroughs. As labor costs in the incumbent power keep increasing with economic development, some of its manufacturing production is shifted to other countries, allowing the rising power an opportunity to achieve a breakthrough in this field.

The size of the aggregate economy represents a country's economic strength. Technology represents a country's innovative ability. Finance represents a country's financing ability, especially importance in international capital markets. Military power represents a country's strength in combat.

Finally, global governance refers to a country's soft power on the international stage, including its cultural and ideological influence, its role in shaping global and regional rules, its influence within international organizations, world public opinion and political discourse, and its influence on other countries.

Reviewing the historical data of the abovementioned five great power competitions, we find that except in the US-Soviet competition, the rising powers all surpassed the incumbent powers in manufacturing and their aggregate GDP reached 60% or more of the incumbent power's GDP. Therefore, we define manufacturing and the size of the aggregate economy as prerequisite fields of great power competition. The rising power's manufacturing capability must approach or even surpass the incumbent power's, and the rising power's GDP must reach 60% or more of the incumbent power's for the two countries to enter the competition stage; otherwise, the relationship between the two countries cannot be considered as great power competition.

Once they enter the stage of great power competition, the two countries compete in the six fields identified earlier. As shown in Fig. 3.1, manufacturing, technology, finance, and military are the core areas of competition, and the two countries typically engage in fierce competition in one of these four fields, while the aggregate economy and global governance play a mutually supporting and enhancing role as the respective internal and external environment for the competition: a country's advantages in the size of its aggregate economy and/or its position in global governance can place it in a favorable position in manufacturing, technology, finance, and military competition; likewise, a country's competitive advantages in manufacturing, technology, finance, and military power can help it gain advantages domestically (in the aggregate economy) and externally (in global governance).

Historically, the outcomes of great power competitions have been closely related to the extent of catch-up by the rising power in the above six fields. Out of the four major great power competitions in the twentieth century—namely, between Britain and Germany during World War I and World War II; between Britain and the United States from the American Civil War to World War II; between the United States and the Soviet Union before the dissolution of the Soviet Union; and between the United States and Japan around the signing of the Plaza Accord—only the US challenge to Britain's world-leading position was successful. The other three competitions—Germany's attempt to catch up with Britain, the Soviet Union's attempt to catch up with the United States, and Japan's attempt to catch up with the United States—all ended in failure for the rising power. So, what was the reason for these failures?

Historical experience shows that only when the rising power surpasses the incumbent power in all of the above six fields will the world order change. If the rising power surpasses the incumbent power in some or even most fields,

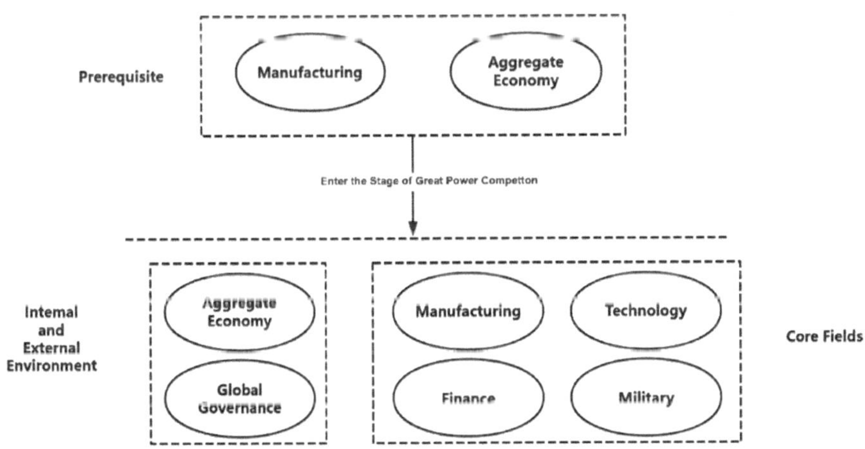

Fig. 3.1 Intrinsic relationship between the six fields of great power competition

the incumbent power may still be able to retain its position with its advantages in the remaining fields.

Table 3.1 summarizes the catch-up status of the rising power in the six fields in five great power competitions, including the ongoing US-China competition.

3.1.1 Britain-Germany Competition

In the first half of the nineteenth century, thanks to the First Industrial Revolution, Britain established the British Empire and became the world hegemon. Britain's strategy was to maintain a balance of power among the major countries in continental Europe, preventing the emergence of a continental European hegemon that could challenge it. Britain's main competitors at the time were France, which held a dominant position on the European continent during the Napoleonic era, and Russia. Britain had a close relationship with Germany at first, but as Germany's strength grew, the relationship between the two countries changed.

Germany's GDP surpassed that of Britain in 1890.[1] By 1913, Germany accounted for 14.8% of world manufacturing output, compared to Britain's 13.6%.

In the field of technology, Germany and the United States were the main leaders of the Second Industrial Revolution, while Britain was relatively lagging in the invention and application of new technologies. The core technological advances of the Second Industrial Revolution included the widespread use of electricity, the invention of internal combustion engines and new transportation tools, the invention of new materials and chemicals, and innovations in communication technologies such as the telegraph and radio. German engineer Ernst Werner von Siemens invented the world's first high-power generator in 1866. Karl Friedrich Benz and others invented the internal combustion engine and automobile in the 1880s. Germany's chemical industry dominated the world, accounting for 90% of global dye supply in 1913. Britain's technological achievements in the Second Industrial Revolution were mainly improvements in steelmaking and steam engines—far less prominent than those of Germany.

In terms of military power, in 1880, the total number of Germany's army and navy personnel was 426,000, surpassing Britain's 367,000. However, Germany was weaker than Britain in terms of naval warship tonnage. At its peak before World War I, Germany's warship tonnage, at 1.305 million tons, was still less than half of Britain's, at 2.714 million tons. Overall, Germany's military strength can be considered to be on par with Britain's before World War I, but it surpassed Britain's before World War II.

[1] Bairoch, Paul. "International Industrialization Levels from 1750 to 1980," *Journal of European Economic History* 11, no. 2 (1982): 269.

Table 3.1 Catch-up status of the rising power in the six fields

Field	*Great Power Competition (Incumbent Power-Rising Power)*				
	Britain-Germany (1885–1945)	*Britain-US (1880s–1940s)*	*US-Soviet Union (1940s–1991)*	*US-Japan (1960s–1990s)*	*US-China (2018–present)*
Manufacturing	Germany surpassed Britain in industrial output in 1910	The United States surpassed Britain in steel production in 1886	The Soviet Union did not surpass the United States in manufac-turing	Japan surpassed the United States in total industrial output in 1995	China surpassed the United States in manufacturing in 2010
Aggregate Economy[a]	Germany's GDP surpassed Britain's around 1890	US GDP surpassed Britain's around 1880	Did not surpass. The Soviet Union's GDP reached 60% of US GDP in 1968	Did not surpass. Japan's GDP reached 60% of US GDP in 1992	Has not surpassed. China's nominal GDP reached 60% of US GDP in 2016
Technology	Germany surpassed Britain around the time of the Second Industrial Revolution	The United States surpassed Britain around the time of the Second Industrial Revolution	Equal. The Soviet Union's military and space technology caught up with the United States in the 1960s	Equal. Japan's electronics and automotive technology caught up with the United States in the 1980s	Has not surpassed
Finance	Did not surpass	The United States surpassed Britain with the establishment of the Bretton Woods system in 1944	Did not surpass	Did not surpass	Has not surpassed

(continued)

Table 3.1 (continued)

Field	*Great Power Competition (Incumbent Power-Rising Power)*				
	Britain-Germany (1885–1945)	*Britain-US (1880s–1940s)*	*US-Soviet Union (1940s–1991)*	*US-Japan (1960s–1990s)*	*US-China (2018–present)*
Military	Germany's military strength surpassed Britain's before World War II	The United States surpassed Britain in military strength around World War II	Equal. Soviet military strength was on par with the United States after World War II	Did not surpass	Has not surpassed
Global Governance	Did not surpass. Germany had far fewer colonies and allies than Britain	The United States surpassed Britain after World War II	Equal	Did not surpass	Has not surpassed
Summary	Germany surpassed Britain in 4 fields and lagged in 2 fields	The United States surpassed Britain in all 6 fields	The Soviet Union equaled the United States in 3 fields and lagged in 3 fields	Japan equaled or surpassed the United States in 2 fields and lagged in 4 fields	China has surpassed the United States in 1 field and still lags in 5 fields

Note [a]The aggregate economy of Britain, Germany, the Soviet Union, and the United States is based on GDP (PPP) data in the Maddison database. By some measures, China's PPP-adjusted GDP has surpassed the United States

Finance was Britain's strength. The seven major wars between Britain and France from 1689 to 1805 were protracted wars. These costly and resource-draining wars urgently required "money, more money." This need triggered a "financial revolution" at the end of the seventeenth century that extended into the beginning of the eighteenth century as both Britain and France developed complex banking and credit systems to pay for their war costs. Britain, in particular, established a reputation in finance, giving it a stronger financial advantage than any other major country at that time, an advantage it maintained until after World War II. Germany was far from catching up to Britain's global financial center status and even had a large gap vis-à-vis France. In 1910, the amount of foreign securities issued by Britain was approximately £200 million, compared to £100 million by France, and £28 million by Germany, illustrating the huge gap between Britain and Germany in the financial field.[2]

In the field of global governance, Britain leveraged its colonial resources and advantageous position in international diplomacy to form alliances. First, it joined the Franco-Russian alliance, then gained the support of the United States, and ultimately held the upper hand over Germany in World War I. Together, Britain, France, and the United States accounted for 51.7% of global manufacturing output in 1913, far surpassing the 19.2% share of Germany and the Austro-Hungarian Empire. The combined steel output of Britain, France, and the United States was 44.1 million tons, while that of Germany and the Austro-Hungarian Empire was only 20.2 million tons. In World War II, the total strength of the Allies, led by Britain, surpassed that of the Axis led by Germany: in the military field alone, the Allies' arms production in 1943 was $62.5 billion, far exceeding the Axis' $18.3 billion. Through the two world wars, Britain ultimately defeated Germany's challenge.

In summary, in the great power competition between Britain (the incumbent power) and Germany (the rising power), Germany surpassed Britain in three of the six fields—manufacturing, economic size, and technology. It was at least on par with Britain in the military field, and only lagged Britain in finance and global governance. Britain, relying on its advantages in those two fields, still beat back Germany's challenge. However, Britain also lost its position as the world's hegemon, ultimately handing over that position to the United States.

3.1.2 Britain-US Competition

In the late nineteenth century, Britain still held the position of world hegemon, but after the end of the American Civil War, the United States developed rapidly and began to catch up economically. In terms of manufacture and aggregate economy, after the 1870s, Britain's industrial development slowed down due to large amount of capital outflows and outdated technical equipment, and it gradually lost its dominant position in world manufacturing and GDP. The United States, on the other hand, abolished slavery and applied new technologies in a timely manner, and its industrial development picked up very fast.

The size of the US economy surpassed Britain's around 1880, and US industrial output surpassed Britain's to rank first in the world in 1894. During this period, tensions between Britain and the United States intensified over issues such as colonization and trade, but Britain's tensions with Germany on the European continent were even more intense. Britain ultimately chose to draw closer to the United States, relying on the latter's

[2] Bersch, Julia, and G. Kaminsky. *Financial Globalization in the 19th Century: Germany as a Financial Center*, 2009. https://api.semanticscholar.org/CorpusID:32751074, accessed on November 29, 2025.

support to counter Germany, thus allowing the United States to develop rapidly without interference.

In the field of technology, the United States and Germany were both leaders in the Second Industrial Revolution that began in the second half of the nineteenth century. Scientists in the United States invented the light bulb, the telephone, and the airplane, promoting the widespread application of electricity, while Britain's achievements in the field of technology during this period were relatively few. By around 1910, the United States had fully surpassed Britain in the field of technology.

In terms of military power, World War I provided the United States with the opportunity to fully realize its hegemonic ambition, and World War II established US superpower status in the global military field. In 1941, the United States produced 26,277 aircraft, compared to Britain's 20,094, marking the first time the United States surpassed Britain in this area. In 1943, US arms production was valued at $37.5 billion, significantly surpassing Britain's $11.1 billion. Undoubtedly, US military strength surpassed Britain's during World War II.[3]

Even before the two world wars, the United States had always been seeking to establish an American-style world order on the back of its strong economic power. But with the onset of the Great Depression in 1929, US relations with the rest of the world became more complex and conflicts escalated. However, the United States ultimately took advantage of the opportunities presented by the two world wars to establish the Bretton Woods system in 1944. In addition, events such as national independence movements in developing countries, beginning with the Suez Canal incident in 1956, hit colonial powers like Britain, weakening its control over the developing world, and allowing the United States to greatly strengthen its influence. Ultimately, the United States successfully surpassed Britain in both finance and global governance, becoming the world's dominant power.

3.1.3 US-Soviet Competition

During World War II, the United States joined forces with Britain (by then known as the United Kingdom) and the Soviet Union to lead the Allied Powers against the Axis Powers represented by Germany, Italy, and Japan. After World War II, the world was divided into two major camps: one led by the United States and the other by the Soviet Union. The Cold War began, and the United States and the Soviet Union engaged in intense competition in various fields.

The Soviet Union's strength in military, science, and technology was at times on par with the United States'. In terms of military power after World War II, while the Soviet Union's navy was inferior to the United States', it had

[3] Kennedy, Paul M. *The Rise and Fall of the Great Powers: Economic Change and Military Conflict from 1500 to 2000*. Random House (NY), 1987.

a larger army and its nuclear projection capability was outstanding. In 1974, the Soviet Union had 1575 intercontinental ballistic missiles (the United States had 1054) and 720 submarine-launched ballistic missiles (the United States had 656). In terms of science and technology, while the United States was stronger in basic science and most cutting-edge technologies, the Soviet Union was at times ahead in areas such as aerospace. For example, the Soviet Union was the first country to successfully launch a satellite and astronauts into space in 1957, one year ahead of the United States.

In the late 1960s and early 1970s, the United States was mired in the Vietnam War; its domestic economy was stagnant, and its relations with economically recovering Western Europe and Japan were also becoming increasingly tense. During this period, the Soviet Union was able to narrow its economic gap with the United States. It provided a large amount of aid to so-called Third World countries and enhanced its influence globally, so much so that its position in the global governance system arguably surpassed that of the United States.

The Soviet Union never surpassed the United States in manufacturing, although its heavy industry was on par with the United States' for a considerable period of time. By the late 1960s, the Soviet Union's GDP reached its peak, at about 60% of the United States'. In the financial area, the Soviet Union did not establish an open financial system and was far behind the United States in financial development and access to world financial markets.

Ultimately, the Soviet Union's domestic economy stagnated as its manufacturing industry was too focused on heavy industry, and it was overly expansionist abroad. In the more than ten years after its invasion of Afghanistan in 1979, economic, social, and political crises in the Soviet Union intensified and it eventually disintegrated, thus losing in the great power competition with the United States.

3.1.4 US-Japan Competition

Japan was defeated in World War II and occupied by the US military. In 1951 and 1960, Japan and the United States signed the "Japan-US Security Treaty" and the "New Japan-US Security Treaty," respectively, allowing the United States to maintain its military bases and large-scale troop presence in Japan.

After its defeat in World War II, Japan's economy was paralyzed and production plummeted. Subsequently, Japan's economy was nurtured by the United States, first through billions of dollars in direct aid, and then through huge "special demand" orders during the Korean War and the Vietnam War. As a result, Japan's economy recovered and developed rapidly, with GDP reaching 60% of the United States' in 1992. Japan's total industrial output surpassed that of the United States in 1995, marking the beginning of a period of competition between the two countries.

From the 1970s to the mid-1980s, Japan opened its domestic financial market, reduced financial regulation, and promoted the internationalization of the yen. But by 1995, the yen accounted for only 6.77% of the world's official foreign exchange reserves, while the US dollar accounted for 58.96%, indicating a significant difference in the yen's international status compared to the dollar. After the 1997 Asian financial crisis, Japan's approach shifted from pursuing the internationalization of the yen in international trade, financial transactions, and reserve asset holdings, to the regionalization of the yen. The Japanese government proposed the idea of establishing an Asian Monetary Fund (AMF) with Japan at the center to provide financial support to countries and regions affected by the Asian financial crisis. This idea was strongly opposed by the International Monetary Fund (IMF) and its largest shareholder, the United States, and had to be abandoned.

Competition between the United States and Japan manifested mainly in the fields of trade and technology. Japan caught up with the United States in some areas of advanced manufacturing and technology. For instance, Japan's steel and automobile production surpassed the United States' in 1980, and its semiconductor dynamic random access memory (DRAM) production surpassed the United States' in 1982.

With the rapid development of Japan's industries, trade frictions with the United States began to intensify. In the early postwar period, there was a large gap in economic strength between Japan and the United States, but by 1965, the trade pattern between the two countries reversed, and the United States began to experience a trade deficit vis-à-vis Japan. By 1980, the bilateral US trade deficit with Japan reached $12.4 billion, accounting for one-third of the total US trade deficit.[4] Trade frictions between Japan and the United States gradually expanded from textiles and steel to other fields, namely color TVs, video recorders, semiconductors, electromechanical products, and automobiles. Taking advantage of their unequal political status, the United States implemented a series of measures to suppress Japan's rise. The following are some well-known examples: in 1981, the United States reached an agreement with Japan for the latter to impose "voluntary export restraints" on its automobile industry to appease US domestic automobile producers; in 1985, the United States forced Japan to increase imports of US agricultural products such as beef and oranges; also in 1985, the United States, Japan, France, Germany, and the United Kingdom signed the Plaza Accord, allowing the dollar to depreciate against the yen and the deutschmark; in 1986, the United States forced Japan to set a minimum price for its semiconductor exports to the United States and guarantee the market share of semiconductors imported from the United States; in 1987, the US government imposed a 100% tariff on electronic products from Japan such as televisions and computers from Japan.

As a result of the 1985 Plaza Accord, the yen appreciated significantly against the dollar and Japan's exports decreased, reducing (but not eliminating) its trade surplus vis-à-vis the United States. This ultimately led to Japan's "lost decade" of sluggish growth and deflation.

[4] The data comes from the United Nations Statistical Yearbook.

In summary, Japan surpassed the United States in manufacturing and was on par with the United States in technology for a time, but lagged in terms of economic size, financial weight, military power, and global governance role. The United States, leveraging its superiority over Japan in those four fields, forced Japan to continually make concessions in their trade and technology competition, causing it to lose its competitive advantage in those areas. This ultimately led to stagnation in Japan's economic growth and the loss of its ability to catch up with the United States.

3.1.5 US-China Competition

In 2010, China's manufacturing output surpassed the United States' and by 2016, China's nominal GDP was 60% of the United States' nominal GDP, marking the beginning of competition between the two countries. The current status of competition has China leading in manufacturing and the United States leading in the other five fields. (In fact, by some measures of PPP-adjusted GDP, China's PPP-adjusted GDP has already surpassed that of the United States.) The competition has just begun, and it will undoubtedly be an earth-shattering event of the twenty-first century. The outcome will determine the direction of the world order in the twenty first century.

Looking at great power competitions in history, it is clear that unless the rising power can surpass the incumbent power in all six areas, there is a high likelihood that it will fail the challenge. Competition in manufacturing capacity, economic size, and military strength tend to attract the most public attention, and it is relatively straightforward for the rising power to concentrate its efforts in these areas. However, catching up with and surpassing the incumbent power in technology, finance, and global governance is more challenging, and the incumbent power can still prevail based on its strengths in these three fields, even if it loses its strengths in manufacturing, economic size, and military strength.

3.2 The Three Elements of Competition

What forces determine the level of confrontation or cooperation between nations? "Who is the enemy, who is the friend" is certainly important, but there are no eternal friends or enemies between nations. National interests, and only national interests, are the ultimate consideration in determining the level of confrontation or cooperation between nations. So, under the premise of maximizing national interests, what are the most important factors affecting the level of confrontation or cooperation between two countries?

Our research shows that the level of confrontation or cooperation between two countries mainly depends on three elements: (1) the relative strength of the two countries; (2) the political and cultural identities of the two countries; and (3) the third-party effect, that is, the impact of a third party on the relationship between the two countries.

3.2.1 Relative Strength

In daily life, when two people have a conflict, the police maintain order and judicial agencies mediate the conflict. A conflict between nations is slightly different from conflicts between individuals because there is no world body authorized to maintain order and mediate conflicts. Conflict between nations is like a two savages fighting over food. Each savage sees both expected benefits (more food) and expected costs (injury) arising from the fight. The primary factor determining the intensity of the conflict between two savages is relative brute strength—only when the strength of both sides is comparable does the conflict become intense.

The expected benefit from a conflict between nations is typically modeled as the probability of winning times a larger share of total output (as represented by the sum of the GDP of the two countries). The expected losses from a conflict between nations can be human casualties as well as the negative impact of the conflict on the economy, such as the impact of the Russia-Ukraine conflict on Ukraine's agricultural production.

How does relative strength affect the likelihood of conflict between two countries? This can be discussed from the perspectives of a small country, a big country, and countries of comparable strength.

Small country versus bigger opponent. A small country that is weaker than its opponent may make two completely different choices depending on its domestic economic situation. If its domestic economic situation is deteriorating, the small country may be more likely to opt for conflict with its bigger rival for two reasons: to divert domestic attention away from the economic crisis and to take the chance that it might win the conflict and thereby obtain more resources and alleviate the domestic economic crisis. If its domestic economy is growing well, the small country is more likely to cooperate with its bigger rival and postpone conflict, so-called hiding one's capabilities and biding one's time.

Big country versus smaller opponent. A large country has little to gain from a conflict with a smaller opponent, so it is likely to cooperate with the smaller rival.

Big country versus big opponent. Two big countries of comparable strength are likely to become more aggressive toward each other. The reason is simple: "One mountain cannot harbor two tigers."

Take China and the United States as an example. In the 1980s, China was still significantly weaker than the United States. A conflict with the United States would not have yielded much benefit to China. Moreover, China's economy was growing rapidly, and a peaceful and stable international environment was conducive to China's domestic development. From the perspective of the (far stronger) United States, China posed no challenge to US dominance in the global market, so there was not much to be gained from a conflict with China. Therefore, at that time, from the perspective of relative strength, choosing cooperation over conflict was more beneficial than harmful for both China and the United States.

But since 2016, China's GDP has exceeded 60% of US GDP, making China the second-largest economy in the world after the United States. The relative strengths of the two countries has changed and objectively, China and the United States have become two big countries competing in the international market.

Take China and Japan as another example. In the 1980s, China's economy was also very weak compared to Japan's, and China-Japan relations were generally friendly and stable. Around 2010, China's GDP caught up with Japan's, and China replaced Japan as the largest economy in Asia. The Diaoyu Islands dispute erupted around that time, and the relationship between the two countries became tense. Ten years later, in 2020, China's GDP was three times that of Japan. While Japan has allied with the United States in the latter's competition with China, its relations with China are gradually easing.

Will a small country that is growing well always choose to cooperate with a big country? The answer is not necessarily. Whether to choose cooperation or conflict also depends on two other elements: political and cultural identity, and third-party effects.

3.2.2 *Political and Cultural Identity*

"Good wine is for friends, and if jackals come, they will be greeted with hunting rifles." This classic lyric vividly illustrates that it is easy for friends to cooperate, while there is more conflict between enemies. Conflicts with people with whom one identifies closely have a high cost relative to the expected benefit, so friends will try to avoid conflict. However, conflicts with people with whom one is less aligned yield relatively less cost compared to the expected benefit.

Similarly, if two countries have a high degree of political and cultural alignment, the expected benefits of conflict are small relative to the cost and they are more inclined to cooperate with each other. Conversely, if two countries have a low degree of political and cultural alignment, such as significant ideological differences, then the expected benefits of conflict are greater relative to the cost and they are more inclined to conflict.

3.2.3 *Third-Party Effect*

In most cases, bilateral relations between two countries are part of multilateral relations and are influenced by third parties outside of the two countries. This situation is referred to as the third-party effect. The influence of a third party on the relations between the two countries is quite complex and can be divided into three situations.

Conflicting parties are major powers and the third party is a small country. For example, in the US-Soviet competition, the United States and the Soviet Union were major powers, while Belgium in Western Europe and Hungary in Eastern Europe were third-party small countries. In this case, the third party has no substantial impact on the conflict between the major powers.

Conflicting parties are major powers and the third party is also a major power. For example, in the Franco-German conflict before World War I, France and Germany were major powers, and the third-party, Britain, was also a major power. In this case, the more independent and powerful the third-party Britain was, the more difficult it was for either France or Germany to defeat the other and dominate Europe, so the intensity of the Franco-German conflict was relatively low. But if Britain leaned toward one side, France and Germany would be more prone to conflict. In fact, shortly after Britain abandoned neutrality and chose to join the French camp, forming the Franco-Russian-British alliance, World War I broke out.

Conflicting parties are small countries and the third party is a major power. If the third-party major power is independent of the dispute between the small countries, then the intensity of conflict between the two small countries would depend on their relative strength and the degree of closeness in their political and cultural identification. If the third-party major power is in the same camp as the two small countries, the two small countries would tend to cooperate under the orders of the camp led by the third-party major power. If the third-party major power is allied with only one of the small countries, then the level of conflict between the two small countries would conform to the level of conflict between a small country and a big country (or camp).

3.3 Five Stages in US-China Relations

Using our framework of six fields and three elements of great power competition, we can categorize past and future US-China relations as five stages shown in Table 3.2.

In these five stages of US-China relations, the first and second stages are historical, and the third, fourth, and fifth stages are forward-looking. For the historical and current situations, we use a bilateral relationship index[5] to carry out a quantitative analysis.

[5] Index source: Yan, Xuetong, and Fangyin Zhou, "Quantitative Measurement of National Bilateral Relations," *Chinese Social Sciences* 06 (2004): 90–103. The index was subsequently updated on the official website of the Institute of International Relations, Tsinghua University. http://www.tuiir.tsinghua.edu.cn/info/1145/5980.htm, accessed on November 27, 2023.

Table 3.2 Five stages of US-China relations

Stage	*Year*	*Characteristics*
Confrontation Stage	1949–1978	• In terms of political identity, there was ideological confrontation between China and the United States • In terms of relative economic strength, China was far behind the United States and developing slowly
Small Country—Big Country Stage	1979–2015	• In terms of political identity, China and the United States established diplomatic relations and normalized relations • In terms of relative economic strength, China's GDP was less than 60% of the United States', making it a small country in comparison; at the same time, the industrial structures of the two countries were highly complementary, and China's economy was growing rapidly • In terms of third-party effects, US attention was distracted by its rivalry with the Soviet Union and later Japan, terrorism, the Global Financial Crisis, et cetera
Great Power Competition Stage I	2016–2035	• In terms of political identity, American protectionism starts to rise, and the US-China trade conflict breaks out after 2018 • In terms of relative economic strength, China's nominal GDP exceeds 60% of the United States', and China becomes the world's second-largest economy, gradually catching up with the United States. In terms of industrial structure, China enters the high-tech industry, becoming a strong competitor to the United States • There are no prominent third-party effects
Great Power Competition Stage II	2036–2060	• China's nominal GDP surpasses that of the United States • China and the United States compete in technology, finance, military, global governance, and other fields
Competitive Coexistence Stage	2061–	• China's nominal GDP reaches 1.5–2 times that of the United States. China, India, the United States, and the European Union become the world's major economies, and the world order enters a stage of competitive coexistence

3.3.1 *Historical Evolution of the US-China Relationship Index*

As shown in Fig. 3.2 of the US-China Relationship Index, the horizontal axis represents time, and the vertical axis is the bilateral relationship index. The higher the index value, the worse the relationship and the more severe the confrontation between the two countries. The lower the index value, the better the relationship between the two countries. The value of the index ranges from –9 to 9, where –9 to –6 is friendly, –6 to –3 is good, –3 to 0 is normal, 0 to 3 is discord, 3 to 6 is tension, and 6 to 9 is confrontation.

The major events marked in Fig. 3.2 are: ① first battle of the Korean War; ② signing of the Korean War Armistice Agreement; ③ signing of the US-Taiwan

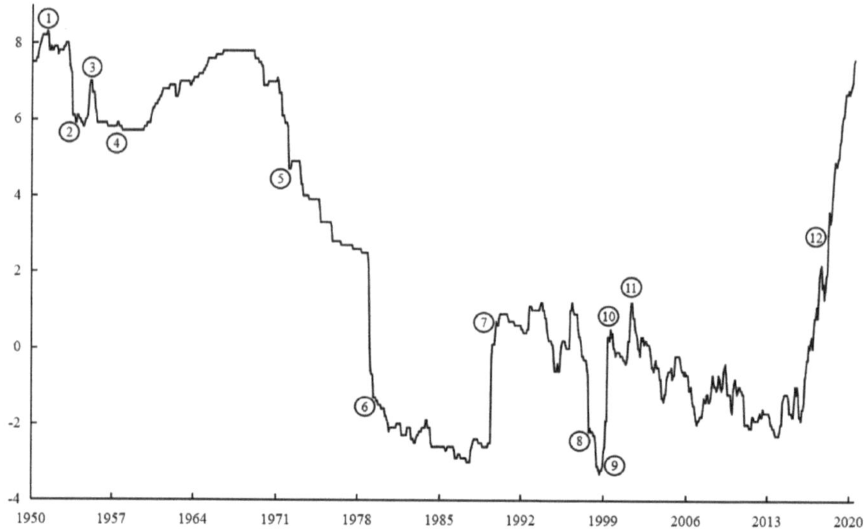

Fig. 3.2 US-China relationship index and major events (*Data source* Yan Xuetong Index)

Mutual Defense Treaty; ④ decision by China and the United States to upgrade consular-level talks to the ambassador level; ⑤ US President Richard Nixon's visit to China and signing the Shanghai Communique; ⑥ establishment of diplomatic relations between China and the United States; ⑦ US imposition of comprehensive sanctions on China; ⑧ China's President Jiang Zemin's visit to the United States; ⑨ US President Bill Clinton's visit to China; ⑩ US bombing of the Chinese Embassy in Yugoslavia; ⑪ US-China aircraft collision in the South China Sea; ⑫ US-China trade war.

Confrontation Stage (1949–1978)

Let's begin with the first stage from 1949 to 1978: the Confrontation Stage. As shown in Fig. 3.2, from 1950 to 1971, the US-China relationship index ranged between 4 and 8, indicating that the relationship between the two countries was confrontational. 1972–1978 marked the transition from the first stage to the second stage; in 1972, US President Nixon visited China, and the relationship between the two countries began to ease. In 1979, China and the United States established diplomatic relations and the relationship between the two countries began to improve.

Using the "six-fields three-elements" framework discussed earlier, we can analyze the reasons for the confrontation between China and the United States in this stage as follows. First, from the perspective of political and cultural identities, there is a political antagonism between China and the United States, pushing them toward conflict. Second, in terms of relative strength, among the six fields of great power competition, China could not compete with the United States in manufacturing, economic size, technology, and finance; however, China's military power was strongly demonstrated in the Korean War and the Vietnam War and in terms of global governance, China had a strong influence in the so-called Third World, making it a force that could not be ignored worldwide. Third, with respect to third-party effects, US-China relations were actually part of a US-Soviet-China triangle: when the Korean War broke out in 1950 and China chose to stand with the Soviet Union, China and the United States were in conflict, and in 1972, when Nixon visited China and China left the Soviet camp, US-China relations began to normalize.

Small Country-Big Country Stage (1979–2015)

The second stage in US-China relations ran from 1979 to 2015: the Small Country-Big Country Stage. After the establishment of diplomatic relations between China and the United States in 1979, political relations between the two countries normalized, and the relationship between China and the United States during this stage was cooperative, mainly for three reasons.

First, in terms of economic size, China was a small country and the United States was a big country. In 1980, China's industrial output was only 11% of that of the United States, and China's GDP was only 6% of that of the United States. The two countries did not meet the prerequisites for great power competition at that time. Because of the great disparity in their economic sizes, plus the fact that China's economy was growing rapidly, China's best strategy was to keep a low profile and focus on its own economic development.

Second, China and the United States were at different levels of development. China had low labor costs and scarce capital and technology, and the United States had high labor costs, advanced technology, and abundant capital, so the industrial structures of the two countries were highly complementary.

Third, during this stage, the United States' attention was distracted by other major countries and regional conflicts—the third-party effect—such as rivalry with the Soviet Union in the 1980s, trade disputes with Japan in the 1990s, and the global anti-terrorism campaign led by the United States after the 9/11 attacks.

Therefore, in the second stage from 1979 to 2015, the overall US-China relationship was relatively stable and good. Even so, as shown in Fig. 3.2, the US-China relationship index did occasionally fluctuate. In 1989, the United States imposed comprehensive sanctions on China, and the US-China relationship index rose from −2 to 1, still more or less within the normal range. After that, there were some favorable events mixed in with minor conflicts from time to time. For example, around the time of Clinton's visit to China in 1998, US-China relations quickly warmed up, while events such as the US bombing of the Chinese embassy in Yugoslavia in 1999 and the South China

Sea aircraft collision incident on April 1, 2001, caused short-term tensions in US-China relations.

Great Power Competition Stage I (2016–2035)

As shown in Fig. 3.2, in 2016, China and the United States entered the Great Power Competition Stage I. In 2018, the US-China trade war broke out, and the US-China relationship index subsequently jumped sharply. The index after June 2019 has already exceeded 6, which means the two countries are in a confrontational state. Overall, from 1949 to 2022, the US-China relationship index has approximated a U-shaped curve. How will US-China relations evolve in the future?

3.3.2 *Current Status and Outlook of US-China Relations*

US-China relations are currently in the third stage, namely Great Power Competition Stage I. In 2010, China's manufacturing output exceeded that of the United States; by 2016, China's nominal GDP had exceeded 60% of US GDP, making China the world's second-largest economy. After 2016, China met the prerequisites for the rising power vis-à-vis the incumbent power, the United States, and from then on, the two countries entered the stage of great power competition. In this stage, China's main task is to catch up in economic size. In 2022, China's nominal GDP was 70% of US GDP, and China aims to catch up with the United States by around 2035.

Assuming that US nominal GDP grows at its potential growth rate of 2% in the next few years, if China wants to achieve the goal of catching up with the United States in economic size in the period 2030–2040, the average annual growth rate of China's GDP over the next decade would need to be about 3 percentage points higher than that of the United States. In other words, to successfully achieve the goal of the first stage of great power competition, China's average annual GDP growth rate needs to reach 5% in the next decade or so.

If China's nominal GDP catches up with US GDP by 2035, then US-China relations will enter the fourth stage, namely Great Power Competition Stage II. The main theme of the fourth phase is still great power competition. In the early part of this stage, China's economic size will surpass the United States, but it will still lag in the four fields of high tech, finance, military strength, and global governance. Therefore, China's main task in this stage will be to catch up comprehensively in these four fields. According to most estimates, this will take about 30 more years, so China could surpass the United States in these four fields around 2060. If China successfully surpasses the United States in all six fields of great power competition, China's nominal GDP could eventually reach 1.5–2 times US GDP. At this time, the relationship between China and the United States will enter the Competitive Coexistence Stage.

How can China maintain the continuous development of its aggregate economy and achieve the goals of the third and fourth stages? This question will be analyzed in detail in the following chapters.

An interesting question is: if China's economy reaches twice the size of the US economy by 2060 and China becomes the world's largest economy, can it replace the United States and become the new world hegemon?

The answer is: unlikely. Why?

According to predictions by international organizations such as the United Nations, the World Bank, and the Organization for Economic Cooperation and Development (OECD), the mid-range forecast for China's total population in 2060 is about 1.2 billion, and by 2100 it will be 1 billion. Assuming stable immigration, the US population is expected to maintain a relatively stable growth rate, with a mid-range forecast of 400 million in 2060 and 500 million in 2100. According to the mid-range forecast, by 2060, China's total population will be three times that of the United States. If China's per capita GDP reaches about 70% of US per capita GDP by 2060, then China's nominal GDP will be about twice US GDP in 2060.

According to these forecasts, the top four economies in the world in 2060 will be China, India, the United States, and the European Union, with their respective shares of the world economy being about 29%, 18%, 16%, and 16%. Even so, China's share of the world economy at its peak would be less than 30%. Britain (including colonies) had over 50% of the world's industrial output when it became the world's leading country in 1860, and the United States also had over 50% of the world's GDP at the end of World War II in 1945. China's share of the world economy is far below the 50% needed to establish a world hegemony similar to that of Britain and the United States. Moreover, due to a declining population, China's share of the world economy will gradually decline after reaching its peak in 2060. Even in 2060, when China's economy becomes the largest in the world, the combined total of any two of the second, third, and fourth largest economies, India, the United States, and the European Union, will exceed China's economy. Therefore, it is unlikely that a hegemonic country similar to Britain or the United States will emerge in the world order after 2060. A more likely scenario is a world order where the top economies compete, cooperate, and coexist.

From now until 2060, China and the United States are in a stage of great power competition. On the one hand, China's economic strength is gradually catching up with that of the United States in terms of aggregate economic size, high tech, finance, and military power, which will inevitably bring about changes in the global governance system. On the other hand, the United States will use its still dominant position in the five areas of economic size, high tech, finance, military power, and global governance to contain China's development and maintain its leading position among the great powers. This kind of great power competition will last for at least 40 years. According to the above theory of the three elements of national conflict, it will not be surprising if conflicts or even intense confrontations occur in US-China relations over the next 40 years.

3.3.3 *The Changes in US-China Relations I Have Personally Experienced*

So far, US-China relations have gone through three stages: Confrontation, Small Country-Big Country, and Great Power Competition I. Interestingly, I happened to be a witness to these three stages of US-China relations. Here I share some stories from each stage that I have personally experienced, to supplement the macro analysis with a micro personal perspective.

A Story from the First Stage

My first impression of the United States in my memory was the slogan: "Down with American imperialism!"

On May 20, 1970, when I was in third grade in primary school, 500,000 Chinese people gathered in Tiananmen Square in Beijing to support the anti-American wars in Vietnam, Cambodia, and Laos. At the rally, Chairman Mao Zedong issued the 5/20 Declaration, calling on the people of the world to unite and overthrow American imperialism. Marshal Lin Biao, Vice Chairman, read Mao's 5/20 Declaration at the rally and shouted the last sentence loudly: "Down with American imperialism and all its running dogs!" One of my primary school classmates climbed the village telephone poles every day, mimicking the shouts of "Down with American imperialism and all its running dogs!" One day, police officers came to the village and arrested this boy, saying he slandered Vice Chairman Lin and was a counterrevolutionary.

I remember our primary school holding a pledge meeting to support the people of Vietnam, Cambodia, and Laos in their fight against America. After the principal finished reading his speech, he would shout this slogan. In my memory of primary school meetings, this slogan would always be shouted. This story illustrates how at that time China and the United States were in a confrontational relationship politically.

Stories from the Second Stage

In 1979, Vice Premier Deng Xiaoping visited the United States, and China and the United States normalized diplomatic relations. Western developed countries, led by the United States, opened their doors to China, and China's economy took this opportunity to quickly integrate into the world economy. The most prominent characteristics of China at that time were poverty and lack of openness to the world, especially in comparison with developed countries like the United States and Japan. The establishment of diplomatic relations between China and the United States brought China the opportunity for economic takeoff.

In 1980, I was studying in the Mathematics Department of Nanjing University, and a classmate brought a Sanyo tape recorder from Japan. The tape recorder was single-card and only the size of a book. The other classmates and I had never seen such a thing, so a large group of students crowded into his dormitory room to observe his tape recorder. Amid the commotion, one student pressed the play button, and a song by Teresa Teng floated out. The gentle, soft voice was something we had never heard before. All the students were instantly quiet. This was the first time I saw imported electrical appliances and heard such "decadent" music, and the impression is still vivid today!

In 1984, I was working at Nanjing Agricultural University, and a classmate came to visit me. He was wearing a high-necked sweater and a tie on the outside, looking very stylish. When I went to the cafeteria with him, many girls looked at him. He proudly said that the tie was an export item that was permitted for domestic sale, and they thought it was beautiful! I also thought the tie was indeed beautiful. When we met again later, he said he was wrong. The girls were looking at him not because the tie was beautiful, but because a tie should not be worn outside the sweater. One can't help but laugh. In the early 1980s, when China was just starting to reform and open up, the gap between China and developed countries in terms of economic development and standard of living was significantly vast.

In early 1990, I received a full scholarship from the Pennsylvania State University, so I prepared to go and study in the United States. Before going abroad, I was a teacher at Tsinghua University, with a monthly salary of 115 RMB. After I went to the United States for my postgraduate studies, my monthly scholarship was $800, which was about 30 times higher than my salary as a teacher in China.

At that time, in the eyes of Americans, China was very insignificant. There was almost no news about China on American television. In the months after I arrived in State College in 1990, the first time I saw a TV news report about China was when they were introducing the Terracotta Warriors in Xi'an. The Terracotta Warriors flashed by in the news, but from beginning to end, the focus was on a few old ladies with bound feet on the streets of Xi'an. I was so angry that I almost smashed the TV.

On my first day of graduate school in the United States, I introduced myself in halting English as coming from China, a major country with a larger population than the United States. My American classmate, Jack, immediately interrupted me, asserting that the United States was a major country, and China was a minor one. From that day, Jack and I would often debate the issue, and every few days, we would revisit it. Eventually, Jack presented data showing that China's GDP was less than one-tenth of US GDP, thus proving his point. I had no rebuttal and could only remain silent.

With Deng Xiaoping's southern tour in 1992, China accelerated its opening up. US-China relations warmed and the globalization of production—mainly through the outsourcing of manufacturing from developed countries like the United States, Japan, and Western European countries to China—developed rapidly. What struck me most at the time was the increasing number of products labeled "Made in China" on the shelves of American supermarkets.

After 1995, while working at the University of Oklahoma, I found that the small refrigerator, hairdryer, TV, and other electrical appliances I bought were all made in China, something unimaginable in the past.

During the Production Globalization Era, due to China's cheap labor, many American multinational companies moved their factories to China. While this significantly increased the profits of American multinational companies, it also led to a decline in American manufacturing and unemployment for many American workers. This sparked dissatisfaction with free trade and globalization within the United States, as well as debates about US-China relations. However, the dissatisfaction and debates abruptly ended with the 9/11 terrorist attacks in 2001.

In 2007, I started working at the IMF in Washington, DC. By then, China had become the country with the largest trade surplus with the United States. In 2008, when Obama won the US presidential election, the topic of "strategic adjustment of US-China relations" once again filled the meetings in Washington. On TV, there was news about China almost every day, and meetings at the World Bank and the IMF, regardless of their scale and theme, would always find a way to discuss China.

From these personal experiences I've shared, one can feel that the changes in US-China relations have always been influenced by the relative strengths of the two countries, their political and cultural identities, and the effects of third parties. These three dynamic variables determine the direction of US-China relations.

Here's a little anecdote I like to share. My former classmate Jack, who initially argued with me about whether China was a major country or a minor country, reunited with me in Washington in 2017, and we had another debate. However, this time he no longer insisted on the view that China was a minor country compared to the United States. Instead, he insisted on using PPP-adjusted GDP to compare the two countries, arguing that China's economy had already surpassed the United States on that basis.

This time, I also had no rebuttal. The facts are indeed as such: in 2014, the IMF calculated that China's GDP had surpassed the United States in terms of PPP. At the same time, China had transformed from a processing powerhouse into a manufacturing powerhouse, and from the "world's factory" into the "world's market." More importantly, "Made in China" had been upgraded to "Innovated in China"—by 2015, China's investment in research and development had surpassed the European Union's to rank second in the world.

Looking Forward to the Third Stage

What is China's main task before 2035? According to the rules of great power competition, the answer is simple: do everything possible to ensure long-term economic growth. You might say, isn't this common sense? Which country doesn't want to do a good job in economic growth?

Actually, it's not necessarily so. When conflicts arise between countries, the scene can become chaotic, and attention can easily be misplaced. For example, everyone might be thinking about ways to "show off their muscles" or "compare the size of their fists," forgetting that at this stage, their first task is actually to focus on "growing taller and stronger." Looking back at the experience of the United States successfully challenging the dominant position of Britain, what did the United States do right? It was to focus on economic development around the time of World War I!

Therefore, the most important goal for China at this stage is to catch up with the GDP of the United States around 2035. As mentioned earlier, achieving this goal requires China's GDP to grow at an average annual rate of 5%.

This goal is realistic. It should be noted that in 2024, the exchange rate of the RMB to the US dollar is roughly between 6.5 and 7.5 RMB per US dollar. In fact, due to the international reserve currency status of the US dollar, the exchange rate of the RMB to the US dollar overestimates the strength of the United States and underestimates the strength of China. Therefore, in the long run, the RMB will appreciate. Considering the long-term appreciation trend of the RMB exchange rate, it is possible for China's nominal GDP to catch up with US GDP by 2035.

But this goal is also a challenging one. If China's GDP is to maintain an annual growth rate of 5%, it needs corresponding development in areas such as technology, finance, military, and global governance, and the United States has certain advantages in these areas. It can be expected that from 2024 to 2040, the competition between China and the United States will unfold in a grand manner, and whether China can "persevere without letting go," maintaining a 5% annual GDP growth rate, will determine the future of US-China competition and the world order.

CHAPTER 4

Analysis of the US-China Tariff War

Why do international trade conflicts arise? They stem from competing overall long-term and/or specific short-term interests between countries. In Chapter 1, we discussed three principles for analyzing international trade conflicts from the perspective of competing overall and long-term interests. In this chapter, we will discuss competing specific and short-term interests between countries, using three well-known theorems of international trade: the Stolper-Samuelson theorem, the optimal tariff argument, and the "Hicks theorem" of technological competition. Then, we will analyze the US-China tariff war within the framework of competing overall/specific, long-term/short-term interests.

In March 2018, the Office of the US Trade Representative (USTR) released the "Section 301 Report into China's Acts, Policies, and Practices Related to Technology Transfer, Intellectual Property, and Innovation."[1] In the report, the US government put forward four reasons for the investigation into alleged actions by China to "encourage or require the transfer of American technology and intellectual property to enterprises in China": they could inhibit US market access to China; they could worsen the US trade deficit with China; they deprive US citizens of fair remuneration for their innovations; and they undermine US manufacturing, services, and innovation.

[1] United States Trade Representative, *Section 301 Report into China's Acts, Policies, and Practices Related to Technology Transfer, Intellectual Property, and Innovation*. 2018. https://ustr.gov/about-us/policy-offices/press-office/press-releases/2018/march/section-301-report-chinas-acts, accessed on November 29, 2025.

J. Ju, *US-China Great Power Competition and The New World Order*,
https://doi.org/10.1007/978-981-95-3762-4_4

But do these reasons hold up? If they don't, then what is the real reason for the United States to initiate this trade war?

We first introduce the Stolper-Samuelson theorem to analyze competing specific interests between countries. Then, we introduce the optimal tariff argument and the Hicks theorem to analyze competing short-term interests between countries.

4.1 Competing Specific Interests: The Stolper-Samuelson Theorem

The Stolper-Samuelson theorem (hereafter abbreviated as the SS theorem)[2] is a fundamental theorem in international trade theory. The SS theorem points out that although free trade is beneficial for a country as a whole, there are definitely winners and losers among different groups of people within the country. In political economy terms, free trade will inevitably lead to conflicts between interest groups within a country.

What different interest groups does a country have? The most important ones are the owners of different factors of production: the owners of labor (workers), the owners of capital (capitalists), the owners of technology, the owners of land, and so on. In theory, free trade benefits the country as a whole, that is, the gains of the winners will be greater than the losses of the losers. But if there are no corresponding domestic policies to use part of the winners' gains to subsidize the losers' losses, then the interest groups represented by the losers will definitely oppose free trade.

Which interest groups are the winners and which are the losers in international trade? The SS theorem proves that the owners of the relatively abundant factors in a country will usually be the winners, and the owners of the relatively scarce factors will usually be the losers. Take China and the United States as examples. China has abundant labor, but technology and capital are scarce; in the United States, it is just the opposite. Through free trade, China exports labor-intensive products and imports technology and capital-intensive products, while the United States does the reverse. Since the 1990s, many American processing factories have closed, and labor-intensive production has been outsourced to China. As a result, the demand for labor in China has increased, and workers have flocked from rural areas to export-processing factories in coastal areas in Guangdong, Zhejiang, Jiangsu, and other provinces—these (Chinese) workers have benefited from China's openness to trade. However, US manufacturing companies will employ fewer workers in their own country and the wages of American workers will

[2] The SS theorem was proposed by American scholars Wolfgang Stolper and Paul Samuelson in 1941. Stolper is a professor of economics at the University of Michigan, and Samuelson is a professor of economics at the Massachusetts Institute of Technology. The latter is not only a Nobel laureate in economics, but also one of the most important representatives of neoclassical economics.

decrease—the interests of (United States) workers will be harmed, so they will oppose free trade.

The cross-sectoral movement of factors of production under free trade also has political economy implications. Suppose free trade leads to a country importing software and exporting steel. As the country imports more software and exports more steel, its domestic software industry will shrink, and its domestic steel industry will expand. Some companies in the shrinking domestic software industry will go bankrupt, its workers will lose jobs, and both wages and investment returns in the industry will decrease. At the same time, new companies will enter the expanding domestic steel industry, employment and investment will expand, and both wages and investment returns in the industry will increase. In short, in the short term, international trade is beneficial to a country's export sector, but it will harm the interests of the import-competing sector.

The SS theorem can explain the market access and trade deficit arguments in the USTR's Section 301 Report. The report notes that China's exports to the United States are much higher than its imports from the United States, and this is impacting the employment of ordinary American workers. This view is supported by some academic research and is referred to as the "China Shock".[3] Mitigating the impact of Chinese exports on American manufacturing employment is one explanation for the United States initiating a trade war with China.

4.2 Competing Short-Term Interests

Economic analysis can be divided into dynamic and static analysis. Dynamic analysis refers to cross-time period analysis over multiple time periods, while static analysis refers to analysis within a single time period. In this book, we use dynamic analysis to refer to the long term, and static analysis to refer to the short term. Dynamic (long-term) analysis focuses on economic growth. Competing long-term interests between countries are highlighted in Chapter 1 using the principle of the growth trap of specialization solidification. Static (short-term) analysis focuses on prices.

The short term usually refers to a period of about a year, when investments in factories and other fixed capital have not yet had time to change. For example, after the outbreak of the US-China trade war, some Chinese textile factories exporting to the United States planned to move their production to Vietnam. The period before they move to Vietnam is considered the short term; the period after they move to Vietnam is considered the medium and long term.

[3] Autor, David H., David Dorn, and Gordon H. Hanson. "The China Shock: Learning from Labor-Market Adjustment to Large Changes in Trade," *Annual Review of Economics* 8, no. 1 (August 8, 2016): 205–40, https://doi.org/10.1146/annurev-economics-080315-015041.

What kind of international trade indicators reflect a country's short-term interests? One commonly used example is the short-term change in a country's export prices relative to its import prices. If a trade policy causes the country's export prices to rise or import prices to fall, then the country benefits from the policy, otherwise it suffers. In international trade theory, the ratio of export prices to import prices is also called the terms of trade. The occasional news report of "worsening terms of trade" generally refers to a drop in export prices or a rise in import prices. Policies affecting the terms of trade include tariffs and technological competition. These are illustrated below using the optimal tariff theory and the Hicks theorem.

4.2.1 *The Optimal Tariff Theory*

In the US-China trade war, tariffs are the focus. From 2018 to 2019, the United States increased tariffs on almost all products imported from China. Does increasing import tariffs benefit the United States?

When the United States imposes a tariff on a product such as washing machines imported from China, it affects three parties. The first party is the domestic consumer: the tariff causes the price of washing machines to rise in the United States; so the American consumer's utility (or "consumer surplus") is reduced. The second party is the domestic producer: when the price of washing machines rises in the United States, American manufacturers of washing machines will benefit from higher "producer surplus." The third party is the government: the tariff revenue increases government revenue.

Therefore, a country's optimal tariff depends on the balance of interests among these three parties, which can be summarized by two indicators: the terms of trade and the volume of trade in the affected product. An improvement in the terms of trade will increase a country's welfare, while a decrease in the volume of trade will usually reduce its welfare.

In international trade theory, countries are categorized as large countries and small countries. Large countries can influence world prices but small countries cannot and can only accept world prices. A country's optimal tariff largely depends on whether the country is a large or small country.

If a large country imposes a tariff on an imported product, it will reduce the domestic demand for the imported product, and consequently reduce the world demand for the product. As a result, the price of the imported product will fall, thus improving the large country's terms of trade and enhancing its welfare. On the other hand, the tariff decreases the volume of imports, thereby reducing the welfare of the country's consumers. The net effect of the tariff depends on the tradeoff between the effects of terms of trade improvement and the trade volume reduction. The so-called optimal tariff refers to the tariff rate that maximizes the country's benefit from the improved terms of trade, net of the loss caused by the decrease in trade (import) volume.

Whether a country can benefit from imposing a tariff depends on whether it can reduce the world price of the imported product by reducing its demand for the product. In other words, if a country can manipulate world prices through tariffs, then the optimal tariff for this country is greater than zero; otherwise, this country should set a zero tariff. A small country cannot affect world market prices because its import demand has no significant impact on the world market. Therefore, for small countries, the optimal tariff is generally zero. However, the optimal tariff for a large country is usually greater than zero because the domestic market of a large country is relatively large, and it can manipulate world prices by using a tariff to suppress domestic demand, and consequently world demand, for the imported product.

While a large country could gain from imposing an optimal tariff on its imports, the exporting country would always lose because it suffers both a worsening in its terms of trade and a decrease in its trade (export) volume.

The premise that a large country will benefit from imposing an optimal tariff on its imports rests on the assumption that other countries do not retaliate. If the other (exporting) party is also a large country, and retaliates by imposing its own optimal tariff, a tariff war will occur between two large countries. A tariff war will reduce the welfare of both countries, which will leave both countries worse off than if they had no tariffs at all.

Returning to the US-China trade war, the optimal tariff theory could imply that the US action of imposing additional tariffs on imports from China is because existing US tariffs on Chinese imports are lower than the optimal tariff, so it would seem that the United States would benefit from increasing its tariffs.

So, what exactly is the optimal tariff rate for US imports from China? Why did Trump want to impose a 25% tariff on imports from China across the board? From the discussion above, we know that the optimal tariff level of the United States depends on its ability to manipulate world market prices. For some products, such as widely used items like lighters and belts, China exports a large amount all over the world and the United States does not have much bargaining power, so its optimal tariff on these products should be close to zero. For other products such as washing machines, the United States is a big market and has stronger bargaining power, so its optimal tariff for washing machines will be higher. So according to the optimal tariff theory, it doesn't make sense for the United States to impose a 25% tariff on all types of products imported from China. China's announcement of a reciprocal 25% tariff on imports from the United States was simply a retaliation for the US action; 25% is not necessarily China's optimal tariff for imports from the United States.

The news media also reported an interesting detail about the trade war: during their negotiations with China, the Trump administration proposed a strange condition that China would not retaliate for the increased US tariffs. The Chinese media noted that this was funny and infuriating at the same time, that the Trump administration would be so unreasonable as to expect that the United States should be allowed to hit China but China would not be allowed to fight back.

But in fact, this condition of the US government can be explained by the optimal tariff theory. If China retaliates for the increased US tariffs by increasing its own tariffs on imports from the United States, there would be an all-out tariff war, which would not be in the interest of the United States. The United States wanted to increase its tariffs on imports from China, but it also wanted to avoid a tariff war with China, so its demand of "no retaliation" was in line with the requirements of the optimal tariff theory. Of course, whether the Chinese government agreed to this condition is another issue.

4.2.2 *The Hicks Theorem*

Other reasons for the United States to initiate its trade war with China are the protection of its intellectual property rights and the protection against China's "forced technology transfer," industrial policy, and state-owned enterprises. These two reasons are actually related to the technological competition between the two countries. To analyze these two reasons, we will use the Hicks theorem about technology competition.[4] The question originates from a problem proposed by British economist John Hicks in 1953: Will a country benefit or suffer from another country's technological progress?

The core of the answer lies in the impact on import and export prices, that is, the terms of trade. Technological progress usually reduces the cost of products, thereby reducing the price of products. A country's technological progress has three possible outcomes for its trading partner. In the first case, if technology improves uniformly in all sectors in the country, reducing the prices of both its exports and its import-competing products and leaving its terms of trade unaffected, the welfare of its trading partners will generally improve. In the second case, if technology improves mainly in the country's export sector, reducing its export prices and worsening its terms of trade, the welfare of its trading partners will improve. In the third case, if technology improves mainly in the country's import-competing sector, reducing the price of its imports and improving its terms of trade, the welfare of its trading partners will deteriorate.

In terms of US-China trade, let's assume that China has a comparative advantage in textiles, producing and exporting textiles, while the United States has a comparative advantage in semiconductor chips, producing and exporting chips. Then, using the Hicks theorem, we can conclude that if China improves its technology in the production of textiles, it will increase the supply and

[4] Paul Samuelson studied the issue of whether the United States benefits or suffers when China's technology level improves, see: Samuelson, Paul, "Where Ricardo and Mill Rebut and Confirm Arguments of Mainstream Economists Supporting Globalization," *Journal of Economic Perspectives*, 18(3), 2004, pp135-146. Jiandong Ju and Xuebing Yang have systematically discussed this issue and summarized it as the "Hicks Theorem," see: Ju, Jiandong and Xuebing Yang, "Hicks Theorem: Effects of Technological Improvement in the Ricardian Model," *International Review of Economics and Finance* 18, 2009, pp. 239–247.

reduce the price of its textiles, thus improving the welfare of the United States, which imports textiles from China. If China improves its technology in the production of semiconductor chips, it will reduce its demand for and hence the price of imported chips, thereby reducing the welfare of the United States which exports chips to China.

Here's an actual example. Around 2010, the selling price of China-made cars was generally about 100,000 RMB. At that time, continuously variable transmissions (CVTs) could not be produced in China and needed to be imported. The import price of a CVT was about 60,000 RMB, accounting for about half of the price of a car. Later, when China began to produce CVTs domestically, priced at around 5000 RMB each, the price of imported CVTs suddenly dropped from 60,000 RMB to less than 10,000 RMB each. From this example, it can be seen that China's technological improvement in high-tech products will inevitably reduce the price of imported high-tech products, which will indeed harm the interests of the high-tech exporting countries.

4.3 The Structure of US Exports to China: The Puzzle of Anti-comparative Advantage

Before analyzing the US-China trade dispute that broke out in 2018, we need to first examine the structure of US exports to China. A major feature of US-China trade is that the United States has a large trade deficit with China. In 2022, China's exports to the United States amounted to $537.013 billion, while US exports to China were $155.785 billion. The US trade deficit with China was $381.228 billion, accounting for 32.2% of the total US trade deficit of $1.18 trillion.[5]

In 2022, China's total trade surplus was $877.603 billion, of which the surplus with the United States accounted for 46%.[6] In fact, China's trade surplus in 2022 was only 4.72% of GDP, a significant drop from the peak of 7.51% of GDP in 2007.[7] So, what are the characteristics of US-China trade and how have they changed over the years?

The US trade deficit with China can be partly explained by the observation that the United States exports only a few products to China. Why only a few? What are the main products that the United States exports to China?

The years 1992–2011 were a period of rapid growth in US-China trade. The total trade volume between China and the United States increased by 25 times, and the share of imports from China in total US imports rose rapidly from 5% in 1992 to 20% in 2011. However, the share of imports from the United States in China's total imports did not increase but actually decreased from 11% in 1992 to 8% in 2011. Correspondingly, the US trade deficit with

[5] Data source: U.S. Bureau of Statistics

[6] Data source: General Administration of Customs, PRC.

[7] Data source: National Bureau of Statistics of China.

Table 4.1 Main US exports to China

Product type	*$ millions*			*Percentage change from 2000 to 2008 (%)*
	2000	*2004*	*2008*	
Waste and scrap	744	2508	7562	916
Oilseeds and grains	1048	2829	7316	598
Semiconductors and Electronic Products	1317	3565	7475	467
Resins, Rubber, Artificial or Synthetic Fibers	660	1630	3523	433
Aircraft and its Parts	1770	2111	5470	209
Total US exports to China	16,253	34,721	71,457	339

Source US-China Economic and Security Review Commission, 2009 Annual Report to Congress, p. 77

China increased by about 150 times, from $1.45 billion in 1992 to $235 billion in 2011.

Table 4.1 lists the top five items exported from the United States to China in 2000–2008, as reported in the US-China Economic and Security Review Commission's 2009 Annual Report to Congress.

Although the share of imports from the United States in China's total imports declined in dollar terms, the amount of US exports to China increased from $16.253 billion in 2000 to $71.457 billion in 2008. The largest increase in US exports to China was in waste and scrap, which grew from $744 million in 2000 to $7.562 billion in 2008, an increase of 9.16 times. The next four most important US exports to China were the familiar oilseeds and grains; semiconductors and electronic products; resins, rubber, artificial or synthetic fibers; and aircraft and parts.

Table 4.2 shows the industry ranking of US exports to China in 2011. If we rank products by the value of US exports to China as a share of US exports to the world, what are the top three products that the United States exports to China? Are they chips and soybeans? No, they are not.

As shown in Table 4.2, the top US export to China in 2011 was waste aluminum, of which China accounted for 71.28% of total US exports; the second was copper waste and scrap copper, of which China accounted for 69.43% of total US exports; the third was waste cardboard, of which China accounted for 67.93% of total US exports. These three types of waste together accounted for 7.04% of total US exports to China (8.58% when we include scrap metal and other garbage). Therefore, in 2011, the most important "product" exported by the United States to China, in terms of share of total US exports to the world, was actually garbage!

After 2012, China began to restrict and gradually ban the import of solid waste from abroad and the share of US waste exports to China in China's total imports began to decline. But when the US-China trade war erupted in 2018

Table 4.2 Ten industries with the largest share of US exports to China in 2011

HS Product Code	*Exports as share of total US exports to China (%)*	*Exports to China as share of total US exports to the world (%)*	*Ranking by share of total US exports to China*	*Ranking by share of total US exports to the world*	*Product name*
760,200	2.63	71.28	4	1	Waste aluminum
740,400	3.37	69.43	2	2	Copper waste and scrap
470,710	1.04	67.93	9	3	Recovered (waste and scrap) unbleached kraft paper/ paperboard/ corrugated paper
120,100	10.09	59.66	1	4	Soybeans, whether or not broken
520,100	2.45	30.43	5	5	Cotton, not carded/ combed
720,449	1.53	17.11	8	6	Ferrous metal waste and Scrap
854,231	2.44	15.09	6	7	Electronic integrated circuits, processors, and controllers
870,323	2.82	12.53	3	8	Passenger vehicles, cylinder capacity 1500–3000 cc
870,324	1.77	10.39	7	9	Passenger vehicles, cylinder capacity greater than 3000 cc
270,112	0.81	5.63	10	10	Bituminous coal

Source UNComtrade

and the United States tightened control over its high-tech exports to China, the share of US waste exports to China began to rise again. For example, US exports of scrap copper to China dropped from 3.37% of China's total imports in 2011 to 0.38% in 2019, and then rose back to 0.98% in 2021.

The principle of comparative advantage discussed in Chapter 1 suggests that a country's export structure should be consistent with its relative efficiency in producing products, that is, the higher the relative efficiency (or the lower the relative opportunity cost) of producing a product, the more likely it is to be exported. Five scholars from Tsinghua University[8] analyzed the structure of US exports to China and found that China's exports to the United States are in line with China's comparative advantage, but US exports to China do not conform to US comparative advantage—the higher the relative efficiency of production in the United States, the less those products are exported to China! They called this abnormal phenomenon of US exports to China the "anti-comparative advantage puzzle."

Why do US exports to China violate the principle of comparative advantage? This is because the United States is unwilling to export the high-tech products in which it has a comparative advantage to China and restricts those exports instead, but it is willing to export waste to China and actively does so. So why is the United States unwilling to make use of its comparative advantage and export more high-tech products to China?

4.4 The US-China Tariff War

The three principles in Chapter 1 (the principle of comparative advantage, the principle of international monopoly profits, and the principle of the growth trap of specialization solidification) and the three theorems discussed in this chapter—the SS theorem, the optimal tariff theory, and the Hicks theorem—provide a framework for analyzing trade wars in terms of competing overall/specific and long-term/short-term interests between countries. The principle of international monopoly profits can be used to analyze competing overall interests between countries. The SS theorem can be used to analyze competing interests among different groups within a country. The principle of the growth trap of specialization solidification can explain competing interests between poor and rich countries when it comes to industrial upgrading and long-term growth. The optimal tariff theory and the Hicks theorem can explain, using the terms of trade, competing interests between countries when it comes to tariffs and technological competition. A country's overall interests and specific interests may be consistent or divergent, and so may its long-term interests and short-term interests. A country's trade policy reflects the balance of and contradictions in its overall/specific and long-term/short-term interests.

[8] Ju, Jiandong, Ma Hong, Wei Ziru, et al. 2012. "The Mystery of the Anti-Comparative Advantage in US-China Trade," *China Economic Quarterly* (in Chinese) 4: 805–832.

The US-China trade war started with the USTR's Section 301 Report in March 2018 and entered a new stage with the so-called CHIPS and Science Act[9] in August 2022, which basically represents the shift of US policy strategy toward China from cooperation to competition. Behind the four main reasons for the US trade actions against China given by the US government are the real reasons that are revealed by our analytical framework, and these real reasons are clearly suggested in the CHIPS and Science Act of 2022.

4.4.1 *Facts*

On March 23, 2018, after the USTR's Office released its Section 301 Report, US President Trump announced plans to impose 25% tariffs on $50 billion worth of imports from China. China immediately responded with plans for retaliatory tariffs on about $50 billion worth of imports from the United States. The tariffs began to be implemented on July 6, 2018.

The first round of tariffs imposed by the United States and China each had their own focus, both aiming to hit the other's pain points. The first batch of Chinese goods that the United States imposed a 25% tariff on was concentrated in products "containing industrially significant technology," which was the area highlighted in the Section 301 Report. The first batch of US goods that China imposed a 25% retaliatory tariff on was concentrated in the agricultural and automotive industries, which are areas that have a significant impact on US domestic politics.

The United States firmly opposed China's retaliatory tariffs, which escalating the conflict between the two sides and leading to further rounds of tariff measures covering a broader range of goods. From July 6, 2018, when the United States and China implemented the first round of tariff measures, to January 15, 2020, when they signed the so-called Phase One Trade Deal in Washington, D.C., the two sides imposed five rounds of tariffs on each other.

According to a report by the US Congressional Research Service, after these five rounds, about 67% of US imports from China were subject to tariffs ranging from 15 to 25%, and about 60% of China's imports from the United States were subject to tariffs ranging from 5 to 25%. Estimates show that the US-China tariff war involved more than $450 billion worth of goods exported by both countries.[10]

Although the Phase One trade deal signed in 2020 temporarily suspended the unprecedented economic and trade tensions between the two countries, the tariffs largely remained in place. The average US tariff rate on imports from China rose sharply from 3.1% before the tariff war to 19.3% after the

[9] "H.R.4346—117th Congress (2021–2022): CHIPS and Science Act," https://www.congress.gov/bill/117th-congress/house-bill/4346, accessed on November 29, 2025

[10] Fajgelbaum, Pablo D., and Amit K. Khandelwal. "The Economic Impacts of the US–China Trade War," *Annual Review of Economics* 14, no. 1 (April 28, 2022): 205–28. https://doi.org/10.1146/annurev-economics-051420-110410.

tariff war, and the China's average tariff rate on imports from the United States also increased significantly from 8% before the tariff war to 21.2% after the tariff war.

The mutual imposition of tariffs by the United States and China has had adverse effects on both countries and even the global economy. In 2022, even though the total value of China's goods trade (imports and exports, in US dollars) maintained a good growth rate of 4.2% over the previous year, the total value of China's goods trade with the United States grew by only 0.48% over the previous year.[11] As for US goods exports to China, by December 2019, they had fallen by 18.6% compared to 2017, and US exports subject to China's retaliatory tariffs had fallen by 26% compared to 2017. In 2020, US goods exports to China recovered to 5.01% below the 2017 level, and it was not until 2021 that they went above the 2017 level. US goods exports to China remained above the 2017 level in 2023 but 3.11% lower than the 2021 level.[12]

4.4.2 Reasons

When we re-examine the reasons for US trade action against China set out in the Section 301 Report and elsewhere, we can see that they are inconsistent with the facts in many places.

US trade deficit with China. The $419.2 billion number for the US merchandise trade deficit with China in 2018 is an overestimate. According to calculations by China's Ministry of Commerce,[13] the US merchandise trade deficit with China in 2018 was about $240.9 billion (not counting the processing trade), and the overall US trade deficit with China in 2018 was about $153.6 billion, only 37% of the bilateral merchandise trade deficit number published by the United States. Moreover, China's trade surplus was on a declining trend in 2018, having fallen 2.5% of GDP from 10% in 2007, according to data provided by the World Bank; and China's trade balance was considered by the IMF to be basically balanced in 2019.

US manufacturing unemployment. Have China's exports exacerbated unemployment in the US manufacturing sector? There are different research results on this issue. For example, Shang-Jin Wei and others[14] point out that previous studies only considered the direct impact of China's exports on

[11] Data source: National Bureau of Statistics website, https://data.stats.gov.cn/easyquery.htm?cn=C01, accessed on November 29, 2025.

[12] Data source: https://www.bea.gov/data/intl-trade-investment/international-trade-goods-and-services, accessed on November 29, 2025.

[13] Data source: http://www.xinhuanet.com/english/2019-06/06/c_138122148.htm, accessed on November 29, 2025.

[14] Wang, Zhi, Shang-Jin Wei, Xinding Yu, and Kunfu Zhu. "Re-Examining the Effects of Trading with China on Local Labor Markets: A Supply Chain Perspective," August 1, 2018, https://papers.ssrn.com/sol3/papers.cfm?abstract_id=3236693.

US export industries and not their indirect impact on upstream and downstream industries in the United States. If we consider that China's exports to the United States have improved the production efficiency of US industries, thereby increasing employment in upstream and downstream industries, then China's exports have helped to increase rather than decreasing employment in US manufacturing. For example, China's steel exports to the United States have indeed reduced employment in the US steel industry, but China's steel exports have also helped to reduce the price of US steel, increasing the production efficiency of the US construction industry that uses a large amount of steel, thereby increasing employment in that industry. Thus, China's steel exports have increased net employment in the United States when the steel industry and construction industry are considered together.

Forced technology transfer. The Section 301 Report accuses China of stealing American technology and forcing American companies to transfer their intellectual property to enterprises in China. This accusation also contains many inaccuracies. For example, in 2018 the United States accused the China National Nuclear Corporation (CNNC) of plagiarizing 70,000 technical documents from the Westinghouse Electric Company. But what actually happened? Westinghouse had sold the technology for its AP1000 nuclear reactor, which could not find a buyer in the United States, to China Nuclear Power Company (CNNP), a subsidiary of CNNC. According to the agreement between the two parties, Westinghouse provided CNNP with the corresponding 70,000 technical documents. This was something CNNP paid for, so how did it become theft?

Non-market policies. The US government has accused China of "unfair" competition because it subsidizes its high-tech industries and state-owned enterprises through industrial policies. This is really an unfair accusation. Most high-tech industries have increasing returns to scale and require a large amount of fixed investment such as in research and development (R&D). Governments in all countries support their high tech industries in various ways. The United States and China have different positions in the global value chain for high-tech industries. US government subsidies are mainly in the R&D stage, while China's government subsidies are mainly in the manufacturing stage, and subsidies in the manufacturing stage inevitably involve direct subsidies to enterprises. The US government seems to believe that subsidies for R&D and innovation are "fair" while subsidies for manufacturing enterprises are "unfair." Even so, the US government has itself now begun to directly subsidize US enterprises. The 2022 CHIPS and Science Act signed by President Biden allocates over $52 billion in fiscal funds to support R&D, manufacturing, and training in the US semiconductor industry in the name of competing with China. The US accusation against China for supporting high-tech industries through industrial policies is hypocritical.

In summary, the reasons put forward by the US government for initiating the trade war with China are not only unfair, but often inconsistent with the facts. So, what are the real reasons for the tariff war? We can analyze this question using our framework of competing overall/specific and long-term/short-term interests.

The first batch of imports from China that was subjected to a 25% tariff by the United States, amounting to $50 billion, was concentrated in the high-tech industry. From the perspective of competing overall interests, we can argue that the US government's aim in imposing these tariffs was to limit the market scale of China's high-tech industry, thereby curbing the technological progress of this industry (which is characterized by increasing returns to scale) and enabling the United States to maintain its dominant position in the high-tech field. From the perspective of competing long-term interests, curbing China's high-tech industry would slow the speed of China's industrial upgrading and economic growth, and help the United States maintain its position as the world's largest economy for as long as possible. From the perspective of competing short-term interests, using the Hicks theorem, we can argue that restraining China's high-tech industry will keep the price of US high-tech exports (such as advanced semiconductors) high, keeping US chip manufacturing companies (such as Qualcomm) profitable.[15] Using the optimal tariff theory, we can argue that because the United States is a large player in the world market for high-tech products, the tariff on China's exports of these products would lower their price, thereby improving the US terms of trade. As for the various domestic interest groups in the United States, the tariffs on imports from China will protect the profits and employment level in US domestic enterprises that produce goods that compete with the targeted imports from China as well as increase the government's revenue.

But have these goals of the United States been achieved?

4.4.3 *Impact on US Welfare*

President Trump liked to claim that the United States would make billions of dollars of tariff revenue from the US-China trade war. However, paradoxically, in September 2020, more than 3000 US companies, including Tesla and Ford, jointly sued the US government, arguing that the tariffs increased the cost of products and parts imported from China, causing them economic losses. The companies demanded that the US government refund the tariff payments with interest. US Treasury Secretary Janet Yellen initially agreed to cancel the tariffs imposed by Trump to help American consumers and alleviate inflation pressure in the United States. However, USTR Katherine Tai insisted on retaining Trump's tariffs to help American workers. So, who is right and who is wrong among Trump, Yellen, Tai, and the more than 3000 US companies? What has been the impact of Trump's tariffs on China and the United States?

[15] Ju, Jiandong, Hong Ma, Zi Wang, and Xiaodong Zhu. "Trade Wars and Industrial Policy Competitions: Understanding the US-China Economic Conflicts," *Journal of Monetary Economics*, January 2024: 42–58.

From July 2018 to June 2019, the US government imposed tariffs of 25% on some $250 billion worth of goods imported from China, which roughly comes up to tariff revenue of $62.5 billion. China also imposed tariffs of 25% tariffs on some $110 billion worth of goods imported from the United States, which roughly comes up to tariff revenue of $27.5 billion. Since the United States collected about $35 billion more in tariff revenue than China did from the tariff war, it's no wonder that Trump has repeatedly claimed that the United States won the tariff game, to the tune of more than $30 billion!

So, was Trump right?

Standard partial equilibrium tariff analysis tells us that a tariff will affect a country's economy in three aspects: consumer welfare, producer welfare, and the government revenue. Recall the example of a tariff on washing machines in Sect. 4.2.1. The tariff will raise the price of washing machines in the United States, thereby reducing the welfare (consumer surplus) of US consumers who purchase washing machines and increasing the welfare (producer surplus) of US producers who make washing machines. Additionally, the tariff will increase the revenue of the US government. In sum, a tariff on washing machines will increase the welfare of US washing machine producers and the US government but reduce the welfare of US washing machine consumers. Therefore, Trump's claim that the United States won the tariff game is not accurate: the net impact of the tariff must take into account the total loss or gain of all three parties. Trump only focused on the $62.5 billion increase in government revenue but did not mention the impact on American consumers and producers.

For a small country that cannot influence world prices, the net welfare impact of a tariff is always negative, that is, the loss to domestic consumers is greater than the gains to domestic producers and the government. However, under optimal tariff theory, a large country capable of influencing global prices may achieve a positive net welfare impact. The critical question is whether the United States can influence world prices. It is generally believed that the United States, as a large country with a huge domestic market, should have this ability.

Surprisingly, research shows that the US market exhibits the characteristics of a small country and it cannot influence world market prices in the short term. Mary Amiti, Stephen Redding, and David Weinstein analyzed the impact of the 2018 US tariffs on world prices and US welfare and found that while the tariffs caused domestic prices in the United States to increase proportionally, the impact on world prices was almost zero. In other words, the tariffs imposed by the United States in 2018 did not manage to reduce world prices, which is a surprising finding. The cost of the US tariffs was almost entirely borne by US consumers and importers, as Chinese exporters did not lower their prices.

Trump's tariffs not only did not increase US welfare, but caused about $8.2 billion in unnecessary losses.[16]

Research by other American scholars has found similar results, that is, the additional US tariffs did not manage to reduce the world prices of the targeted products, so the cost of tariffs has been almost entirely borne by US consumers and importers. Thus, the views of Tesla, Ford, and other US companies that import Chinese parts, as well as US Treasury Secretary Yellen, who believed that Trump's additional tariffs reduced US consumers' welfare, are supported by academic research.

Furthermore, the optimal tariff theory indicates imposing the optimal tariff is beneficial for the large country only if its trading partners do not retaliate. However, when the United States imposed tariffs on imports from China, China retaliated immediately (such as by imposing tariffs on soybean imports from the United States), which further harmed the interests of US exporters (such as farmers).

4.4.4 *Impact on the US Trade Balance*

Let's take a look at the impact of the US tariffs on the US trade balance, which is the main component of the current account balance.[17] China's current account surplus with the United States saw a significant decline in 2018, falling by $146 billion from 2017. However, the US current account deficit did not decrease, but instead increased by $38.3 billion. Why?

The data shows that in August 2018, after the United States imposed tariffs on imports from China, China's exports to the United States decreased by $850 million. However, at the same time, Mexico's exports to the United States increased by $850 million. Therefore, the imports that the United States reduced from China almost all shifted to increased imports from Mexico, showing a clear trade diversion phenomenon. In 2018, the US trade deficit with China decreased significantly, but its trade deficit with Mexico, Japan, Germany, and other countries increased significantly.

In fact, the US trade deficit has continued to increase yearly, from $799.3 billion in 2017 (before the US-China tariff war) to $1.09 trillion in 2021, with only a slight reduction in 2019. The US-China trade war has not improved the US trade deficit.

Can the United States use tariffs to improve its current account deficit? The answer is no. Why? Because a current account deficit means that the country's aggregate saving is less than its aggregate investment, so it is essentially borrowing money from the rest of the world. Successive US administrations

[16] Amiti, Mary, Stephen J. Redding, and David E. Weinstein. "The Impact of the 2018 Tariffs on Prices and Welfare," *Journal of Economic Perspectives*, 2019: 33 (4): 187–210. https://doi.org/10.1257/jep.33.4.187.

[17] The balance of the current account includes the trade balance and the interest income from investments. Since the interest income from investments is relatively small, the balance of the current account is mainly the trade balance.

have been running up the fiscal deficit, which is the main contributor to its current account deficit. After Trump took office, he cut taxes significantly, reducing government revenue, and exacerbating the fiscal deficit. The US Federal Reserve can issue more dollars to fill the gap between government revenue and expenditure. Since the US dollar is the main international reserve currency, the rest of the world is willing to hold dollars and essentially lend money to the United States to finance its current account deficits. This is the root cause of the US trade imbalance. As long as the US dollar remains the main international reserve currency, the United States will be able to keep financing its current account deficits and the basic trend of the US trade deficit will not change, regardless of how US-China trade relations change.

4.4.5 *Impact on US Trade Structure*

We have analyzed the impact of the US-China tariff war on US welfare and the US trade balance. Generally speaking, because tariffs affect consumers, producers, and the government, and there are winners and losers, it is generally believed that the net impact of tariffs on a country's welfare is small, within 1% of GDP. However, the impact of tariffs on a country's production and trade structure can be significant.

After the United States imposed tariffs on imports from China, US domestic production and imports from other countries replaced the imports from China. We refer to the phenomenon of tariffs causing the source of imports to shift from one country to another as "trade diversion." Trade diversion can have a significant impact on a country's trade structure.

For example, take the case of US tariffs on washing machines. In February 2013, the United States imposed anti-dumping and countervailing duties on washing machines from South Korea and Mexico, causing the number of washing machines exported from these two countries to the United States to plummet. South Korean washing machine manufacturers, in order to compensate for losses and reduce costs, moved their production base to China. Within two years, China's share of total US washing machine imports soared to 67% from 7% in 2011. However, most of the washing machines exported from China to the United States were still South Korean brands, such as LG and Samsung. Therefore, the market share of South Korean washing machine brands in the United States increased between 2012 and 2014.

In 2017, the United States imposed anti-dumping duties on washing machines made in China, and China's exports of washing machines to the United States fell sharply. The South Korean brands moved their production base for washing machines to Vietnam and Thailand, and continued to export heavily to the United States. Thus, the US tariffs simply shifted the source of washing machine imports from South Korea to China, and then to Vietnam and Thailand. At the same time, the tariffs increased the price of washing machines in the United States and the higher prices were passed on to US consumers.

As another example, let's look at the case of China's tariffs on soybeans. In 2017, the United States and Brazil were China's main soybean suppliers. In June 2018, China imposed a 25% tariff on US soybeans, after which US soybean exports to China dropped to almost zero and US soybean prices fell in the world market. Meanwhile, Brazil's soybean exports to China increased and Brazilian soybean prices rose in the world market. By October 2018, Brazilian soybeans were 25% more expensive than US soybeans in the world market.

In the above two examples, the tariff led to a shift in the source of imports: from South Korea to China, then to Vietnam and Thailand in the case of US tariffs on washing machines; and from the United States to Brazil in the case of China's tariffs on soybeans. These examples illustrate the effect of trade diversion on a country's trade structure.

4.4.6 Conclusion

This chapter addressed the following questions: How should we understand the Trump 1.0 tariff war that broke out in 2018? What were the root causes that led to the tariff war? What has been the impact of the tariff war? How will the Trump 2.0 tariff war initiated in 2025 evolve?

The reasons put forward by the US government for initiating the tariff war—that China has inhibited US market access, worsened the US trade deficit, forced US enterprises to transfer their technology, and essentially undermined US manufacturing, services, and innovation—are superficial, hypocritical, and even misleading. The real reasons for the US-China trade war are competing overall/specific and long-term/short-term interests between China and the United States. We end this chapter with the following concluding thoughts.

Firstly, as clearly suggested in the 2022 CHIPS and Science Act signed by President Biden, restricting the market size of China's high-tech industry and maintaining US world monopoly in the high-tech field is beneficial to the overall interests of the United States. Curbing the development of China's high-tech industry will slow down China's industrial upgrading and allow the United States to maintain its position as the world's largest economy to the greatest possible extent, which is beneficial to the long-term interests of the United States. Restrictions on China's high-tech industry would increase the price of US exports of high-tech products, increasing the profitability of US high-tech companies, which is beneficial to the short-term interests of the United States. Therefore, imposing high tariffs and other trade restrictions on China's high-tech industry is beneficial to the United States from these three perspectives.

Secondly, the US government is concerned that the country is too dependent on imports from China in some important industries, such as semiconductors, high-power batteries, rare earth minerals, pharmaceutical products, and chemical raw materials. Citing the need for "industrial security," the Biden administration has moved to reduce imports from China in these industries by shifting to domestic production or imports from so-called friendly countries. Although tariffs may have little net impact on a country's welfare, they could have a big impact on trade diversion.

Thirdly, US tariff policy is the result of lobbying from domestic interest groups. Trump's tariffs protected the interests of US manufacturing workers, but they hurt US consumers and US companies that import inputs from China. Will US consumers and importers be able to lobby successfully to remove the tariffs? Will the US government bow to the concerns of consumers and companies struggling with rising production and living costs?

On May 14, 2024, the Biden administration announced tariff hikes on $18 billion worth of imports from China, targeting sectors like electric vehicles (EVs), batteries, steel, and critical minerals. The tariff rate on EVs was raised from 25 to 100%. In climate change-related industries such as EVs and renewable-energy industries, the United States is falling behind China. Hiking tariffs will cause advanced green technology products from China to exit the US market. Will this help the United States to catch up in global green transition or make it fall further behind?

On April 2, 2025, the returning Trump administration launched "Trump 2.0" tariff war. This time is not only targeting China, but also the entire world, aiming to restructure the global trade system by "reciprocal tariffs."

The "Trump 2.0" tariffs set 15% "baseline" duties on almost all imports to the United States, and a second tier of bilateral "reciprocal" surcharges—ranging from 10 to 41% to almost all US trading partners, calculated on Washington's assessment of bilateral trade deficits between the United States and each of its trading partners, and even served as President Trump's diplomatic leverages.

From the perspective developed in this chapter, the "Trump 2.0" package, like its 2018–2020 predecessor, serves short-term domestic interests to raise tariff revenues and protect import-competing manufacturing firms, and long-term interests to reform global trade system so that United States may regain the monopoly power over its competitors. On the other hand, Trump 2.0 tariffs inevitably distort the global value chain and raise production and living costs in the United States. Will tariffs help US economy grow in the long run?

CHAPTER 5

Mirror Tactics: How to Avoid Confrontation?

Tactics are the specific methods and measures for guiding and implementing one's actions in a dispute, and they constitute the plans and pathways to achieve one's goals. What is China's goal in international disputes? The answer is simple: to avoid confrontation and strive for cooperation. This chapter discusses the optimal methods and paths to avoid confrontation and achieve cooperation in international disputes.

In Chapter 3, we described the five stages of US-China relations and noted that they have now entered the third stage, which is the stage of great power competition. So how does the United States understand US-China competition? After the outbreak of the US-China trade war in 2018, President Trump and US Secretary of State Michael Pompeo repeatedly emphasized "America First" and "defeating China." When Joe Biden became President of the United States in 2021, he changed some of Trump's policies but continued the policy of "containing China." In his first foreign policy address, Biden called China the "most serious competitor" of the United States, and said he would prevent China from surpassing the United States to become the most powerful country in the world. In order to compete with China, he said the United States would need to invest heavily in new technologies and ensure that the global trade and investment rules of the twenty-first century are formulated by the United States and its allies, not China.

US Secretary of State Antony Blinken summarized the US approach to China in 2021 as "competitive when it should be, collaborative when it can be, and adversarial when it must be." He elaborated on this in a 2022 speech focusing on three pillars: "invest, align, compete"—specifically, invest in the competitiveness of American industries, their innovation ability and the US

J. Ju, *US-China Great Power Competition and The New World Order*, https://doi.org/10.1007/978-981-95-3762-4_5

democratic system; align with US allies and partners, using regional governance systems and ally relationships to put pressure on China; and compete with China to defend US interests in technology, industry, defense, geopolitics, and other fields. The 2022 CHIPS and Science Act, the 2022 Inflation Reduction Act, and other bills passed by the US Congress have turned the slogan of "containing China" into laws and administrative policies.

In his second term, President Trump focuses on trade confrontations, aiming to reduce the trade deficit, reshoring production and reducing reliance on China. So, how should China respond to the US policy?

5.1 Tactical Principles

The choice between confrontation and cooperation in a trade war can be analyzed using game theory models similar to those used to analyze expansion versus contraction in corporate competition, offense versus defense in sports, and war versus peace in military conflicts.

China's experience during the Revolutionary War period can be distilled into tactical principles and applied to great power competition. During the Anti-Japanese War, the Kuomintang (Chinese Nationalist Party) and the Chinese Communist Party (CCP) needed to come together to resist Japan. However, there was constant friction and fighting between the two parties. Mao Zedong, the leader of the CCP, famously proposed two principles that could bring about a truce with the Kuomintang so that they could unite against their common enemy and win the war against Japan. Mao's principles can be a guide to formulating China's strategy in the great power competition with the United States.

Tactical Principle 1: If others do not offend me, I will not offend them; if others offend me, I will certainly offend them

The current US-China competition has some similarities with the friction between the Kuomintang and the CCP during the Anti-Japanese War. Although some people in the US government take "containing China" as the policy tone for their approach to China, we believe that the people of China and the United States share the same long-term fundamental goal of world peace and development, just as the Kuomintang and the CCP shared the same goal of resisting Japan. Seen in this light, the "containing China" policy by the United States is analogous to the Kuomintang's efforts to destroy the CCP during the anti-Japanese war. As we will show in this chapter, Mao's first principle—"If others do not offend me, I will not offend them; if others offend me, I will certainly offend them"—can become China's tactical principle to avoid confrontation and strive for cooperation in the US-China dispute.

Tactical Principle 2: You fight your way; I fight my way

In March 1965, Mao told Pakistan President Ayub Khan: "Our method of fighting is: you fight your way; I fight my way. Whether it's the Japanese or the Americans, they all can't beat us... There is nothing mysterious about fighting a war. If you can win, fight. If you can't win, retreat. You fight your way; I fight my way."

Economic and trade wars between countries are actually very similar to military wars. In the Art of War, Sun Tzu states: "There are no constants in warfare, just as there are no constant forms in water. Those who can win by adapting to the enemy's changes are called gods." That is to say, the key to victory is to make the best decision according to the changes in the opponent's situation. "You fight your way; I fight my way" not only requires changes according to the enemy's changes, but also requires turning passivity into initiative, creating local advantages, accumulating small victories into big victories and local advantages into overall advantages, and winning the final victory. As we will show in this chapter, Mao's second principle—"You fight your way: I fight my way"—can also become China's tactical principle in its great power competition with the United States.

5.2 Mirror-Tactic Model

"If others do not offend me, I will not offend them; if others offend me, I will certainly retaliate" can be summarized as a "mirror tactic," where one's actions mirror the opponent's, reflecting their strategy as if in a mirror. In a game of cooperation versus confrontation, this strategy translates to: "If you cooperate with me, I will cooperate with you; if you confront me, I will confront you in return."

This section presents a simple model to illustrate what would happen if a country could make a commitment to another country to adopt the mirror tactic. The model is presented in three steps: first, we analyze what would happen with no commitment (that is, if countries cannot commit to adopting the mirror tactic); second, we analyze what would happen if commitment were possible; and third, we find the optimal outcome between the two.

5.2.1 No Commitment

Consider two countries: Home and Foreign. Each country has two choices: cooperate with the other country and attack (confront) the other country.

Table 5.1 describes the game matrix, with Home's choice of actions shown in rows and Foreign's choice of actions shown in columns. The payoffs for Home and Foreign are represented by the four pairs of numbers (x, y) in the matrix, where x represents Home's payoff and y represents Foreign's payoff.

We set cooperation as the baseline state: if both countries choose to cooperate, each gets a payoff of 0. If one country chooses to confront while its

Table 5.1 Game matrix 1

	Foreign		
Home		Cooperation	Confrontation
	Cooperation	(0, 0)	(–10, 10)
	Confrontation	(10, –10)	(–5, –5)

opponent chooses to cooperate, the confronting country gains with a payoff of 10 while the cooperating country loses with a payoff of –10. If both countries choose to confront, both suffer losses. However, both countries mitigate losses than –10 as they both attack. Thus, their losses are less severe than –10. We assume that in this scenario each country gets a payoff of –5.

What is the optimal strategy for Home? From Home's point of view, if Foreign cooperates, Home gets a benefit of 0 if it also cooperates, but it gets a larger benefit of 10 if it confronts Foreign. If Foreign confronts, Home gets a loss of –10 if it cooperates with Foreign and a smaller loss of –5 if it fights back. Therefore, irrespective of Foreign's choice to cooperate or confront, Home's optimal strategy is to confront. The same reasoning applies to Foreign's optimal strategy. Therefore, the equilibrium in this game is that both countries will choose to confront, resulting in losses for both (–5, –5).

Readers familiar with game theory will notice by now that the "no commitment" game is the famous Prisoner's Dilemma.[1] Although both parties could achieve a better payoff (0, 0) by choosing to cooperate, in a no-commitment environment, the optimal strategy for both parties is to confront, resulting in a poorer outcome for both (–5, –5). The reason is actually very simple: without a binding commitment by both countries to cooperate, if one country chooses to cooperate, the other country will definitely choose to confront and gain a payoff of 10, leaving the first country with a loss of –10. To prevent this outcome, the optimal strategy for both countries is confrontation. Thus, confrontation is inevitable, and win–win cooperation cannot be achieved.

5.2.2 Commitment to the Mirror Tactic

To break the Prisoner's Dilemma, Home can commit to adopt the mirror tactic: "If you cooperate, I will cooperate; if you confront, I will also confront." Once this commitment is made, it must be kept. Breaking the commitment results in costs for Home such as loss of trust, credibility, and reputation. We assume that the cost to Home of breaking its commitment is –15.

[1] Refers to a special game between two captured prisoners, illustrating that in a non-cooperative environment, the optimal choice for an individual cannot achieve the optimal choice for the group.

Table 5.2 Game matrix 2

	Foreign		
Home		Cooperation	Confrontation
	Keep the Promise	(0, 0)	(−5, −5)
	Break the Promise	(−5, −10)	(−25, 10)

Table 5.2 describes this game matrix. Foreign still has the same two choices: cooperate and confront. Home's choices are now whether to keep the promise of using the mirror tactic or break the promise.

If Home chooses to keep its commitment to adopt the mirror tactic, this means that if Foreign cooperates, Home will also cooperate, resulting in a payoff of 0 for each country; and if Foreign confronts, Home will also confront, resulting in a payoff of –5 for each country. If Home chooses to break the commitment, this means that if Foreign cooperates, Home will confront, leaving Foreign with a loss of –10, and Home with a net loss of –5 (a gain of 10 minus the penalty of 15 for breaking the commitment); if Foreign confronts, Home will cooperate, leaving Foreign with a gain of 10 and Home with a total loss of –25 (a loss of 10 plus the penalty of 15 for breaking the commitment).

What is the optimal strategy for both countries? From Home's point of view, if Foreign chooses to cooperate, Home gets a payoff of 0 if it keeps its promise and cooperates, and a loss of –5 if it breaks its promise and confronts Foreign. If Foreign chooses to confront, Home suffers a loss of –5 if it keeps its promise and confronts Foreign, and an even bigger loss of –25 if it breaks its promise and cooperates. Therefore, regardless of whether Foreign chooses to cooperate or confront, the optimal choice for Home is to keep its commitment to adopt the mirror tactic. From Foreign's point of view, if Home chooses its optimal strategy of keeping its promise, Foreign will get a payoff of 0 if it chooses to cooperate, and a payoff of –5 if it chooses to confront Home. Therefore, cooperation is the optimal choice for Foreign.

In summary, the optimal strategy for Home is to commit to adopting the mirror tactic and the optimal strategy for Foreign is to cooperate with Home, resulting in an equilibrium where both countries cooperate with each other. Readers familiar with game theory will recognize this as the Nash equilibrium under credible commitment.[2]

The third step, the strategy choice between "no commitment" and "commitment" is shown in Fig. 5.1.

Under the no-commitment scenario, as shown in Table 5.1, both countries fall into the Prisoner's Dilemma: the optimal strategy for both is confrontation

[2] Nash equilibrium is a basic equilibrium of non-cooperative games. If any participant's chosen strategy is optimal when all other participants have chosen equilibrium strategies, then this combination of strategies is defined as a Nash equilibrium.

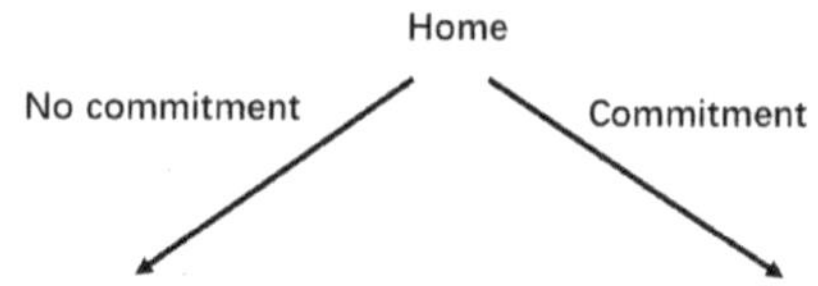

		Foreign	
		Cooperation	Confrontation
Home	Cooperation	(0,0)	(-10,10)
	Confrontation	(10,-10)	(-5,-5)

		Foreign	
		Cooperation	Confrontation
Home	Keep the Promise	(0,0)	(-5,-5)
	Break the Promise	(-5,-10)	(-25,10)

Fig. 5.1 Strategy selection

and the equilibrium payoff is (–5, –5). If Home can make a credible commitment to adopt the mirror tactic, as shown in Table 5.2, both countries reach the Nash equilibrium: the optimal strategy for Home is to keep the promise and the optimal strategy for Foreign is to cooperate, resulting in cooperation by both countries and an equilibrium payoff of (0, 0). Therefore, if Home can commit to adopting the mirror tactic ("If you cooperate, I will cooperate; if you confront, I will also confront"), it can successfully avoid the bad result of both sides choosing confrontation and achieving cooperation instead.

5.3 Asymmetric Structure of Interests

In a trade war, each country's optimal strategy is determined by its interests. China's trade policy is formulated by the central government, which represents the interests of the entire country. But whose interests are represented by China's main trading partners' trade policies? The answer: the interests of certain powerful groups. The trade policies of the United States and the European Union are driven by politicians who represent (or favor) particular interest groups, such as industry unions, local governments, political parties, and enterprises. Whichever interest group gives more political donations will naturally have their interests more strongly represented. The interests of different groups may be conflicting, such as the interests of workers versus capitalists and import-competing industries versus export industries. The interests of different states in the United States and different members of the European Union may also be conflicting. Therefore, there may be internal disagreements over what their most important specific, overall, short-term, and long-term interests are. In other words, China's interests and US interests are determined in different ways—the former through a central authority representing the country as a whole, and the latter through a political process reflecting different degrees of representation for different interest groups.

The fundamental conflict between China and the United States lies in how they view the transformation of the world order. On the one hand, China's rejuvenation and development are good for world economic development, so groups in the United States who support world economic development should also share an interest in China's development. On the other hand, however, China's rejuvenation will end the United States' global domination, and the reform of the world order will certainly touch the "cheese" of some groups in the United States who are obsessed with ruling the world. There will inevitably be contradictions and conflicts among these different groups. Even within a group, long-term versus short-term interests and overall versus specific interests could be contradictory—for example, their long-term, overall interests may support world development and China's rejuvenation, while their short-term, specific interests may oppose China's rejuvenation.

The mirror tactic could help to overcome the problem of conflicting interests in pursuit of cooperation by unifying groups with consistent interests, winning over the groups in the middle, and punishing the groups that take confrontational measures.

5.4 Case Study 1: EU-China Photovoltaics/Wine Trade Dispute

Let's look at a successful example of the mirror tactic: the EU-China photovoltaic/wine tariff dispute.

In 2012, EU photovoltaic manufacturers facing stiff competition from China lobbied first their own governments and then the European Commission, demanding punitive tariffs on photovoltaic products imported from China. In 2013, the European Union initiated an anti-dumping investigation into China's photovoltaic exports, threatening to impose a 47.6% tariff on them.

What should China have done in response? Should it have also restricted its imports of photovoltaic products from the European Union? That would not have been easy to achieve. Why? Because the European Union basically did not export photovoltaic products to China. So, how could China apply the mirror tactic?

The mirror tactic does not necessarily mean that China had to retaliate on exactly the same product. "You fight your way, I fight my way": China could hit back on other EU exports. Although China did not import photovoltaic products from the European Union, it did import a large amount of EU wine. It is interesting that China's Ministry of Commerce almost simultaneously initiated an anti-dumping investigation into EU wine exports. China's anti-dumping investigation of EU wine did not affect EU photovoltaic manufacturers, but did affect EU wine manufacturers and, by extension, the EU parliamentarians and politicians supported by the wine industry.

Looking at the resolution process of the EU-China trade dispute, we found that when the European Union launched an investigation into China's photovoltaic exports, China launched an investigation into EU wine exports; when the European Union stopped its investigation into China's photovoltaic exports, China also stopped its investigation into EU wine exports. China's strategy was like a mirror image of the EU strategy. The dispute between China and the European Union over photovoltaic and wine exports lasted for five or six years, and both sides took basically the same steps. In the end, EU tariffs on photovoltaic imports from China and China's tariffs on wine imports from the European Union stayed at their normal levels. This can be seen as an example of China successfully applying the mirror tactic to avoid tariff escalation.

5.5 Case Study 2: US Long-Arm Jurisdiction and Sanctions on Huawei

The EU-China photovoltaic/wine trade dispute is an example where China used the mirror tactic successfully to avoid tariff escalation. But the mirror tactic did not prevent the US-China trade war, which has seen the two sides launch a tariff war on thousands of each other's exports, and has also extended to technology, finance, global governance, and many other areas. Why didn't the mirror tactic avoid the US-China trade war?

In this section, we focus on another area of the complex US-China trade war, namely US "long-arm jurisdiction" over multinational corporations. In addition to tariffs, an important weapon wielded by the United States against China has been its direct supervision of and sanctions on overseas multinational corporations. What kind of country can effectively supervise and sanction foreign-owned multinational corporations? Of course, only a globally dominant country like the United States can do so. We refer to US supervision of and sanctions on non-US multinational corporations as long-arm jurisdiction.

The most familiar example of US long-arm jurisdiction is the US sanctions against Huawei. On May 15, 2019, President Trump signed an executive order declaring a national emergency over threats against American technology. Subsequently, the US Department of Commerce added Huawei and its affiliates to the so-called Entity List,[3] banning the sale of Huawei's communication products in the United States, and prohibiting American companies from exporting components such as chips and operating systems to Huawei. On

[3] BIS first published the Entity List in February 1997 as part of its efforts to inform the public of entities who have engaged in activities that could result in an increased risk of the diversion of exported, re-exported, and transferred (in-country) items to weapons of mass destruction (WMD) programs. Since its initial publication, grounds for inclusion on the Entity List have expanded to activities sanctioned by the State Department and activities contrary to U.S. national security and/or foreign policy interests.

See https://www.bis.doc.gov/index.php/policy-guidance/lists-of-parties-of-concern/entity-list, accessed on August 29, 2024.

September 15, 2020, the US Department of Commerce imposed a comprehensive embargo on Huawei Companies outside the United States that use American software for technical design or American components for production would also need approval from the US Department of Commerce in order to sell to Huawei and its affiliates. This effectively bans all multinational companies from exporting software and components to Huawei. At the same time, the US government mobilized all its resources to dissuade other countries from using Huawei's equipment in their mobile phone networks and sought to even ban Huawei globally.

5.5.1 *Why Does the United States Want to Strike Against Huawei?*

The reason for striking against Huawei, as Trump made very clear, is that Huawei is a global leader in 5G technology and China is the United States' biggest competitor in the field of artificial intelligence (AI).

Huawei was founded in 1987 and has become a global leader in communication technology, specializing mainly in information and communication infrastructure and intelligent terminal industries. In 2019, Huawei surpassed Apple to become the world's second-largest smartphone seller, second only to Samsung. Having invested in 5G research for over 10 years, Huawei is currently one of the largest patent holders in the world and is at least 12–18 months ahead of its peers in 5G.

In order to maintain its global dominance in the field of communication technology, the United States cannot afford to fall behind in the competition for 5G. Therefore, the United States is intensifying the development of its domestic communication technology and service market on the one hand, while doing its utmost to counter Huawei on the other. The US strike against Huawei is based on its own long-term and overall interests, to maintain its leading position in global communication technology, especially in the 5G industry.

Historical data shows that technological progress has contributed about two-thirds to the growth of the US economy from 1909 to 1949.[4] The value added of the US high-tech industry accounted for 39% of total US GDP in 2016.[5] Although the value added of the information technology (IT)-related industry only accounted for 1.7% of US GDP during the same period, it has

[4] Robert M. Solow, "Technical Change and the Aggregate Production Function," *The Review of Economics and Statistics* 39, no. 3 (August 1, 1957): 312, https://doi.org/10.2307/1926047.

[5] National Science Foundation. "Patterns and Trends of Knowledge- and Technology-Intensive Industries," *NSB 2018 Report*, 2018. https://www.nsf.gov/statistics/2018/nsb20181/report/sections/industry-technology-and-the-global-marketplace/patterns-and-trends-of-knowledge--and-technology-intensive-industries, accessed on November 29, 2025.

contributed 7.6% to economic growth and 32.8% to productivity improvement.[6] Therefore, the IT-related industry is crucial to the long-term growth of the US economy.

Using the analytical framework described in Chapter 1 and Chapter 4, we can see that striking against Huawei is beneficial for the United States to maintain its dominant position in the global high-tech field—thus it aligns with the overall interests of the United States. It is conducive to upgrading the US high-tech industry while crippling the development of China's high-tech industry, thereby accelerating the long-term economic growth of the United States relative to China—thus it aligns with the long-term interests of the United States. By cutting US and world demand for Huawei products, the United States can suppress the price of China's (Huawei) products in the world market and raise the price of US high-tech products in the world market and improve its terms of trade—thus it aligns with the short-term interests of the United States. However, striking against Huawei has different implications for specific US interests: it helps US high-tech companies that are Huawei's competitors but it harms US consumers (individuals, firms, institutions, government agencies, etc.) who are now stopped from buying or using Huawei equipment, as well as US high-tech component and equipment exporters who are now stopped from selling to Huawei.

Could the mirror tactic have prevented the escalating US strikes against Huawei? In the case of the EU-China photovoltaic/wine trade dispute, the friction was mainly driven by the specific interests of EU photovoltaic manufacturers. When China found another specific interest "lever" in the EU, namely EU wine producers, it was relatively easy to use the mirror tactic to avoid a tariff war. In this case, however, Huawei's outstanding development in communication technology has touched a sensitive nerve in the United States which wants to maintain its dominance in the high-tech field. Since it is affecting the long-term and overall interests of the United States, it is far from enough for China to simply find a lever of specific interests to prevent the United States from attacking Huawei.

5.5.2 *How Does the US Government Implement Long-Arm Jurisdiction?*

As outlined above, the US government's strikes against Huawei proceeded in several steps. The first step was to restrict government procurement, by using the so-called National Defense Authorization Act to prohibit US government agencies from purchasing Huawei equipment and services. The second step was to impose a comprehensive ban on Huawei by adding it to the Entity List, prohibiting the sale of Huawei products in the US market and banning US companies from exporting key components to Huawei, such as chips and

[6] Dale W. Jorgenson, Mun S. Ho, and Jon D. Samuels, "The Impact of Information Technology on Postwar US Economic Growth," *Telecommunications Policy* 40, no. 5 (November 28, 2015): 398–411, https://doi.org/10.1016/j.telpol.2015.03.001.

operating systems. In fact, the prohibition on exports to Huawei extended beyond US companies to foreign (non-US) companies that use US technology and components. The third step was to resort to the judicial process. On December 1, 2018, Canadian police arrested Huawei's Deputy Chairman Meng Wanzhou at the request of the US government on charges related to Huawei's alleged violations of US sanctions on Iran.

The strength and means of the United States to protect the high-tech should not be underestimated.

Before its attack on Huawei, in July 2012, the US government threatened to impose export restrictions China's ZTE Corporation over the company's alleged violations of US sanctions on Iran and North Korea. ZTE was founded in 1985 and is China's second-largest telecommunications equipment company behind Huawei. The US action led to a shock in ZTE's production and business activities, as its key components (such as chips) were mainly imported from the United States. After lengthy consultations between the two countries, the US government issued ZTE with a hefty fine of $1.4 billion and also sent regulators to supervise the restructuring and strategic adjustment of its top management. In April 2018, the US government placed a seven-year ban on exports by American companies to ZTE because the company allegedly made false statements during the investigation into sales of its equipment to Iran. Subsequently, a deal was reached with the Trump administration where ZTE agreed to pay a further $1 billion fine and fund a new in-house compliance team staffed by US experts. Altogether, the fines ZTE paid to the US government totaled $2.59 billion, more than 80% of the company's net profit over the past 30 years.

We can clearly see that when a certain company poses a threat to US dominance in technology, the US government will use all its power to severely strike at the company. Is US long-arm jurisdiction specifically targeted at Chinese companies? In fact, it is not. The United States has used long-arm jurisdiction many times to strike at foreign companies, even those of its allies, such as France, Germany, Japan, and the United Kingdom.

One of the most famous cases involved France's Alstom, a leading provider of infrastructure equipment in the world and a symbol of French high-tech since the 1950s. The US government charged Alstom with violating the US Foreign Corrupt Practices Act (FCPA) by paying bribes to government officials around the world, including in Indonesia, Egypt, Saudi Arabia, and the Bahamas. On April 14, 2013, US police arrested Alstom executive Frédéric Pierucci in New York[7] and three more Alstom executives in succession. It was not until Alstom paid a fine of $772 million and sold the company to General Electric that Pierucci was released.

In another case, in 2011, the US government issued a multimillion-dollar fine to a Hungary-based telecommunications company, Magyar Telekom, for

[7] Pierucci, Frédéric. *The American Trap: My battle to expose America's secret economic war against the rest of the world*. Hachette UK, 2019.

allegedly paying bribes to officials in Macedonia and Montenegro. But what does a Hungarian telecommunications company paying bribes in Macedonia and Montenegro have to do with the United States? What gives the United States (long-arm) jurisdiction over this case? The argument given by the US Securities and Exchange Commission was that it had the responsibility to oversee the conduct of a company that traded in the US market.

5.5.3 *Why Can the United States Exert Jurisdiction Over Non-US Multinational Corporations?*

How can US law and foreign policy interests be imposed on non-US multinational corporations? The main reason is that the United States has the power to inflict severe punishments on companies that do not comply with its rules. This power comes from its dominant position in several respects.

First, there is the huge American market. Foreign companies faced with the threat of being kicked out of this major market fear that they will suffer significant losses in profits and global competitiveness. Second, the United States is a global leader in some high-tech areas. Foreign companies faced with the threat of being cut off from key American components fear that they will experience a production shock. Third, there is the US dollar, the most-used currency in international transactions. Foreign companies faced with the threat of financial sanctions and being kicked out of the global payment system, fear that they will not be able to survive. Furthermore, the US government has the capability to monitor and enforce its rules worldwide through its dominant position in global information and intelligence and judicial cooperation with many countries.

Canada, Mexico, and the European Union have laws to counter US extraterritorial jurisdiction. For example, the European Union passed the EU Blocking Statute in 1996, prohibiting EU individuals and companies from complying with third-country laws, such as sanctions imposed by the United States against Cuba and Iran. However, these laws have had no real effect and over the past 20 years, the United States has stubbornly advanced its long-arm jurisdiction over foreign companies despite opposition from other countries. Most EU companies still comply with US sanctions against Iran and trade between the European Union and Iran is essentially barter trade that does not use the US dollar-dominated trade settlement system. The US FCPA has been successfully pushed globally: The United Nations Convention Against Corruption, passed by the United Nations in 2003 with over 170 signatories to date, is essentially a replica of the US FCPA including provisions to strengthen international law enforcement and judicial cooperation between countries.

Can US long-arm jurisdiction be effectively resisted? In the past, the United States has punished multinational corporations from France, Germany, Japan, and the United Kingdom without encountering any substantial resistance. It was not until Huawei that the US government encountered strong resistance to its tactics.

In 2019, Huawei's recorded sales revenue of 858.8 billion RMB, an increase of 19.1% over the previous year, and a net profit of 62.7 billion RMB, an increase of 5.6% over the previous year. On September 24, 2021, the US government suspended its charges and withdrew its extradition request against Meng Wanzhou; no fines were paid and the charges were dismissed in 2022. The following year, Huawei announced the production and sale of 5G products completely free of US components. In September 2023, it released the Mate 60 and Mate 60 Pro mobile phones that use a 7-nm chip designed by Huawei and manufactured by China's chip foundry, SMIC. With the release of its new phone, Huawei's sales volume increased by 84% year-on-year in 2023, and its shipments returned to the top ten in the world and the top five in the Chinese market. In the high-end mobile phone market, Huawei returned to the top three in the world after Apple and Samsung.

According to Huawei's founder Ren Zhengfei, when he finally realized that the United States wanted to kill Huawei, he knew the company had to resist strongly for its survival. In 2021, Huawei established five new so-called legions to focus on industries like digital finance, machine vision, and manufacturing digitalization; and in 2022, Huawei established ten more legions focusing on interactive media, display chips, data center networks, smart airports, and rail links, etc.

When China realized that the United States wanted to contain its high-tech ambitions, it knew it had to go all out to achieve independent innovation and develop its own high-tech industry. To counter US extra-territorial jurisdiction measures, China's Ministry of Commerce introduced its own Unreliable Entity List Regulations and Measures to Block the Improper Extra-Territorial Application of Foreign Laws and Measures. On June 10, 2021, the Standing Committee of the National People's Congress voted to pass the Anti-Foreign Sanctions Law to counter foreign sanctions, interference, and long-arm jurisdiction.

The case of Huawei shows that the United States' targeting of China's high-tech companies is not just about protecting specific US interests (such as its own high-tech companies) but about protecting US long-term and overall interests at the expense of China's. In the EU-China photovoltaic/wine trade dispute, committing to the mirror tactic of "if you cooperate, I will cooperate; if you confront, I will also confront" could avoid confrontation and achieve cooperation at the tactical level. But the United States' aim to curb the development of China's high-tech companies is a higher-level competition between the two sides, with the transformation of the world order at stake. This requires not only tactical choices but also the formulation of strategic directions.

5.6 Case Study 3: US-China Tit-for-Tat Tariff Hikes

During President Trump's second term, the United States implemented a series of global tariffs, leading to a strong response from China. This escalated into a phased agreement between the two nations, illustrating the effective use of "Mirror Tactics."

On April 2, Trump signed an executive order instituting a 10% "baseline tariff" on all countries, with additional tariffs based on the size of the US trade deficit. For China, this resulted in a tariff increase to 34%.

In retaliation, on April 4, China announced it would impose a 34% tariff on all US imports starting April 10, and also strengthen export controls on rare earth elements. Trump, threatening further escalation, warned of a potential 50% tariff increase. China, unyielding, signaled it would not back down. As a result, on April 8, Trump raised tariffs to 84%, and China quickly followed suit with its own 84% tariff hike.

On April 10, Trump escalated further, setting the tariff rate on Chinese exports to the United States at 125%. China responded the next day with a matching increase to 125%, stating that at such levels, US goods would no longer have a market in China. If the United States continued its tariff hikes, China warned, it would cease responding altogether.

China's use of mirror tactics led to significant discontent among voters in US agricultural states, and created mounting domestic pressure on Trump. US trade with China nearly halted, major retailers like Walmart ran out of inventory, inflation surged, and US stocks, bonds, and the dollar plunged—a "triple whammy." The pressure became unsustainable for Trump to maintain tariffs as high as 145%.

On April 11, Trump announced a tariff exemption for electronic products like smartphones. In turn, China lifted tariffs on some US semiconductors and integrated circuits. By May 12, both countries reached a Phase-One trade agreement in Geneva, which included the mutual elimination of 91% of reciprocal tariffs, the suspension of 24% for 90 days, and the retention of a 10% baseline tariff on each other's goods. By November 1, both reached a trade and economic deal in Korea, which included commitments to stabilize and expand trade relations.

In terms of outcomes, a 10% tariff on fentanyl imports was added as part of the deal reached on November 1. Since then, the United States has imposed an additional 20% tariff on Chinese goods, while China imposed a 10% tariff on US goods. Additionally, 24% of the tariffs have been suspended until November 10, 2026.[8]

[8] See: https://www.whitehouse.gov/fact-sheets/2025/11/fact-sheet-president-donald-j-trump-strikes-deal-on-economic-and-trade-relations-with-china/, accessed on December 3, 2025.

CHAPTER 6

Tripod: Structural Changes in the Global Value Chain

6.1 The Problem at the Turn of the Century

Starting from this chapter, we will discuss the strategic directions of great power competition, first introducing structural changes in the global economic fundamental and superstructure in this chapter and Chapters 7, and 8.

Let me take you back to the afternoon of December 31, 1999, in Norman, Oklahoma, in the backyard of my old house near the University of Oklahoma. I took a chair and sat under the walnut tree in the backyard. Golden leaves were all over the ground, and the afternoon sun shone on the walnuts hanging from the branches. School was on winter break, and the neighbors were all preparing for New Year's Eve at home. The neighborhood was quiet, with the occasional dog barking. Beijing had already entered the new century. The sounds of fireworks, cheers, and celebration on the TV echoed in my backyard, where it was still in the old century. The great Y2K disaster, the end of the world that Americans had been hyping, did not seem to be coming. I probably still had time to shake some walnuts down from the tree to bake a walnut cake tomorrow and celebrate the arrival of the new century. The thought of the delicious taste of roasted walnuts made me smile, but my thoughts flew through the walnut tree, up to the blue sky, and toward the distant universe: Would the future disaster still come? How would the world order evolve? Could mankind achieve permanent peace? What kind of world order could achieve permanent peace for mankind?

As I gazed at the distant, azure sky, the word "tripod" suddenly began coming to my mind. A tripod—a structure achieved through competition, restraint, and cooperation among major powers—would support permanent

J. Ju, *US-China Great Power Competition and The New World Order*,
https://doi.org/10.1007/978-981-95-3762-4_6

peace in the world. This is simple logic, not profound. The question is: given that thousands of years of human history have been filled with bloody wars, what is special about the new millennium that would make mankind stop fighting and killing one another and move toward peace, rather than war, chaos, and destruction?

The sun was about to set as I stepped out of the yard. In front of the residential area was a large expanse of grassland. Looking westward, the last sunset of the old century painted the prairies of Oklahoma red. The hammerhead of the oil drilling machine (the "nodding donkey") swung up and down on the grassland. When the hammerhead swung up, it was illuminated red by the sunset, and when it swung down, it turned yellow like the grassland, as if it were constantly switching between heaven and earth. A few cows on the grassland leisurely swung their tails, which also changed colors under the reflection of the sunset. When the cow tails swung up, they were illuminated red by the sunset, and when they swung down, they reflected the yellow of the grassland.

I decided to write an article that would looking forward to the new millennium to answer the questions I was reflecting on. I will refer to the new millennium as the "new world," and the time before that as the "old world." The first question to answer is: What is the essential difference between the new world and the old world that could make humans in the new world stop killing each other and move toward peace?

The most typical characteristic of the new world is that it is innovation driven, and innovation is driven by resources such as knowledge, technology, and human capital. But where does knowledge come from? Knowledge comes from ideas. Robert Lucas, a Nobel laureate in economics, once described ideas as a cloud from the sky, just like the changing sunset glow above my head. What drove development in the old world was physical capital—land, machines, livestock, etc.—like the grassland, nodding donkey, and cows in front of me.

So, what's the difference between knowledge and land? Knowledge is a public good: one person knowing that $1 + 1 = 2$ does not prevent others from having the same knowledge. Land is a private good: if one person occupies the grassland in front of me, others cannot. One of the most important reasons for the wars and killings in the old world was the struggle for land. The infinite "idea cloud" of the new world essentially requires people to cooperate, creating knowledge together and promoting economic development. The finite land supply of the old world essentially brings about possession and deprivation, struggle and war. This is the essential difference between the new and old world—they are as far apart as heaven and earth!

In the old world filled with possession and deprivation, struggle and war, the winner takes the crown, and the world order is inevitably dominated by the hegemon. In the new world of knowledge and innovation, what is the survival rule? Isn't it cooperation, learning, and sharing? Wouldn't the order of the new world be determined by the distribution of human capital? Isn't human intelligence—the basis for human capital—naturally distributed globally, and not just concentrated in a few hegemonic countries? Therefore, the governance system of the new world should be a multipolar system, and a stable multipolar system requires at least three major countries (economies) as supports. After two world wars, Europe has taken substantial steps on the path of integration. The euro was introduced on January 1, 1999. The United States, Canada, and Mexico form a free trade bloc in North America.[1] Europe and North America are undoubtedly two major economic blocs, so where is the third pole of the world? Asia, it must be in Asia!

After the dissolution of the Soviet Union in 1991, the United States held a dominant position globally. In 1992, Francis Fukuyama published his famous book, *The End of History and the Last Man*, claiming that American-style liberal democracy was the end-point of humanity's ideological evolution. With the spread of outsourcing, globalization, and global value chains, the US-led world order will remain stable for a considerable period of time. But how long will it remain stable—ten thousand years, a thousand years, or ten years? Is the new world order stably dominated by the United States or will it evolve into a tripod structure? In short, is the new world order a continuation of a historical cycle of hegemonic iteration, or is it entering a new paradigm of competitive coexistence?

6.2 The Concept of Global Value Chains

The world order is the core of the global superstructure. Economic fundamentals determine the superstructure, and the change in the superstructure usually lags behind the change in the economic fundamentals. To trace the evolution of the global superstructure, we first need to explore the evolution of the global economic fundamentals.

What are the global economic fundamentals? They are the global production, consumption, and trade networks commonly referred to as the global value chain (GVC). We define the global superstructure as the international monetary system and the global governance system built on these fundamentals.

Before analyzing the structural changes in the global superstructure, let's first elaborate on the concept of the GVC. Take the production of shirts as a simple example. Suppose cotton is grown in the United States, processed into cloth in China, and made into shirts in Bangladesh to be distributed for sale worldwide. This process of producing shirts, distributed globally and interconnected upstream and downstream, from raw material to final product,

[1] The United States, Canada, and Mexico signed the North America Free Trade Agreement which entered into force on January 1, 1994. The agreement was renegotiated under the Trump administration as the US-Mexico-Canada Agreement which entered into force on July 1, 2020.

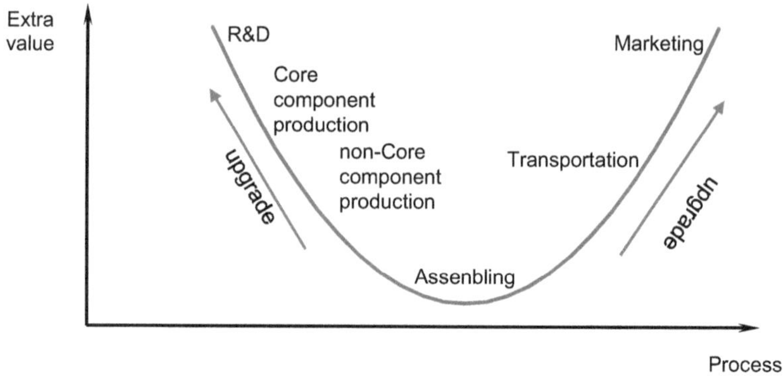

Fig. 6.1 Global value chain "smile curve"

is the GVC. Through the operation of the GVC, this shirt, as the final product, realizes the creation and flow of value.[2]

One interesting feature of the GVC for manufactures is the "smile curve" shown in Fig. 6.1, which explains the contribution of each part of the GVC to the product's value.

Figure 6.1 shows, from left to right, the various upstream and downstream production links in the GVC of a typical manufactured good. The far left is R&D, followed by core component production, non-core component production, assembly, and transportation and marketing of the finished product. We can see that R&D and core component production are on the far left of the curve, and marketing and retail are on the far right of the curve, which often account for the most value added, while the value added of non-core component production, assembly, and transportation in the middle of the curve is relatively small.

Generally speaking, in the GVC of a firm or multinational corporation, the high value-added production links such as R&D, core component production, and marketing are controlled at their headquarters, while the production links with relatively low value added, such as non-core component production, assembly, and transportation, are outsourced globally.

Consider the production of the 2018 Apple iPhone X. The iPhone has over 1000 components, produced by approximately 200 companies worldwide. Apple controlled the R&D and marketing, and produced the core component of the iPhone, the processor. The iPhone's dynamic memory was from Qualcomm, the NAND flash memory was from Samsung in South Korea, the camera was from Sony in Japan, and batteries, speakers, casings, and some

[2] The global value chain is also called the supply chain or global production network. Economists generally use the term "value chain" because it emphasizes the creation, flow, and realization of value. Researchers in the management and engineering fields often use the terms "supply chain" and "production network," considering the steps and processes of production and their geographical distribution.

other components were produced by Chinese companies. The iPhones were mainly assembled by China's Foxconn.

From the example of the iPhone, we can see that the production of some goods has become highly globalized. The global value chain is like a network spread all over the world, achieving seamless connection and collaboration. So, what is the structure of such a network?

6.3 The Tripod Structure of the Global Value Chain

In this section, we will analyze the changes in the structure of the GVC since the twenty-first century in terms of the global economic fundamentals: trade, production, and consumption. We will look at two points in time: the turn of the century in 2000, and the beginning of the US-China trade war in 2019.

6.3.1 *Changes in the Structure of Global Trade*

How has the structure of global trade changed in the 20 years between 2000 and 2019? To visualize the structure of global trade, we use the trade network diagram, which connects each country to its largest trading partner. To determine a country's largest trading partner, we first calculate its trade dependency on each of its trading partners. For example, China's trade dependence on a certain country is calculated as the share of China's imports from and exports to that country in China's total imports and exports. Then, we rank all of the country's trading partners, and the one with the highest trade dependency ratio is the largest trading partner.

Figures 6.2 and 6.3 are the trade network diagrams for 2000 and 2019, respectively. To plot the diagrams, we selected the top 60 economies by global trade volume, plus major economies in East Asia and Southeast Asia. The sample is highly representative, accounting for more than 90% of global trade volume. In 2000, there were 65 economies in the sample; in 2019, there were 68 economies. The economies are grouped into four regions: Europe on the left side of the diagram, Asia at the top, North America on the right, and other economies at the bottom.

First, let's look at the global trade network in 2000 shown in Fig. 6.2. Each economy has a straight line with an arrow pointing to its largest trading partner. Taking China (CHN) as an example, there is a line connecting China and the United States (United States), and the direction of the arrow is toward the United States, indicating that the United States is China's largest trading partner. The United States and Canada (CAN) are connected by a double-headed arrow, indicating that the United States and Canada are each other's largest trading partners.

From Fig. 6.2, it can be seen that almost all European countries have an arrow pointing to Germany (DEU) and only two—Germany and the United Kingdom (GBR)—have an arrow pointing outside Europe to the

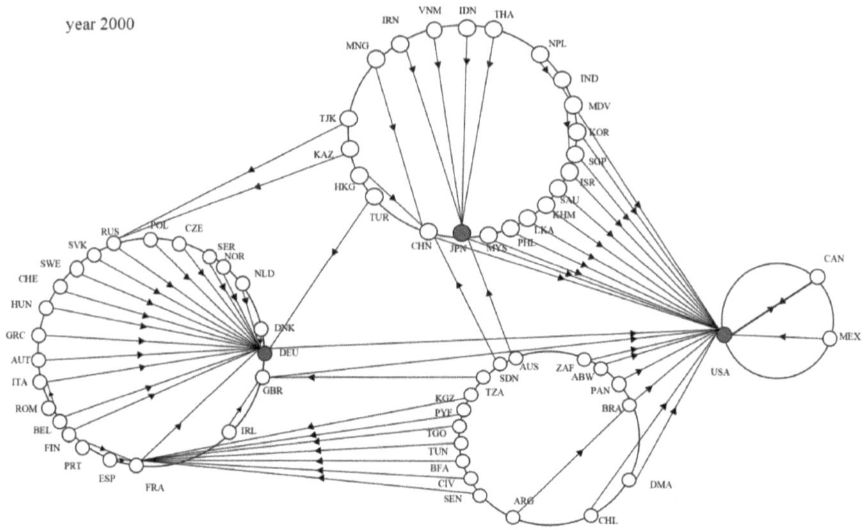

Fig. 6.2 Global trade network in 2000 (*Note* The correspondence between country [or economy] codes and country [or economy] names in this chapter is provided in the footnote[3])

United States. Hence, our first conclusion is that in 2000, Europe's trade was mostly intraregional with Germany as the center. A similar pattern could be seen in North America, with the United States as the center. Asia's trade had a different pattern: a few Asian economies, including Thailand (THA), Indonesia (IDN), and Vietnam (VNM) had Japan (JPN) as their largest trading partner but many more Asian economies, including China, Japan, Singapore (SGP), and South Korea (KOR), had the United States as their

[3] ABW—Aruba; AGR—Algeria; ARG—Argentina; AUS—Australia; AUT—Austria; BEL—Belgium; BFA—Burkina Faso; BGD—Bangladesh; BGR—Bulgaria; BLR—Belarus; BRA—Brazil; BRN—Brunei; BTN—Bhutan; CAN—Canada; CHE—Switzerland; CHL—Chile; CHN—China; CIV—Ivory Coast (Côte d'Ivoire); COL—Colombia; CYP—Cyprus; CZE—Czech Republic; DEU—Germany; DMA—Dominica; DNK—Denmark; EGY—Egypt; ESP—Spain; EST—Estonia; FIN—Finland; FJI—Fiji; FRA—France; GBR—United Kingdom; GRC—Greece; HKG—Hong Kong; HRV—Croatia; HUN—Hungary; IDN—Indonesia; IND—India; IRL—Ireland; IRN—Iran; ISR—Israel; ITA—Italy; JPN—Japan; KAZ—Kazakhstan; KGZ—Kyrgyzstan; KHM—Cambodia; KOR—South Korea; KWT—Kuwait; LAO—Laos; LKA—Sri Lanka; LTU—Lithuania; LUX—Luxembourg; LVA—Latvia; MAC—Macau; MAR—Morocco; MDV—Maldives; MEX—Mexico; MLT—Malta; MMR—Myanmar (Burma); MNG—Mongolia; MYS—Malaysia; NGA—Nigeria; NLD—Netherlands; NOR—Norway; NPL—Nepal; NZL—New Zealand; OMN—Oman; PAK—Pakistan; PAN—Panama; PER—Peru; PHL—Philippines; POL—Poland; PRT—Portugal; PYF—French Polynesia; QAT—Qatar; ROM—Romania; RUS—Russia; SAU—Saudi Arabia; SDN—Sudan; SEN—Senegal; SER—Serbia; SGP—Singapore; SVK—Slovakia; SVN—Slovenia; SWE—Sweden; TGO—Togo; THA—Thailand; TJK—Tajikistan; TUN—Tunisia; TUR—Turkey; TZA—Tanzania; UKR—Ukraine; USA—United States; VNM—Vietnam; ZAF—South Africa.

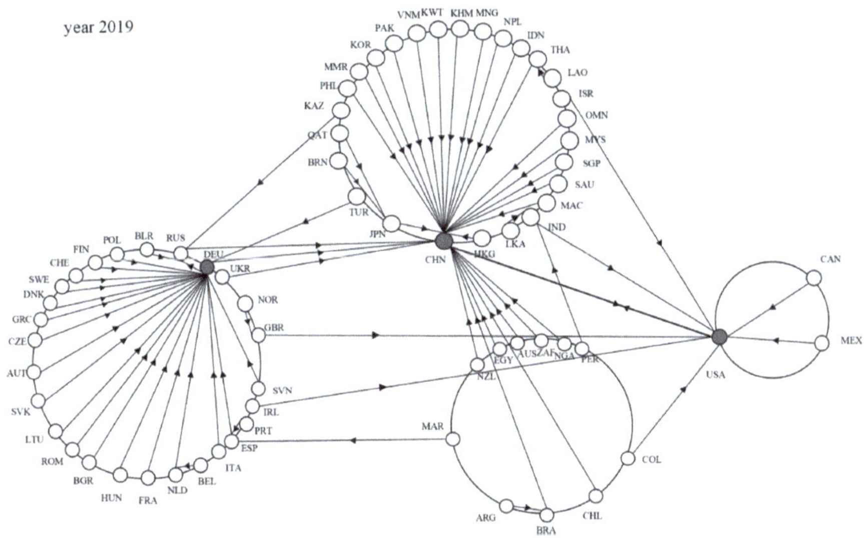

Fig. 6.3 Global trade network in 2019

largest trading partner. In other regions of the world, countries in Latin America mostly traded with the United States and countries in sub-Saharan Africa mostly traded with France (FRA).

It can be seen that in 2000, global trade had a bipolar structure with the United States as the main trading partner of the Asia–Pacific region and Germany as the main trading partner within the European region. Furthermore, Germany, the European center, and Japan, the Asian center, both had the United States as their largest trading partner. Therefore, in 2000, it can be said that the United States was the center of the global trade network.

What did the global trade network look like 20 years later, at the beginning of the US-China trade war in 2019? Fig. 6.3 shows the global trade structure in 2019.

Compared with 2000, Europe's trade structure did not undergo significant changes: most European countries still had Germany as their largest trading partner in 2019. However, Germany, the European hub, had changed its largest trading partner from the United States to China. Similarly, in North America, the arrows from Mexico and Canada still pointed to the center, the United States. But the United States had changed its largest trading partner from Canada to China. Asia's trade underwent tremendous changes: almost all the arrows from Asian economies pointed to China, indicating that China had replaced Japan and the United States as the Asian center and the largest trading partner for most Asian economies in 2019. In other parts of the world, too, countries such as Australia (AUS), Brazil (BRA), Chile (CHL), and South Africa (ZAF) now had China as their largest trading partner.

Comparing Fig. 6.2 with Fig. 6.3, we can conclude that the global trade network has undergone structural changes, evolving from a bipolar trade pattern with Germany and the United States as regional centers and the United States as the global center to a tripod trade pattern with China, Germany, and the United States as regional centers. The global trade structure dominated by the United States, which seemed to have "ended the evolution of ideology" at the turn of the century, changed to a tripod structure just 20 years into the new century. Facts speak louder than words; the structure of the economic fundamentals of a world order that was said to be long-lasting changed dramatically just 20 years later.

6.3.2 *Changes in the Structure of Global Production*

To visualize the structure of global production, we use the production network diagram, which connects each country to its largest trading partner in production inputs (value added, or parts). We can calculate a country's use of value added from other countries in its production based on the international input–output table. Using the production decomposition method in the GVC network, we can identify the source and destination country of each unit of value added in the country's GDP. Then, we can calculate a country's "parts trade dependence" on a certain trading partner as the share of its imports of parts from and exports of parts to that trading partner in its total imports and exports of parts. The trading partner with the highest parts trade dependence is the country's largest trading partner in parts.

Figures 6.4 and 6.5 show the global production networks in 2000 and 2019, respectively. The countries are grouped into the same four regions as in the trade network diagrams, and each country has a straight line with an arrow pointing to its largest trading partner in parts.

The data shows that in 2000, Germany was the largest trading partner in parts for many countries in Europe; Japan was the largest partner for a few countries in Asia; and the United States was the largest partner for North America as well as many countries in Europe and Asia. Similar to the global trade network in 2000, the global production network presented a bipolar pattern with Germany as the regional parts trading center in Europe, and the United States as the regional parts trading center in Asia–Pacific and also the center of the global production network.

In 2019, Germany remained the largest trading partner in parts for many countries in Europe, and the United States remained the largest trading partner in parts for North America and some countries in Europe and Asia. But in the Asia region, China replaced Japan as the regional parts trading center. China also replaced Canada as the United States' largest trading partner in parts. With China's rise in global production, the global production network shifted from a bipolar structure to a tripod structure.

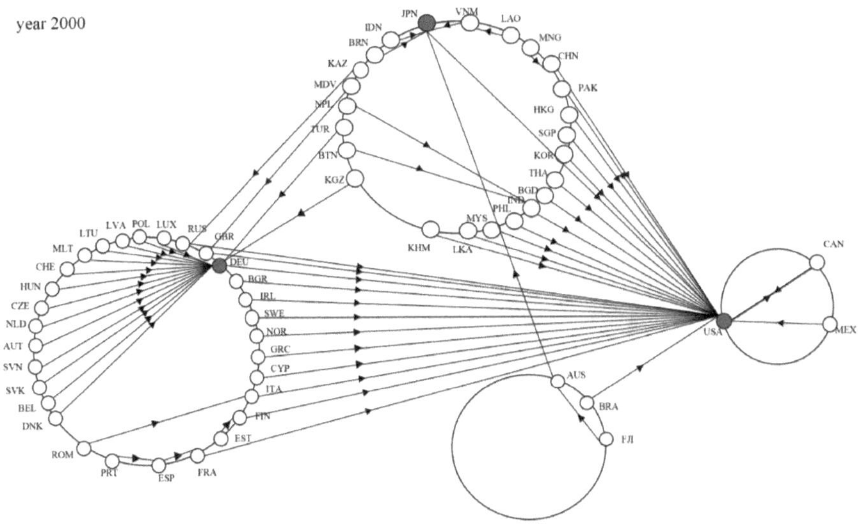

Fig. 6.4 Global production network in 2000

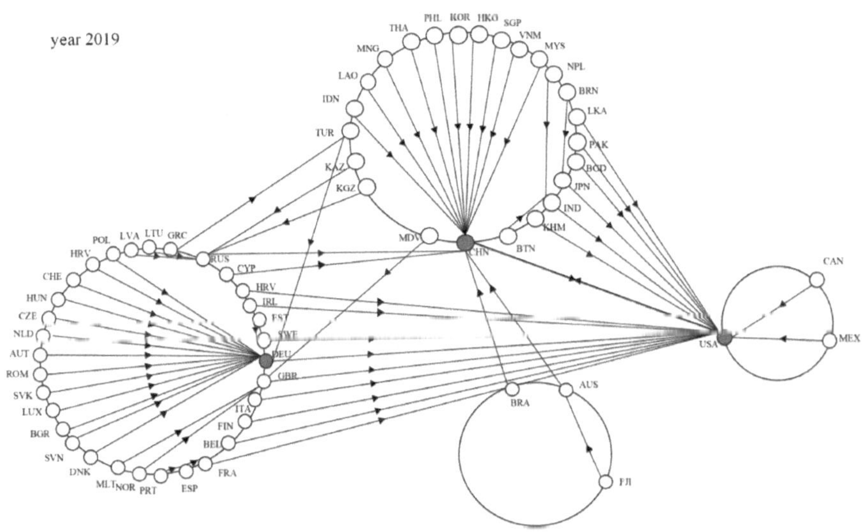

Fig. 6.5 Global production network in 2019

6.3.3 *Changes in the Structure of Global Consumption*

We can analyze changes in the global consumption network between 2000 and 2019 by looking at each country's largest trading partner in final (consumer) goods. Similar to the previous subsection, using international input–output table data, we calculate a country's "consumer goods trade dependence" on a certain trading partner as the share of its imports of consumer goods from and exports of consumer goods to that trading partner in its total imports and exports of consumer goods. The trading partner with the highest consumer goods trade dependence is the country's largest trading partner in consumer goods.

Our results[4] are that in 2000, Germany was the largest trading partner in consumer goods for most countries in Europe, while the United States was the largest trading partner in consumer goods in North America and for the rest of the world. In 2019, Germany remained the consumer goods trading center in Europe and the United States remained the consumer goods trading center in North America, while China became the consumer goods trading center for Asia.

In summary, we can see that in 2000, the GVC presented a European network centered on Germany and an Asia–Pacific network centered on the United States, with the United States being the center in the GVC. By 2019, global trade, production, and consumption had formed a tripod structure with a Europe network centered on Germany, a North America network centered on the United States, and an Asia network centered on China.

6.4 The Regional Network Centers: China, Germany, and the United States

In this section, we will analyze the internal structure of the European, Asian, and North American value chain networks. In general, a value chain network can present two patterns: the "hub-and-spoke" pattern and the "multi-country cooperation" pattern. In the hub-and-spoke pattern (or the "big country-small country" pattern), there is a core (big) country in the network whose GDP exceeds 50% of the region's GDP. The big country has absolute influence on the regional economy, and occupies the "hub" position, while other countries are "spokes." In the multi-country cooperation pattern, the GDP of the core country is less than 50% of the region's GDP, and a few large countries in the region jointly cooperate to lead the regional economy.

The European network includes all EU countries; the Asian network mainly includes East and Southeast Asia, that is, the 10 Association of South East Asian Nations (ASEAN) countries plus China, Japan, and South Korea (collectively known as ASEAN+3). The North American network includes the United States, Canada, and Mexico.

In terms of their share of regional GDP, from 1971 to 2021, the United States accounted for more than 80% of the North America network's total GDP, giving the United States absolute influence in that network. China's GDP was only 16.44% of ASEAN+3 GDP in 2000, but grew to 63.62% in 2021, giving China absolute influence in the Asia network. By 2021,

[4] To save the space, figures for global consumption network are not presented.

therefore, the North American and Asian networks had conformed to a hub-and-spoke structures centered on the United States and China, respectively. Germany's GDP has consistently stayed around 25% of EU GDP, with a slight decline since 2000, indicating that Germany does not have absolute influence on the European network, but co-leads that network with other countries such as France and Italy. Therefore, the European network conforms to a multi-country cooperation model.

Table 6.1 provides more detailed data on the regional proportions of GDP, trade, production, and consumption for the three regional centers: China, Germany, and the United States.

Focusing on the Asian network, in 1980, China was far from being a core country. China's GDP was 12.36% of total ASEAN+3 GDP, China's exports were only 7.0% of total ASEAN+3 exports, and China's imports were only 7.3% of total ASEAN+3 imports. By 2000, China's share in the region by these

Table 6.1 Selected regional economic indicators for China, Germany, and the United States

Year	*2000*			*2010*			*2021*		
Country	*China (%)*	*Germany (%)*	*United States (%)*	*China (%)*	*Germany (%)*	*United States (%)*	*China (%)*	*Germany (%)*	*United States (%)*
Share of regional GDP	16.44	26.77	87.59	40.56	23.36	84.91	63.62	24.78	87.69
Share of regional exports	22.32	25.92	88.31	50.98	23.17	84.80	70.52	23.59	88.35
Share of regional imports	22.37	25.67	88.75	50.97	22.45	85.05	70.48	23.37	88.54
Share of the regional intermediate goods consumption	27.01	25.18	88.07	57.31	22.83	83.88	74.65	22.99	88.39
Share of the regional intermediate goods supply	26.51	25.68	88.12	56.83	23.67	84.02	74.30	22.89	88.32
Share of the regional final goods consumption	17.21	26.14	89.28	41.27	22.06	85.90	64.20	23.78	88.65
Share of the regional final goods supply	17.82	26.14	88.45	42.67	22.67	85.38	65.23	24.34	88.36

Note Calculated based on the World Bank's GDP data and the Asian Development Bank's international input–output table for 2000, 2010, and 2021

three indicators had only reached 16.44%, 22.32%, and 22.37%, respectively. However, by 2021, China's GDP share in the region had reached 63.62%, and its import and export shares were both approximately 71%. Moreover, China's share in the demand for and supply of intermediate goods (parts) in ASEAN+3 reached 74%, and its share in the demand for and supply of final (consumer) goods in ASEAN+3 reached 64%. China's share in ASEAN+3, whether in terms of GDP, intermediate goods, or final goods, exceeds 50%. What does this mean? This means that more than half of the production, consumption, and trade in the region is driven by China. Therefore, in this sense, China's economy is closely related to the economic development of East and Southeast Asia, and the countries in this region will find economically very hard to decouple from China's economy.

6.5 Driving Forces and Prospects of the Tripod Structure

On December 31, 1999, on the eve of the turn of the century, as I looked up at the starry sky on the boundless prairie of Oklahoma, contemplating the pattern of the new world order, the United States' dominant position in the GVC was still as solid as an Antarctic iceberg, and a world order of tripod peaceful coexistence was just a beautiful dream. What force, in just 20 short years, has changed the US-dominated GVC structure into a tripod structure of Asia, North America, and Europe? The answer is globalization and trade!

The formation of the tripod structure was mainly driven by market and production factors. From the market perspective, we find that from 1960 to 2000, Asia's share of world GDP was the lowest among the three regions, and the global economy was dominated by the North America and EU markets. However, after 2000, and especially after the 2008 global financial crisis, Asia's share of world GDP showed a rapid rise. Since 2011, Asia has surpassed North America and Europe to become the world's largest market, and a tripod market structure of Asia, America, and Europe has formed.

From the production perspective, the three markets could basically achieve self-sufficiency with their existing factor endowments. In the North American region, the United States and Canada could provide technology and capital, while Mexico could provide labor. In the Asian region, China, Japan, Singapore, and South Korea could provide technology and capital, while Southeast Asian countries could provide labor. In the European region, developed countries like Germany and France could provide technology and capital, while Eastern European countries could provide labor. Therefore, all three regions developed relatively independent internal factor supplies.

Finally, the cost of forming a regional value chain among countries in the same region is relatively lower due to factors such as lower transportation costs, history of production interdependences, and cultural differences. This is how the tripod GVC gradually took shape.

In Chapter 2, we analyzed the past 500 years during which globalization progressed from the stage of market discovery to the stages of trade, production, and innovation, with the dominance of the hegemonic countries evolving in sync. Each wave of globalization has been accompanied by a break in the dominance of the hegemonic country of the time. 1978 to 2018 was the era of global production, and the globalization of production, or the formation of the GVC, helped to break the hegemonic countries' domination of production geographically. The global center of manufacturing prowess shifted from the United States to Germany and Japan, and then to China. The geographic dispersion of production and the subsequent formation of a tripod structure is an inevitable trend of globalization!

In what direction will this tripod structure of global production develop? According to predictions by international organizations such as the OECD, by 2060, the economies of China and India combined will exceed 40% of the global economy, while the economies of the United States and Europe combined will be less than 35% of the global economy. If anything, the Asian region, with the addition of India, will strengthen its position within the tripod structure relative to the North America and Europe regions.

With the tripod structure in economic fundamentals already formed, what's next for the global superstructure? Where will the current contradictions between the global economic fundamentals and the global superstructure lead the world order? This is the topic of the next chapter.

CHAPTER 7

Fundamental Misalignment in the International Monetary System

In the global economic and financial system, corresponding to the structure of the GVC—which we call the global economic fundamentals—are the structure of the international monetary system (IMS) and the global governance system for global trade, investment, and finance—which we call the superstructure. In this chapter, we focus on the first fundamental misalignment between the global economic fundamentals and the superstructure, that is, the structural misalignment between the structure of the GVC and the structure of the IMS.

As discussed in Chapter 6, over the past 20 years, the structure of the GVC has evolved from one dominated by the United States to a tripartite structure anchored by China, Germany, and the United States. So, should the structure of the IMS adapt accordingly? How will it change? This is the primary issue affecting the order of global economic and financial system. Let's first review the history and current situation of the IMS.

7.1 International Monetary System: History and Current Status

The IMS refers to the arrangements or rules made by countries around the world for the pricing of goods and capital in international trade and cross-border investment, as well as the form of international cooperation established for this purpose. Different countries have different currencies. For international trade and cross-border investments to take place, there must be agreement on the rates of exchange between currencies, and this explains the birth and development of the IMS.

J. Ju, *US-China Great Power Competition and The New World Order*,
https://doi.org/10.1007/978-981-95-3762-4_7

7.1.1 *History*

The starting point of the modern IMS is the gold standard. The most important feature of the gold standard is that the value of each country's currency is based on gold. As depicted in Fig. 7.1, a country's currency is divided into two types: the domestic currency, which is banknotes or paper money; and the international currency, which is gold coins. The domestic currency has a fixed ratio with gold, which is its gold content. In the early gold standard, the gold content of £1 was 7.32238 grams, and the gold content of $1 was 1.50463 grams. That is, the gold content of £1 was 4.8665 times that of $1, so the exchange rate of pound to dollar was 1:4.8665.

The earliest form of the gold standard was the gold coin standard, under which gold coins could be freely minted and exchanged for paper currency at the mint price. Under the gold coin standard, gold could be freely imported and exported, and the fixed mint prices between two countries implied a fixed exchange rate (mint parity) between their currencies. The gold coin standard proved to be unstable and was subsequently replaced by the gold bullion standard and the gold exchange standard.

Fig. 7.1 Basic characteristic of the gold standard

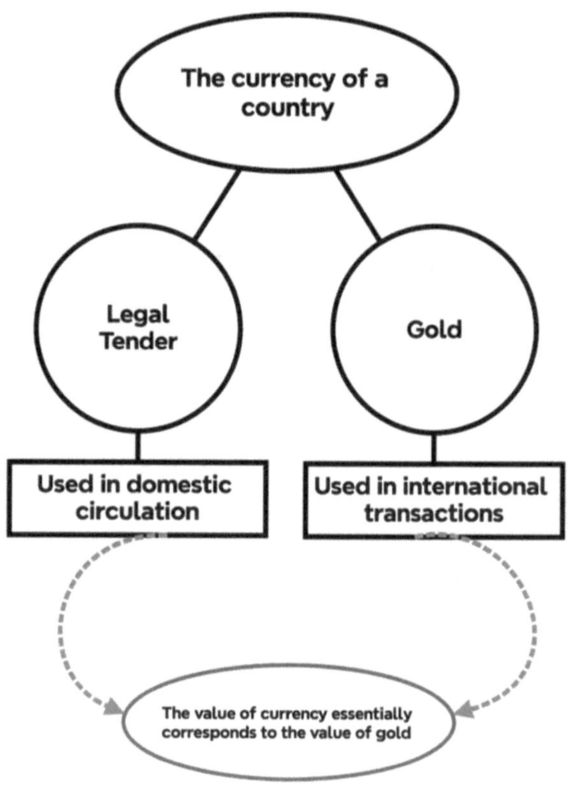

Under the gold bullion standard, gold coins could not be used as money; instead, gold bullion was used for international settlement and countries had to buy and sell gold bullion to back their paper currencies. Under the gold exchange standard, countries would buy and sell not gold bullion but gold-convertible foreign exchange, that is, the currency of a country on the gold bullion standard. The Bretton Woods system centered on the US dollar after World War II was a gold exchange standard.

The history of the IMS can be roughly divided into five periods: (1) the gold standard from 1870 to 1914; (2) the gold exchange standard from 1918 to 1933; (3) a period of monetary chaos from 1934 to 1943; (4) the Bretton Woods system from 1944 to 1973; and (5) the post-Bretton Woods system from 1974 to the present.

Gold Standard (1870—1914)

Britain, the most advanced capitalist economy at the time, adopted the gold standard around 1816. European countries gradually followed suit and by the end of the nineteenth century, most major countries had adopted the gold standard. The gold standard, which lasted for more than 40 years, established the pound as the world currency.

The establishment and development of the gold standard had significant effects. On the positive side, the system was a relatively stable monetary system, manifested in basically stable exchange rates between the currencies of major countries under the system, such as the British pound, the French franc, and the US dollar. The exchange rate stability under this system was conducive for international trade and capital flows and the economic development of the countries participating in this system. On the negative side, this monetary system relied too heavily on gold, and as time went by, world gold production was unable to meet the demand driven by global trade growth. In short, there was not enough gold. Reflecting the huge gap in economic development among countries, the distribution of gold reserves was also extremely unbalanced. International buying and selling of gold became increasingly difficult while the issuance of banknotes was increasing at the same time.

The gold standard lasted until 1914. After the outbreak of World War I, countries suspended gold exports, halted the free exchange of banknotes and gold, and the system disintegrated.

Gold Exchange Standard (1918–1933)

After World War I, in 1922, European countries led by Britain held an economic and financial conference in Genoa, Italy, to discuss the issue of rebuilding a viable IMS. One proposal at the conference was to adopt a gold exchange standard to conserve the use of gold. Under the gold exchange standard, gold would still be the basis of the IMS: countries' domestic currencies would still have gold content, but the banknotes would replace gold in day-to-day transactions. Countries would keep part of their reserves in gold and part in currencies that were directly exchangeable for gold, thus maintaining a fixed exchange rate with gold either directly or indirectly. Only the currencies of major countries—Britain and the United States—could be directly exchanged for gold; smaller countries would have to exchange their currencies for major country currencies to obtain gold. Gold would only serve as a means of payment in the event of a currency crisis.

After this conference, except for the United States still implementing the gold coin standard, and the United Kingdom and France implementing the gold bullion standard, these two monetary systems directly linked to gold, the currencies of other European countries all implemented the gold exchange standard in the form of indirect linkage. That is, small countries can use the currency of major countries as reserves, while major countries use gold as international reserves.

However, the Genoa Conference failed to establish a framework for international policy coordination. There was no mechanism to prevent countries from setting parities that led to a system of misaligned exchange rates. In a situation of insufficient gold reserves, countries with depreciating exchange rates could not intervene in the foreign exchange market to stabilize their currencies by selling gold.

In 1931, foreign investors lost confidence in Britain's commitment to maintain the value of the pound and rushed to exchange pounds for gold in large numbers. The ensuing banking crisis forced Britain to abruptly and unilaterally abandon the gold exchange standard.

Monetary System Chaos (1934–1943)

The Great Depression from 1929 to 1933 forced many countries off the gold exchange standard, including the United States, which officially departed in March 1933. Beginning in the 1930s, the IMS entered a chaotic period lasting over a decade. Countries formed currency groups, such as the pound group, the dollar group, and the franc group. Within each currency group, the currency of a major country served as the main reserve currency and was used for settling transactions within the group. At the same time, the currency groups fought for global dominance in the IMS. This situation lasted until the end of World War II.

Bretton Woods System (1944–1973)

After World War II, the international community reflected deeply on the drawbacks and harms of the chaotic IMS that existed before, and established a new IMS centered on the US dollar, namely the Bretton Woods system. The system was established in July 1944, when representatives from 44 countries convened the United Nations International Monetary and Financial Conference at the

Mount Washington Hotel in Bretton Woods, New Hampshire, in the United States.

The Bretton Woods system established a "double peg mechanism" where the US dollar was pegged to gold and other currencies were pegged to the US dollar. The price of the US dollar was fixed at $35 per ounce of gold; other currencies maintained a fixed exchange rate with the US dollar. Countries held official reserves in US dollars or gold, and they had the right to exchange dollars for gold with the US Federal Reserve at the fixed price. The Bretton Woods system was essentially a gold exchange standard centered on the US dollar.

Why the US dollar? The US economy developed rapidly during World War II due to the war stimulus, and its industrial capacity was at its peak. The United States was the world's largest economy at the time, accounting for more than 50% of world GDP. US military power was also unprecedentedly strong; being the only country in the world at the time with nuclear weapons, its war potential far exceeded other countries.

The Bretton Woods system solved the problem of gold shortage to a certain extent. The fixed exchange rate system stabilized world trade and finance. The International Monetary Fund (IMF) was established to promote international monetary cooperation and provide financial resources to member countries with balance-of-payments difficulties to help reduce the extent of external imbalances. However, the use of the US dollar as the global reserve currency had an inherent problem known as the Triffin Dilemma. Since all countries under the Bretton Woods system needed to hold US dollars as foreign exchange reserves, this inevitably led to an outflow of dollars from the United States, forcing the United States to maintain a persistent current account deficit. But this caused the US dollar to become overvalued relative to gold, and to maintain confidence in the dollar, the United States needed to run a current account surplus (or at least a balance), which was an irreconcilable contradiction.

On August 15, 1971, US President Richard Nixon made a shocking announcement that the US dollar could no longer be exchanged for gold. Italy and Japan decided to de-link their currencies from the US dollar. In March 1973, six countries of the European Community, including France and Germany, tied their currencies together and jointly floated against the US dollar, effectively dismantling the Bretton Woods system of fixed exchange rates.

Post-Bretton Woods System (1974 to the Present)

After the collapse of the Bretton Woods system, the international monetary system urgently needed adjustment and reform. The Interim Committee on the International Monetary System of the Board of Directors in the International Monetary Fund proposed an "Outline for Reform of the International Monetary System" in June 1974, which made principle suggestions on issues such as gold, exchange rates, reserve assets, and international balance of payments adjustments, laying the foundation for subsequent monetary reform.

In January 1976, a committee of the Board of Governors of the IMF met in Kingston, Jamaica, and signed the so-called Jamaica Accords, ratifying the end of the Bretton Woods monetary system. The most significant feature of the Jamaica Accords is that the price of gold was allowed to float with respect to the US dollar and other currencies. This established an exchange rate system of managed floating among major currencies that has continued to the present day.

7.1.2 *Current Status*

The current IMS is still a US dollar-denominated system. The functions of an international currency are serving as a store of value (for savings), a medium of exchange (for trading), and a unit of account (for pricing). As we will show below, the US dollar has a monopoly position in all three functions. Specifically, let's look at the usage of major international currencies in four areas: official foreign exchange reserve holdings; international payments; foreign exchange transactions; and international lending. Overall, we can say that the current IMS consists of "one super and one strong" currency, where the US dollar is the "super currency" and the euro is the "strong currency," less dominant than the dollar but far stronger than other reserve currencies.

Official Foreign Exchange Reserve Holdings

Official foreign exchange reserves are assets held by a country's monetary authorities that can be converted at any time into foreign currency, gold, foreign securities, etc. The IMF compiles detailed statistics on the currency composition of its member countries' official foreign exchange reserves, including reserves held in eight currencies—the Australian dollar, Canadian dollar, euro, pound, renminbi, Swiss franc, US dollar, and yen.

Figure 7.2 shows the changes in the currency composition of the world's official foreign exchange reserve holdings from 1975 to 2022. We can see that the US dollar has always occupied the primary position as an international reserve currency, even long after the collapse of the Bretton Woods system. The two oil crises in the 1970s and early 1980s, the birth of the euro in 1999, and the subprime mortgage crisis in 2008 had a small negative impact but the dissolution of the Soviet Union in 1992, the Asian financial crisis in 1997, and the European debt crisis in 2010 had a positive impact on the reserve currency status of the US dollar. Overall, the US dollar's share in the world's official foreign exchange reserve holdings has always remained around 60%. According to data from the IMF, as of the fourth quarter of 2022, the US dollar accounted for 58.58% of the world's official foreign exchange reserve holdings, whereas the euro accounted for 20.37%, and the renminbi accounted for only 2.61%.

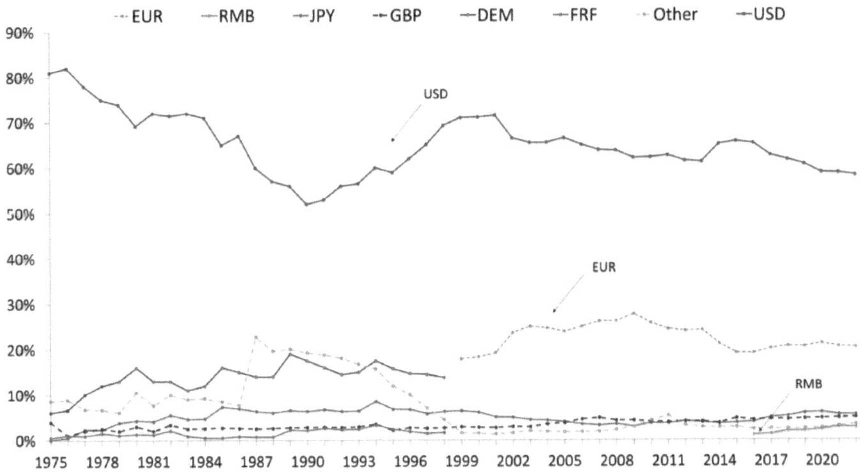

Fig. 7.2 Currency composition of world holdings of official foreign exchange reserves (1975—2022) (*Data source* IMF; Eichengreen et al. [2017][1])

International Payments

An international payment currency refers to a currency used to carry out foreign trade and international capital transactions. For example, businesses engaged in the import and export of goods and services will need to agree on which currency to use for actual payments—the currency of the exporting country, the importing country, or a third country. In international business, the currencies used for actual payments are called international payment currencies. Currently, the two main international payment currencies are the US dollar and the euro. According to data provided by the Society for Worldwide Interbank Financial Telecommunication (SWIFT) in December 2022, the US dollar and the euro were used for 47.89% and 36.34% of all global payments, respectively, far more than other currencies such as the pound (6.08%), yen (2.88%), and renminbi (2.15%).

Foreign Exchange Transactions

The daily trading volume in the global foreign exchange market in 2022 was as high as $75 trillion, far higher than the daily volume of $0.09 trillion in international trade. According to statistics from the Bank for International Settlements (BIS), in 2022, the US dollar accounted for 44.22% of global foreign exchange transactions, while the euro's share was 15.27%, the yen

[1] Eichengreen, Barry, Arnaud Mehl, and Livia Chitu, *How Global Currencies Work: Past, Present, and Future*, Princeton University Press, 2019.

8.35%, and the renminbi only 2.60%. It can be said that the US dollar is by far the most commonly traded currency.

International Lending

In the international bond market, as of the fourth quarter of 2022, 46.73% of international bonds were denominated in US dollars, 37.81% in euros, and 15.46% in other currencies including the renminbi. As for cross-border bank loans, as of the fourth quarter of 2022, 52.16% were denominated in US dollars, 27.53% in euros, and 20.31% in other currencies including the renminbi. Thus, the US dollar still occupies a dominant position in international banking and debt issuance.

In summary, although the global production, consumption, and trade networks have undergone significant structural changes over the past 20 years, evolving from US dominance in 2000 to the current tripod, the IMS has essentially maintained a dollar-dominated structure since 1944.

7.2 The Fundamental Misalignment: Mismatch Between the Tripod Economic Structure and the Unipolar International Monetary System

Let's return to the question raised at the beginning of this chapter: given that the structure of the global economic fundamentals has changed, should the IMS, as one of the core components of the global superstructure, change correspondingly and how?

7.2.1 Theory

Theoretically, the structures of the global economic fundamentals and the IMS should match, that is to say, in an ideal state, a country's share of world GDP should correspond to the share of its currency in global foreign exchange transactions. Let's explain the relationship between a country's currency position and economic position step by step.

First, consider an ideal world where all countries' currencies are freely convertible international currencies and the cost of currency exchange is zero. In this case, a country's currency position has nothing to do with its economic position because trading with any currency is the same, with zero cost difference.

Next, let's get closer to reality. Still assuming that all currencies are freely convertible international currencies, now suppose there is a small cost to convert from one currency to another. In this case, a country will use its own currency for domestic transactions, but which currency will it use for exporting? Since all currencies are equally convenient for cross-border trade but there is a small cost to convert between the domestic and foreign currencies, it will be more convenient for countries to use their own currencies for exporting. Assume that a country's share of global exports is proportional to its share of global GDP. Note that a country's GDP is the total amount of output produced in the country, which is approximately equal to total domestic transactions plus total exports. Therefore, a country's share of global GDP and the share of its currency in global foreign exchange transactions should be equal. So when all currencies are international currencies and can be freely converted, but there is a small cost of conversion, a country's share of global GDP and the share of its currency in global foreign exchange transactions should be the same.

Now let's get even closer to reality. What if some currencies, like the dollar, are convenient to use and have low conversion costs, while other currencies, like the renminbi, are inconvenient to use and may not even be freely convertible? We can predict that the more convenient currency will be used by more countries, while the inconvenient currency will be used by only a few countries. This could result in a mismatch between countries' currency and economic positions, and the share of the convenient currency in global foreign exchange transactions could be greater than its country's share of global GDP.

The use of a currency has strong network externalities, that is, the more widely a currency is used, the more convenient it will be for people to use it. In the course of recent history, there have been one or more dominant international currencies, such as the pound before World War I and the dollar after World War II. The share of the dominant currency in international foreign exchange transactions may exceed the share of its country in the world economy, that is, the structure of the IMS may deviate to a certain extent from the country distribution of world GDP.

7.2.2 *Data*

In the real world, does a country's share in the world economy match its share in the IMS? Fig. 7.3 is a correspondence chart for eight economies (excluding China and the United States) in 2022, where the horizontal axis measures a country's share of the global GDP, and the vertical axis measures the share of the country's currency in global foreign exchange transactions.

Theoretically, the GDP share and currency share of each country should be close to the 45-degree line. In reality, in 2022, the Eurozone's share of total GDP was 14.23%, and the euro's share in total foreign exchange transactions was 15.27%, almost perfectly corresponding. Countries like Australia, Canada, Japan, Switzerland, and the United Kingdom are also quite near the 45-degree line, indicating that the international position of these economies basically matches the international position of their currencies.

But what does it look like when China and the United States are included? From Fig. 7.4, it can be seen that the United States is far above the 45-degree line, while China is significantly below it. The US share of total GDP

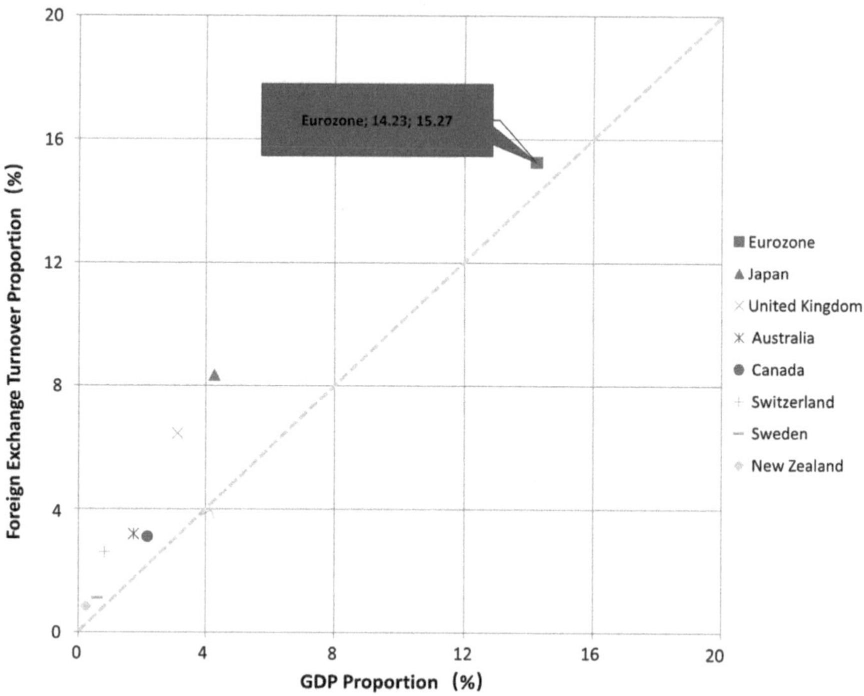

Fig. 7.3 Share of global GDP versus currency share in global foreign exchange transactions in 2022, excluding China and the United States

is 25.74%, and the dollar's share in total foreign exchange transactions is 44.22%—a gap of 19 percentage. Conversely, China's share of total GDP is 17.85%, and the renminbi's share in total foreign exchange transactions is 3.5%, the latter being more than 14 percentage points less than the former. The country's share in the global real economy and its currency's share in the IMS are severely mismatched for both the United States and China. This is the fundamental misalignment between the structure of the global economy and the structure of the IMS! The contradiction between the tripod global economic structure and the dollar-dominated IMS is the fundamental misalignment of the global economic and financial system.

7.2.3 *International Seigniorage*

What are the benefits for the United States of the dollar being the dominant international currency? The benefit is so-called international seigniorage.

Seigniorage is the revenue from issuing currency. Currency can be understood as a special kind of commodity, and the income obtained from issuing this special commodity minus the cost of producing this commodity is seigniorage. The printing cost of a 100-dollar bill may only be $1, but it can

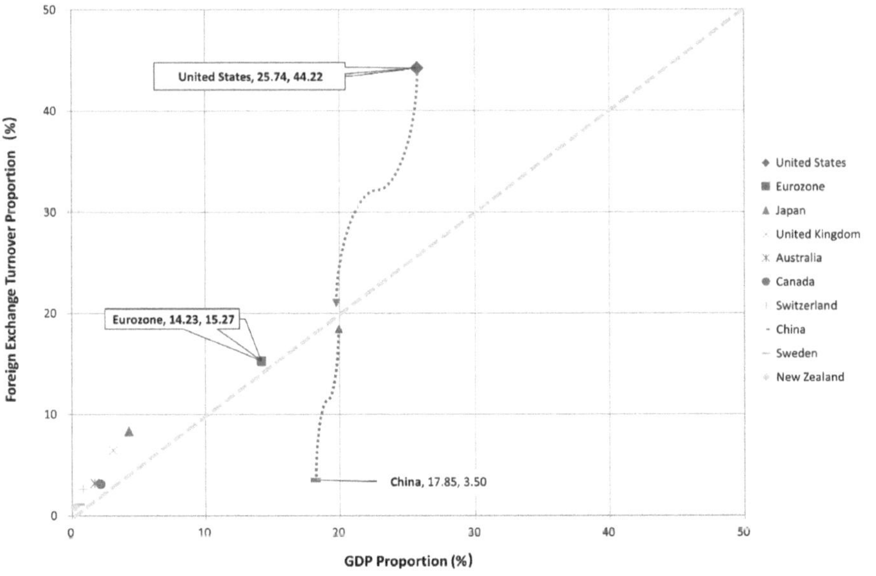

Fig. 7.4 Share of total GDP versus currency share in total foreign exchange transactions in 2022, including China and the United States

purchase $100 worth of goods, and the difference of $99 is seigniorage for the US Federal Reserve, which is an important source of government revenue. In the era of electronic payments, the Federal Reserve issues currency by simply changing a number, with virtually zero cost, so when the Federal Reserve issues $100, the US government's income increases by $100.

There are three types of dollar seigniorage, namely net income seigniorage, opportunity cost seigniorage, and monetary seigniorage.[2] Net income seigniorage equals the interest income earned by the Federal Reserve from its investment portfolio plus service fees minus operating expenses, and opportunity cost seigniorage is the interest generated by the Federal Reserve's investment in US Treasury bonds. Our main interest is monetary seigniorage, which equals the change in the real supply of money by the Federal Reserve (the change in nominal money supply divided by the price level that year). Monetary seigniorage is essentially the increase in the money supply minus the cost of inflation. As the dollar is an international currency, the Federal Reserve's issuance of more money could potentially lead to global inflation, making the income from the dollar issuance owned by Americans while the cost of inflation is borne by the world. Let's discuss this further.

[2] Cutsinger, Bryan P., and William J. Luther, "Seigniorage Payments and the Federal Reserve's New Operating Regime," *Economics Letters* 220 (October 6, 2022): 110880. https://doi.org/10.1016/j.econlet.2022.110880; Zhang Jianhua, Zhang Huaiqing, 2009, "Measurement and application of the People's Bank of China's seigniorage: 1986–2008" *Economic Research* (in Chinese), (7), pp. 79–90.

In a closed US economy, if the Federal Reserve issues an additional $100 but the output of the US economy does not increase, this will only cause the price of goods to rise proportionally, increasing US inflation. Therefore, the Federal Reserve's issuance of more money will not benefit the American people.

In an open US economy, the situation is very different. Even if US output does not increase, the US government can use the additional $100 to purchase goods and services from other countries. Thus, the benefits of the Federal Reserve's money issuance are entirely retained by the United States. However, since the dollar circulates around the world, if global output does not increase commensurately, the issuance of more dollars would lead to global inflation. US GDP only accounts for 25% of global GDP, so the United States could bear only 25% of the ensuing cost of inflation, with the remaining 75% borne by the rest of the world. Theoretically, if the Federal Reserve issues an additional $100, the United States could potentially "fleece" $75 from the rest of the world.

The above example assumes that the US share of the world economy is about 25%, and the share of the US dollar in world foreign exchange transactions is 100%. This is an extreme example in theory, but the underlying logic is clear: if the international structure of the economic fundamentals and the structure of the IMS do not match, the dominant international currency country could make use of the asymmetry between the revenue and inflation cost from currency issuance to levy a "seigniorage tax" on other countries in the world.

We've seen so far that network externalities of currency use tend to cause inertia in the structure of the IMS, so that even when the economic position of the dominant international currency country no longer matches its currency position, its dominant currency status can still be maintained for a certain period. At the same time, the dominant international currency country will be unwilling to give up its ability to use its position to levy a seigniorage tax by shifting the cost of inflation from its currency issuance to other countries in the world—"our dollars, your problem." This constitutes the fundamental misalignment of the IMS: network externalities delay the reform of the IMS, while the seigniorage tax levied by the dominant international currency country eventually prompts resistance from other countries and efforts to promote the structural adjustment of the IMS to make it consistent with that of the global economic fundamentals.

7.3 How to Resolve the Fundamental Misalignment of the International Monetary System?

Historically, this is not the first time a contradiction between the structures of the global economic fundamentals and the IMS has appeared. The last time it appeared was when the world-leading position of Britain was replaced by the United States, as discussed in Sect. 7.1.1.

During the gold standard period, the British pound was the world's most trusted equivalent of gold as an international payment method and reserve currency. In 1913, just before the outbreak of World War I, 40% of the world's foreign exchange reserves was stored in the form of the pound.[3] The challenge to the pound came from the US dollar. US GDP surpassed that of the British Empire (including its colonies) in 1912, and the dollar began to overtake the pound as a global reserve currency in 1924. The dollar completely took over the dominant position of the pound in the IMS in 1944. The mismatch between the economic fundamentals of Britain and the United States and their currencies' positions in the IMS lasted for over 30 years. What happened during those 30 years? The period encompassed two world wars and the Great Depression from 1929 to 1933.

World War I, which broke out in 1914, destroyed the gold standard system centered on the pound. Through war loans and goods trade with Europe, the United States greatly increased its economic strength, becoming the world's largest creditor nation and accumulating rich reserves of gold. This led to the rise of the dollar's influence. At the end of the war in 1919, the United States, which held nearly 40% of the world's gold reserves, was the first country to return to the gold standard. The dollar began to compete with the pound, and the two currencies were on a par in areas such as reserve holdings, foreign acceptance bills, and cross-border payments. The dollar surpassed the pound as the most widely held reserve currency for the first time in 1924, and this advantage of the dollar over the pound continued until the outbreak of the Great Depression.

The arrival of the Great Depression in 1929 ended the competition between the dollar and the pound. The economic strength of the United States and Britain was severely hit; output, consumption, and trade shrank in both countries, and the international status of both the dollar and the pound declined. From 1932 to the outbreak of World War II in 1939, several currency groups emerged, such as the pound group, the dollar group, and the franc group. The international monetary system presented a "center-periphery" structure, with the center being the pound, dollar, franc, etc. The global economic system was in complete disarray and the IMS was also in a chaotic stage until the Bretton Woods Conference in 1944 that rebuilt the IMS with the US dollar at its center.

This period of history reveals two critical insights. First, a mismatch between the IMS and the real economy inevitably calls for reform of the IMS. Second, historically, changes in the IMS have always been accompanied by war or financial crises.

[3] Chiţu, Livia, Barry Eichengreen, and Arnaud Mehl. "When Did the Dollar Overtake Sterling as the Leading International Currency? Evidence from the Bond Markets," *Journal of Development Economics* 111 (October 2, 2013): 225–45. https://doi.org/10.1016/j.jdeveco.2013.09.008.

The rapid development of China's economy has once again brought the fundamental misalignment of the IMS to the surface. Interestingly, until the outbreak of the US-China trade war in 2018, this fundamental misalignment, although present, was not acute, and the global economic and financial order was actually stable. Why? Before 2018, China and the United States complemented and were integrated with each other in the GVC, and they were closely linked in the IMS: the renminbi and the US dollar were almost at a fixed exchange rate; the monetary policies of two countries were basically consistent; and more than half of the US trade deficit was China's trade surplus. In fact, the US dollar ran not only the US economy, but the economies of both China and the United States—as the New York Times columnist Thomas Friedman observed, China and the United States were like two countries operating as one economy.[4] If China and the United States were considered as one economy, their combined GDP would have accounted for about 40% of global GDP, and the share of the US dollar and the renminbi in global foreign exchange transactions would have been about 46% at the time. Therefore, as one economy, the economic and monetary positions of China plus the United States would have been matched, and the global economic structure and monetary structure would have been stable.

Unfortunately, since the outbreak of the US-China trade war in 2018, the economic and financial systems of China and the United States have diverged. The fundamental misalignment of the global economic and financial system has emerged, and the world economy has entered a turbulent stage.

How can this fundamental misalignment be resolved?

7.3.1 Convergence

The first solution raised by the United States would be through "convergence" of the two economies: specifically, for China's economic and financial system to converge toward the US-led economic and financial system. Whether it is through "structural reform," as dictated by Trump, or compliance with the "rules-based international order," as dictated by Biden, the essence would be for China to abandon its independent ability to chart its own development and growth path and submit to the US vision of the world and China's place in it. Convergence would rebind the economic and financial systems of China and the United States together, making them "one economy, two countries." But this "one economy" would be led by the United States, and China would have to operate under the system and follow the rules dictated by the United States. In other words, convergence would require China to be subordinate to the United States in terms of its economic and financial development. As

[4] Friedman, Thomas, "The World Is Faster, Deeper, More Fused, Open and Fragile," *China-US Focus*, April 20, https://www.chinausfocus.com/foreign-policy/the-world-is-faster-deeper-more-fused-open-and-fragile, accessed on November 29, 2025.

China's economy continues to grow, it would be difficult for China to accept such convergence.

7.3.2 Decoupling

The second solution raised by the United States—after China explicit rejected the convergence solution—would be through "decoupling" of the two economies. Decoupling began in the Trump administration and was strengthened and renamed "de-risking" in the Biden administration. Either ways, the essence is "de-Chinaization," which is to isolate or cut off China from the world economy, so that the United States can continue to dominate it.

What would the correspondence chart between share of global GDP and currency share of global foreign exchange transactions (Fig. 7.4) look like if we exclude China's GDP and renminbi foreign exchange transactions? It would look like Fig. 7.5: US GDP would rise to 31.33% of world GDP (without China), and the dollar's share in global foreign exchange transactions (without the renminbi) would rise to 45.83%. With China out of the picture, the entire system would be more "stable" because there would be no negative outlier below the 45-degree line to challenge the US position above the 45-degree line. Therefore, we can understand why some people in the United States are proposing various forms of de-Chinaization.

"De-Chinaization" requires excluding China from the GVC and cutting off China's access to global sources of capital, technology, skilled labor, and other factors crucial for development. To achieve this strategic objective, the United States would need to strengthen its economy and reconfigure the GVC. Since taking office in 2021, President Biden has promoted industrial policy in the United States by increasing R&D subsidies in the high-tech field and trade restrictions to reduce its dependence on imports from China in key industries such as semiconductors, large-capacity batteries, critical minerals, and chemical raw materials. The 2022 CHIPS and Science Act and Inflation Reduction Act, for example, provided huge incentives for US high-tech manufacturing industries such as chips and green energy, to enhance their competitiveness and "counter China." The Biden administration has also made strong efforts to persuade its allies in Europe and Asia to form a united front under American leadership to "de-risk" by reconfiguring the GVC to reduce their trade dependence on China. The idea, it seems, would be to revert the current tripod structure of the GVC back to the US-led GVC structure in 2000.

To achieve this goal, the United States will fully use the dominant position of the dollar in the IMS. Since the COVID-19 pandemic, the Federal Reserve has issued a large amount of money, ostensibly to promote economic recovery, but also to support US industrial policy to counter China. By issuing more dollars and receiving the attendant international seigniorage, the United States can strengthen its real economy and support its efforts to reconfigure the GVC.

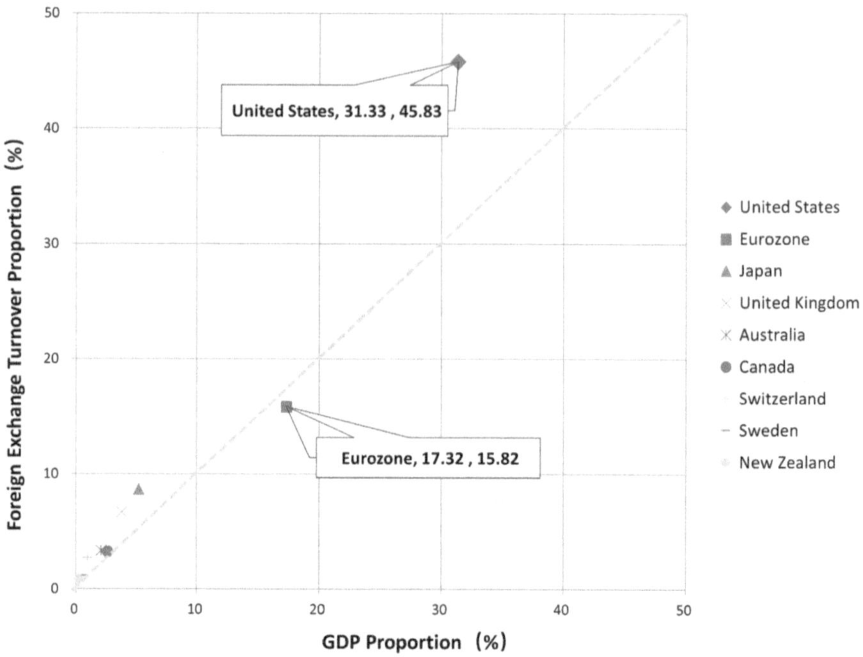

Fig. 7.5 Share of global GDP versus currency share of global foreign exchange transactions, 2022, excluding China

However, ultra-easy monetary policy also brings a certain degree of inflation. In fact, the Federal Reserve has had to raise interest rates quickly to curb inflation pressures brought on by supply shortages due to the US-China trade war and supply chain disruptions due to COVID-19 and the Russia-Ukraine conflict. The US practice of maximizing its international seigniorage has been exacerbating global inflation and the risk of a global economic recession, which could ultimately weaken the international status of the dollar.

7.3.3 *Tripod International Monetary System*

The decoupling solution—which involves the United States using its international seigniorage benefit to reconfigure the GVC—uses the superstructure of the global economic and financial system to change the economic fundamentals. But isn't it the more natural rule for the economic fundamentals to determine the superstructure? Since the GVC has changed to a tripod structure, the IMS should also reflect this change, moving from a unipolar system dominated by the dollar to a multipolar system supported by three currencies. In other words, a more sensible way to resolve the fundamental misalignment of the IMS would be to establish a tripod IMS of the dollar, the renminbi, and the euro that corresponds to the tripod GVC of the United States, China, and Europe.

As a necessary condition for establishing a tripod IMS, the renminbi would need to become a freely convertible international currency like the dollar and the euro. However, free convertibility of the renminbi would require the opening of China's capital account, and opening the capital account could expose China to the risk of capital flight and, in the worst case, a financial crisis. Is there a way to solve this dilemma? Can China open its capital account and still protect itself from the risks of volatile capital flows?

The misalignment between the economic fundamentals and the structure of the monetary system needs to be resolved. The dollar has become the United States' most powerful weapon. In the Russia-Ukraine conflict, the United States used the internationally dominant status of the dollar to impose comprehensive financial and economic sanctions on Russia, which was as powerful a method of attack as a military assault. The weaponization of the dollar by the United States has forced Russia to de-dollarize rapidly, and China, which is regarded as a strategic competitor by the United States, has to prepare for this rainy day. Can the reform of the IMS from dollar-dominated to tripod be peacefully achieved?

We will discuss these issues in detail in Chapter 11. The answer is optimistic. Innovations in capital flow management policies will enable China to open its capital account in an orderly way and minimize the risk of financial crises caused by volatile capital flows, and innovations in monetary technology, that is, the birth and development of digital currencies, may allow the reform of the IMS to proceed on a peaceful path!

CHAPTER 8

Fundamental Misalignment in the World Order

"5, 4, 3, 2, 1, Happy New Year! The new century has arrived!" At midnight on January 1, 2000, there was a cheer in my neighborhood in Norman, Oklahoma, in the United States. My neighbors were students from the University of Oklahoma; two were in my Intermediate Microeconomics class—Mike, a junior philosophy major and Anita, a sophomore marketing major.

Mike knocked on my door excitedly: "Happy New Year, Dr. Ju!" He was waving two bottles of beer: "Come out, Dr. Ju!"

I walked out the door and took the beer he threw at me: "What are you excited about, China is already in the new century." Most of the lights in the neighborhood were on, and there were already quite a few people on the street, Mike and a few students, holding beers.

"Do you know, Dr. Ju? Only now is it the new century. Beijing time doesn't count." Anita waved her beer bottle at me.

"Does New York time count?" I was a bit unconvinced.

"Happy New Year!" Mike clinked his beer bottle against mine: "It's like this: Oklahoma is the heartland, and the redemption of mankind is marked by the redemption of the heartland, so only when the heartland reaches the new year is the new century considered to have arrived."

I smiled at him and said: "Keep boasting. You should switch majors and study marketing, since everything in Oklahoma is number one in the world, from beef to walnuts—even the start of the new century is marked by Oklahoma."

The new century has arrived, but what does the new world order look like? How will it come about?

J. Ju, *US-China Great Power Competition and The New World Order*,
https://doi.org/10.1007/978-981-95-3762-4_8

8.1 History and Current Status of the Global Economic Governance System

The world order needs a global governance system. In the absence of a world government, the global economic governance system establishes and maintains the rules of global trade, finance, and investment. Before revealing the fundamental misalignment of the world order, let's first introduce the history of global economic governance after World War II.

The global economic governance system includes some international organizations that we are very familiar with. In international finance, global governance is mainly represented by the International Monetary Fund (IMF) and the Bank for International Settlements (BIS); in international trade, global governance is mainly represented by the World Trade Organization (WTO); in international economic development and poverty reduction, global governance is mainly represented by the World Bank Group.

Let's first briefly discuss the main developments in the global economic governance system over the past 70 years.

8.1.1 Main Developments in the Global Economic Governance System

As mentioned in Chapter 7, toward the end of World War II in July 1944, representatives from 44 countries gathered for a conference at Bretton Woods, New Hampshire, to design the framework for postwar international economic cooperation. The so-called Bretton Woods conference established the fundamental principles of a new monetary system and created two international institutions to support the structure of the international economic and financial order: the IMF to oversee the international monetary system and the World Bank to finance economic development.

Also in 1944, in the so-called Dumbarton Oaks conference held in Washington, D.C. in August–October and led by the United States, the United Kingdom, the Soviet Union, and China, proposals were made to create the United Nations (UN), an intergovernmental forum for solving international problems and disputes; the proposals were adopted in 1945. Arising from the discussions that took place in a 1947 UN conference was the General Agreement on Tariffs and Trade (GATT), which was signed in October that year.

After the collapse of the Bretton Woods system in 1973, the IMF switched its role from monitoring fixed exchange rates to "exercising firm surveillance over its members' exchange rate policies" and increasing its lending activities to help countries in balance of payments crises.[1] The standard reform package promoted for crisis-affected developing countries by the IMF and the

[1] "Money Matters, an IMF Exhibit—The Importance of Global Cooperation, Reinventing the System (1972–1981), Part 1 of 7." *International Monetary Fund*, September 5, 2001. https://www.imf.org/external/np/exr/center/mm/eng/mm_rs_01.htm, accessed on November 29, 2025.

World Bank (backed by the US government) was known as the Washington Consensus—a set of 10 prescriptions promoting free-market policies such as trade liberalization, privatization, and financial liberalization.

The WTO's creation on January 1, 1995, marked the biggest reform of international trade governance since the end of World War II. From 1948 to 1994, the GATT had provided an avenue for multilateral trade liberalization, but it was a provisional agreement and organization. The WTO, its successor, was established as a full-fledged international organization dealing with the rules of world trade and the settlement of disputes.

The 1997 Asian crisis prompted further rethinking of the global financial architecture. The United States opposed Japan's proposal for an Asian Monetary Fund, which it claimed would weaken lending standards and diminish the role of the IMF. In February 1999, the Financial Stability Forum (FSF), a group consisting of major national financial authorities, was created on the recommendation of the Group of Seven (G7) countries to promote international financial stability.

The United States and other members of the G7 (Canada, France, Germany, Italy, Japan, and the United Kingdom)[2] continued to lead the global economic order until the outbreak of the global financial crisis in 2008, which had originated from the US subprime mortgage crisis the previous year and spread to Europe. The United States' dominant position in the global economic governance began to shake. In 2009, the Group of Twenty (G20)—comprising the G7 countries plus the European Union and 12 major developing countries including China, India, Indonesia, and South Korea—declared itself the main forum for "defining and strengthening global architecture and governance on all major international economic issues."[3] The G20 established the Financial Stability Board (FSB) as a successor to the FSF to monitor and make recommendations for the global financial system.

The outbreak of the US-China trade war in 2018 marked a new stage in the evolution of the world order. Effective operation of the global economic governance system is urgently needed, whether for pandemic prevention, climate change, or economic recovery. Therefore, the restructuring of global economic governance has become a pressing issue.

8.1.2 US Dominance in Global Economic Governance

How is US dominance reflected in global economic governance? Let's first look at the two international institutions of the Bretton Woods system: the IMF and the World Bank. On key decision-making issues in these two international organizations, the United States has effective veto power.

[2] Russia formally joined the group in 1998 and resulted in the Group of Eight (G8). But Russia's membership was suspended in March 2014 due to its annexation of Crimea.

[3] Readers are referred to: https://www.g20.org/en/about-the-g20, accessed on November 29, 2025.

Table 8.1 Shares and voting rights of the top ten countries in the IMF[4]

Rank	*Member Country*	*Share of quota (%)*	*Share of votes (%)*
1	United States	17.43	16.50
2	Japan	6.47	6.14
3	China	6.40	6.08
4	Germany	5.59	5.31
5	France	4.23	4.03
6	United Kingdom	4.23	4.03
7	Italy	3.16	3.02
8	India	2.75	2.63
9	Russia	2.71	2.59
10	Brazil	2.32	2.22

Table 8.1 shows the quota shares and voting power of the top ten countries in the IMF: the United States is at the top with 16.5% of the voting share. The IMF normally makes decisions based on consensus but sometimes takes formal votes. According to its Articles of Agreement, major issues must obtain at least 85% of votes to pass, so if the United States disagrees, they cannot be passed. In this sense, the United States has veto power in the IMF.

The top five countries and their corresponding vote shares (shown in parentheses) in the World Bank are: the United States (15.73%), Japan (7.19%), China (5.58%), Germany (4.27%), and the United Kingdom (3.92%). The World Bank also stipulates that major issues must obtain at least 85% of votes to pass, so the United States has veto power in the World Bank as well.[5]

The WTO, on the other hand, is relatively democratic: all decisions are made by the membership as a whole, unlike the IMF and the World Bank, where power is delegated to a board of directors. Voting is on the basis of "one country, one vote," with the final decision determined by the majority of votes cast, where the majority is typically either 2/3 or 3/4. Major issues, such as accepting a new member, need a 2/3 majority to pass.

As mentioned earlier, the WTO succeeded the GATT as the international organization dealing with the global rules of trade. The United States played a leading role in both organizations. But while the GATT completed eight rounds of negotiations from 1948 to 1994, with significant achievements in tariff reduction, the WTO has made almost no progress in reducing tariffs and other trade barriers. Why has the WTO not been as effective as the GATT? This reflects the gradual change in the US approach to trade liberalization. After the Great Depression, the prevailing view in the United States was in favor of trade liberalization and several bilateral agreements to that end were negotiated with other countries. At the end of World War II, the United States

[4] Data source: IMF official website.

[5] Data source: World Bank official website.

sought to establish an international organization that would be responsible for reconstructing world trade, and the GATT arose from this effort. Therefore, the direction of trade liberalization basically conformed to the interests of the United States, and with its support, multilateral tariff reduction negotiations made significant progress. With the collapse of the Soviet Union in 1991, the United States became very optimistic about "world democracy"; US trade treatment toward so-called nonmarket economies like China was much less favorable than toward its GATT partners. At the same time, there was a dramatic increase in the number of regional trade agreements (RTAs), particularly in Europe but also including the North American Free Trade Agreement (NAFTA) among the United States, Canada, and Mexico, its most important trading partners at the time. By the time the WTO was established in 1995, US interest in multilateral trade liberalization was no longer as great as before. When China was admitted to the WTO in 2001, it had to agree to much harsher conditions than other developing countries, at the insistence of the United States.

In addition to its dominant position in international organizations, US dominance in global economic governance is also reflected in its ability to exercise extra-territorial jurisdiction over other countries' enterprises through long-arm jurisdiction. As we discussed in Chapter 5, US long-arm jurisdiction refers to sanctions and restrictions on non-US companies to protect US domestic and foreign policy interests. US long-arm jurisdiction over global multinational corporations has been increasingly strengthened and effective since the 9/11 terrorist attack in 2001. Whether it's France's Alstom, Germany's Siemens, or Japan's Toshiba, under the big stick of US long-arm jurisdiction, all have paid huge fines and submitted to US supervision. It wasn't until the outbreak of the US-China trade war in 2018 that the United States met with tenacious resistance to its tactics from Huawei.

In summary, the US-led global economic governance system after World War II reflected the United States' strong interest and capabilities in international finance, trade, and investment. Currently, the United States still dominates international financial governance. However, global trade governance is increasingly in trouble, and there is no international organization responsible for global investment governance.

8.2 The Fundamental Misalignment in the World Order

There is no question that after World War II, the United States occupied a dominant position in the world order. US dominance reached a peak after the collapse of the Soviet Union in 1991 but gradually declined after 2008. The fundamental misalignment in the world order is the mismatch between the tripod structure of the GVC and the US-led global governance system. This fundamental misalignment is manifested in three ways: first, the United

States no longer has enough resources to lead super-globalization[6]; second, conflicting interests among domestic groups in the United States no longer support US-led super-globalization; third, the tripod structure of the GVC no longer supports super-globalization.

8.2.1 The Impossible Trinity of Global Governance

Similar to the "impossible trinity" of a fixed exchange rate, free capital flows, and an independent monetary policy in international macroeconomics, we can explain the fundamental misalignment of the world order as the impossible trinity of achieving super-globalization, national sovereignty, and democratic politics simultaneously.[7] This is depicted in Fig. 8.1.

Super-globalization + Democratic Politics

The first case is to choose super-globalization and democratic politics. In this case, the global governance system becomes an enlarged version of the United States, with a super-global government having authority over all countries in the world, similar to the US federal government's relationship with the 50 state governments. This would require all countries to cede sovereignty to the super-global government. Therefore, the world can have super-globalization + democratic politics if all countries give up their national sovereignty. Will this be possible?

The European Union is advancing European integration in this direction. EU members that have adopted the euro hand over their monetary policy autonomy to the European Central Bank but at the same time, each country retains its fiscal policy autonomy. This leads to internal conflicts, which was an

Fig. 8.1 Impossible trinity in the world order

[6] Super-globalization refers to a world with: (1) a GVC linking countries that are consumers/innovators, producers, and resource suppliers; (2) a unified global governance system; and (3) a unified value system represented by the Washington Consensus.

[7] Rodrik, Dani, 2011, *The Globalization Paradox: Democracy and the Future of the World Economy*, New York: W.W. Norton & Company..

important reason for the European debt crisis in 2010. Fiscal union has been mooted as a next step forward for European integration, but this has proven difficult to put into practice.

What is more difficult is requiring all member countries to unify their ideology under the banner of democratic politics. The Russia-Ukraine conflict shows that the eastward expansion of European integration has its limits. How much harder would it be for the world to unify under one political ideology?

The fundamental misalignment of the world order has made it impossible for the super-globalization that was barely achieved before the turn of the century to continue. Whether we are talking about the global governance system or the value system, the United States no longer has sufficient strength and resources to maintain its ambition to dominate the world. The US-led world order and spreading the ideology of the Washington Consensus require huge financial resources. The United States does not have enough money to finance this dream of super-globalization, as evidenced by its withdrawal from the conflicts it initiated in Iraq and Afghanistan, and its turning to the "America First" policy.

Super-globalization + National Sovereignty

The second case is to choose super-globalization and national sovereignty. In this case, super-globalization is achieved through a global unified market for goods, services, capital, labor, and technology but without a super-global government. Countries retain their national sovereignty, but they commit to eliminating all costs impinging on free international trade and capital movements. Thus, national sovereignty degenerates into merely ensuring that domestic policies are consistent with global rules that ensure the global goods and factor markets operate freely. However, as we discussed in Chapter 4, the SS theorem predicts that free trade will increase the income of owners of the relatively abundant factor of production and reduce the income of owners of the relatively scarce factor, and it will cause conflicts between domestic interest groups. In the short term, free trade will make the export sector expand, while the import-competing sector will suffer. Therefore, super-globalization + national sovereignty will bring about sharp conflicts among different domestic interest groups, causing democratic politics to fall into turmoil.

Argentina is an interesting illustration of this case. In the early 1990s, under the influence of Domingo Cavallo, the Harvard-educated Minister of the Economy, the Argentine government implemented typical super-globalization economic policies: establishing monetary stability by fixing the exchange rate of the Argentinian peso to the US dollar at 1:1 and eliminating exchange rate restrictions, accelerating privatization, deregulating markets, and encouraging free trade and capital flows. The free-market policies brought an inflow of international capital and economic prosperity to Argentina. However, the good times didn't last long. When capital flows reversed after the Asian financial crisis in 1997, Argentina's economy quickly deteriorated. In 2002, Argentina experienced a serious financial crisis and its GDP shrank by 12%

in that year alone. The financial crisis caused domestic political turmoil and government changes, which ultimately led to the end of Argentina's super-globalization policy.

Even the United States has encountered conflicts between super-globalization economic policies and domestic democratic politics. Trade liberalization is seen to have exacerbated the decline in US manufacturing employment and the increase in income inequality, leading to protests by the affected groups and the rise in populism. Since the Trump administration, the United States has abandoned its super-globalization policy and embarked on the path of trade protectionism.

The SS theorem tells us that super-globalization will inevitably create winners and losers within a country. If domestic policies cannot adjust in time to compensate the losers and maintain political support, democratic politics will certainly lead to a backlash against super-globalization and change its direction.

National Sovereignty + Democratic Politics

The third case is choosing national sovereignty and democratic politics. In this case, the world operates in a similar way to the institutional arrangement of the GATT: each country retains its sovereign independence and decides its own policies, and countries negotiate over the extent of economic liberalization they will commit to, the only requirement being that they should move in the direction of liberalization and treat all other countries equally. However, national sovereignty + democratic politics cannot even achieve tariff-free trade among all countries—the failure of the WTO's Doha Round is a clear proof—let alone super-globalization involving free international mobility of factors such as capital, labor, and technology. Therefore, national sovereignty + democratic politics necessarily means giving up super-globalization.

The world order of super-globalization led by the United States seemed to be within reach around the turn of the century in 2000. As discussed in Chapter 6, the two ends of the GVC "smile curve" with the highest value added—innovation and marketing—were concentrated in the United States and developed countries. Production, manufacturing, and assembly were in China, and countries in South America, the Middle East, and Africa were the source of resources. Because the United States gained most of the benefits brought by super-globalization, it could use the profits gained from international monopoly status to subsidize the domestic losers of globalization and thus gain political support for globalization within the country, but it had to gain support for globalization in the rest of the world through outlays of American capital, exerting its influence in global governance, and promulgating the Washington Consensus.

However, since 2008, the GVC has evolved into a tripod structure, which has broken the dominant position of the United States. US gains from globalization have declined, and domestic groups that saw themselves as losers under globalization started to call for a reversal of policies, or de-globalization, urged on by populist politicians like Trump. The global governance system led by the United States is no longer operating effectively.

But what is the super-globalization led by the United States? Isn't it Western centrism? So we can say that the emergence of the tripod structure in the GVC has made Western centrism an overly expensive luxury for the United States.

Theoretically, a global governance system would require countries to partially give up national sovereignty. In practice, the global governance system led by the United States requires countries not only to partially give up sovereignty, but also to give up their own ideologies, which can only be achieved through military conquest or financial enticement. With the current tripod GVC, the United States no longer has enough financial resources to invest in countries, as it did with the Marshall Plan after World War II, to redeem their national sovereignty and maintain its leadership in the world order, nor does the United States have enough military power to conquer countries that do not bow to American hegemony.

Morally, even in 2000 when the United States was at its peak, should the United States have wanted to rule the world? Should the United States impose its political ideology on all the people of the world, or should it respect multi-culturalism and the right of the people from other countries to chart their own development paths?

8.2.2 *Turn of the Century Discussion (Part 1)*

Let me take you back to midnight on January 1, 2000, in Norman, Oklahoma.

I sat down with Mike on the bench in front of my house. "Mike, we're both alive, right? Haha, that Nostradamus end of the world, it's nonsense." Mike smiled at me, "Dr. Ju, yes, the new century has begun."

Mike was the best student in my class, minoring in mathematics and Chinese; he was also my neighbor. He always liked to chat with me and learn Chinese after class. The central region of the United States, including states like Oklahoma, Kansas, and Missouri, is commonly referred to as the heartland. People there are relatively conservative, and most are devout Christians. Right before 2000, there were many discussions among the people in the central region, especially in the churches, about an impending major human disaster. Mike and other neighbors even organized a discussion group to meet in his backyard on weekends to discuss Nostradamus' 1999 prophecy. I was also dragged to a few of these meetings. Young people were drinking beer, eating barbecue, and discussing whether humanity would be destroyed. Opinions at the discussion were divided into two factions: one believing that there would be a major disaster, and the other believing that there would not. Anita belonged to the first faction. Before New Year's Day, she stockpiled water, candles, and bread in the cellar in her backyard. Mike, on the other hand, belonged to the second faction. He firmly believed there would not be a major disaster and acted like a prophet, shaking his head and preaching his theory to anyone he met.

I also didn't think there would be a major disaster, and my reasoning was quite simple. I shouted to Anita: "Anita, there's no major human disaster, right? Your Nostradamus is nonsense. Look, the new century has come. You've wasted so much food stored in the cellar."

"Better safe than sorry, Dr. Ju." Anita smiled. "Nostradamus is right. There will definitely be a major disaster. It doesn't necessarily have to be in 1999. We have to prepare for the next one."

Mike tilted his neck back and finished a bottle of beer, getting excited. This little genius was about to preach his theory again. "Anita, Dr. Ju, the new century has come, and there is no major human disaster, which means we have been redeemed. It means He has come again."

"Haha, He has come again, where? Have you seen Him?" I laughed and retorted.

Mike stood up, waving his empty beer bottle. "He has indeed come, but we can't see Him. In classical literature, one conclusion is clear: if any human being claims to be Him reincarnated, that person is definitely a liar, so we can't possibly see Him." Mike looked at me, still waving the beer bottle: "Since there is no disaster today, it means He has come again. Logically speaking, His return can be understood as a redeeming force that has come. You can also understand it this way: the old world has ended, and the new world has begun. It's not like Nostradamus said, that humanity would be destroyed."

I looked at Mike, found it interesting, and patted him on the shoulder: "The new world ruled by America has begun, and Oklahoma rules America, haha."

"No, no, no, Dr. Ju." Mike put down his beer bottle and began to gesticulate. "America can't rule the new world, and no country can rule the new world. Just as no biological person can claim to be Him again, no country can rule the new world. If any country claims to rule the new world, that country must be a liar." Mike continued with his theory: "Every country has mainstream values, under which laws and rules are made, and a system is established. No one holds the truth, so no country holds the truth. Any country that claims to hold the truth must be a liar. The mainstream values of each country only reflect one aspect of human values. So, to approach the truth and human values in a complete and comprehensive way, it is necessary to reflect human values from different aspects, and it is necessary to promote a diversified and pluralistic value and cultural system." Mike was passionately explaining this theory that I had heard dozens of times.

"Well said, Mike, but why does diversity require many countries? Isn't Canada a multicultural country?"

"Dr. Ju," Mike smiled at me, "Canada's 'multiculturalism' is just one aspect. For example, Canada's 'diversity' cannot represent the 'unity' with Islamic culture."

Anita brought a few more bottles of beer. She took off the bottle caps with her teeth and handed the bottles to me and Mike.

I took a sip of beer and asked with a smile: "Mike, your theory sounds good. But why have the English and American hegemonic countries been setting the world's rules for the past few centuries, while the new world becomes diverse?"

Mike tilted his neck back and took a big gulp of beer: "Dr. Ju, the fact is, the human value system has always been diverse. Since the beginning of human civilization, different civilizations have been born in different regions—Africa, Europe, the Middle East, Asia—and each region has its mainstream values. The 'philosophical breakthrough' of the Axial Age around 500 BC that we are familiar with happened in Greece, Israel, India, and China in completely different ways, respectively pushing the civilization of these regions and people's understanding of the universe and life to a new level. These mainstream values are very different, and from a global perspective, the value system is diverse."

Mike continued to drink his beer. "The birthplaces of these cultures in Africa, Europe, the Middle East, and Asia—due to geographical separation, each region seems to exist independently, and each region seems to have the only correct value system. But in fact, they are all just a partial reflection of the human value system. In the past few centuries, Christian civilization has developed strongly and has almost achieved global dominance. However, this is also eliminating the diversity of civilization, culture, and values. Once the diversity of human civilization is eliminated, the truth is eliminated, and of course, humanity will be destroyed. Now that the new century has come peacefully, it means that humanity has been saved. That is to say, the diversity of human civilization is about to be restored."

8.3 How to Understand the World Disorder?

Let's discuss further the fundamental misalignment of the world order.

The COVID-19 pandemic that ravaged the world in 2020 made us acutely aware of the damage that global disorder brings to all countries. National boundaries were meaningless for the COVID-19 virus, and global cooperation was required to prevent a global health crisis. Unfortunately, there was a lack of effective cooperation among countries. At the beginning of the pandemic in 2020, even developed countries were scrambling for masks, ventilators, and other personal protective equipment. The United States politicized the pandemic domestically and internationally, causing partisan conflicts over mask-wearing policies and accusing China of covering up the origin of the virus. The Russia-Ukraine conflict that began in 2022 put Europe on the brink of a hot war, and sanctions on Russia exacerbated the already severe supply disruptions in international trade caused by the pandemic. The US Federal Reserve's continued ultra-loose monetary policy finally triggered global inflation in 2022, with the world economy teetering on the edge of stagflation.

This state of world chaos is very similar to the world disorder before the outbreak of the Spanish flu pandemic in 1918, the Great Depression in 1929, and World War II in 1939.

How to understand the current world disorder? We will start by analyzing the essential differences in the global governance system under the "new world" and the "old world" in different stages of globalization, especially in the global innovation era.

8.3.1 The End of the Eras of Hegemonic Succession

The global innovation era that began in 2018 (also known as the "new globalization" era) has two core characteristics. First, the proportion of service trade, technology trade, and digital trade is increasing significantly and technological innovation is becoming the core driving force of new globalization. Second, new globalization has a tripod structure, with the United States, Germany, and China as the central nodes of North America, Europe, and Asia, respectively, in global trade, production, and consumption networks.

Table 8.2 summarizes the changes in the different globalization eras discussed in Chapter 2.

The "new world" of the global innovation era differs from the "old world" in that the "new world" is driven by innovations based on human capital accumulation, while the "old world" is mainly driven by physical capital accumulation. Science and technology are essentially public goods that can be shared, while physical capital is a private good that is excludable and rival. It is a mistake made by some academics, policy researchers, and practitioners in the United States and Europe, as well as in China, not to recognize that the old world order dominated by physical capital cannot naturally transform itself into the new world order.

8.3.2 The Misleading View of "Great Powers Competing for the World Hegemony"

Over 50 years ago, Charles Kindleberger explored the reasons why the Great Depression of 1929 lasted for a decade. He believed that the core reason for the extent, depth, and duration of Great Depression was "because the international economic system was rendered unstable by British inability and US unwillingness to assume responsibility for stabilizing it."[8] Kindleberger's research, known as "hegemonic stability theory," has become a representative view of the global governance system.

Since then, the academic empirical research on hegemonic stability theory has gone through three stages of development: in the 1970s, it focused on how to measure hegemony and stability; in the 1980s, it mainly explored

[8] Kindleberger, Charles P., *The World in Depression 1929–1939*, University of California Press, Berkeley and Los Angeles, 1973, pp.292.

Table 8.2 Four stages of the global governance system

Globalization stage	*Period*	*Main drivers*	*Ownership of key factors*	*Main global power(s)*	*Global governance system*
Globalization 1.0: Era of Global Discovery	1500–1819	Navigation, ship building and navigation technology	Voyages financed by monarchies	Britain and other hegemonic countries like the Netherlands, Portugal, and Spain	Monarchies
Globalization 2.0: Era of Global Trade	1820–1912	Industrialization (machines, electricity, transportation), international trade	Physical capital concentrated in industrialized countries	Britain	Colonialism led by the British Empire
	1913–1950	Outbreak of two world wars			
	1951–1978	International trade, investment, and capital flows	Physical capital concentrated in industrialized countries	United States	Colonies gained independence; global order dominated by the United States
Globalization 3.0: Era of Global Production	1978–2018	Global value chain, computers and digital technology	Countries around the world in a network of international production and specialization	United States, Soviet Union (before 1991), Germany, Japan	Global order dominated by the United States; rise of regionalism
Globalization 4.0: Era of Global Innovation	2018 to present	Technological innovation, scientific knowledge	Scientific knowledge and technological innovations are more evenly spread around the world	United States, China, Germany	Global governance with tripod regional governance structure

whether American hegemony had declined, thus affecting the international order; and after the 1990s, it focused on the causal relationship between power distribution and the international order. Academic discussions of hegemonic stability theory have declined in recent years, but the hegemonic stability theory is still deeply rooted in people's minds and continues to influence discussions on the future of the global governance system.

The current debate about whether China and the United States are competing for world leadership and whether China will become the new world hegemon is a continuation of the hegemonic stability theory. Since the outbreak of the COVID-19 pandemic, Western scholars have increasingly believed that China will seize the opportunity to seek world leadership. For example, in 2020, Kurt Campbell and Rush Doshi published an article in *Foreign Affairs* arguing that the pandemic had provided opportunities for China's ambitious in the global governance and China was filling the void left by the United States, positioning itself as the global leader in responding to the pandemic.[9] The following year, Doshi published a book in which he argued that China has been formulating a "grand strategy" since the 1980s to replace the United States as the new world hegemon, and that the competition between China and the United States for world hegemony is the crux of restructuring the world order.[10]

In his book, *Destined for War: Can America and China Escape Thucydides' Trap?,* Graham Allison analyzed 16 historical cases where a major rising power threatened to displace a major ruling power and found only four cases where a peaceful transition was achieved. Allison believes that a change in the world order is likely to be accompanied by a major war between the ruling and rising powers. He is pessimistic about where the current power competition between China and the United States will lead, believing that US-China relations have fallen into a terrible vicious cycle, in which mutual accusations have increased suspicion and confrontation, and the two countries seem destined to fight.

Attributing the current world disorder to competition between China and the United States for global leadership is a serious misdirection which could potentially cause great harm, even disaster, to the people of both countries and the world. This is because the competition for global leadership is a zero-sum game, in which there will inevitably be winners and losers, and competition between major powers, especially evenly capable ones, could potentially lead to war.

So why is this view wrong? It is wrong because it overlooks the regime switch from the "old world" to the "new world." As we discussed in Chapter 2, the world has moved from the global production era and entered the global innovation era. The global economic fundamentals have changed from being dominated by the United States to a tripod structure led by the United States, Germany, and China. In line with the generational change from the global production era to the global innovation era, the global governance system must undergo a corresponding change. The core feature of this change is the end of the hegemonic succession that has dominated the evolution of

[9] Campbell, Kurt M. and Rush Doshi, "The Coronavirus Could Reshape Global Order: China Is Maneuvering for International Leadership as the United States Falters," *Foreign Affairs*, March 18, 2020. https://www.foreignaffairs.com/articles/china/2020-03-18/coronavirus-could-reshape-global-order, accessed on November 29, 2025.

[10] Rush Doshi, *The Long Game: China's Grand Strategy to Displace American Order*, 2021, http://dx.doi.org/10.1093/oso/9780197527917.001.0001.

the world order in the past, and the beginning of a new world order of "competitive coexistence." In short, restructuring the current world order is not about the United States defeating China to continue leading the world, nor is it about China replacing the United States as the new hegemon, but rather a paradigm shift in the world order, from being dominated by a hegemonic country to the coexistence of several major countries that compete with and support one another.

According to our "little genius" Mike, the "new world" has arrived and the diversity of human civilization will be restored, with no single country being able to rule the new world. The views of Allison, Doshi, and others on the competition between China and the United States for world hegemony are attempts to explain the new world order with old theories, which is harmful to people in both countries!

8.4 Tripod: A Two-layer New Global Governance

The construction of a new world order of "competitive coexistence" requires new theory.[11] In this section, we explore a new framework for global governance which has a few innovative aspects. For example, we assume a diversity of rules, that is, different countries have different preferences for rules. Furthermore, we assume that the global governance system is not just one set of rules, but a combination of different sets of rules. Rules are public goods, but the governance structure of different rules can vary. For example, climate change mitigation may require a global unified rule, while cross-border investments may require regionally diverse rules. Thus, rule management can be layered, and can be at the global or regional level. Finally, effective world governance, not the distribution of power in the world, is what we see as the establishment of a global order. What kind of new global governance maximizes the welfare of people around the world can be discussed from an efficiency perspective.

8.4.1 Two-layer Governance Architecture: Theory

Let's first discuss the assumptions behind our framework.

Our first assumption is that different countries have different preferences for global governance rules. As the saying goes: "It's hard to please everyone." This assumption stems from the differences in culture, system, and development level of different countries. Take industrial policy as an example: East Asian countries like Japan and China are accustomed to long-term guidance by the government for economic development, while Western countries prefer that the government not directly interfere with economic activities. Developing country governments may prefer to use industrial policy to direct project

[11] For a detailed discussion, see: Jiandong Ju, Wan Peng, Xinding Yu, "A Dual Architecture with a Tri polar Regional Order for Global Governance in the New Globalization Era," *World Economics and Politics* (in Chinese), 2020 (10): 123–154.

investments, while developed country governments may use industrial policy to support R&D.

The second assumption is that the preference heterogeneity varies for different governance issues. Some governance issues, such as climate change mitigation, nuclear weapon non-proliferation, and global disease control, are primarily global and require unified global rules, while other issues, such as transport infrastructure, migration, and capital flows, may be more regional and can be coordinated and governed within a region.

The third assumption is that the cost structure of managing different governance issues varies. The costs of governance are mainly divided into rulemaking costs and day-to-day management costs. Some issues have high rulemaking costs and low daily management costs, while others are just the opposite. For example, the cost of establishing rules for global nuclear weapon non-proliferation is very high, requiring nuclear powers to undertake rounds of negotiation, but the day-to-day management cost is relatively small because nuclear weapons are hardly used on a daily basis. On the other hand, the cost of establishing rules for cross-border or foreign direct investment (FDI) is not very high, as FDI is typically managed by the host country through a negative list, but the day-to-day management cost is high, as almost every FDI project has different issues and different risks.

These three assumptions mean that an efficient or optimal global governance system cannot be one dimensional. Theoretically, an optimal global governance system should have a two-layer architecture consisting of global and regional governance institutions.

The first layer would be global governance institutions, such as the UN and the WTO. Issues for which countries have similar preferences for rules, and where the cost of rulemaking is high but the cost of daily management is low, such as nuclear weapon non-proliferation and climate change mitigation, should be managed by these global governance institutions.

The second layer would be regional governance institutions, such as the European Union, the US-Mexico-Canada Agreement, and a future regional trade governance system in Asia, which should manage issues with large differences in rule preferences, and low rulemaking costs but high daily management costs.

8.4.2 *Two-layer Governance Architecture: Practice*

In various areas like finance, trade, health, and security, a two-layer governance architecture has already emerged: global and regional governance institutions carry out mission division and provide differentiated services to regions. However, the division of responsibilities between the global and regional institutions is not always clear, and both the operating mechanism and governance capacity need to be improved. An example is the coexistence of the WTO and the more than 350 overlapping bilateral and plurilateral RTAs currently in force around the world.

The objectives, capacities, and scope of global and regional financial institutions responsible for public goods, such as financial stability and economic development, vary in the field of international finance. Countries will make targeted choices when seeking different types or levels of financial public goods. International and regional organizations dealing with rules to foster financial stability include the IMF and the Bank for International Settlements (BIS) at the global level, and the Arab Monetary Fund (AMF) and the European Stability Mechanism (ESM) at the regional level. International and regional organizations responsible for fostering economic development include the World Bank Group at the global level and the African Development Bank (AfDB), the Asian Development Bank (ADB), the Asian Infrastructure Investment Bank (AIIB), and the Inter-American Development Bank (IDB) at the regional level. Their objectives, functions, and country coverage are shown in Table 8.3.

International organizations tasked with providing global financial public goods like financial stability and economic development have the capacity to provide (or coordinate) large amounts of financing as well as policy advice and technical assistance. They cover the major economies of the world (with very few countries and regions excluded in the case of the IMF and the World Bank Group) and they have support from their worldwide membership. Regional organizations tasked with providing financial stability and economic development are typically established under the leadership of core countries in the region and under the aegis of the corresponding global organization such as the IMF or the World Bank. Their financial and staff capacity is determined by their core countries and is significantly weaker compared to their global counterparts.

Let's look at the international trade governance system which, as we mentioned earlier, is increasingly in trouble. When the WTO was established in 1995 with a robust dispute settlement system that was an upgrade from the GATT's informal one, no one imagined that the United States would choose to paralyze the system by undermining its appellate body. According to WTO rules, final arbitration of disputes is done by a panel of at least three judges from the appellate body. Since 2017, as the term of several judges ended, the United States has vetoed all appointments to the appellate body over concerns of "judicial overreach"—because it was dissatisfied with some of its rulings. Efforts to reform the dispute settlement system in response to US demands and pave the way for new appointments have been unsuccessful, and the United States has refused to participate in an alternative dispute settlement process set up by other members. If the WTO does not bend to the wishes of the United States, the United States would rather smash it. What is the way forward for the reform of the world trade governance system?

In fact, the governance of world trade does not require the United States to cooperate with China in all aspects. A considerable part of trade flows is intraregional and does not need to be regulated under a global framework. The world trade governance system also has an embryonic two-layer

Table 8.3 Selected international and regional organizations providing financial public goods

Institution	*Global/regional public good focus*	*Main objectives and functions*	*Membership*
International Monetary Fund	Global financial stability	To foster international financial stability by monitoring economic and financial developments in member economies, assisting members with balance of payments difficulties, and providing technical assistance and training	Global: 190 economies around the world
Bank for International Settlements	Global financial stability	To promote international monetary and financial stability through policy dialogue and research, and to act as a bank for central banks	Global: 63 central banks and monetary authorities around the world
Financial Stability Board	Global financial stability	To promote international financial stability by assessing vulnerabilities in the global financial system and coordinating regulatory policies and standards among countries	Global: 24 economies around the world
Arab Monetary Fund	Regional financial stability	To strengthen economic, financial, and monetary stability and lay the monetary foundations for Arab economic integration by correcting balance of payments disequilibria in its member states, improving Arab monetary cooperation, encouraging the development of Arab financial markets, and promoting trade between member states	Regional: 22 countries in the Middle East and Africa

(continued)

Table 8.3 (continued)

Institution	*Global/regional public good focus*	*Main objectives and functions*	*Membership*
ASEAN + 3 Macroeconomic Research Office	Regional financial stability	To contribute to the macroeconomic and financial resilience and stability of the region through surveillance, supporting regional financing arrangements, providing technical assistance, serving as a regional knowledge hub, and facilitating ASEAN + 3 financial cooperation	Regional: 10 ASEAN member countries plus China, Japan, and South Korea
European Stability Mechanism	Regional financial stability	To avoid and overcome financial crises in the euro area and to maintain long-term financial stability and prosperity by providing loans and other types of financial assistance to member states threatened by severe financial distress	Regional: 20 EU member countries that have adopted the euro
Latin American Reserve Fund	Regional financial stability	To promote macroeconomic stability and regional integration by supporting member countries' balance of payments, improving investment conditions for members' international reserves, and contributing to the harmonization of members' exchange rate, monetary, and financial policies	Regional: 9 countries in Latin America

(continued)

Table 8.3 (continued)

Institution	*Global/regional public good focus*	*Main objectives and functions*	*Membership*
World Bank Group	Global economic development	To end extreme poverty and boost shared prosperity on a livable planet by providing loans and technical assistance for capital projects in developing economies	Global: 189 economies around the world
Asian Infrastructure Investment Bank	Regional economic development	To foster sustainable economic development and improve infrastructure connectivity by financing infrastructure development in developing Asia	48 economies in the Asia–Pacific region and 48 economies in other regions
Asian Development Bank	Regional economic development	To foster a prosperous, inclusive, resilient, and sustainable Asia and the Pacific and eradicate extreme poverty in the region by providing loans, technical assistance, grants, and equity investments to promote social and economic development	49 economies in the Asia–Pacific region and 19 economies in other regions
European Bank for Reconstruction and Development	Economic development with a political mandate	To develop open and sustainable market economies in countries committed to, and applying, democratic principles, through projects, business services, and involvement in high-level policy reform	73 economies around the world and, 2 EU institutions

(continued)

Table 8.3 (continued)

Institution	*Global/regional public good focus*	*Main objectives and functions*	*Membership*
Inter-American Development Bank	Regional economic development	To foster sustainable and inclusive development in Latin America and the Caribbean region by providing financial and technical support for member countries and conducting research	26 economies in Latin America and 22 economies in other regions
Islamic Development Bank	Economic development with a religious mandate	To promote social and economic development in member countries by providing Islamic finance for project investments	57 Islamic economies in the Middle East, Africa, and Asia

governance architecture. The WTO undertakes trade governance under the global multilateral system, while the US-Mexico-Canada Agreement (formerly NAFTA) and the European Union are two established regional trade governance systems. If a trade governance system also appears in Asia, then the tripod-based two-layer governance architecture shown in Fig. 8.2 matches well with the tripod structure of the global value chain.

Trade issues that are of global concern and agreed upon by major countries, such as climate change-related trade and border carbon adjustments, can still be managed by the WTO. Most other trade rules can be delegated to regional trade agreements, such as the European Union, the US-Mexico-Canada Agreement, and the future Asian governance system.

The tripod regional trade governance is just an illustration of the framework. In fact, there can be more regional governance institutions, such as in Latin America, Africa, South Asia, and Central Asia. Regional governance not only supplements global governance, but competition among regions can also help to achieve a "competitive coexistence" world order.

If we discard the traditional theory of hegemonic succession, and follow the idea of adapting the world order (superstructure) to the tripod economic fundamentals, if we give up the obsolete idea of power competition for hegemony and follow the new direction of establishing an efficient and beneficial global governance system, if we abandon rigid thinking, and do not insist on unifying all the world's rules under the governance of a hegemonic country, but categorize different economic rules, with multilateral ones managed by multilateral institutions, and regional ones managed by regional institutions—then the world will have a brighter future.

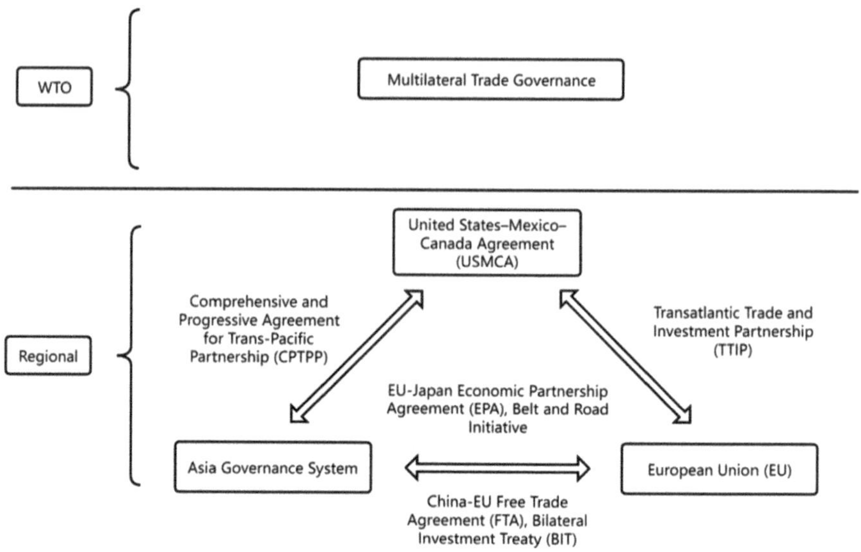

Fig. 8.2 Two-layer governance system of world trade

8.4.3 Turn of the Century Discussion (Part 2)

To end this chapter, let us turn back to the discussion on New Year's Day 2000.

Watching the animated little genius Mike, I continued to ask: "Is the diversity of human civilization the truth?"

Mike looked at me. "Dr. Ju, every one of us, in their own region, in their own cultural system, understands the world based on their own aspect of human values or truth. Once human civilization loses its diversity, humans will not be able to combine all the aspects together, to approach human values in a comprehensive and relatively accurate way." Mike suddenly pointed to his house and continued: "Human values, or truths, are like this house, with walls on the east, west, south, and north, and a roof. Each culture is just one wall, or at most the roof. No matter how great Christian culture is, it is just the roof. If the Christian culture, this roof, destroys the walls on all four sides, the house will collapse. The most important aspect concerning diversity of human culture is the difference between Eastern and Western cultures, which is why I want to learn Chinese."

I nodded with a smile. "Not bad, Eastern and Western cultures are corresponding and symmetrical in many ways. So, where are they corresponding and symmetrical? Mike, let's discuss."

"Sure, Dr. Ju, I'll talk about Western culture, you talk about Eastern culture, let's start."

"Western culture is individualistic."

"Eastern culture is collective."

"Western culture is dualistic. Repay to Caesar what belongs to Caesar and to God what belongs to God."

"Eastern culture is monistic, unity of heaven, earth, and man."

"Western culture starts from individualism, so human rights are the cornerstone."

"Eastern culture is holistic, and the foundation of the whole is morality."

"Human rights and freedom are symbiotic, so the Westerner talks about freedom, and freedom brings innovation."

"Morality and foresight coexist, so the Easterner talks about foresight, and with foresight comes direction."

"Western culture takes individual freedom as its starting point, thus competition is its core, and democracy is its spirit."

"Eastern culture takes the unity of heaven, earth, and man as its starting point, thus balance is its core, and harmony is its spirit."

"So, who is the West and who is the East?" Anita couldn't help but ask.

I looked at them both and said meaningfully: "The east of the East is the West, and the west of the West is the East."

"That's so interesting, so interesting!" Mike spun around excitedly: "Cheers, Dr. Ju!" "Cheers, to the new century!" I held my beer bottle, clinked it with Mike's and Anita's beer bottles, looked around, and realized that the neighbors had all gone back to their houses, and only the lights at Mike's and my front door were still on. "It's already 4 o'clock in the morning. Shall we end our discussion for today? Let's go back and rest." I walked toward the house. "Alright, Dr. Ju, good night." Mike and Anita also started to leave after saying this.

I got to the front door of my house and turned off the light. Mike also turned off the light at his front door. The neighborhood was quiet, the stars in the sky were still shining, and I couldn't help but look toward the East. The first ray of sunlight of the new world was already emerging. Will there still be a major human disaster in the future? How will the world order evolve?

CHAPTER 9

What Determines the Future of US-China Great Power Competition?

Great power competition, also known as the competition between ruling (or incumbent) and rising powers, profoundly affects the lives of every inhabitant on this beautiful planet. What is at stake in contemporary great power competition? In this chapter, we will review seven cases of great power competition since 1500 and show that long-term economic growth represents the outcome of great power competition: countries that win the competition will maintain long-term growth, while those that lose cannot!

As we discussed in Chapter 2, long-term economic growth (measured by GDP) represents both a country's strength and the welfare of its people. What determines long-term growth within great power competition? In this chapter, we will develop an analytical framework to show that the key to maintaining long-term growth is to avoid growth crises. The idea is clear: the outcome of contemporary US-China competition depends on which side can prevent growth crises. What potential growth crises might China and the United States face? How should they prevent them? How might crises develop under US-China great power competition in the coming decades? We will analyze these questions one by one below.

9.1 Historical Review of Great Power Competitions

To find an indicator for measuring success or failure in great power competition, we first look for commonalities in the historical data. Table 9.1 summarizes the results of seven great power competitions since 1500 and the GDP growth of the countries involved during and after the competition.

J. Ju, *US-China Great Power Competition and The New World Order*, https://doi.org/10.1007/978-981-95-3762-4_9

Table 9.1 Review of historical cases of great power competitions since 1500

	Period	*Rising nation*	*Ruling nation*	*Outcome*	*Long-term growth rates*
1	Late fifteenth century	Spain	Portugal	Papal arbitration, peaceful division of the world	Average annual GDP growth rates during 1500–1600 were 0.27% for Spain and 0.06% for Portugal
2	Mid–late seventeenth century to eighteenth century	Britain	Netherlands	Four Anglo-Dutch Wars; Britain ultimately won	Average annual GDP growth rates during 1700–1750 were 1.19% for Britain and 0.41% for the Netherlands
3	Late seventeenth century to mid-eighteenth century	Britain	France	Britain won and expanded overseas hegemony; France lost many colonies	Average annual GDP growth rate during 1760–1820 were 0.80% for Britain and 0.44% for France
4	Early twentieth century	United States	Britain	Peaceful transition of power; United States won	Average annual GDP growth rates during 1914–1939 were 1.96% for the United States and 0.99% for Britain
5	Mid-twentieth century	Germany	Britain	Germany was defeated in World War II; Britain also lost world dominance after World War II	Average annual GDP growth rates during 1944–1954 were 0.64% for Britain, –1.47% for Germany and 1.32% for the United States

(continued)

Table 9.1 (continued)

	Period	*Rising nation*	*Ruling nation*	*Outcome*	*Long-term growth rates*
6	1940s–1980s	Soviet Union	United States	Soviet Union collapsed; United States won	Average annual GDP growth rates during 1990–2000 were 3.44% for the United States and –2.88% for the Soviet Union (original territory)
7	1960s–1980s	Japan	United States	Japan made various concessions and give up challenging the United States economically; United States won	Average annual GDP growth rates during 1985–2005 were 3.17% for the United States and 2.08% for Japan

Source Based on the Maddison database

Spain and Portugal

In the late fifteenth century, Spain and Portugal competed fiercely for ownership of the New World. In 1493, Pope Alexander VI delineated the overseas territories and spheres of influence of Spain and Portugal with the Papal Meridian. Portugal was dissatisfied with this decision, and the two countries were on the verge of war. At a critical moment, Spain chose to give up some of its interests to avoid military conflict, and the two countries signed the Treaty of Tordesillas in 1494 to redraw the colonial spheres of influence, giving Spain ownership of the New World and Portugal dominance over the African route, India, and Brazil. After the Treaty of Tordesillas, the two countries reached a non-competitive state of mutual non-disturbance in overseas colonial expansion. The data shows that both countries maintained normal growth in the subsequent decade.

Britain and the Netherlands

From the mid-seventeenth century to the late eighteenth century, four wars broke out between Britain and the Netherlands. The result was that Britain successfully rose, subsequently achieving rapid economic growth, gaining world financial hegemony, and gradually establishing a vast colonial empire.

On the contrary, the Netherlands failed in the competition, and its economic growth slowed or even stagnated.

Britain and France

After the end of the Thirty Years' War in 1648, France became the dominant land power in Europe. This violated Britain's "continental balance" policy and Britain could not sit idly by when its maritime hegemony and overseas colonies were threatened. In addition, the two countries had opposing religious ideologies. From the mid-seventeenth century, Britain and France engaged in the Nine Years' War, the War of the Spanish Succession, the War of the Austrian Succession, and the Seven Years' War. In 1763, Britain, France, and Spain signed the Treaty of Paris. France ceded all of Canada to Britain and was forced to withdraw from India in the Eastern Hemisphere. Britain saw higher GDP growth, went on to win multiple wars, and became the overseas colonial hegemon, while France's GDP stagnated for a long time.

The United States and Britain

The second Industrial Revolution originated in the United States, greatly improving its productivity. During World War I, the United States was far from the fighting; it transformed from a debtor nation into a creditor nation and the US dollar was established as a world reserve currency. However, Britain was directly hit by the war, leading to a decline in domestic production, a shrinking overseas market, and colonies seeking autonomy after the war. After World War II, Britain lost its military advantage and economic hegemony to the United States and the two countries achieved a peaceful transition. US GDP surpassed that of Britain in 1862 and the British Empire in 1915, and by 1950, the US economy was more than four times that of Britain.

Britain and Germany

After the second Industrial Revolution, both Germany and the United States surpassed Britain in GDP. Britain allied with the United States to defeat Germany in World War II, almost completely destroying Germany's infrastructure and its population. After World War II, Germany was divided and its GDP plummeted. But Britain also lost its position as the world's hegemon.

The Soviet Union and the United States

After World War II, the world saw a Cold War between the socialist bloc led by the Soviet Union and the capitalist bloc led by the United States. After the oil crisis in the 1970s, the Soviet Union, by virtue of its abundant oil and gas resources, enjoyed rapid economic growth. But in the 1980s, the United States forced Saudi Arabia to increase oil production, lowering oil prices and severely damaging the Soviet economy. The Soviet Union eventually collapsed in 1991. After the end of the Cold War, Russia's economy shifted from state control to control by a few oligarchs, with a significant increase in wealth concentration and inequality and a dramatic decline in the aggregate economy.

Japan and the United States

After World War II, Japan's rapid economic development raised the United States' concern. The United States successfully contained Japan's rise through various means, and Japan fell into three "lost decades." This case will be detailed in Sect. 9.4.1.

What do these seven great power competitions have in common? Historical data shows that countries that lost in the competition, such as the Netherlands, France, Britain, Germany, the Soviet Union, and Japan, all experienced stagnation or even a significant decline in their aggregate economic growth, while countries that won the competition all achieved faster aggregate economic growth.

The growth of a country's aggregate economy can be achieved through peaceful means such as improving productivity, or through war and plunder. As described in Chapter 2, the long-term growth of the aggregate economy represents both a country's power and its fundamental interests. The fate of a great power and the evolution of the world order can be measured by the long-term trend of this aggregate indicator. Therefore, we can use the long-term growth of the aggregate economy to measure success or failure in great power competition: countries that win the competition maintain long-term growth of the aggregate economy, while countries that lose the competition cannot maintain long-term growth and the aggregate economy stagnates.

9.2 The Growth-Crisis Model of US-China Competition

Figure 9.1 depicts the historical, present, and possible future economic growth paths of China, the United States, and other countries in the world from 1978 to 2060. The horizontal axis is time, and the vertical axis is aggregate GDP. The GDP growth paths of China, the United States, and other countries are represented by three sets of lines labeled China, USA, and Others. The first 40 years from 1978 to 2018 are history, and the next 40 years from 2019 to 2060 are the present and future. We will first review the history before the outbreak of the US-China trade war in 2018, and then use the data from these 40 years to predict possible long-term growth paths until 2060.

From 1978 to 2018, the average annual GDP growth rates of China, the United States, and other countries were 9.45%, 2.64%, and 2.62%, respectively. China achieved rapid growth during those 40 years. The US economy and other economies in the world maintained steady growth but not as rapid as China's. After the US-China trade war broke out, from 2018 to 2022, the

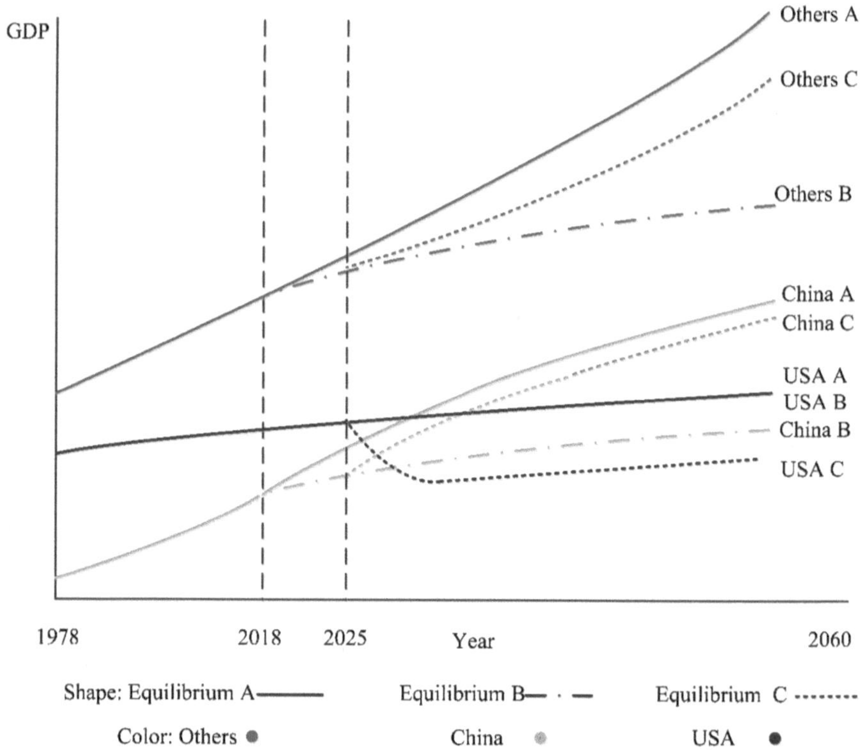

Fig. 9.1 Possible paths of aggregate growth in China, the United States, and other countries in the world from 1978 to 2060

annual GDP growth rates of China, the United States, and other countries were 4.88%, 1.84%, and 1.41%, respectively.

As we discussed in Chapter 2, economic growth relies on the Dual-Wheel Drive Model of innovation and market scale. The period from 1978 to 2018 was characterized by the third Industrial Revolution, where technological innovations were mainly in the area of information technology. The main driving force for market expansion was the third stage of globalization, that is, globalization of production, jointly promoted by China and the United States. In other words, the information revolution and the globalization of production jointly promoted the strong growth of China, the United States, and the world over the past 40 years, enabling the average annual growth rate of world GDP during this period to reach 3.05%. The outbreak of the US-China trade war, coupled with the impact of global and regional crises such as the COVID-19 pandemic and the Russia-Ukraine conflict, reduced the average annual growth rate of world GDP to 2.10% during the period from 2018 to 2022.

According to the Dual-Wheel Drive Model, economic growth of the next approximately 40 years until 2060 will depend on further innovation and global market expansion. Let's first look at innovation. Most people would agree that the fourth Industrial Revolution, represented by AI and the green transformation, has arrived, and its impact on productivity and economic growth may even be more profound and stronger than that of the information revolution of the past 40 years. Therefore, the first wheel—further innovation—is not a problem. Then the trend of economic growth for the next 40 years or so will depend mainly on the second wheel—further global market expansion.

There are four possible growth paths: A, B, C, and D, representing four possible equilibria. In simple terms, equilibrium A represents a win–win situation for China and the United States; equilibrium B represents a situation where the United States wins and China loses the great power competition; equilibrium C represents a situation where China wins and the United States loses the great power competition; and equilibrium D represents a lose-lose situation for both countries.

9.2.1 *Equilibrium A: Win–Win*

The first scenario is that China and the United States will cooperate as they did for the past 40 years before the trade war, and the fourth stage of globalization (the global innovation era) proceeds smoothly. Thanks to the AI revolution and the globalization of innovation, China, the United States, and the rest of the world will all achieve high-speed growth in the next 40 years or so. We call this situation equilibrium A—a win–win situation in which both China and the United States reach their optimal growth potential. This case would be similar to the competition between the United States and Britain in the early twentieth century, when the ruling and rising powers choose to cooperate rather than confront each other. China and the United States have already entered the stage of great power competition. Can they continue to cooperate as they did before 2018? We cannot rule out this possibility, even if it may seem unlikely at the present time.

Suppose China and the United States can cooperate as they did before 2018, and thereby reach their growth potential. What would be the result? In Fig. 9.1, the growth paths for China, the United States, and the rest of the world under equilibrium A are represented by the solid lines "China A," "USA A," and "Others A," respectively.

Let's first consider the United States. According to some forecasts, the annual per capita GDP growth rate of the United States for the next 40 years is 1.58%, and based on the UN population forecast, the annual US population growth rate will be 0.42%. Therefore, we assume that the United States will achieve a potential GDP growth rate of 2% per year. In Fig. 9.1, this is represented by the solid line "USA A."

What about China? Under the dual-wheel drive of the fourth Industrial Revolution and the globalization of innovation, we predict that by 2060, China's per capita GDP will converge to that of developed countries. Under this convergence theory, we assume that China's per capita GDP reaches 70% of US per capita GDP. How to understand this assumption? Currently, the per capita GDP of the United Kingdom and New Zealand is about 70% that of the United States. Therefore, our assumption implies that China's per capita GDP relative to US per capita GDP 40 years from now would be roughly the same as how the United Kingdom and New Zealand compare with the United States in terms of per capita GDP today.

Now, the US population in 2022 was 333 million and US population growth is relatively stable, so we can project that by 2060, the US population will be about 400 million. For China's population in 2060, there are different predictions, ranging from a high of 1.4 billion to a low of 1 billion. Taking the midpoint prediction of 1.2 billion (which is 200 million less than now), this means that China's population will be three times that of the United States in 2060. Multiplied by 70% of US per capita GDP gives us the prediction that by 2060, China's total GDP will be approximately 2.1 times US GDP. To achieve this goal, China would need to maintain an annual GDP growth rate of 2.97 percentage points more than the United States, that is, an annual GDP growth rate of about 4.97%. In Fig. 9.1, this is represented by the solid line "China A."

Boosted by the strong growth of China and the United States, the rest of the world would also enjoy rapid growth over the next 40 years, represented by the solid line "Others A" in Fig. 9.1.

In this scenario, by 2060, China will have an aggregate economy two times that of the United States. For this to happen, China will have to catch up and surpass the United States in finance and technology. This means that the current hegemonic position of the United States in the world economy, international monetary system, and global governance will undergo substantial changes and the world order will evolve into the tripod "competitive coexistence" of the United States (North America), China (Asia), and the European Union that we discussed in Chapter 8. The tripod competitive coexistence era will be an era of rapid growth, prosperity, and brightness.

However, this win–win balance between China and the United States means that the hegemonic status of the United States in the world will end. Judging from declarations by the Trump and Biden administrations and what we know of American public opinion, the United States would not be satisfied with such a future. This is why it initiated the US-China trade war in 2018. The United States would prefer to see itself win and China lose.

9.2.2 *Equilibrium B: The United States Wins, China Loses*

In equilibrium B, the United States wins and China loses the great power competition: the United States achieves optimal (potential) growth, and curbs

China's long-term growth so that by 2060, it still leads China in terms of GDP and dominates the world order. In Fig. 9.1, the United States' growth path is represented by the solid line "USA B" (which is the same as "USA A"), China's growth path is represented by the dotted line "China B," and the growth path of the rest of the world is represented by the dotted line "Others B."

We assume that US long-term growth in equilibrium B is the same as in equilibrium A because China's low growth in equilibrium B would have both positive and negative impacts on the United States. On the one hand, the United States would still dominate the world order and continue to lead the global economy, consolidating its technological leadership and the dollar-dominated IMS, and enjoying all the benefits accruing to it as the world hegemon. On the other hand, China's low long-term growth, far below what it would have enjoyed in equilibrium A, would reduce the scale of the world market, imposing a negative impact on the US economy. We cannot accurately evaluate the magnitude of the positive and negative impacts, so we assume that the positive and negative impacts cancel each other out and the United States maintains a long-term growth rate of 2% as in equilibrium A.

The empirical political science literature suggests that when a rising power attains 80% or more of the power of the ruling power, the world power hierarchy will be threatened.[1] Since China loses in this scenario, we assume that by 2060, its GDP will only reach 80% of the United States'. Then the average annual GDP growth rates of the United States and China over the next 40 years would be 2% and 2.34%, respectively.

In Fig. 9.1, "China B" and "China A" are two different growth paths (in economic growth terminology) or long-term growth steady states (in macroeconomics terminology). We define equilibrium A as the "normal growth equilibrium" and equilibrium B as the "low growth equilibrium" for China. What could cause China to lose the great power competition and end up in equilibrium B? Generally speaking, a crisis could have permanent scarring effects on an economy by changing its economic structure and damaging its growth potential for years or decades. This was what happened, for example, to some Southeast Asian countries after the 1997 Asian financial crisis; to Japan after it conceded the US-Japan trade dispute and its domestic real estate bubble burst; and to the former Soviet Union economies after the collapse of the Soviet Union. If the United States maintains normal growth and China experiences some kind of serious crisis, we could have equilibrium B where the United States wins and China loses the great power competition.

The dashed line "China B" in Fig. 9.1 depicts China's crisis growth path: if a crisis happens in China after 2018, causing permanent scarring in the Chinese economy, China could deviate from the normal growth equilibrium A and end up in the low-growth equilibrium B after the crisis, with an average annual

[1] Organski, Abramo F K, and Jacek Kugler, 1980, *The War Ledger*, Chicago: Univ. Of Chicago Press.

GDP growth rate of only 2.34%, which is about half its average annual GDP growth rate of 4.97% in the normal equilibrium A.

Due to the low growth of the Chinese economy, the total world market shrinks significantly, and the economic growth of other countries also decreases significantly, as shown by the dotted line "Others B" in Fig. 9.1.

9.2.3 Equilibrium C: China Wins, the United States Loses

The third scenario is equilibrium C, where China wins and the United States loses the great power competition, or in other words, the rising power defeats the ruling power, similar to the outcome of the historical Anglo-Dutch rivalry.

In this scenario, the US-China trade war has a negative impact on China's economy in the short term. However, China's economy is resilient and successfully recovers from this setback without any permanent scarring effects, and China returns to its long-term growth path under equilibrium A. In economic terms, the US-China trade war is only a temporary shock and it does not change China's steady state long-term growth. As depicted in Fig. 9.1, China's growth path in equilibrium C, shown by the dashed line "China C," has an adjustment phase for a few years after 2018, during which China's economic growth rate is lower than the normal growth rate of "China A," but after that, China's GDP returns to the normal growth equilibrium A. By 2060, China's GDP will be two times larger than the GDP of the United States.

What happens to the US economy in equilibrium C? Note that as long as the Chinese economy maintains normal growth, China's GDP would surpass US GDP around 2035, and China would gradually catch up with the United States in the four fields of technology, finance, military, and global governance. The misalignment between these global economic fundamentals and the existing US dollar-dominated IMS would intensify and there would be a transition to a new tripod IMS.

The question is: how would this transition occur? One way is a "hard landing" of the dollar-dominated international monetary system, where a crisis erupts in the US dollar and bond markets. The dollar crisis would trigger a global financial tsunami and an economic crisis in the United States and the US economy would collapse. Another way is a "soft landing" similar to the transition from the pound to the dollar as the premier world reserve currency. But this soft landing would require cooperation between China and the United States and equilibrium C already rules this out, so there can only be a hard landing for the dollar in equilibrium C. Therefore, in equilibrium C, if China maintains its normal long-term growth, the dollar-dominated IMS would experience a crisis which would trigger a financial crisis in the United States and cause the US economy to collapse; China would win and the United States would lose. In Fig. 9.1, this growth path for the United States is depicted by the dotted line "USA C."

Of course, when faced with the dollar crisis, the United States could give up the confrontation and decide to cooperate with China and thus achieve a soft landing for the dollar-dominated monetary system and a return to normal growth for its economy. But this is not equilibrium C; it is a return to equilibrium A and the path shown by the line "USA A."

The above analysis suggests that as long as China can maintain its normal growth path, the United States could face a dollar crisis, at which point it would have to decide whether to continue the confrontation and trigger the crisis, or cooperate and avoid the crisis. A dollar crisis would have global repercussions, causing growth in the rest of the world to decrease significantly, as represented by the dotted line "Others C" in Fig. 9.1.

9.2.4 *Equilibrium D: Lose-Lose*

There is also a fourth scenario in the great power competition between China and the United States, which is a lose-lose situation. In this scenario, the competition between China and the United States triggers crises in both countries, and both countries enter a period of slow or even negative growth. This lose-lose equilibrium is similar to the outcome of the historical competition for world hegemony between Britain and Germany, which led to two world wars, resulting in both countries losing their chance at world leadership to two new superpowers, the United States and the Soviet Union.

A lose-lose situation for China and the United States could potentially allow other powers, such as the European Union, India, or Russia, to rise. However, in the short term, it is more likely that the global economy would lose its engine of growth and be mired in a long period of stagnation. The crises in China and the United States would cause the existing world order to collapse, and a new world order would be difficult to establish in a short term, pushing the world into a period of disorder and turbulence.

In Fig. 9.1, therefore, equilibrium D is depicted with the lines "China B," "USA C," and "Others B" for the long-term growth paths of China, the United States, and the rest of the world, respectively.

9.3 Crises

In the previous section, we discussed four possible outcomes of the great power competition between China, as a rising power, and the United States, as the ruling power. In the outcomes, the winner reaches its optimal potential growth rate, while the loser experiences a crisis that leaves permanent scars on its growth potential. Therefore, the key to winning the great power competition is to avoid a crisis. So, what are crises and how can they be avoided?

In economics, a crisis can be understood as a preventable self-fulfilling vicious cycle. This definition contains three key words: "preventable," meaning it can be avoided (under some conditions); "self-fulfilling," meaning that it happens because it is expected to happen; and "vicious," meaning it has negative or harmful effects.

A classic example is a bank run. Under normal circumstances, banks absorb deposits from residents and lend a portion of these deposits to businesses. Residents earn interest income on their deposits, while businesses obtain necessary funds for their operations, and banks earn interest margin income from providing deposit and loan services. However, if a few residents start to worry about the bank going bankrupt and withdraw their deposits, then more people will begin to worry and also withdraw their deposits from the bank. As more and more residents begin to worry, everyone ends up rushing to withdraw their deposits, resulting in a run on the bank. Even a bank that is operating well in normal circumstances would not have enough money to return all its deposits at once. Faced with a run, the bank is forced to declare bankruptcy. After the bank goes bankrupt, a significant portion of the residents' deposits are indeed lost.

The bank run is self-fulfilling. The bank may be operating normally at first, but when a few people suddenly lose their confidence in the bank and start to withdraw their deposits, then more and more people worry about the safety of their deposits and go to the bank to withdraw them, causing the bank to finally go bankrupt. Those who expected the bank to go bankrupt actually caused the bank to go bankrupt.

The bank run crisis is a vicious cycle. As more and more people go to the bank to withdraw their deposits, the risk of the bank being unable to pay increases, and those who were not originally worried about the bank also start to worry and decide to withdraw their deposits. Thus a vicious cycle develops until the bank actually goes bankrupt. Each resident's behavior is rational and optimal. The residents who withdraw their deposits first may be reacting to a perceived risk, while the later ones may simply be following the trend, and the ones after that may indeed find that the bank's risk is increasing. The rational behavior of each one leads to a vicious cycle and a bank run.

The bank run can be prevented. If the central bank can guarantee the deposits in the bank and promise to return all the deposits if the bank is unable to pay, the residents will not worry about the bank going bankrupt. Under the guarantee of the central bank, there will not be a run on the bank and it can return to its normal operation.

The concept of equilibrium in macroeconomics refers to the state reached by the economy when every individual makes rational decisions and maximizes their own interests. There can be more than one equilibrium state for an economy. As mentioned in the previous section, we define the optimal growth path for an economy as the "normal equilibrium" and the low-growth path as the low-growth or "crisis equilibrium." A crisis is a shock to the economy that causes it to move from the normal equilibrium to the crisis equilibrium. The bank run is an example of multiple equilibria: the normal equilibrium, where there is no bank run and the bank operates normally; and the crisis equilibrium, where there is a run on the bank and the bank goes bankrupt.

Another example of a crisis is a currency crisis. A country's market exchange rate may have multiple equilibria. Take Thailand, for example: an exchange rate of 25 Thai baht to $1 could be a market equilibrium, and 40 Thai baht to $1 could also be a market equilibrium. Suppose that under normal circumstances, the exchange rate is fixed at 25 baht to $1. If some Thai residents suddenly worry about a devaluation of the baht, they will sell baht and buy US dollars. When more and more Thai residents sell baht, large-scale capital flight will occur, creating a vicious cycle where falling demand for the baht leads to further depreciation pressure on the baht. Finally, when Thailand's central bank is no longer able to defend the fixed exchange rate, the baht is devalued significantly to 40 baht to $1.

In this case, again, everyone's decision is rational. When Thailand is facing a currency crisis, it is a rational decision for people to dump Thai baht and buy US dollars. It is difficult to change individual behavior during a crisis. The prevention of a crisis can only be achieved by changing the economic environment in advance.

9.4 Potential Crises in China

The key to winning the great power competition between the United States and China, therefore, is which country can prevent crises and achieve their optimal economic growth. US-China competition in technology, finance, military strength, and global governance are external factors affecting the growth equilibrium in the two countries. External factors are conditions, while internal factors are the determining forces for equilibrium. Under great power competition, the growth paths for the United States and China will have multiple equilibria: one or both countries can either grow normally or slide into a crisis. Therefore, each country will try to change the external conditions to prevent a crisis and ensure its own normal economic growth, and at the same time, induce changes in the internal factors of its opponent and trigger a crisis there.

What kinds of crises might the US-China great power competition trigger? In this section, we will first consider six types of crises that could potentially occur in China, the rising power. Based on crises that have occurred historically in great power competitions, these are: (1) a Japan-type crisis; (2) a Soviet-type crisis; (3) a public policy crisis; (4) a financial crisis; (5) a social crisis; and (6) a regional security crisis. The first two are crises that occurred in contemporary rising powers, while the latter four crises were shared by both rising and ruling powers, although the causes and paths of the crisis were different for the two powers.

9.4.1 *Japan-Type Crisis*

The Japan-type crisis specifically refers to the stagnation of industrial upgrading and the resulting growth stagnation. Figure 9.2 describes the evolution of the crisis, which was triggered by an external factor, the US-Japan trade dispute.

The core of the Japan-type crisis is the inability to achieve industrial upgrading. The US-Japan trade dispute in the 1990s interrupted Japan's industrial upgrading path, causing it to move to a low-growth equilibrium. The rising power tends to be a relative latecomer in the field of technology, so it inevitably faces the risk of technological containment by the ruling power. Affected by the ruling power's suppression of its high-tech industries, the rising power may not be able to achieve industrial upgrading and thus lack the driving force for further economic growth, finally ending up in the crisis equilibrium of low economic growth or economic stagnation.

After the World War II, Japan quickly developed into the world's second-largest economy after the United States, with per capita GDP rapidly increasing from $475 in 1960 to $9667 in 1980. Because Japanese products had higher quality and lower prices, they became popular in the US market. By 1985, the US trade deficit with Japan had reached $50 billion, accounting for a third of the entire US trade deficit that year. This triggered the US-Japan trade dispute.

- In 1981, the United States and Japan reached an agreement whereby Japan implemented "voluntary export restrictions" on its automobile industry to ease its relations with the US government.

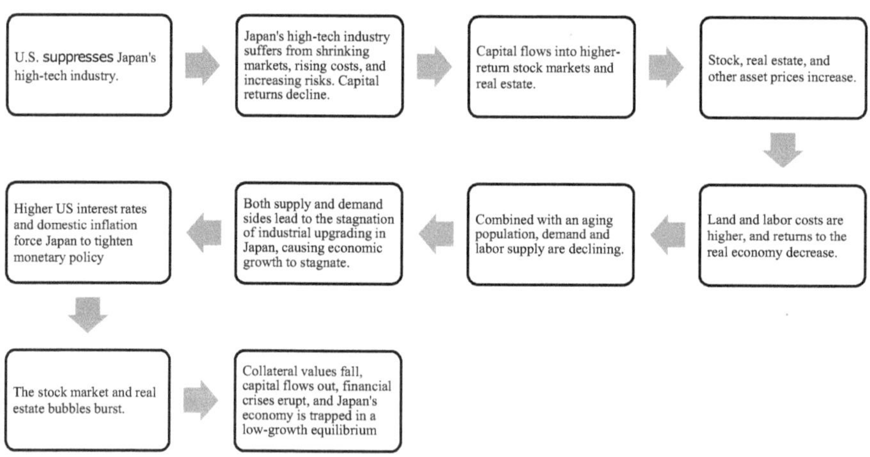

Fig. 9.2 Schematic diagram of Japan-type crisis

- In 1983, to protect Harley-Davidson, the US government imposed a 45% tax on imported motorcycles from Japan, which was not lifted until Harley began to make a profit again in 1987.
- In 1985, the United States forced Japan to increase its imports of American agricultural products, such as beef and oranges.
- In the same year, the finance ministers and central bank governors of the United States, Japan, the United Kingdom, France, and Germany signed the Plaza Accord, agreeing to jointly intervene in the foreign exchange market and allow the US dollar to depreciate against major currencies such as the yen.
- In 1986, the United States forced Japan to sign the Japan-US Semiconductor Agreement, which restricted the quantity and raised the price of Japanese semiconductors exported to the United States, and guaranteed US-made semiconductors a specific market share in Japan.
- In 1987, the US government imposed a 100% tax on electronic products such as televisions and computers from Japan.
- By 1989, the USTR Office had initiated a total of 24 trade disputes against Japan, for all of which Japan made corresponding concessions.

In summary, the United States suppressed Japan's high-tech industry through two channels, and both channels were harsh.

One channel was to suppress the industrial policies adopted by the Japanese government by cracking down on its financial support and subsidies for high-tech R&D and industries. The reason, as we are very familiar with now, was that Japan's industrial policies had disrupted the "fair competition" between US and Japanese companies and did not conform to rules of a market economy. So the US government required the Japanese government to end its support for high-tech industries. At the same time, the United States adopted protectionist trade policies to restrict Japan's market share in the United States through tariffs, quotas, and voluntary export restrictions, as listed above.

The other channel was to discredit and to directly sanction Japanese high-tech companies through long-arm jurisdiction.

In 1982, the US Federal Bureau of Investigation (FBI) carried out a sting operation against Hitachi, a leading company in Japan's semiconductor industry. The operation resulted in indictments against Hitachi and several of its employees on charges that they stole top-secret design materials and computer equipment from IBM. Hitachi became a symbol of Americans' worst suspicions that Japanese companies were stealing American technology.

In 1987, Toshiba Machine, a subsidiary of Japan's Toshiba Corporation, was sanctioned by the United States for exporting high-precision lathes to the Soviet Union in violation of the Paris Coordinating Committee's export controls. The US Department of Defense canceled its originally planned ¥15 billion computer contract and banned new military contracts with Toshiba Machine. The US Congress passed a bill implementing a ban on the import of all products of the Toshiba Corporation for up to five years. Under pressure from the United States, Japan arrested and imprisoned two managers in Toshiba Machine and Toshiba Corporation was forced to publish full-page apologies in more than 50 newspapers across the United States.

Japan's semiconductor industry, especially the five leading companies, Hitachi, Mitsubishi, Fujitsu, Toshiba, and NEC, under the support of Japan's Ministry of International Trade and Industry, started competing fiercely with American companies such as IBM and Intel in the 1970s. By 1985, Japan's global market share in semiconductors exceeded that of the United States. This led the United States to suppress Japan's industry through the channels discussed above, in the so-called US-Japan semiconductor war. As a result, the global market share of Japan's semiconductor components fell from 49% in 1990 to 6% in 2021, as shown in Fig. 9.3.

The late 1980s was the period between the second and third Industrial Revolutions. Partly due to the trade disputes with the United States, Japan's industrial structures were trapped in the industries of the second Industrial Revolution, like electronics, automobiles, and steel, and almost completely missed out on the development of the information technology (IT) and bioengineering industries of the third Industrial Revolution. This stagnation in industrial upgrading shifted Japan from enjoying the high returns and high growth of a virtuous cycle driven by high technology to a vicious cycle of low capital gains, low growth, and low returns. As a result, the share of high-tech product exports in Japan's total manufacturing exports fell from 29% in 2000 to 17% in 2018.

US suppression reduced the returns from Japan's high-tech industry, causing capital to flow into the higher-return real estate industry. At the same time, Japan signed the Plaza Accord in 1985, the yen appreciated, and the

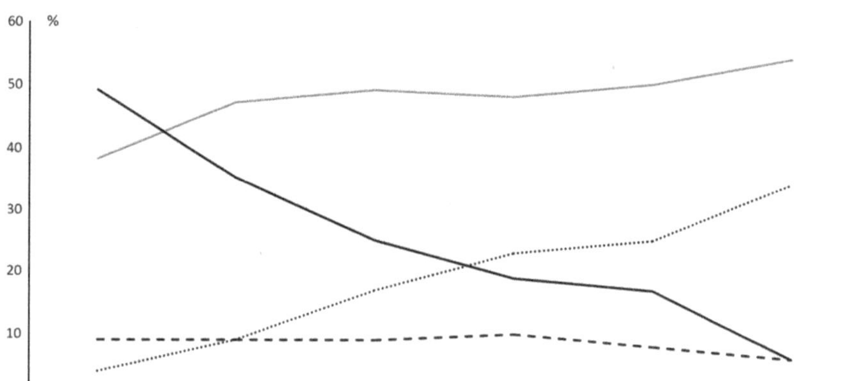

Fig. 9.3 Global market share of semiconductor components (*Source* IC Insights)

Japanese government adopted a loose monetary policy to offset the negative impact of yen appreciation. The appreciation of the yen and financial liberalization attracted a large amount of overseas capital into the stock market. The capital flow surged into the stock and real estate markets triggered bubbles in the two markets. Subsequently, the rise in real estate prices drove up wage costs, which in turn drove up production costs. Coupled with issues such as population aging, it further reduced the returns to capital in Japan's real economy.

Around 1990, the United States entered a cycle of interest rate hikes. Combined with domestic inflationary pressures, this prompted Japan's central bank to tighten monetary policy as well. The Asian financial crisis in the late 1990s further worsened Japan's economy. The bubbles in the stock and real estate markets burst, and the real economy was further hit. Japan's real economy entered a vicious cycle of low capital gains, low growth, and low returns, and it has been sluggish ever since.

Since the onset of the US-China trade war, the United States has similarly been suppressing China's high-tech industry. China's real estate prices and labor costs have also been rising. At the same time, China is also facing the challenge of an aging population. The painful lessons of Japan are worthy of high vigilance. So how to prevent a Japan type crisis? We will discuss this in detail in the next chapter.

9.4.2 *Soviet-Type Crisis*

The Soviet-type crisis refers to the contradiction between a centrally planned economic system and microeconomic vitality. This contradiction was intensified in the great power competition between the United States and the Soviet Union and generated a vicious cycle in the latter. Eventually, the Soviet Union fell into a low-growth equilibrium due to the loss of microeconomic vitality. The contradiction between central planning and economic vitality is typical in rising powers because they need to centralize their resources to catch up with, and to change the international order created and strongly defended by, the ruling power.

The command economy of the Soviet Union required its microeconomic units (state-owned enterprises and collective farms) to obey central planning directives. This nationwide planning directive could coordinate national resources, but it reduced the flexibility and vitality of microeconomic units. After World War II, the Soviet Union had a period of rapid growth but, starting in the 1980s, its industrial and agricultural productivity declined, and it gradually fell behind in economic competition with the United States. The US-Soviet confrontation required the Soviet Union to further strengthen centralized planning directives, leading to a vicious cycle lower production efficiency, slower economic development, greater pressure to confront the United States, and the need to strengthen centralized planning. The ultimate outcome was the collapse of the Soviet Union.

Although post-Stalin Soviet leaders such as Khrushchev, Brezhnev, Andropov, and Chernenko made several rounds of adjustments to the economic system, they never changed the following characteristics: the central government implemented a command economy; there was state ownership of enterprises and collective farming; and enterprises and collective farms lacked autonomous management rights. The centrally planned system also extended to the field of science and technology. For example, a special certificate signed by six experts was required to publish papers, and publications were managed by a special review committee. The Academy of Sciences was responsible for basic research, while applied research in industrial sectors relied on independent research institutes. By the 1970s, there was a lack of innovative talent in Soviet enterprises, and research and production were seriously disconnected.

In the early stage of Soviet industrialization, the so-called price scissors—the difference between industrial and agricultural prices—was used for economic development, whereby the prices of agricultural products were lowered to provide funds for industrial development. Collective farms always had problems with low motivation and efficiency, and grain production in the Soviet Union lingered at a low level for a long time. The economic structure was seriously unbalanced, with light industry lagging far behind.

There were also problems in the management of state-owned enterprises. First, the centrally planned system used only the production completion rate as an assessment indicator, so state enterprises began to hide their production capacity, lower state targets, and even slack off. Second, because funding for production was granted by the state for free, state enterprises were motivated to ask the state for production resources in every possible way. Third, workers' remuneration was not linked to the business situation. These three problems together led to the low efficiency of state enterprises in the Soviet Union.

At the same time, the all-round confrontation with the United States greatly consumed the economic capacity of the Soviet Union. First, military competition occupied economic resources. According to different estimates, during the Cold War, the Soviet Union's annual military spending exceeded 15% of GDP. Second, the United States hit the Soviet Union's oil revenue. After the oil crisis of the 1970s, the Soviet Union, with its rich oil and gas resources, entered a period of rapid economic growth, with a growth rate of 6.4% during its ninth Five-Year Plan (1971–1975). In the 1980s, while the arms race between the Soviet Union and the United States heated up, the United States negotiated with Saudi Arabia to increase the latter's oil production, lowering world oil prices and severely hitting the Soviet Union's economy.

Under a deeply rooted centrally planned system, it is difficult for microeconomic vitality to flourish, and the contradiction between two triggers a vicious cycle. In the decade after the collapse of the Soviet Union and the end of the Cold War, Russia did not achieve its optimal economic growth, nor did it establish an effective market economy. On the contrary, the Russian economy changed from a state monopoly to an oligarchy, the poverty rate of ordinary citizens increased, and the wealth concentration and inequality between the rich and the poor rose sharply. These factors led Russia to fall from being one of the two superpowers during the US-Soviet rivalry to being a lesser economy today.

Chinese socialist market economy system is fundamentally different from the planned economy of the Soviet Union. Private enterprises in China contribute more than 50% of tax revenue, more than 60% of GDP, more than 70% of technological innovations, more than 80% of urban labor employment, and more than 90% of the number of enterprises. Nevertheless, China should learn from the lessons of the Soviet-type crisis and pay attention to handling the contradiction between central planning and microeconomic vitality in its competition with the United States.

China needs to centralize decision-making and carry out overall planning for key high-tech industries and long-term economic growth. Central and local governments should use various policy tools to stimulate innovation efforts in enterprises and research institutions to achieve technological breakthroughs and industrial upgrades. At the same time, China also needs to invigorate local governments, state-owned enterprises, and private enterprises through continuous reforms to maintain long-term high-speed economic growth.

9.4.3 *Financial Crisis*

The rising power always faces an asymmetric IMS dominated by the ruling power, as well as the risk of the ruling power weaponizing its international reserve currency status to launch financial attacks and trigger a financial crisis in the rising power. Therefore, for the rising power, preventing a financial crisis is one of its main tasks during the great power competition.

The anatomy of a typical financial crisis can be outlined as follows. An economic downturn and an increase in foreign interest rates (due to a tightening of foreign monetary policy) make people begin to hold relatively pessimistic expectations for the domestic economy. A self-fulfilling vicious cycle forms where the gap between domestic and foreign interest rates leads to capital outflows, currency depreciation, and balance sheet problems for domestic enterprises with a large amount of short-term debt denominated in foreign currency. Having trouble financing itself, the country experiences a further deterioration of the economy that feeds further capital flight, and so on, eventually triggering a systemic financial crisis.

Take the 1997 Asian financial crisis as an example. In the 1980s and 1990s, Southeast Asian countries such as Indonesia, Malaysia, and Thailand, vigorously promoted labor-intensive export industries, attracted foreign investors by keeping their exchange rates effectively fixed to the US dollar, and loaned excessively to the real estate industry to develop the economy. This approach led to the dual internal risks of over-reliance on exports and a real estate market bubble. Assured by the fixed exchange rate, financial and non-financial corporations borrowed heavily in US dollars.

In the 1990s, the US Federal Reserve raised interest rates to combat inflation, causing capital to flow back to the United States. The currencies of these Southeast Asian countries passively appreciated with the dollar, reducing their export competitiveness. In early 1997, international speculators noticed a slowdown in exports from Southeast Asian countries, the existence of asset price bubbles, and a lack of corresponding capital flow regulation measures, and attempted to short the Thai baht. In June 1997, speculative attacks caused the Thai baht to plummet in value. As it ran out of foreign exchange reserves to defend the baht, the Bank of Thailand abandoned the fixed exchange rate on July 2. The baht depreciated sharply and a large amount of capital fled the country. The currency depreciation resulted in collateral values falling, the ensuing credit crunch caused the economy to deteriorate further, and a vicious cycle was formed.

This financial storm quickly spread to neighboring countries whose currencies depreciated sharply in a short period of time. By the end of March 1998, the Thai baht, Indonesian rupiah, and Malaysian ringgit had depreciated by 39%, 72%, and 40% respectively compared with the beginning of 1997. The collapse of the de facto fixed exchange rate regimes in these Southeast Asian countries triggered a large-scale withdrawal of foreign capital from the region and led to corporate bankruptcies, bank failures, stock market crashes, real estate declines, and rising unemployment rates. Some countries fell into economic recession, or even social instability and regime changes. The storm shattered the rapid development of these Southeast Asian economies, and even affected economies as far away as Russia and Latin America. We will discuss in detail how to prevent such financial crises in Chapter 11.

9.4.4 Social Crisis

A social crisis in a rising power typically has two characteristics: first, social conflicts and economic downturns reinforce each other; second, foreign forces exacerbate the domestic social conflicts, causing them to worsen and eventually erupt into a crisis. A ruling power usually has the dominant ideology, the ability to shape international public opinion, and advantages in other "soft power" aspects, and it will often use its advantages of soft power to attack the rising power and induce a social crisis there.

The anatomy of a social crisis can be outlined as follows. An economic downturn leads to rising unemployment, and worsening income inequality induces social instability. Some interest groups, with support from internal and/or external forces, rise up to oppose the government, leading to social disorder and the attendant economic costs. The economy deteriorates further, conflicts among different interest groups intensify and social disorder escalates in a vicious cycle, eventually leading to an economic and social crisis.

The so-called Arab Spring revolutions in the early 2010s are an example of social crises. The Arab world has long been plagued by differences between secular and religious forces. The drop in oil prices around 2000 caused an economic recession in many countries, while corruption and income inequality made life even worse for the poor. In January 2011, the Ben Ali regime in Tunisia was overthrown by public protests, marking the beginning of a social crisis that quickly spread to other countries in the region and ultimately also brought down the governments of Egypt, Libya, and Yemen.

The social crisis in the Arab region mainly took the form of public anti-government demonstrations organized using modern communication means. The main players were educated, internet-savvy young people who were dissatisfied with the status quo, and they quickly spread their message and coordinated their activities through social media platforms such as Facebook, Twitter, and YouTube.

The Arab Spring led to the so-called Arab Winter, characterized by extensive civil wars, religious wars between Sunni and Shia Muslims, general regional instability, and economic and demographic decline of the Arab League countries. Multiple conflicts are still continuing in the region.

When a country's economy performs poorly, internal conflicts typically emerge among domestic groups. The best way to resolve internal social conflicts is to promote mutual understanding and support, and unite the country to overcome its difficulties, lift the economy out of the doldrums, and return it to the track of normal growth. If the country happens to be the rising power in a great power competition, however, its opponent, the ruling power, would have every incentive to interfere in the internal conflict to aggravate the social crisis and destroy its economic development. In this situation, the rising power would face an external conflict intertwined with its internal conflict, and the best strategy would be to cut off the connection between internal and external conflicts by blocking the hostile forces, the ruling power, from adding fuel to its internal social conflicts.

9.4.5 *Public Policy Crisis*

A public policy crisis refers to a situation where an inappropriate or inadequate policy response to a structural issue affecting long-term growth leads to slowing economic growth, which further constrains policy options to deal with the issue, generating a vicious cycle. Currently, major structural issues of concern for long-term economic growth in countries around the world include climate change, pandemics, demographic changes, and widespread adoption of AI.

Population policy may be one of the most important public policy issues in China because human resources are important factors in determining economic growth and the great power competition. According to data from China's National Bureau of Statistics, the total fertility rate (that is, the average number of children a woman would have over her childbearing years, based on prevailing birth trends) in China dropped from 2.31 in 1990 to 1.22 in 2000. After a brief recovery to 1.44 in 2010, the total fertility rate dropped again to 1.3 in 2020, and is now around 1. Once the total fertility rate falls below 1.5, it is very hard to get it back up toward the level of 2.1 generally thought necessary to sustain a population.

If the trend of low fertility is not curbed, it will lead to a decline in the working-age population (human resources) over time, which will limit market scale effects, discourage industrial upgrading, and dampen economic growth, which could further discourage childbirth, creating a vicious cycle.

China still has the potential to increase its total fertility rate and reverse the ominous decline in population. According to a 2021 survey by China's National Bureau of Statistics, the number of children desired by women of childbearing age in China is 1.8, higher than the "low fertility trap" level of 1.5. The population issue cannot be treated carelessly; it needs the attention of the whole society! How to substantially reduce the costs of childbirth and childcare and boost the total fertility rate back above the low fertility trap level is one of the most pressing public policy challenges for China!

9.4.6 *Regional Security Crisis*

In our "growth-crisis" framework of great power competition, military action by one country is a means to affect the long-term growth of its rival. Military action may have a negative impact on the defending country's long-term growth, which may trigger military retaliation and create a vicious cycle of war and economic recession. We refer to this as a regional security crisis. A regional security crisis is a disruption to a country's normal economic growth that is directly caused by military action, such as losing a war, ceding territory, paying indemnities, and economic collapse, like the outcome of the Britain-China Opium War in 1840, or it can be an economic recession indirectly brought about by military action.

Let's take the Soviet-Afghan war as an example. The Soviet Union invaded Afghanistan in late 1979 and installed Babrak Karmal as the leader. However, the Karmal administration failed to win the support of the population, and the Soviet army fell into a protracted war with the Afghan resistance movement assisted by the United States, the United Kingdom, Pakistan, Saudi Arabia, and other countries. Under military, economic, and diplomatic pressure, the Soviet Union's occupation of Afghanistan was difficult to maintain, and it eventually withdrew its troops in February 1989. After the Soviet withdrawal, Afghanistan fell into a civil war between the government and mujahideen guerrilla forces. Power struggles continued after the government collapsed in 1992, until the Taliban took over in 1996.

The Soviet Union also lost the war. According to official Soviet data, over 68,000 Soviet soldiers were killed, disabled, or missing in the war, and the war directly consumed 45 billion rubles (equivalent to $45 billion today). Its defeat in the war became a catalyst for the collapse of the Soviet Union itself.

For China, the most important regional security issues involve the Taiwan Strait and the South China Sea. Both issues are manifestations of the US-China great power competition. Two characteristics are worth noting. First is asymmetry in interests: for the United States, the Taiwan issue is a means to contain China, but for China, Taiwan is a core national interest—meaning there is much more at stake for China than there is for the United States. Second is asymmetry in military power: the United States possesses superior military power which it deploys to "protect" the Taiwan Strait and the South China Sea to contain China's "ambitions." There is a risk that the United States could use its military advantage to strike at China. To prevent this, China would need to close the gap in military power with the United States, as history shows that the symmetry in military power is the most effective means of preventing military conflicts. At the same time, both China and the United States need to refrain from the use of military power to prevent regional security issues from erupting into larger-scale conflicts.

9.5 Potential Crises in the United States

As the ruling power in the US-China great power competition, the United States also faces the risk of a potential crisis such as a social crisis, cultural crisis, financial crisis, constitutional crisis, public policy crisis, and regional security crisis. Let's analyze them one by one.

9.5.1 Social Crisis

Historically, when a ruling power declines and heads toward the end of its hegemony, it often encounters an outbreak of domestic social conflicts. A social crisis in the United States would likely be rooted in the increasing inequality of income and wealth, which leads to difficulties in the lives of the less well-off. When the economy is down, social conflicts tend to intensify, making it impossible for the government to carry out necessary structural adjustments to restore economic growth. In the short term, the government could respond by increasing fiscal subsidies, which would increase the public debt burden, and/or adopt loose monetary policy, which would drive up asset prices and mainly benefit the rich, leading to more social inequality, more social conflicts, and more social disorder. With increased uncertainty about the stability of the economy, investment would decrease and the economy would weaken further, leading to a vicious cycle that culminates in a social crisis.

Between 1976 and 2018, the income of the top 1% of the US population increased from 11.0% to 20.5% of national income, while the income share of the bottom 50% of the population fell from 21% to 12.7%.[2] Such extreme inequality in the society will inevitably have negative effects on the economy.

Excessive inequality could lead to higher rates of so-called deaths of despair, lowering average life expectancy and harming the quality of human capital in

[2] World Inequality Database, 2023; accessed on November 29, 2025. https://wid.world/

the United States. Research by Nobel laureate Angus Deaton and Anne Case found that between 1999 and 2013, the death rate caused by alcoholism and drug abuse among 45- to 54-year-old White Americans rose more sharply than in other developed countries.[3] According to statistics from the US Centers for Disease Control and Prevention, drug abuse increased rapidly in the United States and the number of deaths due to drug overdoses was almost four times higher in 2018 than in 2000. The high mortality rate caused by behaviors such as alcoholism and drug abuse, along with the rising suicide rate and the persistently high violent crime rate, are collectively weakening the human capital of the United States and could seriously jeopardize its long-term economic growth.

During the 1960s, the US government was able to effectively alleviate social conflicts surfaced by the flourishing civil rights movement by implementing the Great Society federal programs that addressed civil rights, education, medical care, urban problems, rural poverty, and transportation. At that time, the US economy was growing rapidly, there were many job opportunities, and the government had ample funds.

However, today's US politicians seem unable to resolve the country's social conflicts, which are rooted in a failure to adapt to globalization and long-standing racial discrimination, among other things. Some politicians have turned to identity politics and populism, leading to political polarization and further exacerbating social conflicts. The intensification of social conflicts could further discourage investment in the real economy and jeopardize long-term growth in the United States.

9.5.2 *Cultural Crisis*

The expansion of a hegemonic state could bring about conflicts between the majority or dominant racial or cultural group and other groups in the country. If not properly resolved, this could lead to social disorder, discourage investment, and ultimately harm economic growth.

The British Empire expanded greatly during the nineteenth century by ruling and exploiting colonies around the world, which ultimately led to the colonies' struggle for independence. As the contemporary global hegemon, the United States cannot grow without continuously absorbing human capital from other countries around the world. As an immigrant country, the United States has a diverse population with various ethnicities and beliefs. But its basic political structure and ideology have Anglo-Saxon characteristics. Whites and Protestants still dominate the culture, while minority ethnic groups have been subjected to varying degrees of systemic discrimination for a long time. Black

[3] Anne Case and Angus Deaton, "Rising Morbidity and Mortality in Midlife Among White non-Hispanic Americans in the 21st Century," *Proceedings of the National Academy of Sciences* 112, no. 49 (November 2, 2015): 15078–83, https://doi.org/10.1073/pnas.1518393112.

Americans, in particular, have long been subjected to discriminatory treatment in employment, housing, law enforcement, education, healthcare, and other areas.

As the proportion of Whites in the United States slides from a majority to a minority, American culture is beginning its journey from one dominated by Whites and Protestants to one that is multicultural. In the process, conflicts between different ethnicities and cultures are inevitable, with minority groups struggling to eliminate cultural oppression and the majority White mainstream group struggling to "protect their tradition." Such conflicts could develop into a cultural crisis in the United States.

If the US government adopts an overcorrecting approach to enforce racial and other forms of diversity, this could reduce the efficiency of human capital accumulation, causing resource misallocation and affecting the economy's potential growth. Moreover, the overly stringent diversity policies could create a backlash, intensifying the conflicts between racial and ethnic groups, and leading to social disorder, which damages economic growth. A weak economy would further inflame dissatisfaction among minority groups who tend to be poorer than Whites, further worsening the conflict and eventually leading to a cultural crisis.

The Black Lives Matter movement is a manifestation of a social conflict over discrimination and racial inequality in the United States. The movement began in response to several unjustified killings of unarmed African Americans by the police in various US cities and reached its peak in 2020 after the death of a Black man, George Floyd, due to police violence in Minneapolis. The killing sparked nationwide protests in the United States, with large crowds taking to the streets, some rioting and looting, and calling for defunding the police. The demonstrations hindered normal economic activities and caused substantial economic losses (an estimated $2 billion in damage) in the affected areas.

9.5.3 *Financial Crisis*

It should be evident from the discussion so far that what starts out as one type of crisis can quickly develop into another type of crisis. For example, a crisis motivated by socioeconomic factors like inequality or racial discrimination can have serious economic consequences and ultimately turn into a financial crisis. A financial crisis is the most detrimental crisis for the United States as the ruling hegemon. Once a systemic financial crisis occurs, the economic, financial, political, and social systems of the United States could all come under threat and could potentially collapse.

A financial crisis in the United States can develop in different ways. In the 2008 global financial crisis, excessive borrowing caused a bubble in the US real estate market, and the subsequent bursting of the bubble led to severe stresses in the US financial system. The collapse of large financial companies such as Lehman Brothers triggered a panic in financial markets globally.

Investors withdrew their money from banks and investment funds around the world amid uncertainty about each institution's exposure to distressed loans. A global liquidity shortage ensued as everyone tried to sell at the same time and no one wanted to lend. Confidence fell and investment and consumption spending collapsed, leading to a large number of corporate bankruptcies and economic recession. The recession further depressed asset prices, causing a vicious cycle of financial market and macroeconomic distress. The United States and some other economies fell into their deepest recessions since the Great Depression.

As long as the US dollar remains the dominant international currency, the United States has ample room to shift its domestic financial crises to the rest of the world. The 2008 global financial crisis triggered unprecedented interventions by the US Federal Reserve in the form of so-called quantitative easing policies which created excessive global liquidity and caused a surge of capital inflows to other countries, leading to appreciation pressure on their currencies and a build-up of financial imbalances. More recently, in response to the COVID-19 recession, the US Federal Reserve again intervened strongly to increase liquidity, including resuming quantitative easing policies. The surge in global inflation in 2022 stemmed primarily from the extremely loose US monetary policy.

But the edifice of the US dollar-dominated IMS may be beginning to wobble. US government debt is now at an all-time high, well above the level reached during the Great Depression. In 2022, the Federal Reserve had to tighten monetary policy to deal with inflation, which will inevitably cause the cost of US debt to soar. Furthermore, the strengthening of US financial sanctions against Russia in response to the Russia-Ukraine conflict has forced Russia to adopt a "de-dollarization" strategy and is motivating more and more countries to look for alternatives to the US dollar as an international currency.

9.5.4 Constitutional Crisis

A constitutional crisis is a specific form of political crisis that is generally manifested as a conflict that the political constitution is unable to resolve. The conflict can be between different branches of government, between central and local governments, or among different factions within society.

The US Constitution's stability relies not only on legal frameworks but on norms of presidential restraint, particularly during transitions of power. The January 6, 2021, Capitol attack—fueled by then-President Donald Trump's claims of election fraud—exposed how a refusal to concede defeat can incite violence and destabilize democratic processes. Though Trump was impeached by the House for inciting insurrection and later acquitted by the Senate, his 2024 presidential victory highlights unresolved questions about accountability for actions that undermine electoral legitimacy. The 14th Amendment's prohibition on insurrectionists holding office remains untested in this context, as political polarization has stymied its enforcement. A constitutional crisis arises when a president rejects electoral outcomes, incites unrest, or refuses to step down, as such actions erode public trust in institutions and create competing claims to authority. Without a shared commitment to "gentlemanly conduct"—prioritizing democratic continuity over personal or partisan ambition—the United States risks recurring constitutional crises that could fracture its political order.

9.5.5 *Public Policy Crisis*

The COVID-19 pandemic highlighted weaknesses in American public policy that could lead to another similar crisis in the future. The American system is centered on self-interested individuals who operate as a society through the "invisible hand" of the market in economics and democratic elections in politics. This system is often effective when individual behavior has no externalities, that is, when it has no impact on others. However, when individual behavior has strong externalities, the system fails.

The defining feature of a pandemic is contagion, which is a strong externality. Purely from a personal interest perspective, some people did not feel the need to isolate or wear a mask and refused to do so. However, they did not take into account the effect of their decision on others, specifically, that they could transmit the virus to elderly and immuno-compromised people. The US policy response to the COVID-19 public health crisis was chaotic and inconsistent, resulting in 180,000 deaths that could have been avoided.[4] This does not bode well for its handling of future public health catastrophes.

9.5.6 *Regional Security Crisis*

So far in human history, all hegemonic nations have been dethroned in wars, and the United States may be no exception. After World War II, the United States launched three wars in China's periphery, namely the Korean War, the Vietnam War, and the war in Afghanistan. Each ended with a humiliating US withdrawal.

Let's look at the war in Afghanistan. In the summer of 1994, Afghan mujahideen and religious students established the Taliban and controlled the whole of Afghanistan from 1996 to 2001, when they were driven out by a US-led invasion in retaliation for providing sanctuary for Al-Qaeda, the organization responsible for the 9/11 terrorist attacks. The Afghan capital, Kabul, fell in November 2001 and Kandahar, the largest city in southern Afghanistan, fell in December, marking the end of the Taliban regime. But the United

[4] Woolhandler, Steffie, David U. Himmelstein, Sameer Ahmed, Zinzi Bailey, Mary T. Bassett, Michael Bird, Jacob Bor, et al. 2021. "Public Policy and Health in the Trump Era," *The Lancet 397* (10275): 705–53. https://doi.org/10.1016/S0140-6736(20)32545-9.

States then faced a situation similar to the one met by its old rival, the Soviet Union.

The high military and reconstruction expenditures of the war in Afghanistan created a huge fiscal burden, and the unrelenting casualty count caused strong opposition to the war within the United States. In Afghanistan, rising anti-Western sentiments driven by dissatisfaction over the pace of reconstruction, the toll of civilian casualties, and corruption in the government paved the way for the resurgence of the Taliban in 2005.

One month after US forces killed the leader of Al-Qaeda, Osama bin Laden, in Pakistan in May 2011, the Obama administration announced an accelerated timetable for withdrawal from Afghanistan. The United States ended its combat mission in Afghanistan at the end of 2014, and the last US troops withdrew from Afghanistan on August 31, 2021, just as the Taliban swept back into power. The 20-year war in Afghanistan resulted in more than 2200 US military deaths, about 20,000 injuries, approximately $2.2 trillion in military and reconstruction expenditures, and the Taliban back in Afghanistan.

As a ruling power, the United States still possesses an advantage over most of the world in terms of military strength. However, China's military strength is rapidly approaching that of the United States in Asia. If the United States launches a fourth war in China's periphery, just like in the previous three wars, it may fight but not win. But unlike in the previous three wars, if it fights and does not win, US hegemony in Asia may collapse.

9.6 Possible Paths of the US-China Great Power Competition

In the final part of this chapter, we will consider possible paths the US-China great power competition might take and the strategic choices of both sides along the way. We aim to answer three questions: (1) What type of crisis is most likely to erupt? (2) Will there be a military conflict between the great powers? (3) How can a military conflict be successfully avoided?

To begin, we state a rational condition for peace between two great powers, which is that a country will choose peace if the cost of a war is greater than the benefit of the war.

Our analysis will show that the best chances for avoiding a large-scale military conflict between the United States and China and achieving a peaceful transition of the world order are if China achieves robust economic growth, the renminbi becomes an international currency, and China maintains a balance of military power with the United States in China's periphery.

The flowchart in Fig. 9.4 illustrates a possible path that the US-China great power competition could take. Let's go through the flowchart step by step.

The starting point is the US-China trade war, which can be seen as the United States' attempt to instigate a Japan-type crisis in China. As previously mentioned, China's high-tech industry is the core target of US efforts to

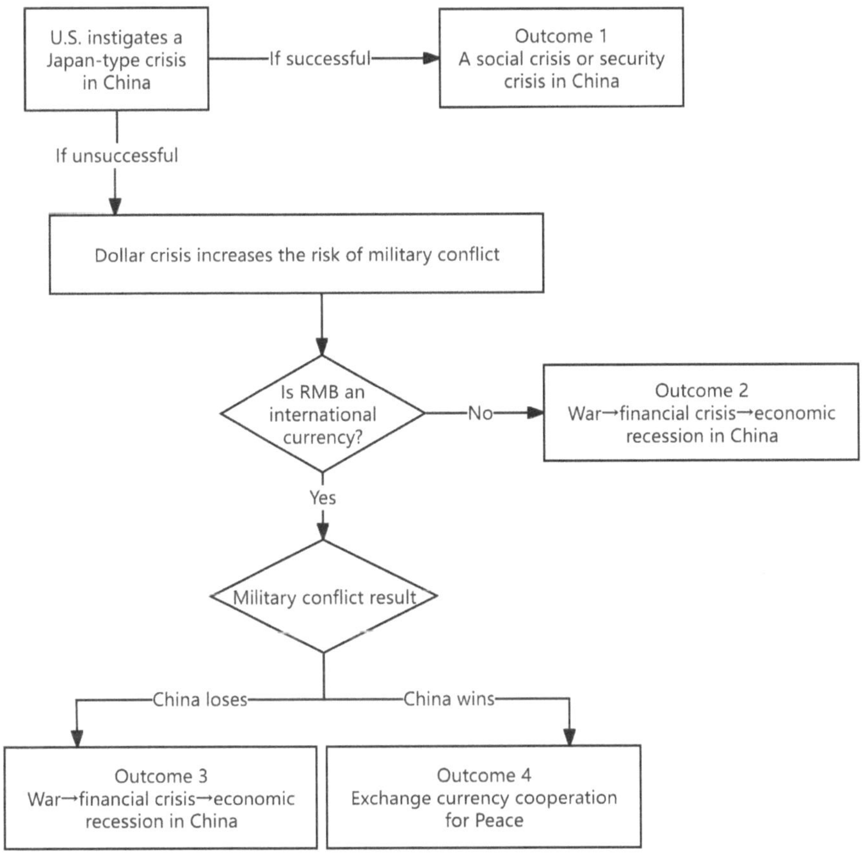

Fig. 9.4 Possible paths of US-China great power competition

contain China. US suppression of China's high-tech industry is directed at three fronts: high-tech companies, technical talents, and industrial policies.

High-tech companies. The United States has added a significant number of China's high-tech companies to the Entity List, cutting off their supply chains. It has engaged in a massive outreach campaign to persuade its allies to avoid telecommunications equipment from Huawei. It has introduced an order to restrict or even ban US outbound investment to China in high-tech areas deemed critical to US national security (advanced computing chips and microelectronics, quantum technology, and AI). It has on various occasions promoted a US-led technology alliance of like-minded countries to compete with China in R&D and technology policy. It has tried to restrict overseas financing for China's high-tech companies by pushing investors to avoid China and threatening to delist these companies from US stock exchanges.

Technical talents. The United States is directly limiting scientific and technological exchanges between the two countries. It has restricted Chinese scholars from participating in academic exchanges and canceled visas for Chinese students and researchers in specific fields under the pretext of security risks. Even though the so-called China Initiative, launched in 2018 to prosecute scientific researchers and academics affiliated with China, ended in failure, the United States continues to increase its scrutiny of the funding sources and research results of Chinese-American scientists.

Industrial policy. The United States has introduced its own form of industrial policy in the CHIPS and Science Act of 2022, and the Inflation Reduction Act of 2022 which provide massive subsidies for US manufacturers of semiconductors, electric vehicles, and clean energy, with the purpose of "countering China" and protecting against its "unfair trade practices." Moreover, the CHIPS and Science Act includes a "poison pill" requiring companies benefiting from its subsidies not to invest in or produce certain high-tech products in China.

9.6.1 Outcome 1

The first scenario is that China fails to prevent itself from falling into a Japan-type crisis, leading to stagnation in its industrial upgrading and sub-optimal long-term growth. This is equilibrium B analyzed in Sect. 9.2.2, where the United States wins and China loses the great power competition.

Will China's losing lead to a peaceful ending of the competition between the two countries? The answer is: unlikely. Instead, we predict that there will be direct or indirect military conflicts between the two countries. Just like its approach to Russia after the collapse of the Soviet Union, the United States would want to take advantage of the situation and completely eliminate China's challenge to US hegemony once and for all by inciting internal conflicts in China, strengthening separatist forces, and provoking a regional security crisis. Faced with this provocation, China will have to strike back with military force, which may escalate into a regional conflict like the Russia-Ukraine conflict, and eventually China will fall into a vicious cycle of war and economic recession.

9.6.2 Outcome 2

The second scenario is that China successfully avoids a Japan-type crisis, and achieves its long-term growth potential, but the renminbi is still not a freely convertible international currency. In this case, China's nominal GDP will catch up with US GDP around 2035. But, as we analyzed in equilibrium C in Sect. 9.2.3, the incompatibility between the tripod structure of the GVC and the dollar-dominated IMS will be increasingly unsustainable and the dollar-dominated system would need to be transformed into a multi-currency system.

If the dollar hegemony collapses, the financial support on which the US military hegemony depends will also collapse. The United States would not sit idly by and let this happen, but would do its utmost to protect the international status of the dollar, likely through military adventurism. As long as the dollar is a safer and more liquid international currency than the nonconvertible renminbi, a military conflict between China and the United States will direct global capital toward the latter. Since dollar-denominated assets will continue to be seen as safe asset when the military conflict occurs, the flow of world capital would be one-way, from renminbi-denominated assets to dollar-denominated assets.

Like the Russia-Ukraine conflict, a regional conflict between China and the United States (using Taiwan, for example, as a proxy) may also become protracted as the United States will not stop creating instability in the South China Sea and other areas around China. As long as the military conflict persists, global capital will flow to dollar assets, strengthening the economic, technological, and military strength of the United States and plunging China into a vicious cycle of war, financial crisis, and economic recession.

9.6.3 Outcome 3

The third scenario is that China successfully avoids a Japan-type crisis and achieves its long-term growth potential, and the renminbi is convertible and achieves international currency status on par with the US dollar. In this scenario, the risks brought about by a military conflict between the United States and China will be symmetrical for both countries: global capital will flow from the losing side to the winning side, so the risks will be mainly borne by the losing side.

Following the condition for peace stated earlier, whether the United States would take military action against China to save the dollar's status in this scenario would depend on whether it thinks it can win a war with China. If China loses the military conflict, global capital will flow from renminbi-denominated assets to dollar denominated assets and China could fall into a vicious cycle of war, financial crisis, and economic recession.

9.6.4 Outcome 4

But if the United States loses the military conflict, global capital will flow from dollar-denominated assets to renminbi denominated assets. The dollar would come under strong depreciation pressure, and the possibility of a financial crisis would increase sharply, depriving the United States of funds to support its military actions. The United States would fall into a vicious cycle of war, financial crisis, and economic recession.

To avoid a further spiraling of crises, the United States might seek to stop the conflict with China and move toward peace. China would likely be willing to exchange currency cooperation for peace, work with the United States to stop the dollar's collapse, and jointly realize the peaceful transition of the IMS from a dollar-dominated system to a multi-currency system.

To summarize, in order for China and the United States to avoid a large-scale military conflict and achieve a peaceful transition to the new world order, China needs to do three things: (1) avoid a Japan-type crisis and achieve strong economic growth; (2) establish the convertibility of the renminbi and promote its use as an international currency; and (3) build up its military power to rival that of the United States.

9.7 The Probability of a War

With the analysis above, we can now assess the probability of a war between the United States and China in the great power competition.

The Benchmark Case

The probability of a war is 1 minus the probability of a peaceful resolution to the US-China competition. The probability of a peaceful resolution is equal to the probability that the cost of a war is greater than the benefit of the war, that is, based on the analysis in Fig. 9.4, it is the probability of the joint event that China avoids a Japan-type crisis, the renminbi becomes an international currency, and China could win the military conflict:

More formally,

$$\begin{aligned}\text{Pr(war)} = 1 - \text{Pr}(&\text{“China avoids a Japan} - \text{type crisis”} \\ &\times \text{“RMB becomes an international currency”} \\ &\times \text{“China could win the military conflict”})\end{aligned}$$

Assuming that three events in the above are independent, we have:

$$\begin{aligned}\text{Pr(war)} = 1 - &\text{Prob}(\text{“China avoids a Japan} - \text{type crisis”}) \\ &\times \text{Prob}(\text{“RMB becomes an international currency”}) \\ &\times \text{Prob}(\text{“China could win the military conflict”})\end{aligned}$$

Let P_1 be the probability of “China avoids a Japan-type crisis, P_2 be the probability of “RMB becomes an international currency” and P_3 be the probability of “China could win the military conflict. ” Then we would have:

$$\text{Prob(war)} = 1 - P_1 \times P_2 \times P_3$$

To begin with, we assume that in the next 10 years P_1, P_2, and P_3 all equal 0.5, then we would have:

$$\text{Prob(war)} = 1 - 0.5 \times 0.5 \times 0.5 = 0.875$$

We next consider the cases where “RMB is not an international currency” versus “RMB becomes an international currency.”

The Case of "RMB Is Not an International Currency"

Figure 9.4 illustrates a possible path for US-China competition, while the order of the events may differ, and correspondingly, the probability of the events will also differ.

Now we move whether "RMB becomes an international currency" to the first event to consider. To save space, the flowchart is not drawn.

The renminbi is not currently an international currency. As noted in Sect. 9.6, the purpose of a military conflict launched by the United States would be to drag China into crises: during the military conflict between the United States and China, global capital will flow from renminbi-denominated assets to dollar-denominated assets in a "flight to safety," which could trigger financial, social, and security crises and lead to a prolonged economic recession.

We first consider the scenario that China falls into a Japan-type crisis. It is hard to evaluate if US military is capable of winning a war against China. However, it is almost certain that the US is capable of creating an uncertainty around China through military conflicts. To completely eliminate China's challenge to the US hegemony, the benefit of a well-designed military conflict initiated by the US is greater than the cost. Therefore, like Russia has experienced, military conflicts between the US and China, directly or indirectly, are almost inevitable in this scenario.

On the side of China, when it has fallen into economic stagnation, separatist movements, directly or indirectly supported by the US, are almost certain to occur. To prevent a comprehensive social crisis, China has to take military actions to stop the separatist movements. As the capital account in China is not open, the expected cost of military action is also relatively low. Furthermore, a military victory may also help China mitigate the domestic social crisis, and even jump out of economic stagnation. Therefore, the risk of military adventure from China is also largely increased in this scenario.

We then consider the scenario in which China avoids a Japan-type crisis and achieves strong growth. In this scenario the US dollar is at the brink of collapse. As the RMB is not an international currency, the risk of military conflict is borne only by the RMB, not the dollar. Again, the purpose of a military conflict launched by the US is only to create uncertainty in the capital market so that the US dollar is saved. It is hard to imagine that the US will not do so in this scenario.

To summarize, in this case, a military conflict between the US and China is almost inevitable. In other words,

$$\Pr(\text{war}) \approx 1$$

Let's now consider the case where the renminbi becomes an international currency.

The Case of "RMB Becomes an International Currency"

If both the renminbi and the dollar are international currencies, the risk of a war to both currencies is symmetric, depending on which country wins the war.

We first consider the scenario that China falls into a Japan-type of crisis and the economy is trapped in stagnation.

The probability of winning a war launched by the US in China's periphery is completely different from that of just creating uncertainty. Furthermore, the challenge to US hegemony is largely reduced as China itself is struggling in economic and social crises. Compared to waiting for a gradually weakening China, the expected benefit for the US of initiating a war against China will be less than the cost.

On the side of China, as the RMB is an international currency (so the capital account has already opened), the expected cost of a military conflict initiated by China is also relatively high.

Thus, in this scenario, that the probability of a war becomes the probability of a "must-win" war, which we assume is largely reduced, to both US and China, and equal to 0.25.

Now we consider the scenario in which China avoids a Japan-type crisis and achieves strong growth. Note that the RMB is already an international currency, and joins the dollar and the euro together to lead the international monetary system. Strong growth in China only makes the RMB stronger and the dollar weaker, but does not necessarily cause the dollar to collapse.

A war against China launched by the United States would not benefit the dollar unless the United States wins the war. Furthermore, a military conflict between the United States and China would likely weaken both the dollar and the renminbi, and strengthen the euro. To win the war, the United States and China would need to boost their own currency against their rival's currency and the euro, which would become much more complicated. Therefore, the probability of a war in this scenario is also largely reduced.

Therefore, we assume that the probability of a war in this scenario is also largely reduced, to both the US and China, and equal to 0.25. That is,

$$\Pr(\text{war}) = 0.25$$

In summary, if the renminbi is not an international currency, a military conflict between the US and China is almost inevitable. However, if the renminbi becomes an international currency, a military conflict between the US and China is largely reduced. The discussion on making the renminbi an international currency will be picked up in Chapter 11.

9.8 Conclusion

In recent years, with the COVID-19 pandemic, the conflicts in Ukraine and the Middle East, global inflation, the threat of climate change, the risks and potential dangers of AI, et cetera, the world has become like a dark cloud before a storm that will bring a torrential flood roaring down. I can't help but recall 1998, when a once-in-a-century flood occurred in the entire Yangtze River basin in China. I was in Oklahoma, watching the developments on TV every day—the soldiers who jumped down the river embankment hand in hand to fight the flood, and the exhausted teachers and students. When I heard that a friend had sacrificed life, I couldn't sleep at night and wrote a poem in Chinese. At this time of global turmoil, I use this poem[5] as the conclusion of this chapter, hoping that both American and Chinese people will guard their homes and welcome a bright tomorrow.

To a Friend

Heroes rise during national crises,
Fierce waves batter the shore.
Monstrous floods invade the land,
A billion soldiers on levees stand.
Noble aspirations last as long as earth and sky,
Rivers run clear and seas comply,
The people are sacred.
Waves for miles wash away the sand,
The moon forever lights the land.

Benefit for all,
Reign by law,
Truth to the people.
Spirits connect past and present,
Waves link the universe in balance.
Though storms may pile like snow on the sea,
Fear not the winds nor darkening lee,
So long as fate we see.
May you walk with strength and pride,
With honor to the land.

[5] The poem is translated from the Chinese.

CHAPTER 10

Technological Competition: The Leader's Dilemma and the Chaser's Trap

Chapter 3 provided an overview of great power competitions in history and identified six fields or areas where competition is concentrated, namely: manufacturing, aggregate economy (GDP), technology, finance, military power, and global governance. Whether China can achieve its goal of catching up with the United States in economic size by around 2035 and avoid the various crises that rising powers may face would depend on how well it fares in competition with the United States in technology, finance, global governance, and military power.

In this chapter, we will discuss the competition in technology. Chapters 11 and 12 will discuss the competition in finance and global governance, respectively. A detailed analysis of military competition is beyond the scope of this book.

10.1 The Story of Kodak

In high-tech competition, where the United States is leading and China is catching up, does the United States have a higher probability of winning? This sounds simple—of course the leader has a higher probability of winning. Similar to a match between two table tennis players, the player with superior table tennis skills should easily win. But what if the two table tennis players switch to badminton? Will the player with superior table tennis skills still easily win the badminton match?

Technological competition between countries is similar in principle to that between enterprises. An example of the latter is the story of Kodak.

J. Ju, *US-China Great Power Competition and The New World Order*,
https://doi.org/10.1007/978-981-95-3762-4_10

Kodak was once the world's leading manufacturer of cameras and color film. For over a century, it made innovations in the industry. For example, it launched a small, lightweight, and user-friendly camera in 1886, and it introduced the world's first commercially successful color film in 1935. At its peak, Kodak's film accounted for two-thirds of the global film market. However, despite being an industry leader, Kodak began to struggle financially in the 1990s and reached its lowest point in 2012 when it filed for bankruptcy.

What happened? Kodak failed to transition from film technology to digital imaging technology in time, so it was eliminated by the new technology.

Was Kodak lagging in digital imaging technology? No, quite the opposite. When Kodak filed for bankruptcy in 2012, its digital imaging technology was not weak at all. Of the more than 10,000 patents owned by Kodak, 1100 were related to digital imaging patent technologies. This technological strength far exceeded that of its competitors at the time. In fact, as early as 1975, the world's first digital imaging was born in Kodak's laboratory, demonstrating the company's potential to become a leader in digital imaging technology. However, this opportunity was voluntarily abandoned by Kodak.

Why? The reason lies in opportunity cost, or what is commonly known as comparative advantage. Although Kodak was leading in digital imaging technology at the time, it was leading more in film technology, meaning its comparative advantage was in film technology, not digital imaging technology. Consequently, Kodak chose to focus on the film production and innovation, which brought huge profits; as the industry leader in film at the time, it would have incurred a high opportunity cost by switching to digital imaging technology. Therefore, Kodak was unwilling to give up its advantage in film technology and treated digital imaging technology as merely a side business. By the time Kodak realized that digital imaging technology had taken over the industry, it was too late.

The case of Kodak is what we refer to as the "leader's dilemma." The counterpart is the "chaser's trap," which refers to the situation where the company (or country) attempting to catch up in technological competition fails to achieve sufficient technological progress and ultimately suffers defeat in the competition. What kind of technological competition could lead to the "leader's dilemma"? What kind of technological competition could lead to the "chaser's trap"? How should China avoid falling into the "chaser's trap"? We will discuss these issues in detail below.

10.2 Classification of Technological Innovations

In this chapter, we categorize technological innovations into two types: incremental technological innovation and disruptive technological innovation.

Incremental technological innovation, as the name suggests, refers to gradual progress and advancements achieved through iterative updates of existing technologies. For instance, microchip technology has evolved from the 28 nm process to the 14 nm, 10 nm, 7 nm, 5 nm, and 3 nm process, et cetera. Moreover, a country can develop 10 nm technology only after mastering the mature 14 nm technology, and once it has achieved then it can upgrade to the 7 nm technology. It is impossible to skip the 10 nm process and upgrade directly from the 14 nm process to the 7 nm process.

Disruptive technological innovation is quite different. It is not about patching up or improving on an old technology but a radical technological transformation. The new technology is not derived from the old one, and adopting the new technology means abandoning the old one. Examples of disruptive technological innovations are: digital imaging technology (new) versus film technology (old); electricity (new) versus mechanical power (old); and electric vehicle engines (new) versus internal combustion engines (old).

10.3 Competition for Incremental Technological Innovation

The nature of incremental technological innovation is different from disruptive technological innovation, so the two types of technological competition are also different. Competition for incremental technology can be characterized as an R&D investment race, where the lagging country is prone to falling into the chaser's trap. In contrast, competition for disruptive technology can be characterized as leapfrogging, where the latecomer surpasses the leading country which is prone to the "leader's dilemma."

We will first discuss competition in incremental technological innovation.

10.3.1 R&D Investment Race

Incremental technological innovation requires the accumulation of existing technology and continuous R&D investment to refine and improve it. The country with the larger accumulation of technology and more R&D investment will make greater technological progress and thus hold an advantage. Therefore, in the competition for incremental technology, the key lies in which party continuously invests more in R&D.

There are many examples of R&D investment races between countries in so-called strategic industries. One example is the long-running competition between the United States' Boeing and Europe's Airbus in the development and technological improvement of large civil aircraft. Other examples can be found in the manufacture of aircraft carriers and the fiercely competitive semiconductor industry.

In the competition for incremental technology, the more R&D investment a country makes, the faster could be its technological progress. The leading country has to continue investing in R&D to maintain its market position. If the lagging (or chasing) country invests more, its technology gap vis-à-vis the leading country will narrow. The smaller the technology gap between the leading country and the chasing country, the more intense their competition in R&D investment will be. Can the chasing country close the technology gap and surpass the leading country? Let's return to the innovation-market cycle discussed in Chapter 2.

10.3.2 The Chaser's Trap

Figure 10.1 illustrates the innovation-market cycle for technology innovation. When a company invests in R&D, it leads to technological advancement; advanced technology helps the company's products gain market share, resulting in higher profits; higher profits enable the company to invest further in R&D. This creates a virtuous cycle where there is a positive feedback relationship linking R&D investment, technological progress, market share, and profits.

The same idea can be applied to countries. If the innovation-market cycle of a country operates in the positive (virtuous) direction, it will make continuous technological progress and gain an increasing share of the global market. It is important to note that when two major countries compete in the global market, an increase in one country's market share implies a decrease in the other country's market share. The country with a higher market share (the leading country) can afford to invest more in R&D and will make faster technological progress, while the country with a lower market share (the chasing country) cannot afford as much R&D and will make slower progress. The innovation-market cycle of the chasing country will operate in the negative (vicious) direction, where lower R&D investment results in slower technological progress, shrinking market share, lower profits, and less funds for R&D—this is what we call the "chaser's trap."[1] Ultimately, the chasing

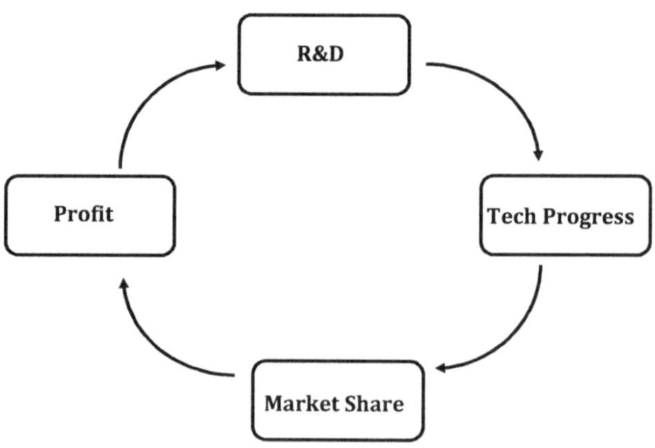

Fig. 10.1 Innovation-market cycle

[1] This book introduces three concepts: the "growth trap of specialization solidification," the "Japan-type crisis," and the "chaser's trap," to discuss the vicious cycles that developing and catching-up countries might fall into. The differences among these concepts are as follows: the "growth trap of specialization solidification" refers to the weakening

country will fail in the R&D race and the result will be an international specialization in technology, where the leading country (the technology leader) produces high-tech products and the chasing country (the technology laggard) produces low-tech products.

As long as the leading country can maintain a positive or virtuous innovation-market cycle, while putting the chasing country on a negative or vicious innovation-market cycle, the leading country will win in the technology competition and the chasing country will fall into the "chaser's trap." The Soviet Union and Japan are examples of countries that have fallen into the "chaser's trap" in technology competition with the United States.

How can a chasing country avoid the "chaser's trap" and establish the virtuous innovation-market cycle to surpass the leading country in technology? There are three conditions it would need to meet simultaneously. First, its R&D investment must be sufficiently high. In 2021, China's R&D investment exceeded 2.79 trillion RMB, an increase of 14.2% compared to 2020, and China's R&D investment intensity (R&D investment funds as a percentage of GDP) reached 2.44%. Currently, China's total R&D investment is second in the world, behind the United States and far ahead of Japan, which ranks third. Second, technological progress in the leading country cannot be too rapid. Productivity growth is driven by innovation and US total factor productivity began to slow down in the 1970s. Third, there must be a sufficient amount of cross-country knowledge spillovers, and the chasing country must possess strong absorption capacity for technology. In other words, the chasing country must be exposed to advanced technology from the leading country, and it must be able to master these technologies through learning and imitation.

If the above three conditions are met, the chasing country will have the chance to catch up with and surpass the leading country in the competition for incremental technology. Of course, the leading country will do all it can to maintain its leading position in technology. One of the most common approaches is to employ technology containment to maintain a "safe" technological gap ahead of the chasing country.

10.3.3 Technology Containment

The practice of technology containment—or even technology blockade—can be traced back to the ancient Roman period over 2000 years ago. During that period, steel smelting technology was the most advanced technology of

of the incentives for high returns on capital, high savings, and high investment caused by capital scarcity countries in an open economy, leading to a specialization solidification and thus falling into a low-growth trap. The "Japan-type crisis" refers to the vicious cycle Japan experienced: "high-tech industries being suppressed, failure to industrial upgrading, capital flowing into real estate and the stock market, the burst of market bubbles in real estate and stock with an aging population, and finally a trap of growth stagnation." The "chaser's trap" refers to the vicious cycle in which a catching-up country produces low-tech products in international specialization during the technology competition, fails to achieve technological breakthroughs, and thus loses in the technology competition.

the time. Mastery of the technology could arm a powerful military force. The ancient Roman legions were once stationed at the border of the Roman Empire to prevent the Celts from invading. When the Roman legions finally withdrew after six years, what did they do besides taking away containers for food and water and demolishing the fortified castles? They dismantled the houses, ruining the iron nails left in the castle or burying them. Why? Because they did not want the Celts to find them. The Romans relied on steel smelting technology to achieve technological leadership in areas such as building irrigation channels, ships, and weapons. They were concerned that if the iron nails were discovered by the Celts, the Celts could develop smelting technology of their own and potentially challenge the dominance of the Roman Empire. Therefore, when the Romans withdrew from the border, the most important thing was to preserve their smelting technology secret.

US Technology Containment of the Soviet Union

During the Cold War, the United States established two technology embargo lists against Eastern Europe and the Soviet Union in 1948. One list was used to prohibit all military supplies to Eastern Europe and the Soviet Union, and the other to prohibit the export of materials that could be indirectly used in military production. At the same time, the United States collaborated with 14 countries to impose a technology blockade against the Soviet Union: the Coordinating Committee for Multilateral Export Controls (CoCom) was established in 1949 in Paris for "security purposes." CoCom maintained a multilateral embargo on atomic energy, munitions, and so-called dual-use items that have both civil and military applications, not only against the Soviet Union, but also against other socialist countries, including China.

CoCom was dissolved in 1994 after the dissolution of the Soviet Union, but the United States continued to control the export of weapons and "sensitive technologies." In 1996, a new multilateral export control agreement was established as a successor to CoCom: the Wassenaar Arrangement has a wide-ranging list of restricted technologies covering munitions and dual-use goods and technologies which include almost all high-tech products, such as advanced materials, electronics, computers, communication products, aerospace products, and AI. The Wassenaar Arrangement has 42 member countries, including almost all major developed countries and technologically leading countries.

How Did Japan Fall into the Chaser's Trap?

As discussed in Chapter 9, in the late 1980s and early 1990s, the United States employed various measures to suppress Japan's technological progress. These actions forced Japanese companies to abandon their challenge to US technological dominance in industries such as semiconductors. The US strategy ensured a virtuous innovation-market cycle for its domestic enterprises, while obstructing the innovation-market cycle in Japan, causing Japan to ultimately fall into the "chaser's trap."

R&D investment. The Japanese government began providing funding for R&D in the semiconductor industry from the 1960s. During the eight-year span from 1976 to 1982, the amount of R&D funded by the Japanese government exceeded 10% of total R&D expenditure in the semiconductor industry. However, in the 1990s, the United States demanded that Japan stop supporting its semiconductor industry through industrial policies on the grounds that it violated the principles of a market economy and constituted unfair competition. Consequently, the Japanese government was forced to abandon its financial support for the sector. Meanwhile, the US government increased its support for R&D in its own semiconductor industry, doing exactly what it had prohibited the Japanese government from doing.

Why does high-tech R&D need government support? Because the required investment in R&D in the high-tech industry is substantial. The first companies to undertake high-tech R&D face significant risks, but once they succeed, there will be significant positive spillovers for the national economy. By providing support in terms of funding and favorable policies, the government can help the high-tech industry to enter a virtuous innovation-market cycle. This idea is certainly well understood by the United States.

Technological progress. US policymakers directly attacked Japan's leading semiconductor companies in various ways. As discussed in Chapter 9, in the 1980s, the US government punished Japanese semiconductor companies like Hitachi and Toshiba for allegedly stealing American technology and for selling sensitive technology to the Soviet Union in violation of the CoCom agreement by hitting them with sanctions, canceling major contracts, and arresting and forcing the resignation of their senior staff. The long-arm jurisdiction and other measures exerted by the United States contributed to the decline of Japan's semiconductor industry. In 1985, Japan had six of the top 10 semiconductor companies in the world; today, it has only one, while the United States has six.

Market share. In 1986, the United States and Japan signed the US-Japan Semiconductor Agreement, which restricted the export of Japanese semiconductors to the United States, reducing Japan's share of the US market, and compelled Japan to open its domestic market to US semiconductors, increasing the US share of Japan's market.

Profit realization. The US government reduced the profits of Japanese semiconductor companies through import tariffs and other trade restrictions as well as through the sanctions mentioned above.

It can be seen, therefore, that the US government suppressed Japan's semiconductor industry at every stage of the innovation-market cycle, destroying its chances of achieving a virtuous cycle of R&D investment, technological progress, market expansion, and higher profits. Japan fell into the "chaser's trap" and its global market share in the semiconductor industry dropped from 49% in 1990 to 7% in 2017.

10.4 Competition for Disruptive Technological Innovation

In the competition for incremental technological innovation, the leading country generally has an advantage. In the competition for disruptive technological innovation, the situation is quite different. Competition for disruptive technology can be explained using the technology leapfrogging model illustrated in Fig. 10.2.

There are two properties of this type of competition that are worth noting. The first is the first-mover advantage: whoever masters the new technology first has an advantage and can lead in that technology for a certain period. The second is that the positions of the leading and lagging countries tend to alternate, as shown in Fig. 10.2. Imagining a group of frogs leaping over one another—leadership alternates from one frog to another as the group moves forward. This is how disruptive technologies advance.

10.4.1 The Leader's Dilemma

As depicted in Fig. 10.2, in the competition for disruptive technology, the leader and laggard tend to alternate. When a new disruptive technology emerges, the leader is surpassed by the laggard in what we refer to as the "leader's dilemma." Why does the "leader's dilemma" occur?

Why do leading and lagging countries alternate in the field of disruptive technologies? Because the new technology and the old technology represent two distinct paths of technological R&D. Unlike incremental technology, where competition is on the same technological R&D path, competition in disruptive technology is a choice between the old technology and the new technology, such as the choice between film cameras and digital cameras in the case of Kodak discussed in Sect. 10.1.

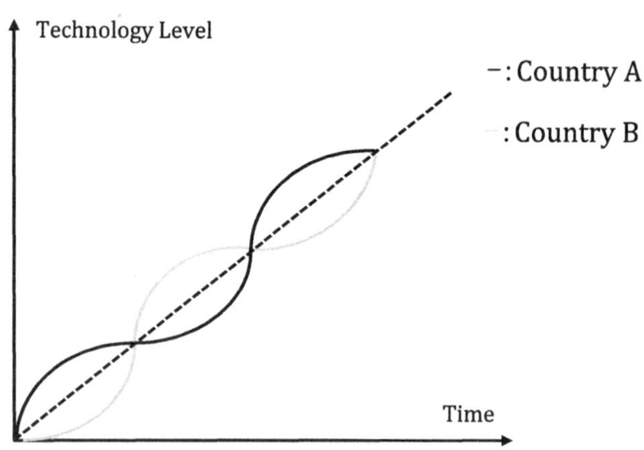

Fig. 10.2 Leapfrogging model

How is the choice between the two technologies made? This is where the concept of comparative advantage comes in. When a new technology emerges, both the leader and the laggard in the old technology are starting more or less from square one in the new technology. The leading country, which has an advantage in the old technology, faces a higher opportunity cost when abandoning the old technology and adopting the new technology. The lagging country, on the other hand, has less invested in the old technology so it has less to lose and more to gain by adopting the new technology. In other words, the leading country has a comparative advantage in staying with the old technology and it will specialize in products based on the old technology, while the lagging country has a comparative advantage in adopting the new technology and it will specialize in products based on the new technology. When the new technology product reaches a certain market share, the laggard overtakes the leader and leapfrogging occurs.

The story of Kodak in Sect. 10.1 is a typical example of the "leader's dilemma." Another classic example of the "leader's dilemma" is the case of Britain and the second Industrial Revolution. The first industrial revolution began in Britain with the invention of the steam engine. During the eighteenth and nineteenth centuries, Britain was far ahead of the United States in industrialization. However, when the second Industrial Revolution, characterized by electric power technology, occurred in the late nineteenth and early twentieth centuries, Britain failed to quickly adopt the new technology. Electric power technology represented a disruptive technological innovation. Britain had accumulated considerable technological capital in steam power and was more willing to stick to that technology. As the steam power-based technology of the first Industrial Revolution was gradually overtaken by the electric power-based technology of the second Industrial Revolution, Britain's competitiveness gradually declined. The United States caught up with and eventually surpassed Britain as an industrial power by 1913.

The development of mobile payments in China and the United States also serves as an interesting example of the "leader's dilemma." Credit cards have been used in the United States for decades; the technology is well developed and credit card payments have become the norm for American consumers. In contrast, credit cards are a relatively underdeveloped payment method in China. This has created a comparative advantage for China to develop mobile payments, where China is currently leading the United States in both technical advancement and market transaction volume. In addition to rapid development in the domestic market, China's mobile payment platforms such as Alipay and WeChat Pay are now also gradually emerging abroad.

10.4.2 Conditions for Leapfrogging

Leapfrogging is typical in the competition for disruptive technology in theory, but leapfrogging by the lagging or chasing country is not guaranteed in practice. It requires relentless efforts by the chasing country, and five conditions need to be met simultaneously.

The first condition is that the new technology should be largely unrelated to the old technology. For example, digital imaging technology is fundamentally different from film technology, and electric power-based technology is fundamentally different from steam power-based technology.

The second condition is that the opportunity cost of replacing the old technology with the new technology must be very high for the leading country. In the case of mobile payments, for example, almost everyone in the United States has a credit card, and individual spending habits, credit histories, and payment networks are all based on credit cards. Therefore, the opportunity cost of giving up credit card payments and switching to mobile payments is relatively high, which would explain the slower rate of adoption of mobile payments in the United States.

The third condition is that the new technology must be cheaper and more efficient for the chasing country than the old technology. Returning to the previous example, mobile payments in China are mainly driven by Alipay and WeChat Pay, which have quickly replaced a large portion of cash transactions. Automatic teller machines are not widely available in China, particularly in underdeveloped areas, but the prevalence of mobile phones is very high, and Alipay and WeChat Pay are regarded by consumers and merchants as convenient and safe options, which would explain the rapid development and spread of mobile payments in China.

The fourth condition is that the cost of producing new technology products (excluding the R&D cost) should be sufficiently low for the chasing country in order to achieve market scale. China's labor costs are lower than that of the United States: based on 2021 data, the average annual salary of a Chinese worker in an urban area is about 22% that an American worker.

The fifth condition is that the market share of the chasing country in the global market for new technology products must surpass that of the leading country. As described by the innovation-market cycle shown in Fig. 10.1, if the chasing country wants to realize technological leapfrogging, it needs to dominate the global market so as to achieve and maintain the lead in the new technology. Although China's Alipay, WeChat Pay, digital RMB, et cetera, started early, rapidly gained popularity in the Chinese market, and are gradually expanding overseas. The United States is now catching up in the global mobile payment market and is actively blocking Chinese platforms while benefiting from the enormous advantage of the US dollar's status as a global currency. In the global mobile payment market, the competition between China and the United States is far from settled.

10.5 US-China Technological Competition

Britain and Japan failed in their technological competition with the United States, falling into the "leader's dilemma" and the "chaser's trap," respectively. What did their companies do wrong? The answer is: British and Japanese companies did nothing wrong. They made choices that maximized corporate profits and that were in line with their country's comparative advantage at the time. British companies chose traditional steam power-based technology instead of the emerging electric power-based technology. Japanese companies chose not to resist American suppression and gave up upgrading their semiconductor industry. These were rational choices made by companies in these two countries in the prevailing environment. Using the definition from Chapter 9, the "leader's dilemma" and the "chaser's trap" are both self-fulfilling cycles and equilibrium states.

So, how can the chasing country overcome the "chaser's trap" in the competition for incremental technology, and how can the leading country avoid the "leader's dilemma" in the competition for disruptive technology? The answer is to use government policies to change the operating environment. For incremental technological innovations, the chasing country needs policies to help domestic companies increase R&D investment in order to challenge the technological dominance of the leading country and achieve technological advancement. For disruptive technological innovations, the leading country needs policies to incentivize domestic companies to switch to the new technology in order not to fall behind in the race. Therefore, the competition between great powers in technology takes place not only in the marketplace, but also in the policymaking sphere.

In this section, we will analyze US-China technological competition through the framework and insights developed so far. In the high-tech field, the United States remains the leading country while China is still the chasing country. The nature of competition between China and the United States differs for disruptive and incremental technological innovations.

10.5.1 US-China Competition in Disruptive Technological Innovation

The risks of climate change and the goal of achieving global carbon neutrality by around 2060 have become a consensus among most countries worldwide. A global energy revolution is underway, with the transition from fossil fuels such as coal, oil, and natural gas to clean energy sources such as wind, sunlight, water, and nuclear power. In this context, clean energy is a disruptive technological innovation compared to fossil fuels. Competition between China and the United States in clean energy products and technologies exhibits properties of the technology leapfrogging model, where the laggard in the old technology (fossil fuel energy) becomes the leader in the new technology (clean energy).

Let's take so-called new energy vehicles (NEVs) as an example to illustrate. NEVs include pure, or battery, electric vehicles (EVs), plug-in hybrid EVs, and hydrogen fuel cell EVs. Currently, China is the world's largest producer and exporter of NEVs. According to calculations by Nikkei Asia based on the data from British research firm LMC Automotive, global production of pure EVs in 2021 was 3.99 million units, of which China accounted for more than 50% (2.29 million units), while the European Union and the United States accounted for 22% and 12%, respectively. According to statistics from China Customs, China exported 498,600 pure EVs (passenger cars) in 2021 while second-ranked Germany exported approximately 230,000 units, and third-ranked the United States exported only 110,000 units. China has also become the largest market for NEVs worldwide. In 2021, China's sales of NEVs ranked first in the world for the seventh consecutive year with 3.52 million units, or 52.15% of the world's total NEV sales. By comparison, only 650,000 NEVs were sold in the United States that year.

Even though automotive powerhouses like the United States, Japan, and Germany began to lay out NEV technology quite early, by 2021, Chinese companies had obtained more than 30,000 patents related to NEVs, accounting for 70% of the global total. Since 2015, China has been leading the global market in the cumulative number of patents related to pure EVs, which are currently the most important type of NEVs.

The development of NEVs is a good example of disruptive technological competition:

- The core technology of EVs is largely independent from that of gasoline-powered vehicles. EVs do not have the same components as gasoline-powered cars such as engines and transmissions, but instead have electric motors and batteries. Traditional automotive components and technology—where traditional car manufacturers have an advantage—are no longer required in the manufacture of EVs.
- At the initial stage of development of NEVs around 2000, the accumulated technology in China was not significantly different from that in Japan and the United States, whose companies were the first to initiate R&D in this field. In terms of pure EV technology, they were basically on the same starting line.
- The rate of development of NEVs is faster than that for traditional gasoline-powered vehicles. The development cycle of a new generation of NEV is 1–2 years, compared to 4–6 years for traditional vehicles.
- China lacks oil resources. Over 70% of China's annual oil consumption comes from imports, so China urgently needs to develop new energy sources to replace fossil fuels. Fortunately, China possesses abundant reserves of critical minerals such as lithium (used for NEV batteries), iron, manganese, graphene, and graphite, which are key materials for NEVs.

- By transitioning from traditional internal combustion engine vehicles to develop NEVs, China has significantly reduced patent barriers to its automotive industry. China has leveraged its profound technical expertise in EVs to become the world's largest supplier of EV batteries, accounting for one-third of the world's capacity.
- China is the largest automobile consumer market in the world. Moreover, due to its large population, China's automobile market is far from saturated. According to statistics from the World Bank, vehicle ownership per thousand people is 837 in the United States, about 600 in Japan and Europe, and only 173 in China. This huge scale of the market and its growth potential provides a solid foundation for the development of the NEV industry.
- The Chinese government has implemented a series of policies to support the development and growth of the NEV industry. Starting in 2001, industrial policies at all levels of government in China have supported the industry through: R&D promotion (2001–2008), demonstration and promotion (2009–2015), consumption incentives (2013–2017), and institutional support (2017 and beyond). The NEV industry in China entered a mature stage in 2017, and its rapid and high-quality development has been mainly driven by market since then.[2]

The development of the automobile industry is crucial for the development of a country's manufacturing industry. The automobile industry did not exist in 1900. In 1920, the value-added of the US automobile industry reached $347 million. By 1929, the United States had become the largest automobile manufacturing country in the world, and the automobile industry had become the largest industry in the United States. Although it started about 30 years later than the United States and Europe, Japan became the world's largest automobile producer in 1980, with an annual output of 13.5 million vehicles.

With the rapid development of the NEV industry, the global market share of China's automobile industry has been increasing. In 2013, China surpassed Japan for the first time to be the world's largest automobile producer. In 2022, China's automobile production and sales were first in the world for the 14th consecutive year, at 27.021 million units and 26.864 million units, respectively. Total retail sales of automobiles reached 4.58 trillion RMB, accounting for 10.41% of total retail sales of consumer goods. NEVs have provided China with the opportunity to leapfrog in the automobile industry, and reshape the global automobile and related manufacturing industries.

When an industry undergoes a disruptive technological change, the whole structure of the industry will change, with the leading companies in the old

[2] Wang Yong, Xu Wan, Zhao Qiuyun, Liu Changzheng, "How China's New Energy Vehicle Industry Achieved Successful Development—An Analysis Based on New Structural Economics," *Economic Theory and Business Management* (in Chinese), 2023, 43(9): 39–54.

technology replaced by new leading companies. For example, in the era of functional mobile phones in 2005, the top five firms were Nokia, Motorola, Samsung, LG, and Sony Ericsson; but in the era of smartphones in 2020, the top five firms were Samsung, Huawei, Apple, Xiaomi, and OPPO—80% of the earlier top five firms had exited the market.

Table 10.1 shows the structure of the automobile industry in 2021. Toyota ranks first in the world in sales (in terms of both units and revenue). However, it ranks second in market value, falling behind EV maker Tesla. Market value reflects the market's expectations regarding a company's future profits. The fact that Toyota's market value is lower than Tesla's indicates that the market is less optimistic about Toyota's future profits. It suggests that traditional automotive companies may not maintain their positions, and there is even a risk that some of them may exit the market.

Why would traditional automotive giants face a greater challenge in transitioning to NEVs? Consider Toyota. Most of Toyota's executives come from the traditional gasoline-powered car business. If Toyota transitions to making NEVs, its current senior executives would have to abandon their considerable human and physical capital investments in the traditional automobile industry and become experts in NEVs. That would be a mission impossible for most of them and they might have to leave their executive positions. Therefore, even if the transition to NEVs aligns with the company's long-term interests, it would not align with the interests of the company's executives. As long as they can still make profits by selling gasoline-powered cars, they will maintain the existing production line and continue to produce gasoline-powered cars.

Table 10.1 Sales, revenue, and market value of top ten companies in the automotive industry

Rank	*Top ten auto companies by sales, 2021 (Ten thousand units)*		*Top ten auto companies by sales revenue, 2021 ($ billion)*		*Top ten auto companies by market value, 2021 ($ billion)*	
1	Toyota	1050	Toyota	25.7	Tesla	728.88
2	Volkswagen	890	Volkswagen	25.4	Toyota	226.46
3	Renault-Nissan-Mitsubishi	763	Daimler	17.6	BYD	121.91
4	Stellantis	667	Ford	12.7	Volkswagen	117.09
5	General Motors	629	Honda	12.4	Mercedes-Benz	77.24
6	Hyundai	538	General Motors	12.2	BMW	58.13
7	Honda	455	BMW	11.3	General Motors	54.84
8	Ford	394	SAIC Motor	10.8	Ford	53.31
9	Suzuki	282	FAW Group	10.1	Stellantis	46.33
10	BMW	252	Hyundai	8.8	Honda	42.69

Source Bufan Think Tank, Fortune and Global Times

However, when the market no longer demands gasoline-powered cars, these traditional automotive giants will fall into the "leader's dilemma" like what happened to Kodak. A large ship is hard to turn around. At that point, the company would be more likely to go bankrupt and exit the market than to achieve a successful transition to NEVs. Just like what happened in the mobile phone industry, 80% of the companies in Table 10.1 that have dominated the global automobile industry for almost a hundred years could end up exiting the industry.

10.5.2 US-China Competition in Incremental Technological Innovation

In the competition for disruptive technological innovation, the United States may succumb to the "leader's dilemma." However, in the competition for incremental technological innovation, China and the United States are engaged in an R&D investment race and the United States is doing its utmost to push China into the "chaser's trap" at each stage of the innovation-market cycle.

R&D investment. The US government has been targeting China's high-tech industry since the 2018 US-China trade war. In the first phase of the trade negotiations, the Trump administration explicitly demanded that China refrain from implementing the high-tech policies outlined in its *Made in China 2025* Ten-Year Plan, arguing that such policies violated market principles and constituted unfair competition. This approach is remarkably similar to the one used against Japan in the 1980s, as described in Sect. 10.3.3. The intention is to reduce China's high-tech R&D investment by curbing government support for it. Under the Biden administration, "countering China" has become a popular political stance in the United States. As noted in Chapter 9, the 2022 CHIPS and Science Act allocates $52.7 billion to the US chip industry, and $200 billion to support US high-tech R&D. Additionally, the Act includes provisions that prohibit companies receiving US federal funding from investing in China's semiconductor sector. The United States is increasing its own R&D investment while suppressing China's.

Technological progress. In October 2022, the United States launched an unprecedented and comprehensive attack on the entire Chinese chip industry chain. High-performance chips and computers were included in the Commerce Control List of items and are subject to export control. The approach aimed to hobble China's development in high-tech industries like supercomputers and semiconductors by preventing Chinese companies from obtaining US equipment, technology, and raw materials. The restrictions extended globally, prohibiting the export of US equipment and technology for manufacturing chips more advanced than the 14 nm process, as well as items produced using such US equipment or technology, to China from any country. Moreover, American citizens are prohibited from engaging in chip development or manufacturing in China without the permission of the US government.

Market share. The US government is using sanctions to reduce the global market share of China's leading high-tech companies. Take the case of Huawei, described in Chapter 5. In 2019, Huawei's smartphone shipments ranked second in the world, capturing 17.6% of the world market, surpassing Apple and only 4 percentage points behind first-ranked Samsung. The US government's crackdown on Huawei led to a sharp decline in Huawei's global smartphone market share. In 2020, Huawei's smartphone shipments fell by 21.5%, and its global ranking fell below Apple to third in the world. In 2021, Huawei divested its Honor smartphone business and fell out of the top five list of global smartphone manufacturers.

Profit realization. The increase in the world market share of US high-tech products has increased the profits of US companies and strengthened their financial position. In the second quarter of 2021, Apple captured 75% of global mobile phone profits even though its global market share was only 13%.

The United States is engaging in intense and comprehensive technological competition with China in all stages of the innovation-market cycle. It is using the same playbook as in the US-Japan semiconductor war in the 1980s, aiming to steer China into the "chaser's trap" like it did to Japan. Will this strategy be successful? What measures should China take to avoid the "chaser's trap"?

Two Misunderstandings About Great Power Technological Competition

Before discussing China's response strategy, two questions need to be clarified. First, can a great power succeed in technological competition without government intervention in the market? The answer is no, sometimes quite the opposite! Second, can a great power succeed in technological competition solely through government interventions without regard to the market? The answer is also no! These two questions represent common misunderstandings about great power technological competition.

In the competition for incremental technology, free-market forces could give rise to multiple equilibria. One equilibrium may be the "chaser's trap," where China specializes in manufacturing using outdated technology. When the United States upsets China's innovation-market cycle, the technological progress of Chinese semiconductor companies will slow down, resulting in a decrease in their market share and an increase in the market share of US companies. As discussed in Sect. 10.3.2, market share has a direct impact on a company's technological progress: companies with a bigger market share not only have higher profits, but also receive more feedback from consumers for improving their product, hence they can make more R&D investments and faster technological improvements than companies with a smaller market share. In other words, US companies like Apple, with their bigger market share, will experience a positive or virtuous innovation-market cycle of faster technological progress, expanding market share, more profits, and more R&D investment, while Chinese companies, with their smaller market share, will experience a negative or vicious innovation-market cycle of slower technological progress, shrinking market share, lower profits, and less R&D investment.

To avoid the "chaser's trap," the Chinese government needs to intervene in the free market through industrial policies, enabling its high-tech companies to jump out of the "chaser's trap" equilibrium with its vicious innovation-market cycle and transition to the equilibrium with the virtuous innovation-market cycle.

The most successful example of government-organized large-scale operations in China is the *Two Bombs One Satellite* project in the 1960s in response to the US government's threats to deploy nuclear weapons against military targets in China. What is the difference between the *Two Bombs One Satellite* project and the current competition in science and technology between the United States and China? The former represented technological breakthroughs carried out under essentially closed market conditions, while the latter is a competition in the open world market. The goal of the former was to strengthen China's military power, while the goal of the latter is to achieve optimal long-term economic growth for China. A large-scale operation like China's nuclear program can be organized and managed in a military way, but long-term economic growth must be based on the market. Innovation-driven long-term growth involves economic activities by thousands of profit-maximizing enterprises over a long period of time, and it cannot be separated from the market. China can only win the competition by changing the market environment for its high-tech firms and helping them to succeed in technological innovation.

Paving the Way for Technological Catch-Up

Let's consider the process of upgrading semiconductor technology. This is illustrated in Fig. 10.3. Chip technology has evolved step by step from the 45 nm process to the 32 nm, 28 nm, and 14 nm and today's 7 nm and 3 nm process. Leading American companies have achieved 3 nm chip technology, while Chinese companies have reached the 14 nm level. The United States is working very hard to block Chinese companies from acquiring technology more advanced than 14 nm.

Why can't Chinese companies catch up to the advanced chip technology by upgrading step by step from the existing 14 nm process technology available domestically to 7 nm process and even 3 nm process technology? The reason is that upgrading from the 14 nm process to the 7 nm process does not simply require a technology breakthrough by Chinese companies, but also requires sufficient market demand to motivate these profit-making companies to develop more advanced chips. Even in the Chinese domestic market, there has been no demand for Chinese-made chips more advanced than 14 nm process. Why? Because demand for high-end chips in China has been met by imports embodying US technology. In this sense, US high-tech companies

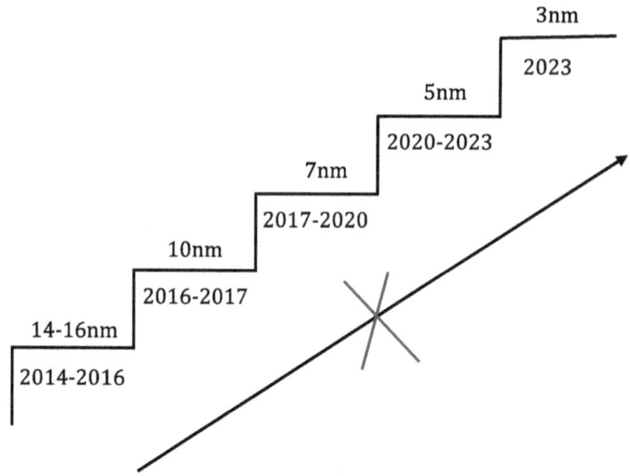

Fig. 10.3 Progress of chip manufacturing process

monopolize China's domestic high-end chip market, creating an insurmountable hurdle for Chinese high-tech companies to develop their own high-end chips.

US containment of China's technological progress is not simply a technological blockade, but rather a deliberate effort to create an environment that shunts Chinese and American companies into separate specializations. To be more specific, the intention is to have American companies specialize in more advanced technology and Chinese companies specialize in less advanced technology so that the United States' dominant position in the high-tech industry is maintained. Therefore, the United States is, in a sense, monopolizing the Chinese market for chips below 14 nm while vigorously blocking Chinese chipmakers from acquiring the technology to make their own high-end chips.

Let's take smartphone chips as an example. Smartphones are usually built on top of a silicon chipset (chip) that serves as the "brain" of the device. The manufacturing process of a chip is typically specified in nanometers—generally speaking, the smaller the nm size, the smaller the internal components of the chip and the better it is for power efficiency and compactness.

The main smartphones sold in China are from Apple, Honor, Huawei, OPPO, Redmi, Samsung, VIVO, and Xiaomi. Advanced chip technology and production are controlled by companies in the United States and its allies, while lower-end smartphone components are made by Chinese companies. Apple uses the 3 nm Apple A17 chip, while Honor, OPPO, Redmi, Samsung, VIVO, and Xiaomi use the 7 nm Qualcomm Snapdragon chip, both of which are owned by US companies. Therefore, the smartphone market in China is still dominated by American technology. When Huawei dared to challenge US dominance in high-end chip technology, the US government banned the sales of equipment to Huawei and sought to persuade its allies to do the same.

If there is no demand for Chinese-made high-end chips in the smartphone market, how can China catch up in chip technology?

The key to catching up is to create market demand for Chinese-made chips through government intervention. Core technology, no matter how advanced, cannot be 100% dominated by foreign companies. Instead, Chinese government can take measures to ensure that a certain share of the domestic market (e.g., 30%) must be occupied by domestic technology. That essentially constitutes a technology security policy. With such a policy, if there is a foreign embargo, at least 30% of the market could still be served by domestic technologies. Moreover, if about 30% of the domestic market share is served by domestic technology, it can also ensure that domestic technology can substitute world advanced technology to a certain extent, thereby preventing undue vulnerability to external pressures.

How should we design a technological catch-up path or technology security policy? Let's take the mobile phone chip as an example.

First, identify smartphone chip as a national core technology.

Second, the national core technology opposes foreign monopolies. The downstream market demand for chips is mobile phones. Any company selling phones in the Chinese market, whether domestic or foreign, must ensure that at least 30% of the phones they sell in China are equipped with domestically produced Chinese chips. For example, companies such as Apple, Samsung, Huawei, Xiaomi, OPPO, Vivo, and others must ensure that 30% of the total phones they sell in the Chinese market use domestically produced Chinese chips.

Third, for example, let's assume "XiaoGuo" is a company selling mobile phones in the Chinese market. If the volume of "XiaoGuo" mobile phones using Chinese domestic chips falls below 30% of its total shipment volume, which leads to a total reliance on foreign chip technology, the "XiaoGuo" company poses a risk to Chinese technological security. The Chinese government should impose taxes on this mobile phone company. The tax rate levied is based on the proportion of Chinese domestic chips used in its total shipment of mobile phones. The smaller the proportion, the higher the tax rate.

Fourth, according to this policy, there will be two types of the same brand of mobile phones sold in the Chinese market. One uses imported chips, referred to as "XiaoGuo A," and the other uses domestically produced chips, referred to as "XiaoGuo B." When the technology of domestic chips is lower than that of imported chips, the quality of "XiaoGuo B" will be lower than that of "XiaoGuo A," and the market price of "XiaoGuo B" may even be lower than its production cost. If this happens, the government can provide subsidies to the company to ensure that "XiaoGuo B" has a certain profit margin.

We refer to such a policy as the "International Technology Anti-Trust Policy." This policy applies to all products recognized as a core technology. Through such an international technology anti-trust policy, it ensures that the market share of domestic produced technology in China reaches 30%. This not only ensures the technological security of the Chinese market but also promotes market competition for core technology products, preventing a global monopoly of core technology products (such as high-end chips, operating systems).

The "International Technology Anti-Trust Policy" serves as a strategic approach to pave the way for technological catch-up and can serve as a theoretical consideration to prevent China from falling into the "chaser's trap." The key for China to form a virtuous "innovation-market" cycle in the context of great power competition lies in its market share. Only by seizing a certain amount of market share and creating a favorable market environment, Chinese enterprises will choose to catch up, innovate, and surpass according to the comparative advantages designed by the government policies.

On August 29, 2023, Huawei introduced its new flagship phone, the Mate 60. The Huawei Mate 60 is equipped with the self-developed Kirin 9000S chip which functions at a level equivalent to the 7 nm process chip. Huawei's technology breakthrough came after three years of relentless efforts by the United States to contain China's high-end chip industry.

It should be pointed out that even a prominent company like Huawei will find difficult to change the competitive environment of the chip market through its efforts alone. The innovation-market cycle for Chinese semiconductor companies cannot be automatically realized by the market and must rely on government policies to nurture and create.

In mid-July 2025, the US government reversed a four-month ban to allow Nvidia to resume exporting its H20 AI chip to China—a device deliberately designed to comply with export rules and priced as a lower-tier offering. This shift aligns with our "innovation-market" cycle theory: the United States aims to preserve its own innovation loop, earn revenue, and keep Chinese firms dependent rather than independent of Western-level chip technology.

By supplying the H20 chip, the United States achieves two objectives: it keeps Chinese firms consuming sub-tier hardware instead of investing in costly full-stack R&D, and it retains commercial presence in a crucial overseas market. In turn, United States revenues can be reinvested into advancing its own R&D and market feedback loop. China's counter is clear: it must institutionalize long-term industrial policies and sustain large-scale investment to avoid the "chaser's trap." Without that coordinated commitment, the H20 move will effectively stall China's drive toward independent AI-chip leadership.

The outcome of technological competition between China and the United States will determine the long-term growth of both countries and the reform of the world order. China has a comparative advantage in disruptive technological innovations, but it needs to strive hard to avoid falling into the "chaser's trap" in incremental technological innovations. The country that can achieve a virtuous innovation-market cycle will win the technological competition.

CHAPTER 11

International Financial Competition

In Chapter 7, we discussed the fundamental misalignment between the global economic fundamentals and the international monetary system (IMS), that is, the mismatch between the tripod structure of the GVC and the dollar-dominated IMS. Because of the dominant position of the dollar internationally, the United States has been able to gain an advantage in international finance relative to other countries. This has been manifested in three main aspects: global inflation, global capital flow volatility, and financial sanctions.

Because of the international status of the US dollar, the United States is able to obtain more seigniorage revenue by issuing a large amount of US dollars through expansionary monetary policy than it could if the dollar were not a dominant international currency. This revenue can be invested domestically in infrastructure, high-tech R&D, and key industries, thereby strengthening the US real economy and reconfiguring the GVC. However, continuous large-scale issuance of US dollars triggers capital inflow surges in other countries and will eventually trigger global inflation. In fact, the massive amount of US dollars issued by the Federal Reserve during the 2008 global financial crisis and the 2020 COVID-19 pandemic has played a significant role in the global inflation that began in 2022.

To combat rising inflation, the Federal Reserve tightened monetary policy and raised interest rates, causing the US dollar to appreciate significantly against other major currencies. As a result, international capital flowed back to the United States, triggering a surge of capital outflows from other countries.

The United States uses the dollar for financial sanctions. When the Russia-Ukraine conflict broke out at the end of February 2022, the United States and other developed economies such as the European Union launched multiple

J. Ju, *US-China Great Power Competition and The New World Order*, https://doi.org/10.1007/978-981-95-3762-4_11

rounds of financial sanctions against Russia. These measures included cutting off major Russian banks from the international payment settlement channel, the Society for Worldwide Interbank Financial Telecommunication (SWIFT), interrupting Russia's US dollar trade settlement; freezing the foreign exchange reserves and related overseas assets of the Russian central bank, controlling Russia's overseas financing channels; and imposing financial sanctions on Russian individuals and entities. As a result of US and EU sanctions, Russia's cross-border foreign exchange transactions shrank by 80% in just a few weeks, and its foreign debt defaults spiraled out of control. In 2022, Russia's GDP fell by more than 1.2%.

Since the onset of the Russia-Ukraine conflict in 2022, the world situation has changed dramatically. The risk of US financial blockades and sanctions against China has greatly increased—the Biden administration has already warned China that it would face consequences if it helped Russia evade sanctions.[1] The competition between the United States and China for leadership in the international financial system has become increasingly fierce. How should China respond?

China's objective is to prevent the risks of a financial crisis and a possible financial blockade by the United States. On this basis, China should promote the internationalization of the renminbi, the reform of the IMS, and ultimately, the establishment of a tripod IMS that matches the tripod GVC structure, thereby resolving the fundamental misalignment between the structures of the global real economy and the IMS.

Preventing a financial crisis requires managing cross-border capital flows. Preventing a financial blockade requires accelerating the opening of China's capital account and the pace of renminbi internationalization. These two tasks seem to point in opposite directions. How can China accomplish these two seemingly contradictory tasks at the same time? The answer is to make disruptive innovations in the international financial system!

Recall the discussion on technological competition in Chapter 10, where the key point was to distinguish between disruptive technological competition and incremental technological competition. As a latecomer to the current international financial system, China has a comparative advantage in disruptive innovations. In this chapter, we will highlight two disruptive innovations in the international financial system: one is the innovation of new monetary policy tools, and the other is the innovation of new digital currency technology. But first, we will describe the anatomy of a financial crisis, and then discuss how to prevent risks of international financial crises and financial blockade risks through these innovations.

[1] See: https://www.reuters.com/world/white-house-adviser-discuss-russias-war-ukraine-with-chinas-top-diplomat-source-2022-03-13/, accessed on November 29, 2023.

11.1 Financial Crises

As discussed in Chapter 9, a financial crisis can be described as a self-fulfilling, preventable vicious cycle. Historically, there have been many types of financial crises, such as currency crises, banking crises, and debt crises, and what starts out as one type of crisis can quickly develop into another type. The Asian financial crisis in 1997 was a classic and painful case.

11.1.1 The Asian Financial Crisis

The crisis started in Thailand. Before 1997, Thailand had a de facto fixed exchange rate policy, with $1 exchanged for 25 Thai baht. In the early 1990s, Thailand maintained high growth in exports and GDP. At that time, Thailand's capital account was open, and it was easy to borrow money from abroad without exchange rate risk. As a result, a large amount of foreign capital flooded into Thailand. In 1996, Thailand's foreign debt exceeded 60% of its GDP. What was all this foreign debt used for? A large amount of it was invested in real estate across the country. According to *Bangkok Post Economic Review Year-End 1996*, loans from financial institutions to property developers in Thailand totaled 264 billion baht in 1993; by the end of June 1996, the loans reached 768 billion baht.[2]

In the mid-1990s, the rise in US interest rates led to the appreciation of the US dollar, and the Thai baht also appreciated accordingly. The appreciation of the baht, coupled with China's strong export growth, contributed to a decline in Thailand's export competitiveness. Thailand's exports fell, resulting in a huge trade deficit after 1996. The bubble in Thailand's real estate market burst, and the stock market fell by 60%. A large amount of foreign capital fled from the country.

The economic problems created an opportunity for foreign investors to launch a speculative attack on the Thai baht. Financial tycoon George Soros saw that there were severe asset bubbles in Thailand's property, stock, and foreign exchange markets, and that Thailand had almost no restrictions on capital flows. Soros' financial attack was simple and brutal: he borrowed a large amount of Thai baht from Thai banks, then sold the baht and bought dollars at the official exchange rate of 25 baht to $1, betting on unwinding the transaction at a devalued exchange rate. Rumors of a currency devaluation caused massive sales of the Thai baht in exchange for dollars and the baht faced strong devaluation pressure. Although the Bank of Thailand used a large amount of its foreign exchange reserves to intervene in the market in an attempt to maintain the fixed exchange rate, it was too late—the momentum of devaluation was like an avalanche. On July 2, 1997, Thailand was forced to

[2] Parnsoonthorn Krissana 1996 "*Year-End 96 Economic Review*" Bangkok Post, December, 1996.

abandon the fixed exchange rate. The Thai baht depreciated by 17% on that day, triggering the shocking Asian financial crisis.

How big was the impact of this financial crisis? The depreciation of the Thai baht reached 40%; more than half of the country's financial institutions declared a halt to business; and more than 10,000 companies went bankrupt. The number of unemployed reached 2.7 million, and almost all of Thailand's GDP for 1997 was lost. Shi Lihua, a manager of a stock investment company in Thailand, was a billionaire before the financial crisis. During the bubble years, he invested all his money in real estate. When the real estate bubble burst and housing prices plummeted by more than 45%, Shi went bankrupt overnight and had no choice but to make a living selling sandwiches made by his wife on the street every day. If this could happen to a billionaire, one can only imagine the plight of ordinary people in Thailand. Soaring prices and the sharp increase in unemployment led to a rising crime rates, and the Prime Minister, who had just taken office less than a year ago, had to resign.

The financial crisis not only severely damaged Thailand's economy, but also spread to other Asian economies such as Indonesia, Malaysia, and South Korea, leading to a wave of financial crises that swept across Asia. After Soros and other speculators successfully shorted the Thai baht, they swept across Southeast Asia. In October 1997, they turned to Hong Kong, which had been handed back to China less than three months earlier. The comprehensive attack on the Hong Kong dollar in the foreign exchange, stock, and futures markets lasted for more than ten months. At a critical moment, China's central government announced that the renminbi would not depreciate and expressed firm support for the Hong Kong dollar. Under the strong resistance of the Hong Kong Special Administrative Region government, the hedge funds failed to destroy the Hong Kong dollar and they retreated in defeat.

The situation after 2022—with the reversal of the Federal Reserve's monetary policy, the appreciation of the US dollar, and large-scale capital flows back to the United States—has many developing countries (emerging market economies) concerned about a possible repeat of the Asian financial crisis. Why do financial crises happen? This is what we will explain in the rest of this section.

11.1.2 Self-Fulfilling Vicious Cycle

A currency crisis (or exchange rate crisis) is typically defined in the empirical academic literature as a situation where a country's currency depreciates by more than 15% against the US dollar within a certain period, accompanied by a sharp drop in the stock market, a surge in unemployment, and a decline in total economic output. According to our definition in Chapter 9, this malign depreciation of the exchange rate is a self-fulfilling vicious cycle, as illustrated in Fig. 11.1.

The foreign exchange market is in a state of dynamic equilibrium. In economics, market equilibrium typically refers to supply equaling demand,

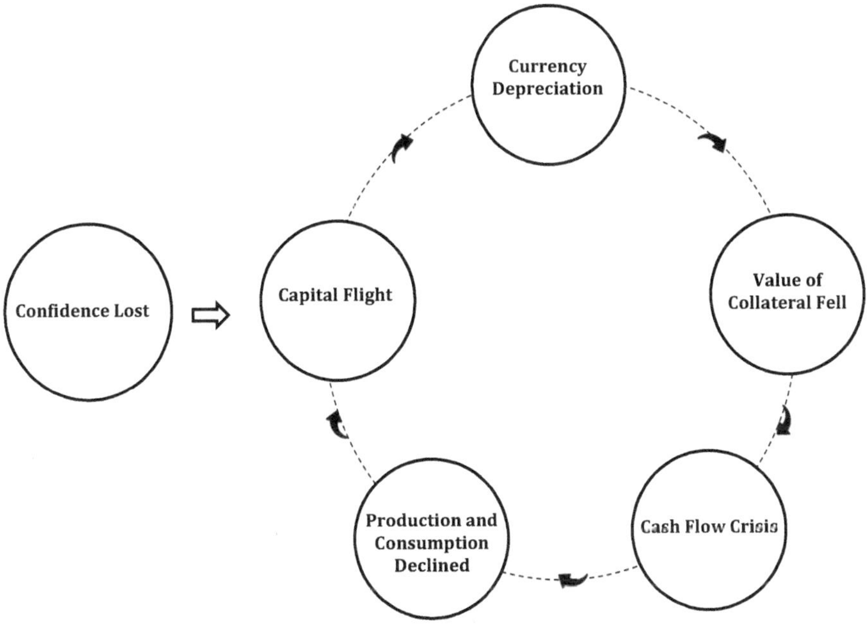

Fig. 11.1 Currency crisis: a self-fulfilling vicious cycle

and the equilibrating factor is price. The price in the currency market is the exchange rate, that is, the price of the local currency in US dollars. All else constant, when demand for the local currency rises, the exchange rate appreciates (the price of the local currency in US dollars goes up); when the demand for the local currency falls, the exchange rate depreciates (the price of the local currency in US dollars goes down). There exist multiple solutions, or exchange rates, that can equilibrate the demand for a currency with its supply. In other words, there are multiple equilibria in the foreign exchange market. For example, $1 to 25 Thai baht could be an equilibrium exchange rate, which we call the normal equilibrium, and $1 to 40 Thai baht could also be an equilibrium exchange rate, which we call the crisis equilibrium. If everyone has confidence in the Thai baht, the exchange rate would settle in the normal equilibrium. If everyone loses confidence in the Thai baht, the baht would depreciate until it reaches the crisis equilibrium.

As illustrated in Fig. 11.1, once confidence in a currency is lost, it will bring about a self-fulfilling vicious cycle. When Thailand's real estate and banking sectors plummeted, investors expected the Thai economy to contract. Under this pessimistic expectation, capital flowed out of the economy, causing the exchange rate to depreciate. The depreciation of the exchange rate caused the value of collateral (such as real estate) in US dollars to fall. The fall in the dollar value of collateral made it more difficult for firms and banks to borrow from abroad, which caused investment, production, and consumption to further decline, confirming investors' pessimistic expectations of the Thai economy, and triggering capital outflows again, in a vicious cycle that continued until the exchange rate reached its new (crisis) equilibrium of $1 to 40 baht. Moving from the normal equilibrium to the crisis equilibrium came at a cost: Thailand's GDP fell by 10% compared to before the crisis, and the stock market fell by 60%.

Although financial crises may originate in the financial market, they can cause a huge blow to the real economy. After the Asian financial crisis, it took many years for the real economies of the affected countries to recover.

To understand why financial crises happen, we need to understand an important concept in international finance called interest rate parity.

11.1.3 Interest Rate Parity

From the example of the Asian financial crisis, we find that there are three key variables in a currency crisis: the exchange rate, the interest rate, and the degree of liberalization of capital flows. The relationship between the exchange rate and the interest rate is enshrined in a basic concept in international finance called interest rate parity (IRP). The IRP formula is an arbitrage condition.

To illustrate, let's suppose that both China and the United States have free capital mobility, meaning that a Chinese resident can freely exchange renminbi for US dollars and invest in the United States, and a US resident can freely exchange US dollars for renminbi and invest in China. Suppose you have 70,000 RMB in China. The annual deposit interest rate in a bank in China is 3%, and the annual deposit interest rate in a bank in the United States is 1%. Assuming today's (spot) exchange rate is 7 RMB to $1, where would you invest your 70,000 RMB?

The first option is to deposit it directly in a Chinese bank. With 70,000 RMB at a 3% interest rate, you will receive 2,100 RMB in interest after one year, and your total principal plus interest will be $70{,}000 \times (1 + 3\%) = 72{,}100$ RMB.

The second option is to deposit it in a US bank. You will first need to exchange your renminbi for US dollars before you can deposit it in a US bank. At today's spot exchange rate, your 70,000 RMB can be exchanged for $10,000, which, at a 1% interest rate, will yield $100 in interest after one year, and a total principal plus interest of $\$(10{,}000 \times (1 + 1\%)) = \$10{,}100$. Then you will need to change this back to renminbi using the one-year forward exchange rate, so the total in renminbi will be equal to $10,100 times the forward exchange rate.

If the forward exchange rate is equal to today's spot exchange rate, that is, the renminbi does not appreciate or depreciate and the exchange rate stays at 7 RMB to $1, then $10,100 will be equal to 70,700 RMB after one year, which is less than the 72,100 RMB you would get from depositing your funds in a bank in China. In this case, everyone would choose to deposit their money in China. But if the renminbi is expected to depreciate in a year, for example, to an exchange rate of 7.50 RMB to $1, then depositing your funds in a US bank for a year would yield 10,100 × 7.50 = 75,750 RMB, which is more than the 72,100 RMB you would get from a bank in China. In this case, people would choose to deposit their money in the United States.

In fact, there are many investors in the market making such decisions every second. This arbitrage condition is the (covered) IRP formula[3]:

$$1 + \text{RMB interest rate} = \left(\frac{\text{Forward rate}}{\text{Spot rate}}\right)(1 + \$\ \text{interest rate})$$

Looking at this formula, we can see that only when both sides of the equation are equal—that is, when a return of $10,100 is equivalent to a return of 72,100 RMB one year later—will Chinese residents be indifferent between depositing their funds in China or the United States today, and the foreign exchange market will be in equilibrium. The one-year forward exchange rate that would ensure this equilibrium is equal to 72,100/10,100 = 7.14 RMB to $1. If the one-year forward exchange rate is higher than 7.14 RMB to $1, then everyone will prefer to deposit their money in the United States. If the one-year forward exchange rate is lower than 7.14 RMB to $1, everyone will prefer to deposit their money in China. As long as the forward exchange rate does not meet the IRP condition, arbitrage opportunities will exist.

The IRP formula links the interest rates of China and the United States and the current and expected future exchange rates in a situation where capital is allowed to flow freely in and out of both countries. The interest rate is the central tool in monetary policy: a lower interest rate indicates an expansionary monetary policy, while a higher interest rate indicates a contractionary monetary policy.

Here is a question: can a country simultaneously maintain a fixed exchange rate, an independent monetary policy, and allow free capital flows? The answer is no, which leads us to the famous "trilemma" or "impossible trinity," which we will discuss next.

11.1.4 *The Trilemma*

The so-called trilemma in international finance theory is that a country can only achieve two of the following three conditions simultaneously: (1) free capital mobility (that is, an open external capital account); (2) a fixed exchange rate; and (3) an independent monetary policy. This is usually explained using a picture like Fig. 11.2.

[3] Covered interest parity (CIP) is a no-arbitrage condition involving forward contracts to hedge exchange rate risk, making it risk-free. Uncovered interest rate parity (UIP) is based on the expectation of future exchange rates and carries inherent risk due to exchange rate uncertainty, that is, there are no forward rate contracts, and it uses only the expected spot rate.

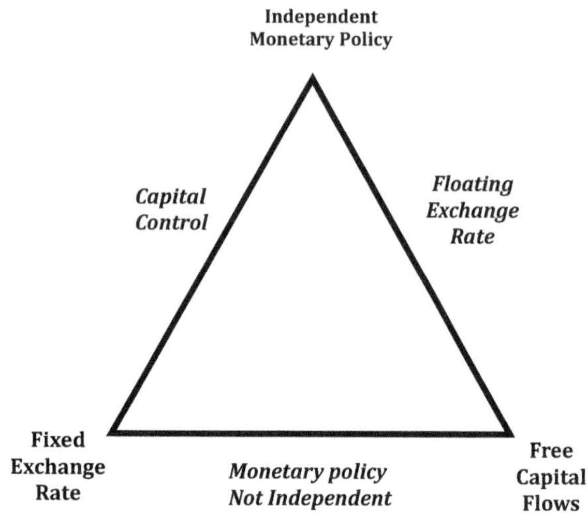

Fig. 11.2 The trilemma

Scenario 1: Free capital mobility + fixed exchange rate → monetary policy cannot be independent. Suppose China has a fixed exchange rate vis-à-vis the US dollar and its capital account is fully open. Since Chinese residents can invest their renminbi in China or exchange their renminbi to US dollars and invest in the United States, the IRP condition must hold. And since the exchange rate is fixed, the forward exchange rate will be equal to the spot exchange rate. Therefore, the IRP condition becomes: *RMB interest rate = US dollar interest rate*. Since the interest rate is the main monetary policy tool, this means that China's monetary policy will be tied to US monetary policy. This is the situation in Hong Kong, China: the Hong Kong dollar is pegged to the US dollar, and capital flows freely in and out of Hong Kong, so Hong Kong's monetary policy is tied to US monetary policy; and therefore Hong Kong's monetary policy is not independent.

Scenario 2: Free capital mobility + independent monetary policy → exchange rate cannot be fixed. Suppose China has an open capital account and independence to conduct its own monetary policy. As in the first scenario, the IRP condition must hold. If China's monetary policy is independent of US monetary policy, the RMB interest rate need not equal the US dollar interest rate. Then the forward exchange rate will not be equal to the spot exchange rate. In other words, the exchange rate cannot be fixed; there must be some form of floating exchange rate system. This is the situation in many developed countries, like Japan and the United States.

Scenario 3: Fixed exchange rate + independent monetary policy → capital cannot be allowed to flow freely. China can maintain a fixed exchange rate and yet have the independence to conduct its own monetary policy (that is, set its interest rate independently of the US interest rate) only if the IRP condition does not apply. This means that the capital account cannot be fully open. Before December 2019, China was close to this third scenario: it had a basically fixed exchange rate, an independent monetary policy, and it maintained restrictions on cross-border capital flows.

In summary, a country can choose one of the three scenarios described above, but an open capital account, fixed exchange rate, and independent monetary policy cannot coexist. Attempting to achieve all three at the same time inevitably leads to a currency crisis. This is the famous trilemma in international financial economics.

Of course, a country's exchange rate and monetary policy regime can change as time goes by. During the Bretton Woods system from 1944 to 1973, exchange rates between major developed countries were fixed, and countries like Japan, Germany, the United Kingdom, and France had restrictions on capital flows to maintain a certain degree of monetary policy independence. In the post-Bretton Woods era, as countries increasingly liberalized their capital accounts, it became more and more difficult for them to tie their monetary policy to US monetary policy. In 1973, the Bretton Woods system collapsed, and these countries had to abandon their fixed exchange rate to the US dollar and let their currencies float.

Now let's return to the initial question of why financial crises occur. As discussed earlier, the foreign exchange market does not necessarily have a unique, stable equilibrium: when investors expect the exchange rate to depreciate for some reason, market forces may not automatically restore the exchange rate to its original equilibrium but instead, may trigger a self-fulfilling vicious cycle of capital outflows and further pessimistic expectations from investors until the exchange rate actually does depreciate. Of course, many factors can trigger the expectation of an exchange rate depreciation, such as the bursting of a real estate market bubble, an economic downturn, and so on. However, one of the lessons learned from the Asian financial crisis is that a fixed exchange rate system with an open capital account may bring the risk of a currency crisis. On the one hand, a fixed exchange rate is beneficial for price level stability and export growth. On the other hand, the fixed exchange rate leaves the country without monetary policy tools to respond to sudden capital inflow and outflow surges that tend to happen with an open capital account.

11.1.5 China's Exchange Rate Reforms

China's monetary system is undergoing reforms. In the past, China mainly adopted a fixed exchange rate vis-à-vis the US dollar. At the same time, because China's development stage and business cycle differed from those of the United States, China needed to be able to conduct its own monetary policy independent of the United States'. As we know from the trilemma, this required that China's capital account not be fully open, and there had to be certain restrictions on cross-border capital flows into and out of China.

The reform of the exchange rate regime from a fixed exchange rate to a floating exchange rate is progressing step by step. Here are two examples of the reform of the exchange rate regime in China.

The 8.11 Exchange Rate Reform

On August 11, 2015, the People's Bank of China (PBOC) changed the reference pricing mechanism system for the renminbi exchange rate to better reflect market developments. The reform established that the central parity of the renminbi's exchange rate against the US dollar would be set with reference to the previous trading day's closing price. This policy change was combined with a 1.9% devaluation of the renminbi relative to the dollar.

The announcement of the reform caused the financial markets, already nervous about a sharp slowdown in growth in China and the sharp drop in the Chinese stock market, to panic. The renminbi depreciated by more than 3% in four trading days, and there were indications of large-scale capital outflows from China. The PBOC quickly started selling dollars and buying renminbi in the foreign exchange market to stabilize the exchange rate, it consumed nearly $1 trillion of its foreign reserves in less than a year. The 8.11 Exchange Rate Reform was a brave attempt to move toward a more flexible and market-driven exchange rate, but it was not successful and was eventually abandoned.

In February 2016, the PBOC implemented a new rule where the central parity rate would take into account not just the previous trading day's closing price, but also the (theoretical) exchange rate that would keep the index of the China Foreign Exchange Trade System, a 24-currency basket, unchanged over the previous 24 hours. This new rule managed to stabilize market expectations and alleviate capital outflow pressures. Later, in July 2017, the PBOC introduced counter-cyclical factors into its rate-setting formula and selectively used them according to market conditions, in order to correct for "big market swings" and limit the flexibility of the renminbi exchange rate to a certain extent.

The Renminbi "Breaking 7"

On August 1, 2019, the day after the twelfth round of US-China trade talks ended, the United States suddenly announced plans to impose a 10% tariff on approximately $300 billion of goods imported from China. The rapid shift in market sentiment caused the renminbi to depreciate. The markets expected the PBOC to use various means such as selling foreign reserves to keep the exchange rate below the psychologically important threshold of 7 RMB to $1. But on August 5, 2019, the renminbi depreciated to more than 7 RMB to $1 for the first time in ten years. The PBOC did not intervene to stop the depreciation, and panic did not occur—the markets showed surprising calmness, with no one-sided depreciation expectations and no wave of Chinese residents buying foreign currency. After that, two-way fluctuations of the renminbi exchange rate became more accepted and exchange rate flexibility increased. After "breaking 7" the renminbi is basically on a managed floating regime, according to the PBOC.[4]

11.2 Financial Sanctions

In addition to taking action to prevent a financial crisis, China also needs to protect itself against possible financial sanctions by the United States. As mentioned in Chapter 9, the United States has often used its dominant position in the IMS to impose financial sanctions on its enemies. Besides Russia, countries such as Afghanistan, Iran, Myanmar, North Korea, and South Africa have been subjected to US financial sanctions.

Financial sanctions by the United States may include the following measures: freezing the assets and/or transactions of sanctioned entities or individuals (government officials, entrepreneurs, et cetera) under US jurisdiction; restricting sanctioned enterprises from accessing the US stock or bond markets for financing, cutting off their ability to obtain US dollars; restricting access to the infrastructures and institutions that execute international payments such as the SWIFT network, disrupting all cross-border economic activities of the sanctioned party requiring international payments; and prohibiting financial institutions in the United States and other countries from providing direct or indirect financial services to the sanctioned parties.

Take Iran as an example. The United States has imposed sanctions on Iran since 1979 after the seizure of the US embassy in Tehran. Iranian banks are barred from directly accessing the US financial system. In July 2010, the United States introduced the Comprehensive Iran Sanctions, Accountability, and Divestment Act which included mandatory banking sanctions targeted at foreign banks that knowingly facilitate, among other things, significant transactions with Iranian-linked banks designated by the United States. When China's Kunlun Bank was found to have violated this law, the US government prohibited US banks from opening or maintaining correspondent accounts in the United States for Kunlun Bank, effectively cutting off its direct access to the US financial system. In 2018, when the United States re-imposed financial sanctions against Iran, the US government told SWIFT that it was expected to comply with the US sanctions against Iran or it could itself face US sanctions; SWIFT subsequently announced that it was suspending some Iranian banks' access to its messaging system.

[4] Renminbi (RMB) is not completely floating. Instead, it operates under a managed float system. The People's Bank of China (PBOC) sets a daily reference rate and allows the RMB to trade within a certain band around this rate. This allows the exchange rate to fluctuate in response to market forces, but within limits set by the central bank.

Take Russia as another example. After the 2014 Crimea crisis broke out, the United States put certain Russian individuals and entities (banks and companies) on its so-called Specially Designated Nationals and Blocked Persons list (SDN list). Individuals and entities on the SDN list have their US assets frozen, and all persons and companies in the United States are barred from doing business with them. After the 2022 Russia-Ukraine conflict broke out, the United States significantly increased the number of sanctioned Russian individuals and entities on the SDN List. The United States and its allies cut off several major Russian banks from the SWIFT system, greatly limiting Russia's cross-border payments, and directly hit the Russian central bank, freezing more than $300 billion of its foreign exchange reserves and assets held in Western countries.

As discussed in Chapter 9, the risk that the United States initiates a military conflict with China is there. If China succumbs to a Japan-type crisis and its technological upgrading and economic growth stagnate, the United States is likely to take advantage of the situation by boosting separatist movements in China and provoking China into a military conflict. If China's economy maintains strong growth and avoids a Japan-type crisis, the contradiction between the tripod structure of the GVC and the dollar-dominated IMS will intensify, and the probability of a dollar crisis will increase. To protect the dollar and strike against the renminbi, the United States could launch a military conflict with China by using a regional proxy like Taiwan. Once China and the United States are involved directly or indirectly in a military conflict, the United States is likely to deploy financial sanctions against China. Therefore, the risk of US financial sanctions against China is real, and China must be prepared for it!

11.3 How to Prevent the Dual Risks of Financial Crisis and Financial Sanctions?

Theoretically, according to the trilemma, if China wants to have exchange rate stability and the ability to conduct its own monetary policy, it will need to manage cross-border capital flows, and maybe even close the capital account, to prevent a financial (currency) crisis. However, closing the capital account and prohibiting cross-border capital flows are exactly the goals that financial sanctions want to achieve. If cross-border capital flows are stopped, China's economy will be effectively closed to the outside world, and China's economic growth will be severely hit—which is also a situation that China would want to avoid. To prevent a currency crisis, China needs to manage cross-border capital flows. To protect itself from financial sanctions, China needs to accelerate the internationalization of the renminbi and the opening up of the capital account. This is a dilemma.

It should be noted that the US dollar has an absolute advantage over the renminbi in the existing IMS. Therefore, using the framework of technological competition in Chapter 10, we can call the United States the leading country and China the chasing country, and we can think of a currency crisis and a financial blockade as two possible chasers' traps for China in the competition between the two countries in the current international financial system. To reverse its disadvantage in the competition, China needs to create "disruptive innovations" in the international financial system so that it can sidestep the United States' advantage in the existing system and induce it to fall into the leader's dilemma.

What are the possible disruptive innovations in the international financial system? We will discuss two possibilities below. The first is a disruptive innovation in capital flow management. The second is a disruptive innovation in international payment technology. We will also discuss how China may use these two types of disruptive innovations to prevent the dual risks of financial crises and financial blockades.

11.3.1 *Disruptive Innovation in Capital Flow Management: Progressive Tax on Cross-Border Capital Flows*

The essence of a financial (currency) crisis is the self-fulfilling vicious cycle, so to prevent a currency crisis, we need to break a link in the vicious cycle in Fig. 11.1. To do so, we propose to add a firewall against capital flow surges—this firewall would not affect the free flow of capital during normal times, but it would slow or stop large-scale capital outflows during crisis times, which could prevent investors' pessimistic expectations from snowballing and thus avert a currency crisis.

The firewall would take the form of a progressive tax on cross-border capital flows. The tax rate would be 0% for "normal" capital flow transaction amounts, and beyond that, the tax rate would increase with the size of the transaction. If the highest marginal tax rate is set sufficiently high, the tax would discourage speculators from attacking the renminbi in order to make a profit.

For example, consider an investor who exchanges renminbi for US dollars in the normal course of business every day, and his average capital transaction is $100 million per day. The tax rate on this normal capital flow is 0%. Suppose the progressive tax thresholds are set at $300 million, $400 million, and $500 million per day, with corresponding marginal tax rates of 5%, 10%, and 30%. This means that for capital flow transactions of less than $300 million per day, the tax rate is 0%; for transactions from $300 million to $399 million, the marginal tax rate is 5%; for transactions from $400 million to $499 million, the marginal tax rate is 10%; and for transactions more than $500 million, the marginal tax rate is 30%. Such a tax could effectively control the scale of capital flight and the extent of currency depreciation during a crisis.

Why would this progressive tax on capital flows prevent a currency crisis? Because a currency crisis is triggered by a speculative attack: short-term, large-scale, malicious speculative trading of currencies. Unlike normal cross-border capital flows, such as foreign direct investment flows and portfolio and equity investment flows, speculative attacks would involve the buying and selling of large amounts of renminbi. With a progressive tax on cross-border capital flows in place, speculative attacks on the renminbi would be much less profitable, so large-scale capital outflow surges would be less likely to occur. If investors do not see a large-scale capital outflow, they would be less likely to panic and behave like a herd by selling off renminbi, and the risk of a large renminbi depreciation would be diminished.

The progressive tax as described above has a loophole: since the tax rate is progressive, won't investors try to evade the tax, for example, by opening several accounts? Since the tax is levied on transactions starting at $300 million, an investor wishing to move $800 million could just open three accounts, with each account having a transaction of less than $300 million.

Indeed, this is a problem. The solution is simple: just add an account opening fee. The firewall would then include two parts: one part being the progressive tax—the larger the capital flow, the higher the effective tax rate; and the other part being the account opening fee—the more accounts an investor opens, the larger the account opening costs. Our calculations show that an appropriate combination of these two parts can ensure that no investor would have capital flows exceeding three times than the normal daily level and no investor, no matter how large his capital flows, would open more than five accounts.

Will adding such a firewall hinder normal cross-border capital flows? The answer is no. Under normal circumstances, the capital flow transaction size would be below the threshold, so the tax would not be activated and the flow of capital would be unimpeded. Only when there is an abnormal surge in capital flows will the tax be activated, in order to prevent speculators from profiting.

Of course, the progressive tax on cross-border capital flows is still an idea at this stage, and further study would be needed to construct a feasible combination of the marginal tax rates and account opening fee. There could be different designs depending on the type of capital flow (bonds, securities, insurance, bank loans, et cetera), the direction of capital flow (inflow or outflow), and the duration of borrowing. Nevertheless, the idea of building a firewall against capital flow surges is a theoretical innovation in capital flow management.[5]

The progressive tax on cross-border capital flows would give China an additional policy tool in its international financial competition with the United States. It would enhance China's policy space for managing the risks of capital flows while maintaining exchange rate stability. For example, when the Federal Reserve tightens monetary policy and raises US interest rates, China

[5] Linear capital flow tax scheme currently adopted by many emerging economies, yet our study shows that does not help to eliminate multiple equilibria and cannot prevent financial crises. In order to prevent financial crisis, we propose that the capital flow tax should be nonlinear, that is, the marginal tax rate increases along with the amount of capital flow. For a detailed discussion, see Ju, Jiandong, Li Li, Guangyu Nie, Kang Shi, and Shang-Jin Wei, "Nonlinear Capital Flow Tax: Capital Flow Management and Financial Crisis Prevention in China." *China & World Economy* 27, no. 4 (July 1, 2019): 1–28. https://doi.org/10.1111/cwe.12284.

could increase the basic tax rate for capital outflows without the need for renminbi depreciation. If the progressive tax on cross-border capital flows can be realized, then the international financial competition between China and the United States would be like two people fighting with bayonets: the dollar would be the strong man, bare-chested, swinging a big knife, while the renminbi would be the scholar, holding a three-foot sword, but wearing armor!

11.3.2 Disruptive Innovation in International Payment Technology: Digital Currency Cross-Border Payment Platform

The key threat of US financial sanctions is the loss of access to the international payment infrastructure. China faces a dilemma: to establish an effective renminbi cross-border payment system would require the renminbi to be freely convertible and the capital account to be open, but this could leave the economy vulnerable to the risks of large and volatile capital flows. The idea of a progressive tax on cross-border capital flows is to manage the risks of large and volatile capital flows while opening the capital account. But while the renminbi is not yet freely convertible and the capital account is not yet open, the idea of a cross border payment platform for central bank digital currencies (CBDCs) could erode US dollar dominance in the international payment system.

For more than a hundred years, money has evolved from minted coins to paper (fiat) currencies, and now to CBDCs. In the existing IMS, the US (fiat) dollar has a central position, and the US government and financial sector enjoy the privileges. However, with the development of CBDCs, the United States could face what we called in Chapter 10 the leader's dilemma—the stronger the advantages of the US dollar, the higher the opportunity cost for it to switch to a CBDC. This could provide an opening for China and other countries to build a new IMS based on CBDCs that could leapfrog over the current US dollar-dominated IMS. The main feature of digital currency technology is the decentralized blockchain network, whereas the existing IMS is centered on the US dollar. The decentralization blockchain would imply de-dollarization.

Let's look at the current dollar-dominated international payment system. The core of the current system is the SWIFT network, which is responsible for cross-border financial information transmission, and the Clearing House Interbank Payments System (CHIPS), which is responsible for US dollar cross-border transaction settlement and clearing. Today, SWIFT is the global leader and standard setter for cross-border financial information transmission services, and its financial communication services cover more than 11,000 financial institutions and corporate customers in more than 200 countries and regions. CHIPS controls the vast majority of global US dollar cross-border payments through connections with the SWIFT system.

The main payment method in the current system is the correspondent banking model. Specifically, when the payer and payee do not have accounts at the same bank, and there is no direct (correspondent) account connection between the banks where the payer and payee are located, the two banks can effect cross-border payments and settlements through a so-called correspondent bank. For example, to clear cross-border payments in US dollars, each bank would have its own SWIFT code and banks would confirm financial transaction information and payment clearing instructions through standardized messages and communication standards using the SWIFT platform. Due to the convenience of SWIFT, almost all banks with international businesses have joined the system, and the SWIFT network has become the key infrastructure for the current international payment system.

The current international payment system has very strong network externalities. The value of the services that market participants receive from this system is directly proportional to the number of entities connected to it. In simpler terms, the more people use it, the easier it is to do business. Once this system is accepted by most banks worldwide, its convenience is hard to surpass, and the system spontaneously forms a stable network with user stickiness.

However, the current international payment system has two main pain points: First, the transaction cycle from initiation to settlement is long, usually requiring 3–4 days. Second, the transaction cost is high. During the first quarter of 2024, transferring money internationally had an average transfer cost of 6.35% of the total transaction, according to the World Bank's Remittance Prices Worldwide database.[6] The main reasons for these two problems lie in the fact that there are too many intermediary banks involved in cross-border transfers. Generally speaking, the entire process involves 2–4 banks.

For a new international payment platform to succeed, it would need to overcome two key challenges. The first is how to attract enough users and generate network externalities to challenge the reach of the current system. The second is how to determine a reasonable exchange rate between CBDCs and fiat currencies. The exchange rate must be attractive to users and prevent speculative capital from using different platforms for aggressive arbitrage.

A promising development is the Multilateral Central Bank Digital Currency Bridge (mBridge) project which aims to build a new cross-border payment settlement platform based on CBDCs. The mBridge project is a collaboration between the Hong Kong Monetary Authority, the Innovation Center of the BIS (Hong Kong), the Central Bank of Thailand, the Digital Currency Research Institute of the PBOC, and the Central Bank of the United Arab Emirates. The mBridge platform maps the CBDCs of multiple parties to the same distributed ledger, enabling transactions to be settled synchronously across borders through smart contracts.

Compared with the traditional correspondent banking model, mBridge has a decentralized governance structure, higher efficiency, and lower cost. The mBridge platform can significantly improve transaction efficiency, reducing the

[6] "Remittance Prices Worldwide |MAKING MARKETS MORE TRANSPARENT," https://remittanceprices.worldbank.org/, accessed on November 29, 2025.

cross-border transaction time from 3–5 days to 2–10 seconds. The traditional correspondent banking model needs to go through multiple intermediaries, while the multilateral transaction model of mBridge can directly achieve peer-to-peer transactions, eliminating the intermediaries, and its transaction speed can be as fast as seconds. Estimates by PwC suggest that the transaction cost of mBridge will be 50% lower than the correspondent banking model. The mBridge platform has reached the minimum viable product stage and is broadening its international reach. The Saudi Central Bank is joining mBridge as a full participant and there are also now more than 26 observing members.

11.3.3 The Development in Stablecoins

While the People's Bank of China (PBOC) has actively developed and piloted its own CBDC, the digital renminbi (e-CNY), across major cities and international trade zones, the rapid rise of stablecoins—a class of privately issued digital tokens designed to maintain a stable value, typically pegged to the US dollar—has introduced a new frontier in monetary innovation. Operating on public blockchains, these tokens offer a low-volatility means of value transfer and have become integral to cryptocurrency trading, cross-border payments, and decentralized finance (DeFi). Though they account for less than 10% of total crypto-asset market capitalization, stablecoins play a critical role as a liquidity layer in the digital financial ecosystem, increasingly resembling a digital extension of the US dollar.

By mid-2025, the global market capitalization of stablecoins exceeded $250 billion, marking over 20% growth since the start of the year.[7] The market remains highly concentrated, with three fiat-collateralized tokens—Tether (USDT), USD Coin (USDC), and Binance USD (BUSD)—comprising more than 90% of total supply. These tokens are typically backed by liquid assets such as short-term US Treasury securities, enabling issuers to maintain price stability while also channeling global liquidity into US sovereign debt. In this way, stablecoins extend the reach of dollar-denominated assets into blockchain environments, reinforcing the architecture of US financial dominance.

In July 2025, the US Congress enacted the *Guiding and Establishing National Innovation for US Stablecoins Act* (GENIUS Act), the first federal legislation governing the issuance and operation of payment stablecoins.[8] The law mandates 100% reserve backing, dollar denominated collateral, regular disclosures, and compliance with anti-money laundering (AML) rules under the Bank Secrecy Act (BSA). Alongside it, the *Digital Asset Market Structure and Clarity Act* (CLARITY Act) establishes regulatory oversight: it assigns jurisdiction over payment stablecoins to the Commodity Futures Trading

[7] See: https://www.reuters.com/business/finance/stablecoins-market-cap-surges-record-high-us-senate-passes-bill-2025-06-18/, accessed on November 29, 2025.

[8] See: https://www.congress.gov/crs-product/IN12522, accessed on November 29, 2025.

Commission (CFTC), while reaffirming the Securities and Exchange Commission (SEC)'s authority over tokenized securities. Together, these laws create a dual regulatory framework that legitimizes dollar-backed stablecoins as tools of US monetary influence.

In contrast to the proliferation of private stablecoins in the United States, the US federal government has refrained from issuing a retail CBDC. Legislative initiatives such as the *CBDC Anti-Surveillance State Act* have explicitly sought to prohibit the Federal Reserve from launching a direct-to-consumer digital dollar,[9] citing concerns over financial privacy and the potential expansion of federal oversight. This policy stance has further solidified the role of privately issued stablecoins as functional stand-ins for a digital dollar.

Unlike stablecoins, which operate on public blockchains and are issued by private entities, the CBDC is a sovereign digital currency running on a centralized infrastructure. This divergence underscores a growing strategic contrast: the United States is pursuing a market-driven, private-sector path to digital dollarization, while China is building a state-led model of digital monetary sovereignty.

In international financial competition with the United States, China is currently in a catching-up position and faces the dual risk of financial crisis and financial sanctions. A progressive tax on cross-border capital flows could help to avert a financial crisis while opening up the capital account. Competitions in the field of digital currency will also determine the future of IMS.

11.4 Conclusion

The Federal Reserve's monetary policy has flipped from extreme easing since the COVID-19 pandemic in 2020 to tightening in 2022, and probably back to easing again under the pressure of the Trump administration in 2025, leaving the world financial markets in a nervous state. I can't help but think of the eve of the 2008 global financial crisis.

In October 2007, finance ministers and central bank governors from around the world gathered in Washington D.C. to attend the IMF-World Bank Annual Meetings. The impact of the US subprime mortgage crisis attracted the attention of the participants. On the afternoon of October 22, after the meetings ended, I strolled out of the IMF building and came to the Kennedy Center for the Performing Arts by the Potomac River. Looking west, the Potomac River was lined with colorful trees, and the sunset was reflected in the red leaves. As the sun set and the sky darkened, I turned to look east, where a bright moon was slowly rising. The IMS may be like the small boat I saw gradually leaving the Potomac River, drifting toward the Atlantic to endure the stormy waves—but where will it finally head? The scene was unforgettable, and I wrote a Chinese poem:

[9] See: https://www.congress.gov/bill/118th-congress/house-bill/5403/text, accessed on November 29, 2025.

Autumn Water

October 2007, Washington DC, USA[10]
One small boat with autumn flows,
Red trees meet white clouds and far sky.
View both shores with countless woe,
Unaware of spring and summer's glow.
No matter how winter's cold raises dark waves,
A bright moon always greets sunset clouds.
Through endless storms eastward I track,
Crossing the sea, home I go.

[10] The poem is translated from the Chinese.

CHAPTER 12

Competition in the Global Governance System

At 8 a.m. on January 1, 2000, in Norman, Oklahoma, the sunlight of the new century filled the room... and I seemed to have returned to my hometown in Rugao, Jiangsu—Jusha Village. How could the thousand-year-old ginkgo tree that had been cut down still stand there at the entrance of Jusha Primary School? The stout ginkgo tree takes more than three people to embrace it, and the canopy of the tree covers an acre. The main trunk stood about 20 meters high; four branches grew from it—each taking a person to embrace—standing tall toward the sky, supporting the canopy. At the top of the main trunk, also known as the "Sky Disk," there was enough space to put a square table for eight. Over time, the leaves have supported a thick layer of mud on the Sky Disk; in the middle, which is as thick as a bowl, a loquat tree had grown in an S shape. It seemed like I was climbing up to the Sky Disk, standing up, and looking toward Lujia Village to the east. The wheat fields were golden, and the canola fields next to them were green. A layer of white mist drifted from the green canola fields to the golden wheat fields. The basin-sized red sun behind the white mist rose slowly from Lujia village, higher and brighter.

... Was someone calling me? Was I dreaming in returning to my hometown, or was I dreaming in my hometown? Or was I dreaming of returning to my hometown dreaming of Oklahoma?... I forced my eyes open and struggled to sit up. Looking at the sunlight filling the room, a poem in Chinese[1] escaped my lips:

[1] The poem is translated from the Chinese.

J. Ju, *US-China Great Power Competition and The New World Order*,
https://doi.org/10.1007/978-981-95-3762-4_12

Dawn's light through eastern pane,
Homeland's scent in nights remain.
Sitting up and pondering deeply,
Where lies the dreamland?

I thought back to the early morning discussion with Mike and Anita about Eastern and Western cultures, multiculturalism, the East within the West, and the West within the East. Just like my dream, Oklahoma was in Rugao, and Rugao was in Oklahoma. Will the global governance system also achieve a harmonious blend of East and West, gradually evolving into a better state? The competition between China and the United States in the global governance system is essentially a struggle of value systems, a conflict of old and new cultures. So where will the culture of the new world be born?

"Dr. Ju, Dr. Ju!" The knocking on the door was getting louder. It was Mike's voice. I got up and opened the door: "Mike, good morning!"

"Good morning, Dr. Ju!"

"Was it you knocking?"

"Yeah, I've been knocking for a while."

"Haha, I thought I was dreaming. Mike, what's up?"

"Dr. Ju, the discussion last night about Eastern and Western cultures was so interesting. Can we continue it?" Mike was holding two cups of coffee.

"You've brought coffee! Let's go to my backyard." I took Mike to the backyard and sat down: "Go ahead, what are your new thoughts?" He had come early in the morning, and he must have had some novel ideas.

12.1 Where Will the New Culture Be Born?

Mike held the coffee in his left hand and started waving his right hand: "I didn't sleep all night yesterday. I've been thinking about a problem, a major problem: the new century, that is, the new world, is fundamentally different from the past. So the new world must have a new culture fundamentally different from traditional culture. Will this new culture be born in the United States, or China, or somewhere else?" True to his philosophy major, he went straight to the core issue.

I smiled at him: "Today's sunshine is as bright as yesterday's. What's fundamentally different?"

Mike waved his hand: "The sunshine changes every day. We just don't feel it. Quantitative changes lead to qualitative changes, and now we're experiencing a qualitative change."

"So where will the new culture be born if the new century is a qualitative change? Oklahoma? Norman? Haha, is little genius Mike inventing a new culture." I couldn't help but tease him.

Mike looked at me slyly. "We can rule out Oklahoma, but we can't rule out the little genius Mike. Dr. Ju, shall we discuss the conditions for the emergence of a new culture?"

"You go ahead, I'm listening." I took a sip of coffee, looking at Mike who was becoming serious.

He put his coffee on the ground and waved his two hands: "First, the internet connects the world, unifying the virtual and physical world. The driving force of world development now is innovation, knowledge, human capital. Consciousness and matter are unified too. Therefore, the new culture must be a monistic culture, not a dualistic culture, a unity of heaven, earth, and man! In this way, the new culture will definitely be born in a region with a monistic culture."

I looked at him and said: "You are sharp. The first condition has already ruled out Oklahoma. What's the second condition?"

"Second, the new culture is a destructive creation of traditional culture, so it won't be born in a region where traditional culture is strong, but in a region where traditional culture is weak, or has even been overthrown. As your Chairman Mao said, a blank sheet is best for drawing the newest and most beautiful pictures; without destruction there is no creation!"

I took another sip of coffee. "You are sharp, ruling out Oklahoma again. You've learned Chinese philosophy quite well."

Mike grinned happily, showing off his Chinese: "I can also speak Chinese philosophy in Chinese: unity of heaven, earth, and man; without destruction there is no creation!"

"Hmm, Chinese with an Oklahoma accent. What's the third condition?"

"Third: on the one hand, the new culture must be created through destruction; on the other hand, it must be born in a place of cultural prosperity, openness, inclusiveness, and development. Fourth, a new culture that influences the world can only be born in a powerful and influential country, so the new culture is most likely to emerge in an economically strong nation."

"Isn't that China? Mike!" I shouted.

Mike looked at me with a smile: "China meets the first and second conditions, but does not seem to meet the third and fourth conditions. It is said that Chinese people are now busy making money and have no time to develop culture. Moreover, the world's six largest economies by GDP are the United States, Japan, Germany, the UK, France, and China, with China only ranking sixth. China's per capita GDP ranks 134th in the world, and is less than 5% of the United States per capita GDP. Even in Asia, China's total GDP is less than a quarter of Japan's. China still has a long way to go to catch up with Japan, so it is not yet a strong economy." He picked up his coffee from the ground, looked at me sympathetically, and asked: "Dr. Ju, did I kill this discussion?"

"No," I looked at him. "China doesn't meet the third and fourth conditions. The U.S. doesn't meet the first and second conditions. Is there any country that meets all the conditions?"

Mike looked at me, "Not yet, maybe there will be one in fifty years."

"Which country is more likely to meet these four conditions?"

"I don't know!"

Mike stopped talking. He silently climbed the walnut tree in my backyard, and jumped back into his own backyard. The sunlight refracting in the azure sky of the new century suddenly pressed on my head, chest, and entire body. I was a bit breathless and couldn't help but feel a surge of emotion. I felt the urge to write. I returned to my room and browsed the Chinese news online. The first thing that caught my eye was news of the election of a new leader in the Taiwan Region of China. The approval rating for Chen Shui-bian, the candidate of the Democratic Progressive Party advocating Taiwan independence, was higher than that of Lien Chan, the candidate of the Kuomintang. It was possible that the Kuomintang's half-century rule in Taiwan would be brought to an end, with attendant implications for peace in the Taiwan Strait.

After the disintegration of the Soviet Union in 1991, the United States became the only superpower in the world, leading its allies to form a world order with one superpower and multiple secondary powers. In Asia, the United States and Japan dominated the region's economy and security. In Europe, 11 members of the European Union launched the euro on January 1, 1999, unifying their currencies. European integration finally took a new step after half a century of setbacks and perseverance. However, the birth of the euro was followed by the Kosovo War. From March 24 to June 20, 1999, the United States led the North Atlantic Treaty Organization (NATO) countries in launching a series of air strikes against the Federal Republic of Yugoslavia. The Kosovo War completely demolished the last vestige of the former Soviet camp on the Balkan Peninsula. But it also hit the ambitious euro, sending a clear signal to the international financial markets that the dollar, and only the dollar, was the king. The spirited euro depreciated significantly in the wake of the NATO bombing of Yugoslavia, and the US dollar returned to its leading position in the IMS.

The United States was conquering and thriving in Asia and Europe. The twenty-first century seemed undoubtedly to be the century of the United States. So much so that Francis Fukuyama argued that world history had ended and the world order led by the United States had entered a steady state.[2]

If Mike is right and the new world is a multicultural world, then Eastern culture should be revived. If Mike's four conditions are correct, then East Asia needs not only strong growth but also to learn from Europe and make a qualitative leap in regional economic integration. I opened my notebook and wrote down the title of an article: "The Proposal of the Huaxia Community."[3]

> "Approximately 1/4 of the global population, living on every piece of land in the world, the Huaxia people of all ethnic groups who have been around for thousands of years are building a brand new world."

[2] Francis Fukuyama, *The End of History and the Last Man*, 1992, http://ci.nii.ac.jp/ncid/BA14011847, accessed on November 29, 2025.

[3] See Ju, Jiandong, 2000, "*The Proposal of the Huaxia Community*," Working Paper.

"In the global trend of economic integration, ... the Huaxia people of all ethnic groups are deeply divided by trade barriers, and direct trade between some regions is even prohibited. Trade barriers hinder the effective allocation of resources and slow down economic development. Eliminating trade barriers and implementing free trade is the general trend and the public's desire. ... The establishment of the Huaxia Community, first implementing free trade, then realizing the free flow of production factors, and then unifying the currency, is the need for historical progress and the inevitability of economic development."

Turn the clock forward to the present day, more than 20 years later. The United States, which was in its prime at the turn of the new century, unexpectedly suffered three crises over just 20 years: the 9/11 terrorist attack in 2001, the global financial crisis in 2008, and the COVID-19 pandemic in 2020. It is now in a precarious state. Meanwhile, the tripod world order, like a sapling in a rock crevice, has broken free from the stone's grasp, raised its head, grown robustly, and displayed its spirited posture in the storm.

In this chapter, we will discuss the third key field of great power competition: competition for the global governance system.[4] Global economic governance is divided into international financial governance and international trade governance. As discussed in Chapter 8, international financial governance is still dominated by the United States and the US dollar. But in international trade governance, whether in the multilateral trade system of the WTO or in regional economic governance, the competition between China and the United States is becoming increasingly fierce. Therefore, this chapter will focus on the competition between China and the United States in international trade governance.

12.2 The Dilemma of the World Trade Organization

The WTO is an international organization that maintains the global rules of trade and symbolizes the multilateral trade governance system. Two of its key functions are providing a forum for trade negotiations and settling trade disputes. Both functions have essentially stalled.

In November 2001, at its fourth Ministerial Conference in Doha, Qatar, the WTO launched a new round of multilateral trade negotiations that covered a broad range of issues including agriculture, non-agricultural tariffs, services, intellectual property, anti-dumping and subsidies, trade and the environment, and trade and development issues. The Doha Development Round—the first since the WTO inherited the multilateral trading system from the GATT in 1995—was originally expected to conclude by January 2005, but no agreement was reached and negotiations broke down after July 2008. Nearly 20 years have passed, and progress in resolving issues in agriculture, development, and rules is slow. New issues reflecting the reality of international trade

[4] We will focus on global economic governance in this chapter.

in the twenty-first century, such as e-commerce and investment facilitation, have not been addressed in a timely manner.

The United States has been blocking appointments and reappointments of members of the WTO Appellate Body, which holds the final judgment power in international trade disputes and is known as the Supreme Court of international trade. As mentioned in Chapter 8, by December 2019, the Appellate Body was left with only one judge, and the term of that last judge expired at the end of November 2020. Due to the lack of judges, the Appellate Body cannot accept any new cases, and at the time of writing, the future of the WTO's dispute settlement system is uncertain.

Underlying these functional problems is the fact that the four principles that the WTO considers to be the foundation of the multilateral trading system are increasingly subject to disagreement among its members.

Non-discrimination. The principle of non-discrimination involves two aspects: most-favored-nation (MFN) treatment, which means that a tariff reduction (or lowering of a trade barrier more generally) applicable to one country should be applied to all countries, and no country should be discriminated against; and national treatment, which means that domestic and foreign goods and services should be treated equally in the domestic market. But there are exceptions to the MFN principle. For example, countries can join regional trade agreements (RTAs) that apply only to goods and services traded within the group. There is a very important exception in the principle of non-discrimination, which is that developing country members of the WTO are allowed special and differential treatment from other members, including more time for implementing trade liberalization. The United States has accused China of using its status as a developing country to avoid WTO rules and gain an unfair advantage and has called for disallowing countries to self-declare their developing status in order to receive special treatment.

Fair competition. The principle of fair competition means that countries should not adopt trade practices that inhibit or distort competition, such as subsidizing exports and "dumping" (exporting products below cost to gain market share). Establishing what is fair or unfair is a complex issue. There is significant institutional diversity across major trading economies such as China, the United States, and the European Union. The United States and the European Union have accused China of unfairly subsidizing its industries, but WTO rules do not prohibit industrial policies per se. Market economies can operate in diverse ways—they do not necessarily have to follow the US model. The economic system in countries like China, where both the market and the government play an active role, has proven to be successful in practice. Furthermore, new sectors like high-tech and AI have strong economic externalities and market structures that do not fit the traditional model of perfect competition. In fact, as discussed in Chapter 10, developed economies like the United States and the European Union are themselves increasingly relying on industrial policies to promote technological advancement.

Trade liberalization. The ultimate goal of the WTO is to achieve freer trade globally by encouraging all countries to continuously lower tariff and non-tariff barriers to trade. But trade liberalization has been, and continues to be, the subject of controversy, especially in sectors like agriculture. Developed economies like the European Union, Japan, and the United States, still implement strong trade protection measures for their domestic agricultural products and deny market access to developing economies. Additionally, the trend of deindustrialization and rising manufacturing unemployment in developed economies has led to shrinking support for trade liberalization and growing support for trade protectionism and unilateralism.

Transparency. WTO agreements require countries to make their trade laws, regulations, administrative rules, and judicial decisions clear and public, so that everyone—domestic and foreign—doing business in or with the country can understand them.

Ideally, the multilateral trading system would form a global super value chain under the governance of the WTO. But with so many countries in the world and such large differences in their development levels, it is nearly impossible for the WTO system to manage global trade under one consistent set of values. The WTO principles, which followed from the GATT principles established by the United States and its allies after World War II, are no longer in line with US interests. Therefore, the stagnation and disorder of the WTO multilateral trade system are almost an inevitable trend.

12.3 The Rise of Regional Trade Agreements

Will global trade fall into disorder because the WTO is in a predicament? Not necessarily, because in addition to multilateral trade governance under the WTO, there are RTAs. RTAs refer to treaties signed between two or more economies (not necessarily in the same region) that define the rules of trade for them. Examples of RTAs are the European Union, the USMCA (the successor to NAFTA), and the ASEAN Free Trade Area (AFTA).

You might ask: since the European Union only eliminates tariffs among its member countries, isn't this discrimination against economies outside the European Union, and doesn't this violate the non-discrimination principle of the WTO? This is a good question.

Article 24 of the GATT (the WTO's predecessor) allows for the formation of RTAs, provided that RTA members do not increase trade restrictions on other countries while promoting trade liberalization among themselves. For example, when the United States, Mexico, and Canada signed the USMCA, each signatory was supposed to ensure that its tariffs on imports from non-USMCA countries (such as China) would not be higher than their levels before the agreement was signed.

There are two main types of RTAs. One is a customs union, such as the European Union, where there are zero tariffs on trade between EU members, and all EU members levy the same tariffs on imports from non-EU countries. The other is a free trade area (FTA), such as the USMCA, the Regional Comprehensive Economic Partnership (RCEP) of 14 countries including China, and the Comprehensive and Progressive Agreement for Trans-Pacific Partnership (CPTPP) signed by 11 countries in the Asia–Pacific region. FTAs have zero tariffs between members, but members' tariffs on imports from economies outside the FTA can be different. In order to prevent arbitrage by non-members, that is, exporting products from outside the FTA to the member with the lowest tariffs and reselling them to the other FTA members at zero tariffs, FTAs must specify "rules of origin" to determine whether goods entering an FTA member country are eligible for preferential treatment such as zero import tariffs.

There are two main types of RTA structures. One is the multi-country cooperation model, where members are of comparable scale and there is no one dominant country in the RTA. AFTA is a typical example of this model, where the 10 ASEAN members (Brunei, Cambodia, Indonesia, Laos, Malaysia, Myanmar, the Philippines, Singapore, Thailand, and Vietnam) jointly promote the process of economic integration. The European Union is also a multi-country cooperation model, with Germany, France, and Italy taking the lead in promoting European economic integration. The other is the hub-and-spoke model, where there is one core member (the hub) and several smaller members (the spokes). The core member has a significant scale advantage over other members and occupies a dominant position in the RTA. The USMCA is a typical example of this model, with the United States accounting for over 80% of production, consumption, and trade in the FTA.

At a time when the WTO is struggling, RTAs have been flourishing. By 2022, there were 358 operating RTAs worldwide (see Fig. 12.1), accounting for over 50% of total global trade. The global trade governance system is currently driven by RTAs alongside the WTO. Since the 1990s, there has been a debate concerning the relationship between the multilateral trade governance system and RTAs—are they substitutes or complements? In an ideal world, the WTO on its own should be sufficient for regulating and promoting global trade. But, as noted in the previous section, the WTO's near-universal membership is a disadvantage when it comes to reaching agreement on many trade issues, whereas smaller RTAs tend to have more success in areas not covered by WTO agreements. In the current situation where the WTO is at a standstill, it can be expected that RTAs will accelerate their development.

12.4 The European Experience

Let's take a look at the most successful and influential economic union in the world: the European Union.

World War II dealt a heavy blow to Europe. Western European countries were deeply pained and hoped to enhance cooperation to avoid more wars. In addition, there were two opposing superpowers in the world at that time:

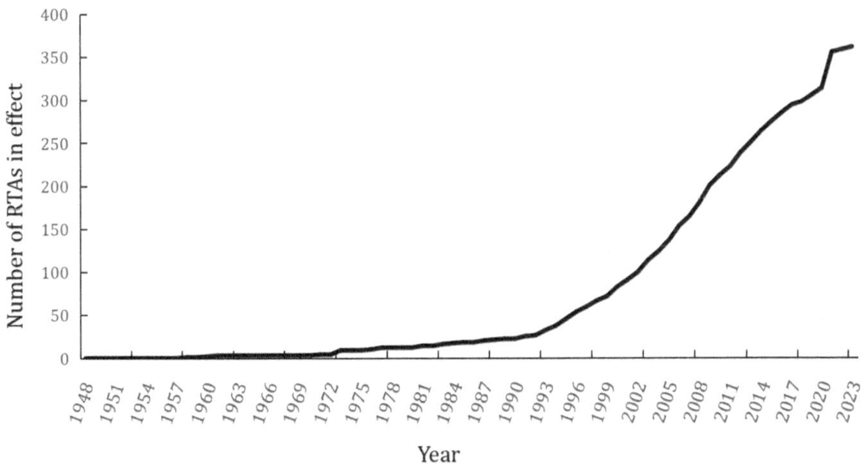

Fig. 12.1 Number of regional trade agreements in effect, 1948–2023 (*Source* World Trade Organization [WTO])

the United States and the Soviet Union. Western European countries could no longer maintain their original status in the world individually, so they also hoped to enhance the status of the region through cooperation. In September 1946, British Prime Minister Winston Churchill proposed to create a "United States of Europe." This vision has been realized in stages, with each stage involving deeper and broader levels of integration.

On May 9, 1950, French Foreign Minister Robert Schuman proposed a plan to pool their coal and steel production to prevent another war between France and Germany. Based on the Schuman Plan, six Western European countries (Belgium, France, Germany, Italy, Luxembourg, and the Netherlands) signed the Treaty of Paris on April 18, 1951, establishing the European Coal and Steel Community. This was the first step in the process of European integration after World War II.

Subsequently, the six founding members agreed to expand their cooperation beyond coal and steel by signing the Treaty of Rome on March 25, 1957, creating the European Economic Community (EEC). One of the main goals of the EEC was to create a customs union and a common market. In July 1968, all tariffs and trade restrictions were eliminated among the six EEC members and a common external tariff was set for imports from the rest of the world. Denmark, Ireland, and the United Kingdom joined the EEC in January 1973, Greece in January 1981, and Spain and Portugal in January 1986, bringing total membership to 12.

In 1986, EEC members signed the Single European Act, launching a six-year program to complete a single European market: "an area without internal borders, in which the free movement of goods, persons, services, and capital should be guaranteed." On January 1, 1993, the European single market was established with the free movement of goods, services, labor, and capital.

On February 7, 1992, the 12 members of the EEC signed the Treaty on European Union in Maastricht, the Netherlands, stipulating that an economic and monetary union would be established by January 1, 1999, entailing a common currency, a common central bank, and a common monetary policy. The EEC was renamed the European Community and integrated into the newly formed European Union in 1993. Austria, Finland, and Sweden joined the European Union in 1995. In December 1995, it was officially decided that the name of the unified European currency would be the euro. On July 1, 1998, the European Central Bank was officially established. On January 1, 1999, the euro was officially launched for 11 EU members (excluding Denmark, Sweden, and the United Kingdom). The period from 1999 to 2001 was the three-year transition period preceded the introduction of the euro: on January 1, 2002, euro notes and coins became legal tender in the 11 founding members and Greece.

Ten countries (the Czech Republic, Estonia, Hungary, Latvia, Lithuania, Poland, Slovakia, Slovenia, Cyprus and Malta) joined the European Union in 2004, followed by Bulgaria and Romania in 2007, bringing the number of EU members to 27. Croatia joined in 2013 and the United Kingdom left in 2020. Currently, the euro is the official currency of 20 out of 27 EU members.[5]

Figure 12.2 shows the main milestones in European integration. The process of European integration illustrates the four stages of economic integration.

The first stage is the integration of the goods market, generally referred to as the common market. This stage proceeded sector by sector (starting with the coal and steel sector and expanding to other industries) and "block by block" (eliminating trade barriers among members, and then unifying the external tariffs of members).

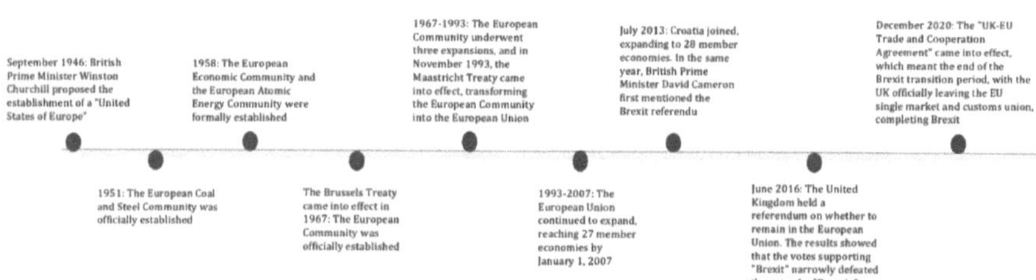

Fig. 12.2 Milestones in European integration

[5] Although all EU countries are part of the Economic and Monetary Union (EMU), 20 of them have replaced their national currencies with the single currency—the euro. These EU countries form the euro area, also known as the Eurozone: Austria; Belgium; Croatia; Cyprus; Estonia; Finland; France; Germany; Greece; Ireland; Italy; Latvia; Lithuania; Luxembourg; Malta; the Netherlands; Portugal; Slovakia; Slovenia; Spain.

The second stage is the integration of the factor market, generally referred to as the community. This stage was achieved with the establishment of the European single market, which ensured free movement of factors of production (capital and labor), as well as goods and services among members.

The third stage is the integration of economic policies, such as monetary, fiscal, and structural policies. The European Union has achieved monetary policy integration but is still striving for fiscal policy integration.

The fourth stage is the integration of politics, diplomacy, and defense. The aim would be to establish a powerful European Federation, which is the highest stage of European unification. How far the European Union can go in this stage remains to be seen.

12.5 Asia's Predicament

Asia—by which we generally mean the group of countries in East and Southeast Asia—lags significantly behind Europe in the process of regional integration, and it has fallen into a predicament. In June 2020, Singaporean Prime Minister Lee Hsien Loong published an article highlighting Singapore's dilemma.[6] Why? Because Singapore relies on the United States to help maintain security in Asia, but it also relies on China economically. Now that there is a competition between China and the United States, the United States is asking Singapore to take sides, so Singapore is in a dilemma. In fact, it is not only Singapore, but other Asian countries like the Philippines, Malaysia, Vietnam, and even Japan and South Korea, all have this feeling of being in a dilemma. How did Asia fall into this predicament?

12.5.1 Fundamental Structural Changes in Asia's Economy

Starting from the 1970s, Asia's economic and trade structure formed a V-shaped "flying geese" pattern: Japan was the leading goose, and other economies, such as the Four Little Dragons of Asia (Hong Kong, Singapore, South Korea, and Taiwan), the Four Asian Tigers (Indonesia, Malaysia, the Philippines, and Thailand), and Mainland China, were the geese behind it on both sides. Japan was dependent on the United States for military and political support, while other economies, except China, were dependent on the US market for trade. Therefore, the Asian economic order in the last three decades of the twentieth century was controlled by the United States.

Figure 12.3 shows China's and Japan's share in the total GDP of East and Southeast Asia.[7] From the figure, we can see that before 2010, Japan was the

[6] Readers are referred to: https://www.foreignaffairs.com/articles/asia/2020-06-04/lee-hsien-loong-endangered-asian-century, accessed on November 29, 2025.

[7] Here East and Southeast Asia represents 10 ASEAN members plus China, Japan, and South Korea.

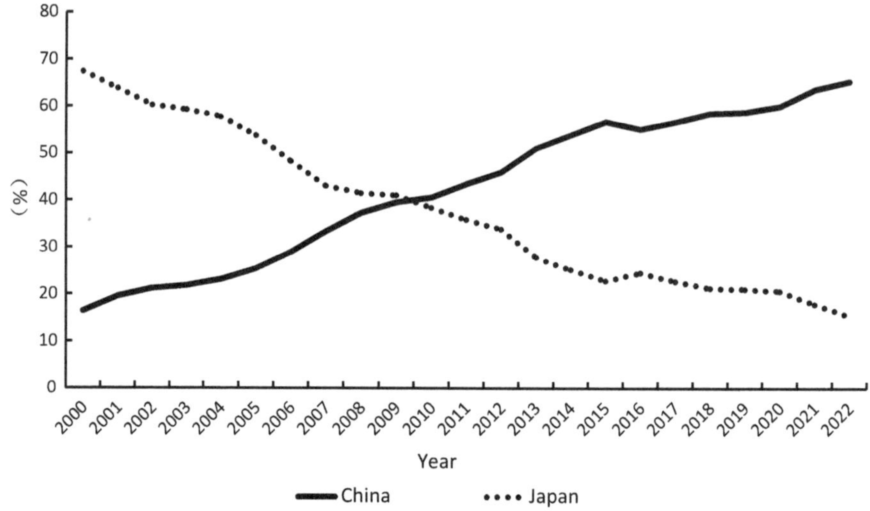

Fig. 12.3 Share of China and Japan in GDP of East and Southeast Asia, 2000–2022 (*Data source* World Bank database)

largest economy in the region. In 2000, Japan's GDP was four times that of China's.

After joining the WTO in 2001, China's economy experienced rapid development. In 2010, China's GDP overtook Japan's and by 2020, it had reached nearly three times Japan's GDP. As shown in Fig. 12.3, since 2014, China has accounted for over 50% of East and Southeast Asia's total GDP. Asia's economic and trade structure has changed from the flying geese pattern with Japan in the lead to a hub-and-spoke pattern with China at the core.

However, there has been no corresponding transformation of the economic order in Asia. The United States is suppressing China's influence in the Asian economic order every way it can. According to US President Biden, "China should not participate in the formulation of global trade and technology rules."[8] This is the first reason for Asia's predicament.

12.5.2 Fragmentation of Asia's Trade Governance

The second reason for Asia's predicament is its fragmented trade governance. The most active regional economic cooperation organization in the region is ASEAN. Founded in 1967, ASEAN currently has 10 members (Brunei, Cambodia, Indonesia, Laos, Malaysia, Myanmar the Philippines, Singapore, Thailand, and Vietnam). ASEAN is an FTA. In January 1992, at the 4th ASEAN Summit held in Singapore, ASEAN members signed an agreement

[8] See: https://www.washingtonpost.com/opinions/2021/06/05/joe-biden-europe-trip-agenda/, accessed on November 29, 2025.

to establish the AFTA within 15 years from January 1, 1993. The objective of AFTA was to increase ASEAN's competitive advantage as a production base for the world market by reducing tariffs for goods originating within ASEAN to 0–5% and eliminating non-tariff barriers to trade.

In October 2003, the ASEAN Economic Community (AEC) was established with the aim of creating a single market and production base where goods, services, capital, and skilled labor could flow freely. The AEC came into effect in December 2015, and the completion of the common market is targeted for 2025.

ASEAN currently has bilateral free trade agreements with Australia and New Zealand; China; Hong Kong, China; India; Japan; and South Korea. On November 15, 2020, ASEAN plus China, Japan, South Korea, Australia, and New Zealand, a total of 15 Asia–Pacific countries, signed the RCEP agreement. The agreement came into effect on January 1, 2022, creating the largest RTA in the world in terms of combined GDP and market size.

Another important RTA in Asia is the CPTPP, a free trade agreement signed in March 2018 by 11 Pacific Rim countries: Australia, Brunei, Canada, Chile, Japan, Malaysia, Mexico, New Zealand, Peru, Singapore, and Vietnam. The background of the CPTPP is quite interesting. The CPTPP began as the Trans-Pacific Partnership (TPP), which was itself at expansion of the Trans-Pacific Strategic Economic Partnership signed in July 2005 by Brunei, Chile, New Zealand, and Singapore. The TPP was a proposed FTA covering these four countries plus Australia, Canada, Japan, Malaysia, Mexico, Peru, Vietnam, and the United States. On November 14, 2009, US President Obama announced that the United States would participate in the TPP negotiations, emphasizing that the agreement would promote US employment and economic prosperity, make a significant contribution to setting twenty-first-century trade agreement standards, and establish a high-standard, innovative, multi-field, and wide-ranging Asia–Pacific regional integration cooperation agreement. On February 4, 2016, the 12 countries officially signed the TPP agreement in Auckland, New Zealand. But in the United States, the agreement was not ratified due to domestic political opposition and on January 20, 2017, the newly inaugurated President Trump announced the United States withdrawal from the TPP. The remaining 11 countries signed the agreement, renamed the CPTPP, in Santiago, Chile, in March 2018. The CPTPP, which entered into force in December 2018, retains over 95% of the original TPP provisions, only shelving 20 of them, 11 of which are related to intellectual property rights.

On September 16, 2021, China officially applied to join the CPTPP. Interestingly, Obama saw the TPP as his most important diplomatic achievement and a key strategic move for the United States to return to Asia. Joining the TPP, known as the "economic NATO" and jokingly referred to as "ABC (Anyone But China)" was a strategic arrangement by the United States to reassert its dominance in the reign, and keep China out of, the formulation of economic and trade rules in the Asia–Pacific region. Many provisions of the TPP, such as strict labor standards, provisions against state intervention in markets, and strict requirements for subsidies, were specifically designed to exclude China. Yet it was the United States that withdrew from the TPP due to domestic political conflicts. China, on the other hand, believes that most of the provisions of the CPTPP are consistent with its direction of opening up to and deepening its integration with other countries in the region. Joining the CPTPP would allow China, as the largest economy in the group, to participate in and influence the formulation of economic and trade rules in the region.

The evolution of RTAs in Asia shows that current trade governance in the region is highly fragmented. The geographical scope, driving goals, and standards and rules of FTAs such as AFTA, RCEP, and CPTPP vary greatly. AFTA and RCEP prioritize economic and trade cooperation goals, while the CPTPP considers political goals to a greater extent. RCEP is based on AFTA rules, with a relatively flexible pace of trade liberalization, while the CPTPP is modeled on North American rules and standards, and reflects the demands of North American companies for strong protection of intellectual property rights. In terms of rulemaking, RCEP adopts an ASEAN-led, multi-country cooperation model. Without the United States, the CPTPP also adopts a multi-country cooperation model.

The fragmented state of trade governance in Asia is due to the decline of the Asian order once controlled by the United States on the one hand, and United States attempts to suppress China's influence in Asia, on the other. The competition between the United States and China in Asia has reached a stalemate. ASEAN, which emerged from a small country cooperation model, is actively trying to fill the vacuum in the Asian order but Asia has already formed a hub-and-spoke economic structure with China at its core, and a multi-country cooperation model of governance driven by 10 relatively small countries—or any governance system that excludes China—does not reflect the region's economic reality.

12.6 The Asian Community and Reconstruction of the Asian Order

The dilemma of Asia's trade governance, reflected in its state of economic integration, is that it remains at a relatively low level and is full of contradictions. Compared with Europe, economic integration of Asia is still at the stage of an FTA. Important factor markets (technology, capital, and labor) are not unified. There is also no effective regional cooperation on important social issues such as climate change, pandemic prevention.

Taking European economic integration as a reference, the next step for Asia's economic integration is the unification of the factor market, that is, the construction of an Asian Community. An Asian trade governance system will be a crucial part of the global trade governance system. The development of this system will naturally be affected by the competition between China and the United States in global trade governance. Therefore, what we need to analyze first are the competition strategies of China and the United States as they fight for control of global trade governance.

12.6.1 US Competition Strategy Against China for Global Trade Governance

In a 2022 speech, US Secretary of State Antony Blinken summarized the Biden administration's approach to China as "invest, align, compete"[9]: that is, investing in the United States strengthening alignment with its allies, and competing with China. This strategy serves two main purposes: first, it aims to reduce China's presence in the global value chain (GVC), by relocating key industries such as chips, high-power batteries, chemical raw materials from China to the United States and its allies in order to reduce US reliance on China and safeguard national security; and second, to curb China's technological and industrial upgrading and ensure the global hegemony of the United States in high-tech industries. The US strategy of forming alliances for international trade would serve the above two purposes, by marginalizing China and isolating it from regional and global trade governance.

How can the United States achieve this goal? We can use Fig. 12.4 to analyze the US de-Sinicization strategy. The CPTPP and RCEP in the Asia–Pacific region, the USMCA in North America, and the Japan-EU Economic Partnership Agreement (EPA) are large RTAs, represented by solid lines in the figure. The Transatlantic Trade and Investment Partnership (TTIP) between the United States and the European Union has not been signed and is represented by the dashed outline in the figure.

Japan is a member of the CPTPP, EPA, and RCEP, and an ally of the United States. To marginalize China, the United States only needs to take three steps. First, it could join the CPTPP, and corral Japan, Australia and other allies to lead the formulation of trade rules for the 12 Pacific Rim countries and keep China out of the CPTPP, furthermore, it can leverage its influence over these countries in the CPTPP to obstruct the realization of regional economic integration goals beneficial to China in the RCEP. Second, it could sign the TTIP which would integrate two of the largest economies in the world. Finally, with the United States connected to the CPTPP, USMCA, and TTIP, it can amalgamate the three RTAs to form a giant RTA covering the world's major economies, excluding China—thus achieving the de-Sinicization of global trade governance.

To be sure, conflicting domestic interests in the United States currently prevent it from realizing the above three steps, but this reflects unwillingness rather than inability. Once domestic opposition eases, the above de-Sinicization plan can be put into practice.

[9] See: https://www.state.gov/the-administrations-approach-to-the-peoples-republic-of-china, accessed on November 29, 2025.

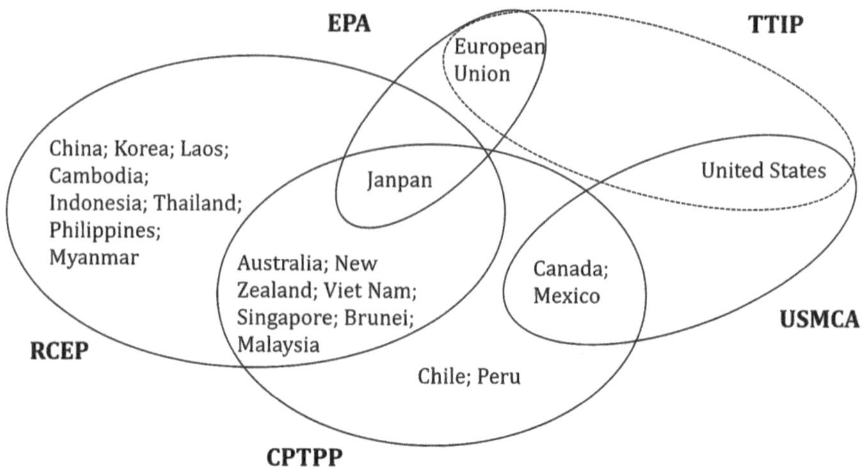

Fig. 12.4 Current and potential large regional trade agreements

Even if there is insufficient domestic political support for returning to the CPTPP and the TTIP, the Biden administration has already started to implement an alternate de-Sinicization strategy. In late 2021, it initiated a technology partnership with Japan, South Korea, and Taiwan to build a semiconductor supply network without China. The so-called Chip 4 Alliance held its first meeting in February 2023 to discuss the semiconductor supply chain and ways to cooperate in the future.

In May 2022, the Biden administration launched the Indo-Pacific Economic Framework (IPEF) with 13 Asia–Pacific countries: Australia, Fiji, India, Indonesia, Japan, Malaysia, New Zealand, the Philippines, Singapore, South Korea, Thailand, and Vietnam. The IPEF focuses on four pillars: trade; supply chains; clean economy (clean energy, and de-carbonization); and fair economy (tax and anti-corruption). The supply chain pillar, in particular, entails the establishment of a Supply Chain Council that will develop sector-specific action plans to "strengthen resilience in critical sectors and key goods"—in other words, to achieve a de-Sinicization of the global value chain in strategic sectors. The Agreement Relating to Supply Chain Resilience was signed in November 2023 and entered into force in February 2024.

The purpose of the US de-Sinicization strategy for the global value chain in strategic sectors is to prevent the United States from falling into the "leader's dilemma" and leading China into the "chaser's trap" discussed in Chapter 10. In the competition between China and the United States, China has an advantage in manufacturing, while the United States has an advantage in technology. Under the Trump administration, the United States launched a comprehensive tariff war against imports from China but the tariff war, while damaging to China's exports, also increased prices in the United States, harming the interests of its own consumers and producers. The Trump administration also eschewed international alliances and RTAs in favor of an "America First" approach. The Biden administration adjusted the US competition strategy against China by targeting its suppression of China in the field of high tech and pushing its allies in Asia and Europe to join its efforts.

Trump administration 2.0 takes place on January 20, 2025, continuing the effort of de-Sinicization, with much hard efforts to reform the global trading system. Trump's Tariff 2.0 represents a deliberate pivot away from multilateral, rules-based free trade toward a transactional, sovereignty-first trade doctrine, with two strategic pillars: first, dismantling reliance on WTO norms, using emergency powers to impose baseline and sector-specific tariffs, and converting tariff revenues into a primary fiscal tool, and second, applying extreme tariff pressure on China, incentivizing reshoring of critical manufacturing (especially semiconductors, metals, and autos), and taxing US firms' China-linked revenues.

Trump's Tariff 2.0 signals a long-term US shift toward protectionism, strategic autonomy, and bilateral deal-making—even at the cost of global trade stability.

12.6.2 *How Should China Respond?*

In the face of the US global trade system reform and de-Sinicization strategy, what is China's optimal response?

We can discuss three possible strategies for China. The first is, of course, to do nothing and accept US de-Sinicization of the GVC. We call this strategy "passive acceptance." The second is to counterattack and promote a global trade governance system led by China, not only for goods trade but also for trade in services including the digital economy, technology, and finance, to counter the current US-led order. We call this strategy "global counterattack." The third is to promote a trade governance system led by China for Asia and countries with close economic ties to China. We call this strategy "limited counterattack."

How to judge the pros and cons of the above three strategies? As discussed in Chapter 9, the goal for China is maintaining strong long-term growth while preventing crises. Therefore, the strategies should be evaluated based on which is most beneficial for China's long-term economic growth.

It should be noted that the United States is in a leading position in technology (see Chapter 10) and international finance (see Chapter 11). If China chooses to passively accept its fate, the United States could achieve a de-Sinicization of global governance system in these areas. This would significantly increase China's cross-border transaction costs and ultimately lower China's economic growth. Therefore, "passive acceptance" is not a superior strategy.

Is "global counterattack" a superior strategy? We do not have data to evaluate the benefits and costs of this imagined global counterattack, but we can refer to the results of the full-scale trade war against China launched by the Trump administration in 2018 and continued by the Biden administration.

In 2018, the United States was already behind China in manufacturing. Trump's tariff war targeted manufactured products from China, aiming to curb the growth of China's manufacturing exports and reduce their importance in the GVC. Instead, China's manufacturing exports increased to $3.321 trillion in 2022 from $2.318 trillion in 2018, and China's share of world manufacturing output increased to 21.72% in 2022 from 17.82% in 2018. The US trade deficit with China increased rather than decreased, to $404.138 billion in 2022 from $323.327 billion in 2018.[10] The Trump and Biden administrations have also done their utmost to block the growth of China's high-tech industry. But China's NEV exports increased by 623% between 2018 and 2022, and Huawei's Mate60 mobile phone returned to the high-end mobile phone market in September 2023 (see Chapter 10). These facts show that the United States is not successful in containing China's manufacturing industry.

While the United States lags China in manufacturing output, China is even further behind the United States in technology and finance. If China wants to launch a comprehensive counterattack against the United States for leadership of global governance in technology and finance, it does not have much areas of leverage. It could protect its own high-tech industries by raising tariffs on high-tech imports from the United States, but this could instead hinder its technological progress. Alternatively, it could form alliances with some developing countries to compete with the United States in technology and finance. However, developing countries are not the main global markets for technology and finance, and the benefits to China would be limited.

The above analysis shows that China's optimal strategy should be a "limited counterattack." In key areas such as trade in digital services, technology, and finance, China cannot afford to be marginalized in Asia or it will be isolated globally. Asia is the largest and fastest growing market in the world. If China can maintain its relevance in Asia, it can ensure that it is not isolated globally. The United States may "de-Sinicize," but it cannot "de-Asianize." As long as China can economically integrate with the rest of Asia, it can promote the restructuring of the global trade governance system. A "limited counterattack" means promoting economic integration in Asia, that is, establishing an Asian Community. What should China do to make this a reality?

12.6.3 History and Goals of the Asian Community

China is part of ASEAN+3, a regional grouping comprising the 10 ASEAN countries plus China, Japan, and South Korea. ASEAN+3 was established in

[10] See: http://english.customs.gov.cn/statics/report/monthly2023.html, accessed on November 29, 2025.

1997 and has at various times taken the role of community building in East and Southeast Asia.

The concept of an Asian Community was not first proposed by China. Its prototype can be traced back to the proposal for an East Asian Community (EAC) by Japanese Prime Minister Junichiro Koizumi in a speech in Singapore in January 2002.[11] Koizumi envisioned the EAC to start with Japan and ASEAN, and widen to include China, South Korea, Australia, and New Zealand as core members. At a summit in Tokyo in 2003, Japan and ASEAN affirmed their desire to establish the EAC. In September 2009, incoming Japanese Prime Minister Yukio Hatoyama actively promoted the concept of the EAC with Chinese and South Korean leaders, positioning it as the world's "third pole" alongside the United States and the European Union. In the second China-Japan-South Korea Trilateral Summit in October 2009, the three countries agreed to jointly build the EAC. In 2012, the East Asia Vision Group II,[12] an eminent persons' group established by ASEAN+3 to make recommendations for regional cooperation and community building, submitted a report proposing to establish an East Asia Economic Community by 2020 which would focus on: a single market and production base; financial stability, food and energy security; equitable and sustainable development; and constructive contribution to the global economy.

However, due to Asia's complex geopolitics, historical issues, the ups and downs of great power games, and the interference of the United States, the EAC did not materialize. In addition to the timing and conditions not being ripe, the early vision of the EAC also lacked a focus on issues that could effectively build consensus.

From a historical perspective, although the progress toward an Asian Community has been halting, it has never been completely abandoned. The idea of the Asian Community is "new wine in old bottles": the name has not substantively changed—which is conducive to historical continuity—but the content has undergone substantial changes. The previous Asian Community was proposed and led by Japan, reflecting Japan's dominant position in the region's economy at the time. Now it is led by China, reflecting China's central position in the current hub-and-spoke structure of the region's economy. Furthermore, the new Asian Community would be a key element in the competition between China and the United States for trade governance in Asia.

The goals of the Asian Community can be specified in three stages: short-term, medium-term, and long-term. In the short term, the goal is to liberalize the flow of technology and data, which would help break the international technology blockade that the United States has imposed on China. In the

[11] See MOFA: Speech by Prime Minister of Japan Junichiro Koizumi: https://www.mofa.go.jp/region/asia-paci/pmv0201/speech.html, accessed on November 29, 2025.

[12] See: https://aseanplusthree.asean.org/wp-content/uploads/2020/01/Report-of-the-EAVG-II.pdf, accessed on November 29, 2025.

medium term, the goal is to strengthen the Asian Community by integrating existing multilateral cooperation platforms such as RCEP, AMRO, and the AIIB to achieve free trade and the free flow of capital and labor within the community. In the long term, the goal is to establish an Asian economic union similar to the European Union but with Asian characteristics, which would be an important pillar in the global tripod economic governance system.

12.6.4 *The Path to Building the Asian Community*

Building a non-discriminatory, fair, free, and transparent trading system in Asia is beneficial for China in the short term, and for Asia and the world in the long term. However, in the short term, it will certainly face strong opposition from the United States, and it may not gain the support of US allies like Japan and South Korea. Therefore, the construction of the Asian Community must rely on China's leadership and promotion in the short term.

China's leadership can be labeled as the "market for rules" strategy: China can unilaterally open its domestic market to member economies, while not requiring member economies to reciprocally open their domestic markets to China, but requiring member economies to abide by the rules of the Asian community. The member economies gain access to Chinese market in exchange for the support of the rules of the non-discriminatory, fair competition, free trade, and transparent in Asian technology market.

The path to building the Asian Community can be summarized in the following ideas: unilateral opening; bilateral negotiations; easy first and difficult later; and orderly entry.

China can unilaterally open its entire market for goods, services, labor, and capital to those economies willing to become members of the Asian Community. For example, RCEP has a 20-year schedule for product market opening but China can unilaterally open its product market earlier, and it can also open up its market for services and other areas not mentioned in RCEP or other agreements. This would allow other members to gain access to the huge Chinese market. In exchange, they would need to agree to support the rules of trade in the Asian Community. The four major rules of the WTO—non-discrimination, fair competition, free trade, and transparency—have been abandoned by the United States. China cannot restore the WTO, but it can restore the four major WTO rules in the Asian Community. For example, in return for access to China's market, Asian Community member countries should commit to opening their economies to all members in the future, although they would be free to specify the transition period needed, such as 5 years, 10 years, or even longer. More importantly, member economies must support the free flow of trade in goods and services and commit to not enacting discriminatory trade barriers or blockades against other member economies.

As the core, or axis, of the Asian Community, China would take the lead in rulemaking. The approach should be to adopt bilateral negotiations in sequence, that is, negotiating with one country at a time. Membership in the Asian Community would not necessarily be limited to countries in the geographic region. There are many countries with close economic and trade relations with China outside Asia, such as Argentina, Brazil, and Peru in South America, Ethiopia and Tanzania in Africa, and Russia and the United Kingdom in Europe. As long as they are willing to abide by the rules of non-discrimination, fair competition, free trade, and transparency, and do not seek to block, contain, or discriminate against China in the high-tech supply chain, they can all become members of the Asian Community.

In East Asia, the most important and difficult countries to persuade would be Japan and South Korea, but China can build the Asian Community by starting with the easier countries before moving to the more difficult ones. For example, China can first invite friendly countries like Cambodia and Laos to become members of the Asian Community, and then invite resource-rich developing countries like Indonesia, Kazakhstan, and Pakistan. Note that these countries do not have much advanced technology, so building a unified Asian technology market and not discriminating or containing China in technology do not cost them anything, and they will benefit greatly from the full opening of the Chinese market. The rational choice for these countries should be to join the Asian Community. As the Asian Community expands, countries that have not yet joined would be more and more at a disadvantage. Therefore, Malaysia and Vietnam may join next. Finally, when the cost of being marginalized by China and the Asian market becomes very high, South Korea and Japan could decide to become members of the Asian Community.

When China established the AIIB, it adopted a similar strategy. At first, many developed countries felt that China would not succeed, but China negotiated bilaterally with one country after another, and as a result, many countries were willing to join. As the lineup of members grew, the United Kingdom couldn't wait to express its willingness to become a member of the AIIB. Subsequently, Argentina, Brazil, and Belarus all joined one after another. Now, the AIIB has more than 100 members spread over six continents. China should follow the same snowballing method it used with the AIIB to establish the Asian Community.

12.7 Conclusion: Will a New Culture Be Born in Asia?

On September 15, 2022, the European Parliament passed a resolution condemning Hungary for seriously violating the democratic norms of the European Union and emphasizing that it had to do everything possible to bring Hungary back to a fully democratic regime that conforms to European values.

There is no similar set of jointly held values in East and Southeast Asia, and this has always been considered a barrier to building an Asian Community.

The stories I encountered in my research for this chapter also illustrate this issue.

On New Year's Day 2000, when I was thinking about the new world order, how to build an Asian governance system similar to the European Union was the key issue. Democracy is the consistent value system of EU member economies. I hoped to find a common value system among Asian economies. The Chinese (Huaxia) civilization is the largest and most long-standing cultural system in East Asia. Therefore, promoting deep cooperation among economies in the Chinese cultural sphere and establishing an economic community against the background of Chinese culture became the direction of my thinking about the Asian order, and I named the article "The Proposal for a Huaxia Community."

In 2002, I took an academic leave of absence from the University of Oklahoma and returned to Beijing to work for a year, eagerly promoting the concept of Huaxia Community. However, the academic community in Beijing at that time was passionately discussing joining the WTO, catching the express train of globalization, and embracing "universal values." Unexpectedly, yet understandably, this article about a tripod world order bumped against the wall everywhere and found no place for publication. I gave two academic lectures on the Huaxia Community at Peking University and Tsinghua University, but apart from a wave of skepticism, it hardly sparked any discussion, so I had to give up.

Ten years later, in 2012, after the global financial crisis, the world structure underwent significant changes, and the tripod GVC structure began to emerge. I held an academic discussion on "The New Stage of China's Opening Up and a Proposal for the Huaxia Community" at the School of Economics and Management at Tsinghua University and began to promote the idea of Huaxia Community in Asia.

My first stop was South Korea to attend an academic conference and promote the concept of Huaxia Community. The scholars at the conference responded positively to the content of the proposal but questioned the term "Huaxia," believing it carried the flavor of Greater China. They had a heated discussion and suggested a relatively neutral name: because many countries in East Asia use the lunar calendar, they proposed renaming it the Lunar Calendar Community.

My second stop was Japan to attend an academic conference and promote the concept of the Lunar Calendar Community. The Japanese scholars also responded positively to the content of the proposal, but disagreed with the term "Lunar Calendar" because Japan had abandoned the lunar calendar and uses the solar calendar. Some scholars suggested changing the name to the Confucian Community, but others opposed it, feeling that the term "Confucian" lacked inclusivity in value orientation. Later, one scholar suggested finding a cultural symbol common to the people of China, Japan, and South Korea as the name of the community. After much discussion, everyone agreed that chopsticks are used in the three countries, so they suggested changing the name to the Chopsticks Community.

My third stop was Singapore to attend an academic conference and promote the concept of the Chopsticks Community. The scholars at the conference also responded positively to the content of the proposal but disagreed with the term "Chopsticks" because Southeast Asian countries like Malaysia and Indonesia do not use chopsticks. After much discussion, the only name accepted by East and Southeast Asian countries was a geographical name, that is, the Asian Community. In fact, the name "Asian Community" had already been proposed at an ASEAN+3 leaders' meeting earlier. So from then on, I've used the name Asian Community.

This story reflects the cultural differences and diversity of values in East and Southeast Asian countries, but is this an obstacle to the construction of the Asian Community?

In the past, Southeast Asian leaders like Singapore's Prime Minister Lee Kuan Yew and Malaysia's Prime Minister Mahathir Mohamad have pointed to a set of Asian values emphasizing collectivism that differ from mainstream Western values emphasizing individualism. But such Asian values have been questioned and opposed by many. It seems that Asia does not have a set of Asian values accepted by all parties, but is this an obstacle to the construction of a new culture?

If we agree with little genius Mike's judgment that the new world and the old world are essentially different, then the new culture is a disruptive innovation to the existing culture, similar to what we talked about in Chapter 10. Then, compared to the European Union, which was about to expel Hungary for not being fully democratic, Asia is precisely a blank canvas on which to paint the newest and most beautiful pictures, possessing the latecomer's advantage of the possibility of leapfrogging. If we agree with little genius Mike's four conditions that the birthplace of the new culture needs to meet—monism; overthrow of traditional culture; openness and inclusiveness; and a strong economy—then Asia will be the place where the new culture is born, grows, and flourishes.

CHAPTER 13

The Innovative World

On the afternoon of January 1, 2000, the discussion with Mike in the morning kept me thinking about the essential differences between the new and old worlds. "Little genius" Mike emphasized that the cultures of the new and old worlds would be essentially different. As an economist, I was more concerned about differences in the driving forces of economic and social development. Only by understanding the essential differences between the driving forces of development in both the new and old worlds can we understand why the world order will undergo a paradigm shift from hegemonic succession to competitive coexistence!

The sunlight of the new world shone through the still-hanging walnuts, landing on the small table in my backyard. I opened my manuscript and wrote vigorously:

> The times are different. Human capital, technology, and other creative resources have surpassed physical capital, rivers and land, and other material resources in total quantity and play a leading role in development. Therefore, the old way of development, in which humans achieve the redistribution of material resources through deprivation, struggle, and war is being replaced by the new way of development, in which economic growth is achieved through cooperation, learning, and innovation.

The essential difference between the driving forces of development in both the new and old worlds is the difference in the leading factors of production. In the past ten thousand years of human society, what determined economic development was the distribution of physical capital: land, machinery, and

J. Ju, *US-China Great Power Competition and The New World Order*,
https://doi.org/10.1007/978-981-95-3762-4_13

factories. But since the 1990s, human capital has gradually replaced physical capital as the dominant force in economic development. The entrepreneurial elite has also changed, from the big landlords and manufacturing tycoons of the past to tech geniuses like Bill Gates and Elon Mask today.

Human capital and technological development stem from innovation. But what exactly is innovation? Is it a flash of inspiration from heaven, or can it be owned by humans? If it can be owned, what are the laws of ownership?

13.1 How to Describe the Innovation Process?

Over the past decades, a lot of research on innovation has been done in the field of economics. In the 1990s, Nobel laureate Paul M. Romer introduced the concept of human capital accumulation into the traditional economic growth model, positing that learning (the accumulation of knowledge) would improve total factor productivity and promote economic growth. Romer's endogenous growth theory embodied the process: ideas → technological progress → economic growth.[1] Nobel laureates Robert Lucas and Edward C. Prescott also made significant contributions to the macroeconomic theory of innovation and endogenous growth.[2] Jonathan Eaton and Samuel Kortum developed a microeconomic framework linking the process of individual idea generation with the distribution function of enterprise productivity. The Eaton-Kortum model lays the analytical framework for the process: ideas → innovation → technological progress → market realization.[3] Figure 13.1 illustrates this innovation process.

The source of innovation is the so-called idea cloud. Ideas are intangible and do not exist in physical form. However, ideas can be good or bad, and they can be evaluated based on their quality. The better (higher-quality) the idea, the more it can help to create useful knowledge and better technology that improves the quality of goods and services. How is the idea cloud formed? We assume that people all over the world generate ideas at every moment. These ideas come together, like droplets of water or tiny ice crystals condensed from water vapor. They merge and mix in the air, forming a cloud floating above us—this is the idea cloud: the collection of ideas generated by people on Earth from ancient times to the present.

Contemporary economic literature assumes that at any point in time, in any region of the world, there exists an idea cloud, which is represented in

[1] Paul M. Romer, "Endogenous Technological Change," *Journal of Political Economy* 98, no. 5, Part 2 (October 1, 1990): S71–102, https://doi.org/10.1086/261725.

[2] Robert E. Lucas, "On The Mechanics of Economic Development," *Journal of Monetary Economics* 22, no. 1 (July 1, 1988): 3–42, https://doi.org/10.1016/0304-3932(88)90168-7.

[3] Jonathan Eaton and Samuel Kortum, "Trade in Ideas Patenting and Productivity in the OECD," *Journal of International Economics* 40, no. 3–4 (May 1, 1996): 251–78, https://doi.org/10.1016/0022-1996(95)01407-1.

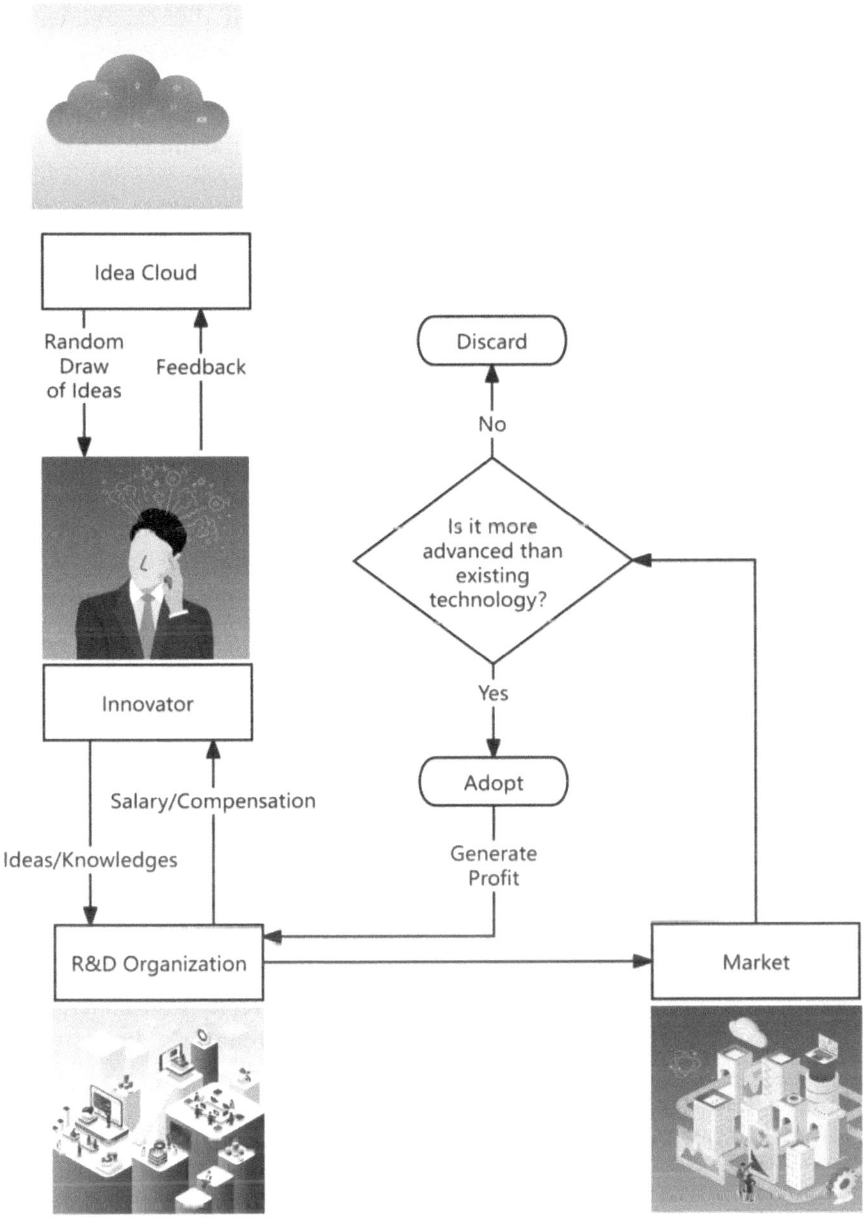

Fig. 13.1 The innovation process

the top left corner of Fig. 13.1. We assume that ideas are discrete and countable, meaning there can be one idea, two ideas, three ideas, and so on, up to an infinite number of ideas. We use a probability function to describe the process of ideas entering the human brain. What does this mean? It means that the probability of any number of ideas falling into the human brain (one idea, two ideas, *k* ideas...) within a certain period (say, one second) is given by a mathematical function. Of course, the number of ideas falling into the human brain in one second is uncertain: the smaller the number, the greater the probability.[4] We also assume that the quality of ideas is random: the higher the quality, the smaller the probability.[5]

As shown in Fig. 13.1, the innovation process includes two cycles: the first cycle is between the innovator and the idea cloud; the second cycle encompasses the innovator, the R&D institution, and the market. In the first cycle, the innovator gets one or more new ideas in his brain (that is, he makes a random draw from the idea cloud), and as he adjusts, refines, or builds on them, the modifications feed back into, and form part of, the idea cloud. In the second cycle, when the innovator obtains an idea of a certain quality, he engages in R&D to produce a new technology. The higher the quality of the idea, the better the new technology created. The new technology then has to be compared with the existing technology in the market. This comparison process is actually the process of market testing and realization. If the market does not accept the new technology, it is abandoned. If the new technology is better than the existing technology, it is adopted for a new product or production process and put on the market to realize profits. Part of the profits will be returned to the innovator as compensation for his or her efforts and to continue the next stage of innovation.

Let's use the invention of WeChat by Mr. Zhang Xiaolong and his team as an example to illustrate this innovation process.

First is the interactive cycle between the innovator and the idea cloud. In 2010, ideas (information) about instant messaging software for the mobile internet, such as MiChat, TalkBox, Kik, WhatsApp, kept falling into Zhang Xiaolong's brain. Zhang came up with the idea of creating a new communication tool for Tencent and reported this idea to Tencent's chairman, Ma Huateng. On November 19, 2010, Tencent's WeChat project was launched with Zhang in charge.

Next is the cycle with the innovator, R&D, and the market. Ma gave Zhang 100 million RMB to form his own team. On November 20, 2010, a WeChat product team of seven people was officially formed, with their office located on the 10th floor of the Southern Communications Building at 1 Huajing

[4] In the literature, the Poisson distribution function is used to represent the number of ideas entering people's minds: the probability that the number k of ideas entering the mind within a certain time period is given by $\Pr(X = k) = \frac{\lambda^k}{k!}e^{-\lambda}$.

[5] The quality of ideas is typically described by the Pareto distribution function. The probability that the quality of an idea x is less than q is $F(q) = \Pr(x \leq q) = 1 - (\frac{q}{\underline{q}})^{-\theta}$.

Road, Guangzhou. Zhang combined his idea of a new communication tool for Tencent with 100 million RMB in funds, a team of seven people, and an office on the 10th floor of the Southern Communications Building to start the development of WeChat. In early 2011, WeChat was launched and entered the market. Zhang introduced a new function that could send free text messages on WeChat 1.0.

The two cycles are constantly iterating and interacting. When it was first launched, WeChat did not have a large user base. To attract users, Zhang's team kept coming up with new ideas, such as adding more user-friendly features to WeChat, including Find People Nearby, Moments, Shake, Drift Bottle, et cetera. After the Find People Nearby feature was introduced, the number of WeChat users grew steeply. After the Shake feature was released, the number of users exploded. In March 2012, WeChat had over 100 million users. As of December 2021, WeChat was the social networking software with the most active users in China, and it had over 1.2 billion active users worldwide. The massive user traffic for WeChat has brought huge revenues for Tencent, and part of that revenue has been reinvested in Zhang's WeChat team for continued innovation.

We can summarize the innovation process discussed above in four stages: generating ideas; transforming ideas into knowledge; applying knowledge to enhance productivity; and realizing value from increased productivity.

Ideas. Ideas are intangible. They are generated by human thinking, and they are information that has yet to be stored and communicated publicly.

Knowledge. Knowledge includes codified (explicit) knowledge, and tacit (implicit) knowledge. The former refers to knowledge that can be recorded, stored, and disseminated through books, audio recordings, et cetera. The latter refers to knowledge that is difficult to record in written or audiovisual form and is typically manifested as experience that needs to be transmitted face-to-face, through in-person training, learning by doing, et cetera.

Productivity. When ideas and knowledge are applied to the production of goods and services, they contribute to productivity. Productivity can be measured or inferred to some extent through the quantity of production inputs used to produce a given quantity of output. It is the concrete manifestation of innovation. Researchers often use indicators such as total factor productivity and labor productivity to represent it. Only when ideas and knowledge are applied to R&D, develop into innovative technologies, and lead to improved productivity, will they have a real impact on the economy. An increase in productivity can be manifested as a reduction in production costs, an improvement in product quality, or the creation of new products.

Valuation. Although knowledge is essentially a public good, in order to promote scientific and technological innovation, human society has established ways to protect intellectual property rights. For example, the patent system ensures that patented knowledge and technology can only be used by its owner (or transferred to others with the owner's consent) within a certain time and space. In this way, the economic rent from their intellectual property helps innovators to realize economic value from their innovations. Beyond economic value, the creation of knowledge and technology also brings non-economic value to innovators, such as reputation. Innovation can also have social value (positive externalities) by improving people's quality of life. Finally, to the extent that innovation helps to deepen the understanding of the laws of the universe and life, it can enhance the humanity of innovators.

In sum, the innovation process develops from abstract to concrete. The idea cloud is the largest set of ideas. Only a subset of ideas is stored in some form and can be communicated as knowledge. Only a subset of knowledge can enhance productivity and help innovators realize value from their innovations.

13.2 How to Measure Innovation?

There are various forms of innovation. One is the creation of new products. New products can be new brands or modifications of existing products, such as new clothing styles, or products that did not exist before, such as electric lights that replaced kerosene lamps, mobile phones that replaced landline phones. New products improve people's quality of life.

Another form is process innovation. New production processes, technologies, or management models can lower production costs and improve product quality. For example, Walmart pioneered a supply chain management method that reduced inventories and costs, improving retail efficiency. But the classic example is the pin factory described by Adam Smith in 1776.[6] Smith observed that a worker on his own might not be able to make a single pin in a day. But by breaking up the pin manufacturing process into stages, such as drawing iron wire, straightening, sharpening the wire, making round heads, and assigning workers to each stage, a small factory of 10 workers could produce 48,000 pins a day. The process innovation called division of labor improved workers' proficiency, saved time from switching work procedures, and provided more feedback for improving the machinery—all of which led to increased output.

Here is an example from China. In 1997, Wu Ruiqiu of Dafen Oil Painting Village in Shenzhen received an order for 400,000 oil paintings to be completed in 40 days. He recruited 200 painters, calculating that each person would need to complete 50 paintings per day to fulfill the order. But the reality was that the skill level of the painters varied greatly. When they worked individually, neither the quality nor the quantity of their work met his requirements. So, Wu set up an oil painting assembly line, requiring each painter to paint only a part of each composition. For example, to make copies of Van Gogh's self-portrait, one person would outline the figure, the second would sketch the head, the third would sketch the face, the fourth would sketch the

[6] Adam Smith, "*An Inquiry Into the Nature and Causes of the Wealth of Nations*," in Oxford University Press eBooks, 1776, https://doi.org/10.1093/oseo/instance.00043218.

clothes, and the fifth would apply the colors. Five people formed a team, and each team could complete 450 paintings in a day, maintaining a consistently high quality. The order was easily completed within 40 days.

Innovation can also spawn new industries and reshape production structures. In the internet era, many network-based service industries have flourished, such as mobile payments and food delivery, changing the structure of the retail industry and making courier services a rapidly developing industry.

Given the different forms that innovation can take, how do we measure its scale and effect? Fig. 13.2 provides three indicators at the input and output ends to measure innovation. The first indicator measures the (quantity and cost of) inputs needed for innovation, for example, total expenditure on R&D and total number of R&D personnel. Modern corporate financial statements detail R&D expenses and costs, including labor, capital, and intermediate input costs. The second indicator measures the output of R&D, for example, the number of published articles and patent applications. The third indicator measures the change in productivity due to innovation.

Now let's look at these indicators for China and how it compares with other countries.

Innovation Input Index

The innovation input index includes indicators such as the number of R&D personnel (in full-time equivalents) and the ratio of R&D expenditure to GDP.

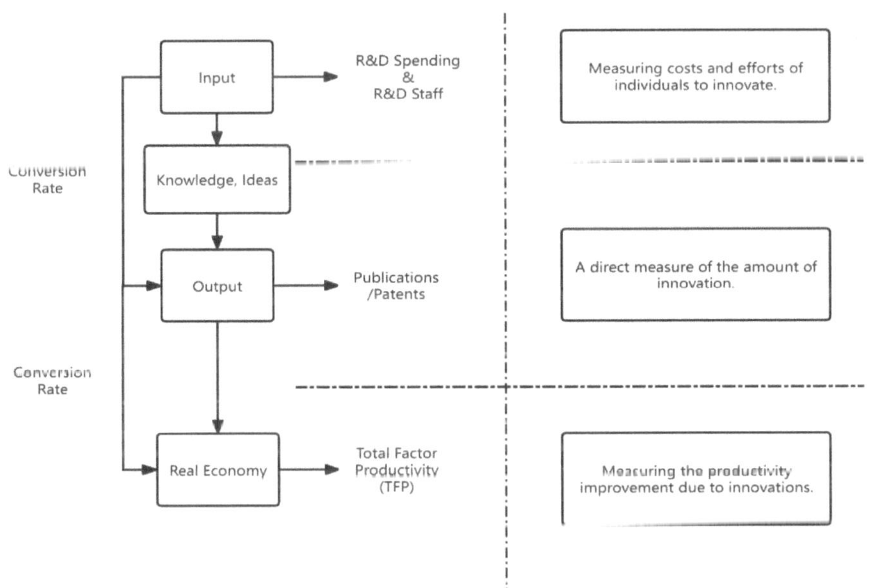

Fig. 13.2 Measurement standards for innovation

From a base value of 100 in 2005, China's innovation input index rose to 219 in 2021. China's R&D expenditure increased from 1.32% of GDP in 2005 to 2.44% of GDP in 2021—an increase of 84.8%—while its R&D full-time equivalents increased from 136.48 million person-years in 2005 to 571.6 million person-years in 2021, an average annual growth rate of 9.4%. This demonstrates that in recent years, the number of scientific researchers in China has shown a steady upward trend.

How does China compare against major economies like the European Union, Germany, India, Japan, Russia, and the United States? Among these seven economies, China's R&D expenditure ranked second to last in 2000—slightly higher than India's and 1/9 that of the United States. But China's R&D expenditure increased from $39.8 billion in 2000 to $514.8 billion in 2019, nearly a 13-fold increase in nearly 20 years, with an average annual growth rate of 14.5%. By 2020, China's R&D expenditure had risen to the second highest in the world, surpassing the European Union's and second only to the United States.

Innovation Output Index

The innovation output index includes indicators such as the number of scientific papers per 10,000 people. From a base value of 100 in 2005, China's innovation output index reached 353.6 in 2021. In 2021, China published 2.034 million scientific papers, more than twice the 943,400 papers in 2005.

Internationally, China published over 400,000 papers in the field of science and engineering in 2016, surpassing the world's leading country, the United States, for the first time (but fewer than the 600,000 papers of EU countries as a group). However, in terms of the number of articles with the highest citation rates (the top 1%), China ranks third after the United States and the European Union but ahead of Japan. The average citation rate of Chinese papers is slightly lower than the world average. Therefore, while China has significantly increased its output of internationally published papers in science and engineering, there is still room for improvement in the quality and impact, as measured by their citation rates.

Thanks to its large national scale and population base, China's total number of patent applications is high. China's patent applications increased from 51,900 in 2000 to 1.5857 million in 2021, a 30.55-fold increase in 21 years, with an average annual growth rate of 17.68%. Since 2010, China's patent applications have far exceeded those of the six other major economies (the United States ranks second and the European Union third). China also ranks first in the number of patent applications approved, with the United States second and the European Union third. Therefore, China has not only seen an increase in the number of patent applications but also a faster growth rate of successful applications. However, China's patent approval rate remains lower than that of the United States. In 2021, China had 1.5856 million patent applications and 695,900 approvals, yielding an approval rate of 43.9%. In comparison, the United States registered 591,500 patent applications in 2021, with 327,300 approved, yielding an approval rate of 55.33%. While China's patent applications and approvals far exceed those of the United States in absolute terms, its patent approval rate still needs to catch up with the United States'.

Overall, whether it's R&D expenditure, patents, or papers, by 2020, China's annual innovation output was the first or second highest in the world. However, due to the late start of scientific research efforts, China has lagged behind the United States in patent application approval rates and paper citations. The quality of innovation in China still requires further improvement.

Innovation Effectiveness Index

The innovation effectiveness index includes indicators such as the ratio of new product sales revenue to main business revenue. From a base value of 100 in 2005, China's innovation effectiveness index reached 189.5 in 2021. In 2021, the sales revenue of new products of industrial enterprises above a designated size in China was 29.6 trillion RMB, nearly 12 times the 2.28 trillion RMB in 2004.

13.3 Five Assumptions About the Idea Cloud

In the economics literature, the idea cloud is a theoretical construct describing the innovation process. What is the idea cloud? The sum of all ideas of all people since the birth of humanity constitutes a part of the idea cloud. Ideas are the source of innovation, so the nature of the idea cloud determines the basic properties of innovation. We can summarize the properties of the idea cloud in the following five assumptions.

The Quality of Ideas Follows a Pareto Distribution

In 1897, Italian economist Vilfredo Pareto studied wealth and income distribution patterns in nineteenth-century Britain and other countries, and he concluded that the distribution of wealth among a population is unbalanced, with 20% of the people owning 80% of the society's wealth. Over time, many people found that the 80/20 rule could be applied to other outcomes, for example, the distribution of IQ in a population, the distribution of paper citations in a group of researchers, et cetera. Pareto used an exponential function to describe the data distribution pattern he observed, which is called the Pareto distribution. The Pareto distribution is generally used to describe an unequal distribution in economic and social activities, though not necessarily exactly 80/20; it can reflect the 80/20 rule under certain specific parameters.

We assume that the quality of ideas follows a Pareto distribution. To explain this, let's suppose we randomly select 100 stock investors to predict the closing price of the Shanghai Shenzhen 300 Index the next day. Each investor makes an independent prediction according to their own ideas. The more accurate the prediction, the higher is the quality of the investor's idea about the Shanghai Shenzhen 300 Index on that day. Out of 100 stock market investors, typically around 20 people's predictions will be relatively accurate, meaning that they will deviate less from the actual value, while the predictions of the other 80 people will deviate more from the actual value. In other words, if the quality of their ideas follows a specific Pareto distribution, then out of 100 randomly selected people, approximately 20 people will have good quality ideas and 80 people will have poor quality ideas.

Here's another example: suppose a teacher asks everyone in his class to independently write an essay on "A Tripod World Order" in 10 minutes. After 10 minutes, the teacher collects the essays and grades them. If the number of students in the class is large enough, say 1,000, the teacher might find that the quality of the essays approaches a specific Pareto distribution: 20% of the essays will deserve a good grade, while 80% of the essays will deserve only average or lower grades.

The Quality Distribution of Ideas Differs Across Regions

The quality of ideas in each geographic region follows a Pareto distribution, but the parameters of the distribution may be different in different regions. For example, suppose there is an economics lecture in Room 101 and a mathematics lecture in Room 201 at 10 a.m. today. The content of the ideas in Room 101 and Room 201 will be different—Room 101 will have more economics ideas and Room 201 will have more mathematics ideas. But the quality of ideas in Room 101 and the quality of ideas in Room 201 both follow a Pareto distribution, although the shape and scale of the distribution could be different.

Ideas can travel across regions. People in one region can acquire ideas from another region through communication. Suppose Mike goes to Room 101 to attend the economics lecture, and Grace goes to Room 201 to attend the mathematics lecture, and suppose the lectures in the two classrooms are also livestreamed online. Then even though Grace is in Room 201, she can listen to the economics lecture on her phone, and she can acquire economics ideas from the lecture in Room 101.

But there are costs associated with the spread of ideas. The closer you are to an idea, the easier it is to acquire it. Mike is more likely to acquire economic ideas than Grace because he is in Room 101 and he can directly ask the lecturer questions about economics. Even if Grace can livestream the economics lecture in Room 201, it is not convenient for her to interact with the lecturer in Room 101. The cost for Grace to acquire economic ideas would be higher.

The Quality Distribution of Ideas Is History-Dependent

Knowledge is about the accumulation of ideas; therefore, ideas have the property of history-dependence. Specifically, the quality of tomorrow's ideas depends on the quality of today's ideas, and the quality of today's ideas depends on the quality of yesterday's ideas. For example, one of my graduate students is working on a doctoral thesis on US-China technological competition. His current research idea is based on papers he has read over the past two years related to the international trade course he took for his master's degree, the intermediate microeconomics course he took as an undergraduate, and the mathematics course he took in high school. In short, his current research idea is based on his long-term accumulation of knowledge.

Ideas Have the Attributes of Public Goods

Ideas themselves have the attributes of public goods, that is, non-rivalry in use and non-excludability of benefits. Rivalry refers to the fact that when one person uses (consumes) a product, the amount of that product available for others to use is reduced. For example, if there is only one bottle of milk on the table and Mike drinks it, then Grace cannot have any milk. Ideas are non-rivalrous because when one person uses an idea, it does not reduce the number of ideas available for others to use. For example, if Mike knows the correct answer to the exam, it does not prevent other students from knowing the correct answer.

Non-excludability means that no one can be excluded from enjoying the benefits of the product. Ideas are non-excludable because there is no way to prevent someone from getting an idea. For example, I have always had the idea of singing at the Wudaokou subway station after retirement, but I cannot prevent other professors at Peking University from having the same idea. (Of course, which professor can actually sing at the Wudaokou subway station after retirement depends on individual effort and luck.)

The Evolution of Ideas Is Objective and Subjective

What determines the quality and quantity of ideas in the idea cloud? Each person's thinking activity is influenced by existing ideas, the material environment, labor, capital, and other inputs (such as scientific research instruments and materials) in the innovation process. At the same time, each person's thinking activity also contributes new ideas to the idea cloud. We call the former the objective evolution of ideas and the latter the subjective evolution of ideas. The process of accepting ideas is also the process of creating ideas, so ideas are both objective and subjective.

If ideas are only generated from existing objective knowledge, then there would not be original innovation or creating something out of nothing. The meaning of original innovation is to create new ideas that do not currently exist. Material resources are objectively existing resources, facts, and laws, so ideas cannot come solely from material resources. At the same time, ideas are more than just exogenous events. People create new ideas in the process of thinking, that is to say, ideas are not only objectively but also subjectively generated in the process of thinking and exploring the unknown.

13.4 The Innovative World Model

Based on the above five assumptions, we can develop a model of the innovative world. This model can be roughly described as follows.

There are about 8 billion people in the world, and the innovation process of each person is as shown in Fig. 13.1. The generation of each person's ideas is random, following a Poisson distribution function.[7] The quality of each person's ideas is also random, following a Pareto distribution function with certain parameters. The generation of ideas by each person is a random draw process, similar to a lottery, with equal probabilities ex ante (before the event) and heterogeneous outcomes ex post (after the event). That is to say, everyone has the same chance to generate high-quality ideas at the start of the innovation process, but the quality of ideas actually generated by everyone will be different—some will have high-quality ideas and some will have low-quality ideas.

The spread of ideas across geographic regions takes time, and the length of time it takes is random. After a person receives an idea, it is transformed into knowledge and disseminated through language, symbols, text, and other means; the process of dissemination requires a certain amount of time.

Each company will choose the best quality ideas from all of its researchers' ideas and compare them against the existing technology. If a new idea is of higher quality, it will be adopted as the future production technology; otherwise, the idea will be abandoned and the existing technology will be retained. Each company will combine its winning new ideas with capital, labor, and other inputs to produce new or improved products and put them on the market at the highest possible price to obtain the highest possible profit.

Each company's productivity follows a random distribution function. It is rigorously proven in the economic literature that the productivity of a company generated by the above "idea → innovation → technological progress → market realization" process follows a Fréchet function.[8]

How can such a mathematical model be tested? A company's productivity can be measured by the total factor productivity (TFP). The data we can measure are the companies' TFP. A large number of empirical studies on the

[7] A parameter is a pre-determined variable within a functional relationship that, aside from the independent and dependent variables, influences the relationship between them. For example, in the Poisson distribution function $\Pr(X = k) = \frac{\lambda^k}{k!}e^{-\lambda}$, λ is a parameter.

[8] The productivity of firms follows a Frechet distribution. Specifically, the probability that the productivity Z_i of firm i is below z is given by $F_i(z) = \Pr(Z_i \leq z) = e^{-T_i z^{-\theta}}$

distribution of company TFP have found that the Fréchet distribution function can indeed describe the distribution of companies' TFP, which indirectly test a series of assumptions of the idea cloud and the innovation model.

The Innovative World model and the Quantum Mechanics model, born a century ago, have many similarities, as shown in Table 13.1.

Both the Innovative World Model and the Quantum Mechanics Model explore the laws of motion that are invisible and intangible, and both are described by probability distribution functions. But, of course, there are fundamental differences between the two. The Innovative World Model describes the non-material world, while the Quantum Mechanics Model describes the material world.

So, what insights does the mathematical similarity between the Innovative World Model and the Quantum Mechanics Model give us? First, just as fundamental particles are unmeasurable, individual ideas are also unmeasurable. However, this does not prevent the idea cloud from having a stable, measurable distribution, with individual ideas being just an observed value of the idea cloud. Second, the stable distribution of the idea cloud allows us to explore the laws of the idea cloud. Third, the unobservable laws of the idea cloud can be indirectly described and revealed by the observable distribution of firms' productivity. Fourth, just as quantum mechanics' exploration of the

Table 13.1 Similarities between the Quantum Mechanics Model and the Innovative World Model

	Quantum Mechanics Model	*Innovative World Model*
Basic Unit	Basic Particles	Ideas
Micro perspective	Particles have heterogeneous energy	The quality of ideas is heterogeneous, following a Pareto distribution
Macro perspective	The wave function is used to predict the possible position and speed of particles, and the propagation process of waves in space and time is described by the wave equation	The quality distribution of ideas can be indirectly measured by the distribution of firms' productivity. The diffusion of the idea cloud also has the property of spatial decay with geographical distance and time lag
The principle and meaning of uncertainty	The state of a particle before observation exists in the form of a probability distribution, and once an observation is made, what is observed is the collapse of the distribution to a specific state with a probability of 1	Ideas exist in the form of a probability distribution. The generation of an idea is the result of drawing a certain idea from the idea cloud

laws of the basic particles has greatly advanced our understanding of the world, promoted the development of productivity, and changed our lives, the exploration of the laws of the idea cloud will also advance our further understanding of the world and transform our lives.

13.5 Conundrums in the Innovative World: The Game of Finding Water in the Desert

In the twenty-first century, humanity has entered a new world. The Innovative World Model establishes a theoretical framework for understanding and analyzing this new world. So, what features does this new world have that are different from the past? How can these new features help us understand the competition between great powers and the construction of the new world order?

Ideas are the source of innovation. In this section, we present a game of "finding water in the desert" to analyze the basic conundrums of the new world. In this game, water is similar to ideas, and finding water is similar to innovation.

Let's imagine this scene: a group of 100 people are moving forward in the desert. There is not enough water in the desert. Once they finish drinking the water they carry with them, they must find water. If they can't find water, they can't survive to get out of the desert.

However, just knowing that you need to find water is far from enough. Next comes a series of challenging questions. Should these 100 people go in the same direction to find water, or should each of them find water separately? After finding a water source, does it belong to the person who found it, or is it shared equally among all? Should they spend time looking for water themselves, or buy water from others who have found water already? Each question is real and relates to the survival of these 100 people. If you were one of them, what would you choose?

The above three questions, when put in the context of innovation, become three basic conundrums of innovation. Should innovation be centralized or decentralized? Should the results of innovation be public or private? Should we innovate independently (creation) or innovate through imitation? There is no single correct answer to these questions, but by analyzing these three conundrums, we can better understand innovation in the new world.

13.5.1 The First Problem: Concentration or Dispersion?

We make two assumptions about the 100 people looking for water in the desert: they are homogeneous ex ante, meaning each person has the same chance of finding water—20%; and they are heterogeneous ex post, meaning those who find water will survive and those who do not find water will die. These 100 people need to make a decision: act together and search for water as a group, or disperse and search for water independently?

The probability of finding water in any one direction, whether for 100 people acting together or just one person, is the same: 20%. If these 100 people group together and concentrate in one direction to search for water, what would be the result? The result would be: either they are lucky and find water, and all 100 people survive; or they don't find it, and everyone dies of thirst. What is the probability that they can find water and all survive? It's 20%. If they disperse and act independently, with each person going in a different direction to look for water, then out of 100 people, there might be 20 people who find water (because the probability of finding water is 20%), but there will be 80 people who don't find water. This means that 20 people will survive, and 80 people will die. The difference between dispersion and concentration is that if they disperse, 20 people are likely to survive, and 80 people are likely to die; if they concentrate, either all die or all survive, but either way the probability of survival at the outset is the same: 20%.

So, should they concentrate or disperse in their search for water? The expected results of concentrating and dispersing in the search for water are the same, but each option has its own advantages and disadvantages. Concentrating in the search for water is fair beforehand and fair afterward: if they are lucky, all 100 people survive together; if they are unlucky, all 100 people die together. Dispersing in the search for water is fair beforehand but unequal afterward: in the group of 100 people, some (the lucky ones) will survive, but the unlucky ones will die.

Concentrating in the search for water is similar to government-led centralized innovation, while dispersing in the search for water is similar to market-led, decentralized innovation. The centralized decision-making of the government and the decentralized decision-making of the market are different processes, each with its own advantages and disadvantages.

Other factors might come into play. For example, if the 100 people searching for water as a group could find an experienced leader who has been in the desert before and has a higher probability of finding water (say, 30% or 40%), everyone would be willing to listen to him. In this case, centralized decision-making would be better than decentralized decision-making. Or if the 100 people searching for water separately all have phones and can communicate with one another, those who see traces of water in one direction could let others know, and in the end, there might be more people, say 30 or 40, who will find water and survive. If information sharing is possible, then dispersing in the search for water might be better than concentrating. Concentration and dispersion can even complement each other—it may be possible to design more complex mechanisms that can better utilize the advantages of both options to increase the probability of finding water successfully.

Nonetheless, concentration versus dispersion is the first conundrum in the process of innovation. Concentration makes everyone go in the same direction. There will be the power of unity. If the direction is right, the power is multiplied, but if the direction is wrong, the whole army will be wiped out. Dispersion gives everyone a chance, but some people will definitely be eliminated, and there will be inequality ex post.

13.5.2 The Second Problem: Public or Private?

Suppose the 100 people have decided to disperse in their search for water. Now let's assume that any water source they find will be enough for all 100 people. Further assume that each person has $1,000 and satellite phones can be used in the desert at a cost of $100 per call. Given the 20% probability of success, 20 people will find a water source, while 80 people will not. Should the lucky 20 who find water call to notify their companions?

The question is: is the found water source public, shared by all who arrive at it, or is it private, belonging to the first person who finds it? This question applies to innovation too: ideas are public goods, but is the new technology invented by the lucky ones who get high-quality ideas first public or private?

If the water source is public, this means that the person who finds it first and spends $100 to call and inform his companions of its location cannot charge them for this information or prevent anyone who arrives at the source from drinking the water. If everyone is selfish and only considers their own interests, those who find a water source will not spend $100 to save their companions' lives. If some of those who find a water source are not so selfish and are willing to spend money to notify their companions, then more people will be able to survive and leave the desert. So the outcome depends on how selfless the people who find water sources are. If Tom finds a water source and calls his companion Mike, who should pay for the $100 call—Tom or Mike? What if Mike refuses to pay for the call after drinking the water?

If the water source is private, this means that whoever finds it owns it. If 20 people find water and 80 people do not, but each person who finds water can help four companions who don't have water, then everyone could survive. Suppose Tom finds a water source and it now belongs to him. If he has a business mind, he might call his good friend Mike and ask Mike to pay him $100 for the call and partner up with him to guard the water source. They would sequentially notify Bob, Grace, and Diana, each one of whom would have to hand over all the $1,000 they have before they are allowed to drink water. The money handed over by Bob, Grace, and Diana will be split evenly between Tom and Mike. If they do not pay, Tom and Mike will fight them off and not let them drink the water. Such a sharing system is established through force, but once it is established, it becomes effective. If all 20 people who find water act like Tom and recruit a helper like Mike, it would be possible for all 100 people to drink water and leave the desert. But inequality would rise: 40 people would have $92,000 and 60 people would be left without money.

What if the probability of finding water is not 20%, but 1%, and Tom is the lucky one who finds the water source? He can call his good friend Mike and the two of them can sequentially call the remaining 98 people to the water source and collect $1,000 from each one in order to drink water. Now two people would have $90,100 and 98 people would be left with no money. Tom and Mike's privatization of the water source and their profiteering from it would cause great inequality. In a harsh survival environment like the desert, such great inequality is likely to lead to unrest. For example, after Bob receives the call, he might gather a group of people to seize the water source from Tom and Mike.

If water sources are public, those who find them have no incentive to inform their companions, and the efficiency of water utilization will not be high. If water sources are private, inequality will rise, leading to social unrest. Just like in this game, whether the results of innovation should be public or private is a conundrum for the innovation process.

The idea cloud is a public good, so innovation derived from it also has the attributes of a public good. This is because the cloud of ideas is formed by the thoughts of everyone on this planet: it contains your ideas and my ideas, the ideas of Chinese people and Americans, the ideas of contemporary people and our predecessors. These ideas are constantly generated, condensed, mixed, and altered before a droplet falls into a lucky mind, takes root, and becomes a truly valuable innovation. The innovations of Einstein, Jobs, Musk, and others didn't come out of thin air. Their ideas cannot be separated from the education and professional training they received, the scientific research accumulated by their predecessors, and the academic environment, laboratories, equipment, and teams provided by the entire scientific community. Behind any great innovation there is always a group of great scientists who, through a long process, build up collective wisdom and effort, paving the way for one genius to complete the final sprint at a certain critical point in time. The applause and glory certainly belong to this genius, but can we say that the innovation is entirely his contribution? Of course not. Ideas cannot be generated or realized independently by one person alone.

Since ideas are public goods that anyone can use, the question is: if the results and benefits of innovation cannot be attributed to oneself, who would still have the motivation to innovate? In order to encourage the generation of new ideas and promote the development of new technologies, we must privatize knowledge and technology to a certain extent through intellectual property rights protection. The privatization of knowledge and technology versus the public-good attribute of innovation is the second basic conundrum in the innovation process.

13.5.3 The Third Problem: Imitation or Creation?

The two most common paths of innovation are the endogenous path and the exogenous path. The endogenous path refers to one's own thinking, experiments, exploration, and independent innovation, while the exogenous path refers to learning from others, imitation, and making improvements or iterations based on others' innovations. So, should we innovate independently or innovate by imitation?

Let's go back to the 100 people spreading out to look for water in the desert. As before, the probability of finding water is 20%. This means that among the 100 different paths they can take to find water, 20 will have a water source. Suppose the water source is private, meaning the finder will own the property rights. Suppose Tom is the first to find a water source. After discovering it, he calls Mike to join him in guarding it and making money from it. Mike comes. Then Tom calls Bob, telling him to come to the water source to drink if he pays $1,000 RMB. Bob has two choices: he can either go to Tom's water source to drink water and survive, but hand over all his money, or he can continue to search for a water source on his own. The first choice corresponds to the process of innovation by imitation, and the second choice represents the process of creation. Should Bob choose the first choice or the second choice?

Since the first water source has been discovered by Tom, this leaves 19 water sources to be discovered and 99 directions in which to look. If Bob continues to search for water sources on his own, his probability of finding a water source is 19/99. If he finds a water source, he can, like Tom, find a partner to guard the water source and sell the water to three people for $1,000 each. Since it costs $300 to make three phone calls, he and his partner would make $2,700. Bob needs to decide whether he should continue searching for a water source by himself to survive and make money (but with the risk of dying of thirst), or pay $1,000 to go to Tom's water source to drink water and survive (without the risk of dying of thirst).

In the context of innovation, if you choose to innovate independently, the risk of failure is greater, but if successful, the technology you master will be more advanced, and the profits will be higher. If you choose to innovate by imitation, you will depend on core technology from elsewhere, but the risk of failure is lower and you can quickly produce the latest products. However, innovation by imitation carries the risk of being stopped from advancing if the source country for the needed core technology decides to restrict its technology exports. Creation versus imitation is the third conundrum in the innovation process. Of course, in the real world, creation and imitation may not be mutually exclusive, and it may be possible to combine them, but still, there would always be the question of whether it is better to focus on one versus the other.

13.6 The New World Order and the Conundrums of Innovation

Concentration versus dispersion, public versus private, imitation versus creation—these three questions constitute the fundamental conundrums of the innovative world. Neither centralized innovation + public ownership + imitation, nor decentralized innovation + private ownership + creation is a stable and efficient innovation mechanism in the long term. A good innovation system strikes a balance in each of these three areas, with varying emphases at different times.

Let's talk about dispersion versus concentration first. Dispersion—market-led decentralized innovation—is suitable at the forefront of technology, when the future is uncharted territory and no one knows which direction is the most fruitful. Moving beyond the technological frontier could involve incremental technological innovation, requiring long-term efforts to improve the cutting edge of existing technology, or disruptive technological innovation, requiring the courage to abandon old technology and develop new technology. When there is no one ahead to lead the way, one cannot know for sure which direction is best to take. In this situation, decentralized, market-led innovation may be more appropriate. But if we are not at the forefront of technology but rather in the catch-up stage, the direction of innovation is more or less known. In that case, centralized government-led innovation may be more appropriate for organizing and concentrating R&D resources in the right direction.

Now let's talk about private versus public ownership of ideas. A certain amount of reward in the form of private ownership of successful ideas, can provide the right incentive to stimulate innovation. On the other hand, public ownership of ideas will allow more people to benefit from—and possibly build on—the successful innovations. To balance these considerations, intellectual property rights could be granted and protected for a certain period.

Finally, let's discuss creation versus imitation. We can think of creation as endogenous innovation, that is, creating ideas by oneself, and imitation as exogenous innovation, that is, not creating ideas by oneself, but imitating and learning from existing ideas by others. Technologies developed through creation belong to the creator, but the process is slow and difficult. Technologies developed through imitation are not original and generally do not become core technologies, but the process is relatively fast and easy. In general, a large economy must have the ability to create, and it must have a complete and open innovation system. If a country does not develop its own core technologies, it risks being too dependent on, and held hostage by, its competitors. Moreover, creation advances the ability to learn—one cannot master postgraduate courses at the primary school level. However, according to the Innovative World Model, ideas are distributed globally, and countries are at varying distances from the technological frontier. Therefore, openness, learning, and imitation are crucial for a country to reach, or remain at the forefront of technology.

In conclusion, an innovation system should be open, encouraging learning and imitation of all advanced technologies. A large economy, like United States or China, should be competitive in key technology areas, and it should encourage strategically important industries to reach the global technological frontier or even move it forward. To achieve this, it should restrict foreign monopolies of core technologies and protect its own technological security, for example, it could ensure that the domestic market share of foreign technologies does not exceed a certain threshold (say, 70%) and that indigenous (domestically developed) technologies do not lag world-leading technologies by a certain threshold (say, one or two generations).

13.6.1 The Driving Force of Development in the Innovative World

The new world is driven by innovation, and innovation comes from ideas, so the continuous generation of high-quality new ideas is the driving force of development in the new world. When everyone actively pursues ideas, the new world will generate a greater quantity and higher quality of ideas, and thereby achieve faster growth. We can think of this as maximizing the total number of quality-weighted ideas, and this is the driving force of development in the innovative world.[9]

How to understand this? When a person maximizes their total number of quality-weighted ideas, this will bring them the highest profit, maximizing their personal interest. Assuming this person's individual maximization behavior does not affect others' ability to obtain high-quality ideas, their contribution to society's accumulation of knowledge and their understanding of the world are also maximized. Overall, assuming one person's maximization behavior does not hinder other's maximization behavior, then everyone's pursuit of maximizing their total number of quality-weighted ideas would serve their own personal interests as well as the interests of society and humankind as a whole.

However, the quality of ideas is relative. A person might try to prevent others from getting more and higher quality ideas that could overshadow their own ideas to maintain a form of monopoly on ideas. Such behavior would maximize the person's individual interests but not the interests of society or humankind. This so-called monopoly of ideas is the fundamental issue in the innovative world.

13.6.2 The Fundamental Issue of the Innovation World: Can Ideas Be Monopolized?

There are two ways to form a monopoly on ideas: one is through the market or, what people sometimes call Big Tech, and the other is through the government, that is, state monopolies.

First, let's talk about market monopolies. In the twenty-first century, Big Tech companies have emerged, and they are growing larger in scale. Apple's market value once exceeded \$3 trillion—more than the GDP of the United Kingdom, making it the world's "fifth-largest economy" after the United

[9] Suppose the set of quality space is denoted by Z, where z represents any idea within the quality space, and $n(z)$ represents the number of ideas with the z quality produced by one person. The "quality-weighted ideas" for this person are then defined as the sum of the products of the idea's quality and the number of ideas of the same quality, i.e., $\sum_{z \in Z} z \times n(z)$.

States, China, Japan, and Germany. The economic size of Big Tech companies now exceeds that of most countries.

The emergence of Big Tech is a characteristic of the innovative world. The important products of the new economy are knowledge, information, and software products, all of which originate from the idea cloud and have the properties of public goods. The fixed costs of producing these products are enormous. For example, developing a new operating system requires hundreds of billions of dollars in R&D investment. But the marginal cost of producing these products, such as an app download or a software copy, is almost zero. New economy products often have higher productivity with more data flow, and Big Tech companies often make money from large-scale databases. Many new products such as Facebook, WeChat, Amazon, and Alibaba are platform products that have strong network externalities: the more people participate in the network, the larger the traffic, the more convenient and efficient it is. All these characteristics mean that new economy companies have increasing returns to scale—the larger the company, the higher its efficiency—which makes them natural monopolies. The market structure for key industries in the new economy is not perfect competition, but a monopoly.

Next, let's talk about government or state monopolies. R&D investments are increasingly concentrated in a few large countries, making innovation also increasingly concentrated in these countries. Against the backdrop of great power competition, the US government is increasingly using all its powers to curb innovation in China.

Whether it's market monopolies or state monopolies, as long as they exceed a certain scale, they are not conducive to innovation! Because monopolies have no competition, and they have no incentive to keep generating new ideas and innovating to thrive.

There is no shortage of monopolies in the world. But monopolies in the old world controlled physical resources like land and oil, while monopolies in the new world control data, technology, and potentially even ideas. The concept of monopolizing ideas is discussed by Yuval Harari in his 2016 book *Homo Deus: A Brief History of Tomorrow*. Harari predicts that with advancements in AI, machines will eventually outperform humans in various jobs, including workers, lawyers, doctors, high-frequency stock traders, and even artists, and ordinary people will become redundant or controlled by AI. However, some people may evolve into superhumans or godlike humans, who will control AI algorithms, which in turn will control the ordinary people.

Harari's predictions may not be far off. Elon Musk's Neuralink is inventing a human brain chip that, once implanted, could potentially enhance cognitive abilities, restore physical functions, treat Alzheimer's disease, transplant or delete memories, and even connect to the internet. If such a chip is successfully developed, it could lead to the emergence of a group of godlike human beings with superintelligence. The technology of the brain chip is Musk's, and he can certainly make different grades of brain chips and decide who gets to use the highest grade, who gets to use the lower grades, and who doesn't get to use the chip at all. Those with the high-grade brain chip can more efficiently generate and apply high-quality ideas and innovate. They can essentially monopolize the idea cloud and ultimately control all of humanity, just like Tom finding and privatizing the water source in the desert and holding the rest of the group to ransom. Ideas and technologies should belong to and serve all of humanity and not be used to turn a small number of people into godlike beings that control all of humanity.

If a technological "genius" like Musk monopolizes the brain chip, even if he wishes to serve humanity and not become a "godlike" being, he cannot. As long as there is a monopoly, the power of monopolistic capital will prevent him from serving all people. The profit-driven nature of capital will use the brain chip to enslave humanity, exploiting every ordinary person outside the "godlike" elite.

Once a technological "genius" like Musk monopolizes the brain chip, can he and his closest friends comfortably become "godlike" beings and control all of humanity? He cannot! From the first day that a "genius" like Musk monopolizes the brain chip, he and his closest friends will immediately live in fear and turmoil. Who doesn't want to be a "godlike" being? Who is willing to be enslaved? From the first day of the "genius" monopolizing the brain chip, the enslaved ordinary people will surely rise up and rebel, and soon, the "godlike" beings will be overthrown, eliminated, and discarded, and the successful rebels will become the new "godlike" beings, continuing to monopolize the brain chip and enslave all of humanity. Then there will be new uprisings and new "godlike" beings, and so on in a cycle. As long as the brain chip can be monopolized, the immense temptation to become a "godlike" being and control all of humanity will plunge the world into continuous turmoil and war, preventing any lasting peace.

Since the beginning of humanity, everyone has been free to dream—just as the old saying goes, "In dreams, anything can happen." But should technological "geniuses" like Elon Musk monopolize brain chips, the freedom to dream may slip away from most of us.

Should humanity allow the monopoly of ideas and its consequences, or should we prevent the monopoly of ideas so that everyone is equal before the idea cloud? Returning to the game of searching for water in the desert: if a map accurately depicting the location of the water source appears, should we allow the group to fight over it, with the winner becoming the king and the rest becoming slaves? Or should we design a mechanism to give everyone equal access to the water source information?

To prevent the monopoly of ideas in the market, the government needs to step in to check the market monopoly's power. And to limit the monopoly of ideas by the government, other countries need to be able to compete and check the government's power. But even a relatively big economy like Italy—the eighth-largest economy in the world—cannot single-handedly contend with Big Tech companies like Apple, Amazon, Google, Facebook, and Tesla, let alone future Big Tech companies. The only governments that are able to provide a counterbalance to Big Tech are the United States, China, and the European Union.

The governments of the United States, China, and the European Union need to work together to prevent a global monopoly of products like brain chips. For example, they could collaborate to ensure that Big Tech companies do not occupy more than 50% of the market share in each of their economies, which means that each economy would have at least two brain chip companies. If the United States, China, and the European Union each have at least two brain chip companies, there will be at least six companies competing globally, which will prevent any single economy from dominating the market.

The monopoly of ideas will bring serious ethical issues. Ensuring fair competition in the market for brain chips and similar products and protecting everyone's freedom to generate ideas, thoughts, and dreams will lay the foundation for peace, stability, and development in the new world. Ensuring equality before the idea cloud is a fundamental challenge for the new world, one which a tripod world governance system should provide a foundation for addressing.

13.6.3 Conclusion

Under the blue sky and among the white clouds, we are observing an ever-changing world. In late July 1997, shortly after Hong Kong returned to China, I went to Hong Kong to attend the Far East Conference of the Econometric Society. After the conference, the plane roared away from Hong Kong, where the five-star red flag and the Bauhinia flag had just been raised. In this place where East meets West, observing the world between heaven and earth, I saw the Pacific and the sky merge into one color under the sunlight. I was filled with thoughts and wrote a poem, which is a fitting conclusion for this chapter.

Reflections
July 1997, Hong Kong[10]

Ten thousand mountains stand high and low, a thousand flowers fragrant,
A thousand waters flow fast and slow, ten thousand moons bright.
Sitting down, one travels a million miles with the earth,
Looking up, a billion eras have passed.
East winds and west rains build the great way,
Rivers rush to the ocean's bay.
Water carries the universe in one hue set,
Sun's light captures all in a golden net.

[10] The poem is translated from the Chinese.

CHAPTER 14

China's Competition Strategy for the Next Ten Years (2025–2035)

According to the five stages of US-China relations in Chapter 3, we are currently in the third stage, that is, the first half of great power competition. The main feature of this stage for China is catching up with the United States in economic size, as measured by (nominal) GDP. Therefore, the success or failure of China's competition strategy can be measured by one indicator: whether China's (nominal) GDP can catch up with the United States' by 2035.

14.1 How Realistic Is China's Goal?

GDP is a macroeconomic indicator of the size of the economy. For China to achieve the strategic goal of catching up with US GDP by 2035, it would have to steadily narrow the gap with the United States in the still lagging areas of technology, finance, military strength, and global governance. This would provide a foundation for China to gradually surpass the United States in these four areas during the second half of the competition stage (2036–2060). According to Chapter 9, to achieve this strategic goal, China would have to successfully prevent six types of crises—a Japan-type crisis, a Soviet-type crisis, a financial (currency) crisis, a social crisis, a public policy crisis, and a regional security crisis—to achieve strong economic growth.

In 2022, China's GDP of $17.96 trillion is approximately 70.5% of US GDP ($25.46 trillion). China's population is approximately 4.24 times the US population: China's population was 1.41218 billion, and the US population was 333.29 million. Hence China's per capita GDP of $12,700 is only 1/6 that of the United States ($76,400).

J. Ju, *US-China Great Power Competition and The New World Order*,
https://doi.org/10.1007/978-981-95-3762-4_14

By 2035, according to some predictions, China's population will be 1.401 billion, while the US population will be 350 million. Thus, China's population will be four times that of the United States.[1] If China's per capita GDP reaches 1/4 of US per capita GDP by 2035, China's GDP will have caught up with US GDP. This would require China's average annual GDP growth rate from 2025 to 2035 to be about 4% higher than that of the United States. This goal is both realistic and challenging.

Japan's experience is worth learning from. Figure 14.1 shows the per capita GDP and GDP of Japan relative to the United States from 1960 to 2020. Japan's per capita GDP in 1960 was $475, about 1/6 of US per capita GDP ($3007). In the following ten years, Japan's economy grew rapidly, at an average rate of 8.47% per year; by 1970, Japan's per capita GDP had increased to $2056 or 39% of US per capita GDP ($5234). By 1987, Japan had caught up with the United States in per capita GDP. But Japan never caught up with the United States in GDP: the peak was in 1995, when Japan's GDP reached 72% of US GDP. After that, Japan's economy stagnated: the average GDP growth rate from 1995 to 2005 was only 1.11% per year. In 2005, Japan's GDP had fallen all the way to 37% of US GDP.

Comparing Japan during that period with China today, which stage in Fig. 14.1 is China at? Let's first look at per capita GDP. China's per capita

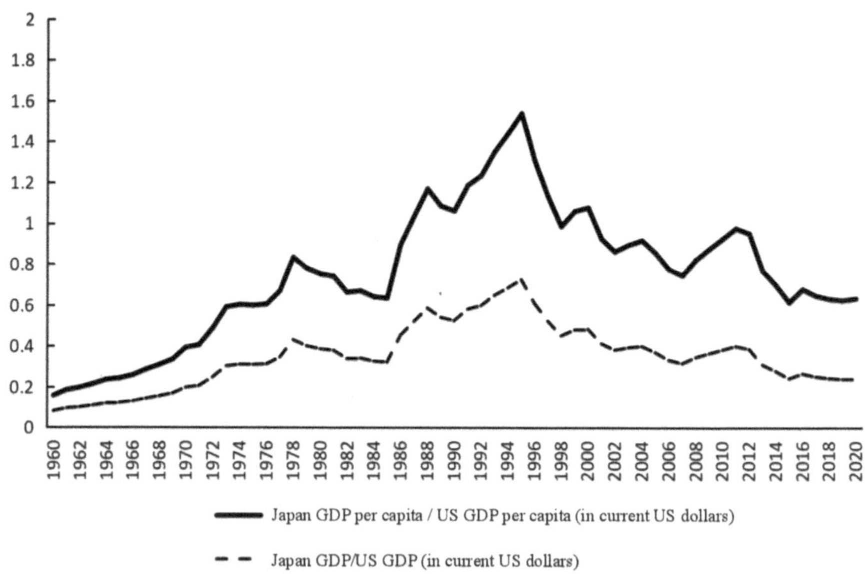

Fig. 14.1 Per capita GDP and GDP of Japan relative to the United States

[1] Data Source: *World Population Prospects* 2022, https://population.un.org/wpp/Download/, accessed on November 29, 2025.

GDP in 2022 was about 1/6 of US per capita GDP, so China today is equivalent to Japan in 1960 in terms of per capita GDP relative to the United States. Similar to Japan in the 1960s, the next ten years is expected to be a period of rapid growth for China. Even if China does not reach the average annual GDP growth rate of more than 8% that Japan saw from the 1960s to the 1980s, as long as China can maintain an average annual GDP growth rate of 5% over the next ten years, its per capita GDP should reach 1/4 of US per capita GDP by 2035, and catching up with US GDP should be an achievable goal.

In terms of nominal GDP relative to the United States, China today is comparable to Japan in 1995. China could face a Japan-type crisis in the next ten years. If it falls into a similar trap as Japan did from 1995 to 2020, the gap between China's GDP and US GDP could even widen in the next ten years, and catching up with the United States in GDP will be a daunting challenge.

Is China today more similar to Japan in 1960 or Japan in 1995? On the one hand, China's per capita GDP is only 1/6 that of the United States—similar to Japan in the 1960s—and there is still vast room for development. On the other hand, China's GDP has already surpassed 70% of US GDP—similar to Japan in 1995. The competition between China and the United States is becoming increasingly intense, with the United States doing all it can to suppress the development of China's high-tech industry and curb China's economic growth. Moreover, China's GDP has already reached 18% of world GDP, and it is increasingly difficult to expand China's share of the global market. We refer to the impact of per capita GDP development level as the "level effect" and the impact of the share of aggregate GDP in the world market as the "total volume effect." From the perspective of the level effect, China's economy still has the potential for high-speed growth, while the total volume effect suggests that the strategic goal of catching up with US GDP in 2035 will be a challenging one. China's economy is already a behemoth in the global economy and its growth space in the global market, especially the European and American markets, is being strongly squeezed. This will pose a challenge for China's continued rapid growth.

Our strategic policy recommendation is for China to promote the positive role of the level effect and minimize and, if possible, avoid the adverse total volume effect.

To avoid the adverse effect of the total volume effect, China should neither over-expand globally nor lose its base. We call this strategic policy: "Not Seeking Hegemony; Anchoring Asian Market." The strategic policy to promote the positive role of the level effect can be represented by "Anchoring Asian Market; Sharing for All."

The key is anchoring an Asian market, which refers to establishing an Asian Community of economies closely linked to the Chinese economy, with a total population of 2–2.5 billion, as discussed in Chapter 12. This can reduce the adverse total volume effect and help China to realize the GDP growth needed to achieve its strategic goal. In other words, China anchoring an Asian market is equivalent to establishing an Asian order!

China's ten-year strategy from 2025 to 2035 can be summarized as: "Not Seeking Hegemony; Anchoring Asian Market; Sharing for All." The following is a detailed discussion.

14.2 Not Seeking Hegemony

Competition between countries has similarities with competition between firms. The market structure of an industry is reflected by the market shares of the leading firms in the industry. Similarly, the structure of the world market is reflected by the market shares of the major countries. Since the Industrial Revolution, the United States and developed countries in Europe have become the dominant forces in the world market. The rise of emerging economies led by China will inevitably change the structure of the world market: the world market shares of developed economies such as the United States and the European Union will decline, and the world market share of emerging economies such as China will expand.

China's share of the world market (proxied by GDP) has reached 18%. Its further expansion will inevitably squeeze the market share of the developed countries and trigger intense competition among the major trading economies.

According to the innovation-market cycle in Chapter 2, the rise of China's share in the world market will lead to more profits, which feed into R&D investment and innovation, forming a virtuous cycle. The key question for China's strategy is the scale of the market it should seek to lead: the world market, the regional market, or just the domestic market? Our argument in this book is that China should seek to be the core, or anchor, of the regional (Asian) market. China should neither over-expand with a view to dominating the global market, nor should it allow itself to be cut off from the world market and retreat into its domestic market. Not being isolated means building an Asian market with China at its center. Not over-expanding means not seeking hegemony, or not trying to dominate the world, that is, not trying to replace the United States as the world hegemon and not seeking to co-govern the world with the United States.

14.2.1 Not Attempting to Replace US Hegemony

There are three reasons why China should not attempt to replace US hegemony: because it is not feasible, not beneficial, and not appropriate. It is not feasible because China's share of global GDP is not sufficiently large to dominate the world market. It is not beneficial to China because the cost of dominating the world market would exceed the benefits. And it is not appropriate because it would reduce world welfare.

Figure 14.2 is a schematic diagram showing China's welfare, US welfare, and world welfare under different assumptions about the scale of the market that China could lead (or dominate). The horizontal axis represents the size of the market led by China, measured by the ratio of China's GDP to world

GDP. The minimum market size is the Chinese domestic market, represented by x^0. In 2023, x^0 =16.9%. The middle point, represented by x^*, denotes a market size that includes the GDP of China plus East and Southeast Asia and other economies closely linked to China, which we collectively call "Asia."[2] The maximum market size would be the entire world market, represented by $\overline{x}$, where $\overline{x} = 1$. Welfare can be approximated as the benefit minus cost, or net gain, from a given market size. We postulate that the welfare curves of China and the world both reach their highest points at market size x^*, when China leads the "Asian" market, while the US welfare curve declines as the size of the market led by China increases.

It is not feasible for China to attempt to replace the United States as the new world hegemon. According to projections of the OECD, by 2060, the global economic landscape will be reshaped, with China leading as the world's largest economy, commanding approximately 26% of global GDP. India is expected to emerge as the second-largest economy with around 18% share, followed by the United States at 15%. The Eurozone-17 countries are projected to account for about 10% of world GDP, rounding out the top four economic powers.[3] According to our analysis of the five stages of US-China relations in Chapter 3, even under very favorable conditions, China's GDP will only be twice as much as that of the United States by 2060. Although

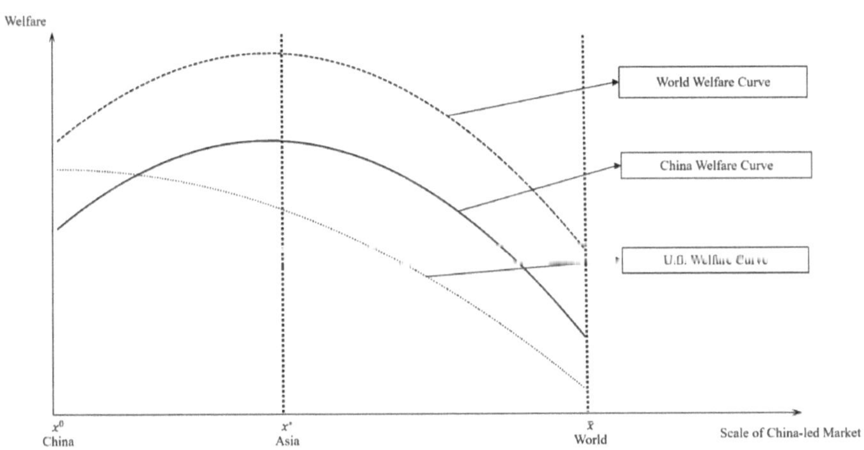

Fig. 14.2 Welfare curves and scale of China-led market

[2] We use "Asia" to represent the economies in Asia and other regions that are closely connected to the Chinese market. In 2019 when US-China trade war just began, the top 30 economies most reliant on trade with China were: Mongolia, Kyrgyzstan, Guinea, Iran, Australia, Armenia, Tajikistan, Laos, Venezuela, Chile, Peru, Brazil, Vietnam, Philippines, South Korea, Benin, Malaysia, Tanzania, New Zealand, Russia, Indonesia, Pakistan, Japan, Panama, Saudi Arabia, Kenya, Kazakhstan, Uzbekistan, Kuwait, and Malaysia.

[3] Data Source: https://www.oecd.org/en/data/indicators/real-gdp-long-term-forecast.html, accessed on November 17, 2024.

it will be the world's largest economy, China will not account for more than 30% of the world's GDP. Moreover, after 2060, the negative effects of China's declining population will gradually increase, and China's share of world GDP may also decline. For China to dominate the world market, it would need to unite with the other two major economies to achieve a share of the world market bigger than 50%. In other words, China would need to lead India and the European Union to dominate the world market, which is unrealistic.

The benefits of dominating the world market for China are less than the costs. Dominating the market brings benefits to the dominant country. As its market expands, scale returns will increase because average production costs will come down, and monopoly profits will also increase. In addition, product diversification could increase, and product quality could improve. All economies in the market will benefit from the increase in market scale, but the dominant country will get a larger share of the scale returns and monopoly profits. But the dominant country would also need to take the lead in governing the market. This includes providing input for the formulation and supervision of trade rules, the construction and maintenance of market infrastructure, and the maintenance and guarantee of market safety. Market order is a public good. Small economies have neither the power nor the incentive to set the rules of trade and are usually "price takers" in this regard. The dominant country has the responsibility to take the lead in setting the rules and must bear the attendant costs.

We can think of the scale returns of the market minus the cost of governing the market as the net benefits that a given market scale brings to the country—this is labeled as welfare in Fig. 14.2. When China tries to dominate a market larger than "Asia," the cost of establishing market order will rise sharply and exceed the benefits of scale returns. Therefore, in Fig. 14.2, China's welfare curve reaches its highest point at the market scale represented by x^* and then declines. In other words, the marginal benefit of China replacing the United States as the new world hegemon is less than the marginal cost. It's not worth it!

In Fig. 14.2, the world welfare curve also reaches its peak at x^*, when China leads the "Asian" market. The current world order is transitioning from US hegemony to a new world order of competitive coexistence of large trading economies. The United States is no longer able to dominate the world market, and the GVC has evolved into a tripod structure. As the size of the market led by China expands from China's domestic market to the "Asian" market, the world order should follow the structural changes of the GVC and global welfare should rise. However, if China goes beyond the "Asian" market and attempts to dominate the world market, the world order would become incompatible with the tripod structure of the GVC and global welfare would decline. For the sake of global welfare, China should not replace the United States as the new world hegemon.

14.2.2 Not Co-Governing the World with the United States

In 2005, C. Fred Bergsten proposed that the United States and China form a Group of Two (G2) to provide the global public goods that the world needed. The idea of the United States and China co-governing the world gained some traction in the Obama administration. The argument was that the United States and China are the world's two most important economies—the United States leads the developed economies and China leads the emerging market economies, and each group accounts for about half of world output—therefore the two countries should work together to lead the world order.

The purpose of the G2 would not be to change the US-led world order by creating a new governing entity to supplant existing multilateral organizations like the IMF and the WTO or international economic steering committees like the G20. Instead, its chief purpose would be to supplement the existing institutions—in other words, to have China help the United States to manage the world under the existing US-led system. This sounds like the convergence theory we discussed in Chapter 7, where China would bind its economic and financial systems to the United States.

This idea of a G2 is fundamentally flawed because it misses the transformation of China's economy, the phase changes in US-China relations, and the evolving interests of the two countries. In Chapter 3, we divided US-China relations into five stages, with 1979–2015 being the second stage of small country-big country relations. In this stage, the main goal of China's economic development was industrialization, characterized by the large-scale transfer of surplus rural labor to urban manufacturing centers. China and the United States complemented each other's advantages, and their economic interests were basically mutually consistent. The combination of US technology and capital and China's low-cost labor together promoted the rapid development of globalization. During that stage, China joining the US-led global economic order was in the interest of both parties. After 2016, however, China's GDP reached and surpassed 60% of US GDP, and the two countries entered the stage of great power competition. China has developed from an industrializing economy focused on manufacturing to a knowledge-based economy focused on technological innovation. Chinese high-tech companies are already competing with US high-tech companies in the global market.

When the Obama administration floated the idea of the G2 in 2010, US power was in decline after the 2008 global financial crisis and US-China interests were already beginning to shift from complementary to competitive. The perception in China was that the United States wanted to freeze US-China relations in the small country-big country stage by offering to cooperate with China to run the US-led world order. The Trump administration changed the US approach to China, initiating a trade war and accusing China of seeking international domination. The Biden administration largely continued Trump's trade policies although it focused more on restricting trade with China in a small group of strategic (high tech) industries under the so-called small yard, high fence approach. Trump's second-term China policy is confrontational and deal-driven, combining record-high tariffs, supply chain decoupling, investment restrictions, and AI deregulation with coercive corporate concessions, all under an "America First" approach that favors bilateral leverage over multilateral cooperation.

Four successive US administrations have had different approaches to China, but all with the same purpose: to suppress China's rise and maintain the leading global position of the United States. As discussed in Chapter 10, the G2 approach aims to make China fall into the chaser's trap where China specializes in manufacturing while the United States specializes in high tech, and experience a Japan-type crisis of growth stagnation, thereby destroying its hopes of catching up with the US economy by 2035.

After 2018, the fundamental misalignment of global economic fundamentals and the international financial system, that is, the mismatch between the tripod structure of the GVC and the dollar-dominated IMS, has intensified. This fundamental misalignment cannot be reconciled with the United States and China co-governing the world: either the United States continues to be the world hegemon and proceeds with de-Sinicization of the GVC, or the IMS moves from a unipolar to a multipolar system and the world order changes from US hegemony to the competitive coexistence of great powers. According to our analysis in Chapter 12, the United States choosing the de-Sinicization option and China choosing the limited counterattack option could be the Nash (competitive) equilibrium. US-China co-governance would essentially be the option of passive acceptance for China, but this is not China's optimal choice.

14.3 Anchoring Asian Market

In Fig. 14.2, China's welfare and world welfare both reach their peak when China leads the Asian market. Therefore, China's goal should be to serve as the core of a stable and prosperous market in Asia.

The United States can be expected to oppose this goal. As the size of the market led by China increases, what impact will it have on US welfare? Let's start with the situation where China only dominates its own domestic market. As China expands beyond its domestic market into Asia (that is, as we move rightward along the horizontal axis in Fig. 14.2), the US share of the Asian market will decrease, which will reduce US welfare. At the same time, the global market will become more diversified and competitive, which would be beneficial to all consumers (including American consumers), but we assume that this gain to American consumers does not outweigh the loss from the reduction in United States dominated market size. Of course, when the size of the market dominated by China expands beyond Asia to the whole world, the size of the market dominated by the United States falls even further. Therefore, Fig. 14.2 depicts US welfare as a downward-sloping curve. This means that an expansion of the China-led market to cover the Asian region would not align with the economic interests of the United States. Therefore, anchoring the Asian market will require China to succeed in the great power competition.

Anchoring the Asian market includes establishing an Asian governance system, ensuring technological security in the Asian market, and ensuring a stable Asian capital market. We discuss each of these in turn below.

14.3.1 Building an Asian Order

Establishing a system of trade governance for an Asian market of 2–2.5 billion people is the key to building a tripod global governance system. If China can anchor the Asian market, the tripod global economic structure of an Asian value chain centered on China, a North American value chain centered on the United States, and a European value chain centered on Germany will be stable. If China cannot, it will be left with only its domestic market, and eventually, it might not even be able to hold onto that. China will be shut out of international capital and technology flows dominated by the United States, and the global economic structure will return to a US-dominated structure. Therefore, the Asian market is the prize that China and the United States are battling for.

For China to be the anchor for the Asian market, it would need to establish an Asian order by developing the Asian Community discussed in Chapter 12. We envision that anchoring the Asian market would entail the following aspects. To begin with, China would need to take the lead in the formulation of the trade rules and governance system of the Asian Community. Governance of the Asian Community, that is, maintaining the Asian order, is a public good, and as the key member of the community, China should be responsible for initiating its construction. Related to this, China and other member countries should ensure an open Asian Community with voluntary entry and exit. Countries can apply to enter the community if they agree to abide by its rules, and members who violate the rules should exit. As the largest economy in the community, China should bear a commensurate responsibility for maintaining the stability and prosperity of the Asian Community. It should also lead the coordination of the Asian Community's economic relations with the rest of the world.

We can compare the strategy of anchoring an Asian market with building the Great Wall in China's history and with the implementation of the Monroe Doctrine in US history.

The Great Wall

Building an Asian Community and building the Great Wall both have similar purposes: to stabilize the social, economic, and military situation within a region, accumulate strength, and seek peaceful development in the region. But there are essential differences in strategic direction between the two.

The Asian Community is about openness, not isolation. The Great Wall was built to protect China from outside aggression. Building the Asian Community is not a defensive strategy like building the Great Wall, but rather an offensive strategy. Building an Asian Community is not meant to keep out specific countries or regions. Instead, it focuses on the construction of a system of governance for the market, for example, through the rules of trade and the entry and exit mechanism. The rules serve as a virtual wall that encircles the market, but the wall is not insurmountable. In fact, the Asian market transcends geographical Asia to include economies that are closely linked to China. For example, some Latin American, European, and African countries may be geographically far from China yet have close economic links to the Chinese market—they can also be members of the Asian market. The degree to which some countries and regions depend on the Chinese market can be expected to change over time. If an economy is highly dependent on the Chinese market, the benefits of joining the Asian Community will outweigh the perceived costs of abiding by its rules. Otherwise, it will exit or choose not to join. By allowing only economies that abide by the rules of the Asian Community to enter and making those that violate the rules exit, we have a stable governance system in the Asian Community.

The Great Wall was built partly with the purpose of enabling the emperor to consolidate his hegemony inside the walled region. But building the Asian Community has the purpose of not seeking hegemony. The purpose of building an Asian Community anchored by China is to build a tripod world governance system, and not for China to ultimately become the world hegemon. It is aimed at coexistence, not hegemony. As we discussed in the previous section, it is infeasible, unbeneficial, and inappropriate for China to replace the United States as the world hegemon. China's ultimate goal is to anchor a stable Asian order that will form part of the new world order of competitive coexistence.

The Monroe Doctrine

In 1823, US President James Monroe delineated two separate spheres of influence: the Americas and Europe. He asserted that the United States would not interfere in the internal affairs of European countries, nor would it allow European countries to interfere in the political affairs of the Americas. So, is China anchoring an Asian market an Asian version of the Monroe Doctrine? Does China want to claim Asia as its own sphere of influence and not allow interference from the United States and Europe? Of course not!

As explained earlier, the Asian Community or Asian market is not a geographical concept but more of an economic concept: it is a common market of economies closely connected with the Chinese market. For example, some African countries that are highly dependent on the Chinese market can be members of the Asian Community. Because China is the largest economy in this community, it inevitably bears the responsibility of providing public goods, specifically, the Asian order. The Monroe Doctrine, by contrast, advocated geographical division: it regarded the Americas as the backyard of the United States, and did not allow other world powers to interfere in it.

The Monroe Doctrine originated from the independence movement of the Spanish colonies in the Americas, but it later became a synonym for US interference in the sovereignty of Latin American countries. By contrast, the Asian order respects the sovereignty of all countries. The Monroe Doctrine sought to establish a regional hegemon by marking the Americas as the sphere of influence of the United States, essentially justifying US intervention in the internal affairs of Latin American countries. In the Asian Community, China would not interfere in the internal affairs of members. Countries decide for themselves whether to join the Asian Community and abide by the Asian order or not. If a member violates the Asian order, China would not instigate a coup or overthrow the government like the United States has done, but would only ask the member to withdraw from the Asian Community.

The original Monroe Doctrine opposed European colonialism in the Americas, which meshed with the goals of the Spanish colonies in Latin America seeking independence. At the time, the political system of the United States injected new choices into the international community, representing the direction of development of that era. However, later, especially after the United States dominated the world in the twentieth century, the Monroe Doctrine evolved into an ideological cudgel: during the Cold War, the Monroe Doctrine was invoked to prevent the spread of communism in Latin America. The Asian Community would encourage and respect the cultural and institutional diversity of all member economies and would not seek to export China's ideology.

Finally, the Monroe Doctrine was isolationist but the Asian Community would be open. As discussed above and in Chapter 8, the Asian Community would be one of the three legs in the tripod structure of the new global trade governance system (the other two being the USMCA and the European Union).

Before concluding this section, two points are worth highlighting. First, not seeking hegemony and anchoring Asian market are two sides of the same coin in the strategy of great power competition. If China is unable to anchor Asian market, then not seeking hegemony would likely lead to de-Sinicization of the GVC and the isolation and marginalization of China in world trade. Conversely, if China expands everywhere and all at once, competing with the United States for global dominance, it will not be able to build the soft and hard infrastructures needed to agree a stable set of trade rules even for Asia, let alone the world. Determining the proper size of the market that China can effectively anchor, that is, the scope of the Asian market, and establishing the Asian order in an effective manner is the soul of the current strategic stage! Second, anchoring an Asian market is not about defending cities or establishing geographical spheres of influence but about establishing stable market structures and trade rules in the global market, especially in the global market for ideas, data, and factors of production.

14.3.2 *Ensuring Technological Security in the Asian Market*

As the anchor of Asian market, China should foster innovation in the region and prevent over-reliance on foreign monopolies. To do so, it would need to establish a virtuous cycle of innovation, R&D, new products, and profits in the technology sector and enforce anti-monopoly policies to safeguard competition in the Asian technology market.

In the era of innovation, everyone is equal before the idea cloud: everything else being the same, everyone should have the same probability of being struck with a new idea. Concentrating all innovation resources in one company is not an efficient way to advance the technological frontier. However, as discussed in Chapter 13, concentration versus dispersion is a conundrum in the new (innovative) world. Concentration of market power is a matter of degree. Anti-monopoly policies aim to safeguard competition and prevent an over-concentration of market power. What would be considered an over-concentration of market power? The most extreme form of market power concentration is a monopoly. If there is only one company in a sector, there is no competition and the sector is over-concentrated. In general, an over-concentration of market power is undesirable and if a company's market share in any sector exceeds 50%, an anti-monopoly investigation should be initiated.

For important sectors such as large language models, online payments, social platforms, operating systems, search engines, railway transportation, power supply there should be at least two companies to maintain a minimum level of market competition. But what if the companies are foreign, that is, headquartered outside the Asian region? Suppose the Asian market relies primarily on one or two foreign companies for core technologies. For ease of exposition, we will refer to them as a foreign Big Tech monopoly. A foreign Big Tech monopoly is different from a garden-variety (domestic) monopoly. Foreign Big Tech monopolies are often government-supported. In great power competition, a strategic goal of the ruling power (the United States) is to suppress high-tech advancements in the rising power (China). Over-reliance on a foreign (US) Big Tech monopoly puts China's technological security at risk. China's government does not have jurisdiction over foreign Big Tech monopolies in their home countries and it cannot safeguard market competition by splitting the company.

Let's take smartphone operating systems as an example. Currently, the two main mobile operating systems are Google's Android system and Apple's iOS system, both from the United States. These two operating systems account for more than 95% of the global market. They also account for more than 95% of the Chinese market. Although the Android system has 80% of the market share in China, the competition between Android and iOS is fierce.

In 2019, the US government banned Huawei from using the Android system. In fact, the US government may at any time ban all Chinese mobile phones from using the Android and iOS systems. The immediate effect of this would be chaos in China's smartphone market. It is simply too big a risk to China's technological security for the government to allow over 95% of the mobile operating system market to be occupied by two US companies. China needs to encourage homegrown mobile operating systems and help them gain market share. Only when indigenous technology reaches a certain share of the market can China (and the Asian market more generally) have the ability to withstand a foreign technology blockade. We believe that 70% is an appropriate limit for the market share of foreign Big Tech monopolies in China, which means that foreign technology should not account for more than 70% of China's market.

Core technology is the most intense area of competition between the United States and China, which has been discussed in detail in several chapters of this book. In the rest of this section we consider three issues that have not been addressed elsewhere: Why didn't China restrict foreign Big Tech monopolies in the past and why should it do so now? How will restricting foreign Big Tech monopolies affect world welfare? And how should China restrict foreign Big Tech monopolies?

Why Didn't China Restrict Foreign Big Tech Monopolies in the Past and Why Do So Now?

Technological backwardness is the norm for developing countries. From 1978 to 2018, China was lagging in most core technologies, which were the domain of foreign (developed) countries. However, China's growth during that period was still rapid. So why does China need to change its policies now to limit foreign Big Tech monopolies? The answer is because China's stage of economic development and industry structure have changed.

From 1978 to 2018, China's economy was in the industrialization stage and manufacturing was the leading industry. A large amount of surplus labor was transferred from rural areas to urban manufacturing centers, which increased China's total factor productivity and led to its rapid economic development. China embraced the wave of globalization. Based on its comparative advantage in labor-intensive industries, China vigorously developed its processing and manufacturing industries, and encouraged the switch from agriculture to industry. At this stage, technological innovations in China mainly took the form of process innovations, technology transfer, and innovation by imitation rather than the invention of new technologies—China did not have the ability to compete with developed countries like the United States in the invention of original technologies.

After 2018, China's economy completed its industrialization phase and the era of surplus labor dividends ended. The Chinese economy has now moved to the innovation stage. The processing and manufacturing industry is no longer the dominant industry in the Chinese economy, which is now becoming a knowledge-based economy, focused on the high-tech industry and services. The increase in total factor productivity brought about by innovation and the continuous upgrading of high-tech industries are the main driving forces of China's economic growth. The Chinese economy now needs more indigenous innovations in new technologies and products, so it needs to foster a virtuous innovation-market cycle. This requires domestic companies to have a certain amount of market share in core technologies for sustainable development. Only by restricting the domestic market share of foreign Big Tech monopolies in core technologies can this goal of advancing indigenous technological innovations be achieved.

Is Restricting Foreign Big Tech Monopolies Good for the World?

China should restrict foreign Big Tech monopolies to protect its technological security. The United States and the European Union also use industrial policy to protect their industrial and national security. As mentioned in Chapter 9 and Chapter 10, the United States passed the CHIPS and Science Act and the Inflation Reduction Act in 2022 to support its own high-tech industries and reduce its dependence on China in batteries, chemical raw materials, and rare earth minerals. In his second term, the Trump administration has pursued a tech security strategy that couples rapid AI deregulation and heavy investment in data and cloud infrastructure with strict export controls on advanced semiconductors, bans on Chinese investment in key sectors, and supply chain realignment. In that sense, trade restrictions in the name of national, industrial, or technological security are not uncommon among the major global economies.

Will China's limits on foreign Big Tech monopolies diminish global scale returns and reduce the efficiency of global production? This question needs to be discussed from three angles.

The first is the balance between scale returns and variety. Increasing returns to scale means that the average cost of producing a product decreases with the scale of production, that is, the larger the quantity produced, the lower the cost of producing each unit or equivalently, the higher the production efficiency. Most high-tech products (especially software products) have increasing returns to scale. Because the larger the enterprise, the higher its production efficiency, left to market forces, the increasing returns enterprise will tend to keep growing until it owns the whole industry, becoming what is called a natural monopoly. However, although a global monopoly can achieve a high degree of production efficiency, it reduces the variety available since it is the sole supplier. For example, if Volkswagen's car production exhibits increasing returns to scale, will the world be better off driving only Volkswagen cars? Probably not, because research has shown that people prefer to have choices, like Toyota, Mercedes-Benz, et cetera.

The second is the balance between scale returns and industrial security. For example, the production of commercial aircraft exhibits increasing returns to scale. But is it optimal to have only one aircraft manufacturer in the world? Of course not. If Boeing is the only company supplying all the commercial aircraft in the world and there is a problem with Boeing's production, then there will be no new airplanes produced worldwide. But now, when Boeing has a problem, there is still Airbus. Therefore, for the safety of the global airline industry, we cannot rely on one large aircraft manufacturer.

The third is the balance between scale returns and innovation. Big Tech companies like Microsoft have monopolized the global computer operating system market since the 1990s, by buying out small businesses that come out with innovations that could potentially challenge its monopoly. Under the big tree, no grass grows! A large amount of academic research has shown that innovation relies on small and medium-sized enterprises, and monopolies hinder innovation. Besides, as discussed in Chapter 13, there cannot be a global monopoly on ideas. Restricting Big Tech monopolies, especially in cutting-edge products like brain chips, is also necessary for human development and security in the era of innovation.

How Should the Asian Community Counter Foreign Big Tech Monopolies?

The Asian Community should counter foreign Big Tech monopolies using anti-monopoly policies. Small countries, in general, are powerless against Big Tech monopolies, so only the governments of large economies like China, the United States, and the European Union have sufficient clout to implement anti-monopoly measures.

As emphasized in Chapter 10 and Chapter 13, it is necessary to cultivate indigenous technology. To do so, it is necessary to give indigenous technology a certain market share so that it can enter the virtuous innovation-market cycle described in Chapter 10. Therefore, a certain degree of trade protection is unavoidable to counter foreign Big Tech monopolies.

Let's take mobile phone operating systems as an example. Google's Android and Apple's iOS occupy more than 95% of the Asian Community market, so they can clearly be considered a foreign Big Tech monopoly. In 2019, the US government banned Huawei from using any hardware or software created by American companies, including Android. Not long after that, Huawei came out with its own mobile operating system, HarmonyOS. By early 2024, HarmonyOS had overtaken iOS to become the second-largest mobile operating system in China. Huawei's resilience and technological process are truly laudable, but the technological breakthrough of a single enterprise may not be sufficient to establish a virtuous innovation-market cycle in China and the Asian Community. Is there something that China's government can do to stimulate innovation and help more of its own high-tech companies achieve similar positive outcomes?

It can regulate the mobile phone sector (manufacturers and importers). The Asian Community could require that at least 30% of the mobile phones sold in the Asian market run on operating systems developed within the community. Mobile phone makers and importers that do not meet this requirement should be taxed and the tax rate would be higher the smaller the proportion of mobile phones they sell with indigenous operating systems installed. At the same time, manufacturers of mobile phones running on the indigenous operating system would be subsidized to ensure that they remain profitable.

Compared to the complete ban on China's 5G technology in the United States and its allies, a policy like the above to restrict foreign Big Tech monopolies is much softer. The United States demanded that China open its mobile phone market to provide market access for Apple and other US mobile phone makers, yet at the same time, it blocked China's ability to develop advanced chips, operating systems, and other technologies under the pretext of opposing "forced technology transfer" and protecting intellectual property rights. China and the Asian Community need to guard against such actions. If developed countries like the United States want market access to the Asian Community, they must allow their technology to enter the market as well.

14.3.3 *Ensuring a Stable Asian Capital Market*

A stable Asian market needs to avoid excessively volatile capital flows. Resolving the fundamental misalignment between the regionalization of the GVC and the dollar-dominated IMS requires the development of an Asian monetary system and the integration of the Asian capital market. In the process of building the European monetary system and integrating the European capital market, the German mark played the role of the regional core currency. Similarly, the process of making the renminbi the core currency in the Asian market needs to be accelerated. How can the renminbi become the core currency of the Asian market? First, it needs to be decoupled from the US dollar and float freely. Then currencies of other Asian economies that are pegged to the dollar should gradually switch to peg to the renminbi instead.

After the RMB/$ exchange rate "broke 7" in the second half of 2019, the PBOC withdrew from regular intervention in the foreign exchange market and the renminbi took substantial steps toward a market-determined floating exchange rate. In the second half of 2022, the renminbi appreciated vis-à-vis the dollar, putting pressure on China's exports. In 2023, however, the renminbi faced depreciation pressure. Should the PBOC intervene to stabilize the exchange rate? The free floating of the exchange rate is a necessary condition for the renminbi to serve as the core currency of the Asian market. The renminbi floating exchange rate system shouldn't be traded for short-term exchange rate stability.

As explained in Chapter 7, to guard against the dual risks of financial crisis and financial blockade, China should open up its external capital account while setting a fire wall to separate domestic financial risks from risks stemming from the dollar-dominated global financial market.

Why can't China just open up its capital account once the renminbi is freely floating, like other developed countries did after the Bretton Woods system collapsed in the 1970s? When developed countries such as France, Germany, Japan, and the United Kingdom floated their currencies and opened their capital accounts after the collapse of the Bretton Woods system, there was no competition among major currencies in the IMS. The competition between the US dollar and the renminbi in the IMS today is part of the great power competition between the two countries, like the competition in advanced semiconductors, where the United States is in a leading position. Research in the IMF and elsewhere has shown that unrestricted capital flows (a completely open capital account) have risks as well as benefits. Thus, allowing free capital flows without protection against excessive volatility is not an optimal choice for China. Financial development in China takes time and a fire wall against capital flow surges is needed for protection until the Chinese financial system catches up with the United States. As discussed in Chapter 11, a progressive tax on cross-border capital flows could serve as such a fire wall. When the renminbi is under extreme depreciation pressure, China can raise the capital outflow tax rate to curb capital flight and thus alleviate the depreciation pressure on the renminbi.

In summary, ensuring a stable Asian capital market does not involve building a Great Wall but rather actively formulating capital market rules to avoid risks from excessive capital flow volatility. The combination of a floating renminbi exchange rate and a progressive tax on cross-border capital flows would help to ensure a stable Asian capital market. China should take the initiative to open up its capital market responsibly and make a quantum leap in the internationalization of the renminbi.

14.4 Sharing for All

China's healthy and rapid economic growth will drive global economic growth, including that of the United States. Therefore, China's strategic goal to achieve an average annual GDP growth rate of about 5% over the next ten years is consistent with the improvement of welfare for people worldwide. As China's per capita GDP gradually approaches that of the United States, China's economic size (GDP) will be twice that of the United States around 2060. The world order of hegemonic succession will end and a new world order of competitive coexistence will arrive.

China's strategy is to share the fruits of its long-term growth with the people of all countries in the world.

- It would be the world's largest consumer market. With the healthy growth of China's economy, the size of China's consumer market will quickly surpass that of the United States, becoming the most important source of profit for global enterprises.

- It would (continue to) be the world's largest manufacturing country, a position it has held since 2010. China is expected to maintain its position as the world's largest, most resilient, and most efficient manufacturing country for the foreseeable future, with positive implications for the safe and efficient operation of the GVC.
- It would be the world's largest source of and destination for capital flows. China is the country with the most savings and largest net capital exports (current account surplus) in the world. In 2022, its outward foreign direct investment was $146.5 billion, among the top three in the world, and its inward foreign direct investment was $189.1 billion, second only to the United States. China's capital market, once opened, will be an important source of and destination for global investment.

As the anchor of the Asian Community, China will provide public goods to the world, including a stable tripod world order, combating climate change, and reining in global technology monopolies. In the era of global innovation, the creation and sharing of ideas, knowledge, and scientific and technological findings is paramount. China's achievements in scientific research, innovation, and higher education already rank either first or close to first in the world. As noted in Chapter 13, in 2022, China's R&D investment reached $457.7 billion (second only to the United States); it had the highest number of patent applications and grants in the world; and it published more scientific and technological papers than any other country in the world. In 2022, China had 3013 universities (the third largest number in the world) with 46.55 million students (the largest number in the world).

We discussed the three conundrums of the innovative world in Chapter 13 and concluded that neither centralized innovation + public ownership + imitation, nor decentralized innovation + private ownership + creation is a stable and efficient innovation mechanism for the long term. A good innovation system strikes a balance in each of the three conundrums, with different emphases at different times.

After World War II, the United States became the center of global scientific research and higher education. Students from all over the world flocked to the United States for postgraduate education, conducted R&D in American universities, research institutions, and companies, and spread the results of their technological innovations to the world. At the same time, the United States also established technological hegemony and obtained high monopoly rents based on these innovations.

The US system relies on decentralized innovation, private ownership, and independent innovation. It does not recognize that ideas and knowledge, as the source of innovation, are essentially public goods nor that the breakthrough technological achievements of great scientists are built on the efforts of countless other scientific researchers that came before them, that innovation is essentially a collective effort. The US scientific research and higher education system encourages individual freedom but ignores the disproportionate accumulation of monopoly rents by Big Tech companies. This system has given the United States technological hegemony over the world, and the power to reap monopoly rents in the world market and contain technological advancement in other countries.

This will not be China's approach. The Scripture of Ethics says: "The way of heaven benefits but does not harm; the way of the sage acts but does not contend." Innovation in the new world has four essential requirements: it has the participation of all humankind; the results are shared by all humankind; it promotes world development; and humanity is sublimated in innovative activities. The American innovation system may meet the first requirement but it does not meet the other three. China should bring a co-creation, sharing, common development, and common sublimation innovation and education system to the new world.

14.5 Conclusion

Let me turn back the clock to February 19, 2000, the fifteenth day of the first month of the Year of the Dragon in the Chinese calendar. In Norman, Oklahoma, the outlook for the new millennium that I had started writing on the first day of the new century had finally come to the conclusion part. I spread out the manuscript on the wooden table under the walnut tree in my backyard. The afternoon sun shone through the branches and remaining walnuts, casting a golden glow on the leaves at my feet. The neighbor's dog was still barking cheerfully in bursts. Outside the yard, a few cows on the Oklahoma prairie were leisurely swishing their tails, and the large hammerhead of the nodding donkey was swinging rhythmically.

What is the ideal of humanity in the new world? What are the basic principles of the new world? Thinking about these questions, the distant sky seemed to surge with a continuous sound pressing on my head.

The ideal of humanity is, of course: "*A Fulfilling Life, A Harmonious World.*"

The basic principles of the new world need to balance the conundrums of dispersion versus concentration, private versus public, creation versus imitation. Individual progress can be represented by "*Self-reliance, Strive for Improvement.*" Social progress can be represented by: "*Learn from Each Other, Progress Together.*"

The innovation of the new world is the common innovation of humanity. The sublimation of humanity is manifested in the continuous understanding and mastery of the laws of the world and the operation of the idea cloud, so the social ideal of the new world can be represented by: "*Rule by Law, Dao Returns to the People.*"

Innovation and development in the new world originate from ideas. The distribution function of the idea cloud is stable, so the development path of the new world can be represented by the words: "*True and Reliable.*"

Dark clouds gradually blocked the afternoon sun, and the sound from west of the Pacific on the TV intersected with the dark clouds east of the Pacific above my head. The clouds were getting denser and heavier, and the wind was rising! I buried my head and wrote quickly:

> On our constantly rotating planet, the East and the West have always been relative. The east of the East is the West, and the west of the West is the East. After two thousand years of baptism by blood and fire, the West of believing in God but ignoring heaven and the earth, and the East of delving into heaven and the earth but forgetting the people, meets again in this vast sky and sea. The natural law revealed by more than 730,000 sunrises and sunsets is: the east of losing the West will lose the way to tomorrow, and the west of losing the East will be endless darkness.
>
> If the East and the West fight, there will be no winners; if the East and the West unite, they will form a complete world.
>
> Wiping off the gunpowder on your body, washing off the blood on your face, along with the European Union, the North American Free Trade Agreement, the Asian Community and other large and small, crisscrossed, rugged roads, we help each other, crawling, and finally arriving at the gate of the New World.
>
> On the left of the gate is written: "***Self-reliance, Strive for Improvement***"
>
> On the right of the gate is written: "***Learn from Each Other, Progress Together***"
>
> Across the gate is written: "***Rule by Law, Dao Returns to the People***"
>
> Behind the gate, the "***True and Reliable***" path leads to the ideal world in the far distance. The rising sun, the flag of the ideal world, flutters in the wind, vaguely visible. It reads:
>
> "***A Fulfilling Life, A Harmonious World***"

Appendix: Summary of Chapters

Chapter 1: Why Do Trade Conflicts Occur?

Beginning with an introduction to the book's theme: rationality and coexistence, this book uses a rational approach to analyze the competitive coexistence of great powers.

As Arrow's impossibility theorem shows that social preferences do not exist, we cannot establish a globally optimal benchmark for conflicting national interests. Consequently, our rational analytical framework explains "what is and why", not "what should be". That is, we take a positive approach, rather than a normative approach of the analysis. Our concept of competitive coexistence also goes beyond the traditional thinking of the world order characterized by hegemonic succession over thousands of years.

International trade conflicts arise when countries have competing overall, long-term, and/or specific, short-term national interests. An analytical framework for the overall, long-term conflicts of interest between countries is provided by the three principles of international trade disputes established in this chapter.

The first principle is the classic principle of comparative advantage, which explains how countries benefit from free trade: when countries export goods that have a relatively lower opportunity cost for them to produce and import goods that have a relatively higher opportunity cost, the efficiency of resource allocation across borders improves.

The second principle is the principle of international monopoly profits: in international trade activities, a country that holds a dominant position in the world market can use this advantage to advance its overall interests (obtain the most gains from trade) at the expense of its trading partners.

The third principle is the principle of growth trap of specialization solidification: even in the ideal perfect competitive market, free trade may make wages and the returns to capital of poor countries and rich countries converge in the long-run. For poor countries, this means that because of their

J. Ju, *US-China Great Power Competition and The New World Order*,
https://doi.org/10.1007/978-981-95-3762-4

comparative advantage, they will be trapped forever producing and exporting labor-intensive goods to, and importing capital-intensive goods from, rich countries. The efforts by poor countries to escape the growth trap caused by specialization can lead to trade conflicts with rich countries.

While the first principle explains how the global output pie can be enlarged through the international specialization, the second and third principles explain the conflicting national interests in dividing the global output pie.

Chapter 2: How Do Economies Grow?

A country's long-term and overall interests are typically represented by the long-term growth of its GDP. Classic growth theory identifies innovation as the most crucial driver of economic growth. Chapter 2 proposes micro- and intermediate-perspectives of economic growth. In terms of micro-perspective, we propose the "Dual-Wheel Drive Model" of economic growth, where a country invests in research and development (R&D) to generate technological innovations, and when the products of innovation are sold at sufficient scale, they earn profits to support more R&D, promoting more innovation, and so on—the larger the market scale, the greater the profits, and the faster the economic growth. In terms of intermediate perspective, this leads to our "growth theorem", which states that a necessary and sufficient condition for an economy to maintain long-run growth is the continuous upgrading of its industrial structure.

We divide the history of globalization into four stages, marked by different forms of global dominance by the hegemon(s) of the period: the era of global discovery (1500–1819), marked by global dominance of trade; the era of global trade (1820–1978), marked by global dominance of production; the era of global production (1979–2018), marked by global dominance of innovation; and the era of global innovation (starting in 2019), where this pattern of hegemonic succession should come to an end.

Chapter 3: How Do Great Powers Compete?

Great power competition refers to competition between the world's current most powerful country (the ruling power) and the country that is catching up to it (the rising power). Chapter 3 defines "six fields, three elements, five stages" of great power competition. The competition is for leadership in six key fields: manufacturing, GDP, technology, finance, military power, and global governance. The relationship between the two countries is determined by three elements: the relative strength of the two countries, their political and cultural identity, and third-party effects. Based on this, we delineate five stages in the relationship between China and the United States: confrontation (1949–1978), small country-big country (1979–2016), great power competition I (2017–2035), great power competition II (2035–2060), and competitive coexistence (starting from 2060).

Once the total manufacturing output of the rising power surpasses that of the ruling power and the former's GDP reaches 60% of the latter's, the two countries are considered to enter the stage of great power competition. China and the United States entered this stage in 2016. In stage I, China's main goal is to catch up with US GDP around 2035. In stage II, China aims to catch up with US leadership in the remaining four fields (technology, finance, military power, and global governance) around 2060.

Some forecasts indicate that in 2060, the world's top four economies will be China, India, the United States, and the European Union, each with a global share of GDP about 29%, 18%, 16%, and 16%, respectively. After 2060, since the global share of the largest economy, China, will be far less than 50%, the world order of hegemonic succession since 1500 is likely to end, and the world order will enter a new stage of competitive coexistence among great powers.

Chapter 4: Analysis of the US-China Tariff War

Chapter 4 picks up again on the reasons for international trade conflicts, using the Stolper-Samuelson theorem to explain competing specific national interests, and the optimal tariff theory and the Hicks theorem to explain competing short-term national interests. Competing goals driven by specific interest groups could lead to trade conflicts between countries: according to the Stolper-Samuelson theorem, free trade creates winners and losers in a country, and this can lead to a backlash against trade openness if there is no system for the winners to compensate the losers. In some instances, policies that are in a country's own national interests may harm other countries in the short term, leading to trade conflicts: when a country's tariff policy or technology policy improves its terms of trade (that is, increases the price of its exports relative to the price of its imports), its own welfare improves in the short term at the expense of its trading partners.

The US-China trade war was initiated in March 2018 by the Trump administration, which accused China of inhibiting US access to its market, worsening the US trade deficit, forcing US enterprises to transfer technology, and essentially undermining US manufacturing, services, and innovation. Our analysis reveals that these reasons do not hold water. The real reasons for the US-China trade war are competing long-term/overall and short-term/specific interests of the two countries, as clearly suggested by trade policies targeting China's high-tech sector in the Biden administration's 2022 CHIPS and Science Act and Inflation Reduction Act.

Chapter 5: Mirror Tactics: How to Avoid Confrontation?

The Biden administration's approach to China has been characterized as "competitive when it should be, collaborative when it can be, and adversarial when it must be." China's goal is to avoid confrontation and strive for cooperation.

Chapter 5 draws on game theory and China's historical experience to discuss the mirror tactics. The first principle is that "If others do not offend me, I will not offend them; if others offend me, I will certainly offend them," which reflects the opponent's actions like a mirror image. The second principle is that "You fight your way; I fight my way."

A simple game theory analysis shows that, given the choice of two actions, confront or cooperate, if a country can credibly commit to adopt the mirror tactic against another country, the result is a Nash equilibrium that avoids confrontation and realizes cooperation between the two. The EU-China trade dispute over photovoltaics and wine is an example of how the mirror tactics successfully averted a tariff war.

However, the mirror tactics did not prevent the US-China trade war from escalating. This is partly due to the US ability to exercise long-arm jurisdiction over non-US multinational corporations—an important weapon that only the United States, as the global hegemon, can wield against countries that do not act in alignment with its foreign policy interests. Because of the conflict involving long-term and overall interests, the US-China dispute requires not only the selection of the optimal strategy at the tactical level, but also the formulation of the strategic competition based on the strength.

Chapter 6: Tripod: Structural Changes in the Global Value Chain

The root cause of US-China great power competition is the fundamental misalignment between the global economic fundamentals and the global superstructure, that is, the international monetary system and the global governance system built on these fundamentals. Chapter 6 discusses structural changes in the global economic fundamentals, that is, the global production, consumption, and trade networks commonly referred to as the global value chain (GVC). The structure of the GVC has changed from bipolar in 2000, with the United States and Germany as regional centers, to a tripod in 2019, with China, Germany, and the United States as regional centers of the Asian, European, and North American value chains, respectively. The Asian and North American value chains have a "hub-and-spoke" pattern with China and the United States as the respective hubs, while the European value chain has a "multi-country cooperation" pattern.

Chapter 7: Fundamental Misalignment in the International Monetary System

The first component of the global superstructure is the international monetary system (IMS). Chapter 7 explains the fundamental misalignment between the structure of the global economic fundamentals (or GVC) and the IMS. While the structure of the GVC is now a tripod with Asia, Europe, and North America as the three legs, the IMS is still a unipolar system dominated by the US dollar. This is partly due to inertia caused by strong network externalities of using the dollar. But the United States is also loath to give up the benefits it enjoys from the international dominance of the dollar, specifically, the ability to collect international seigniorage (that is, gaining revenue from printing money while passing the inflation cost to the rest of the world) and to impose crippling financial sanctions on other countries.

To resolve the mismatch between the tripod GVC and the unipolar IMS, China could be forced to either converge to the US-led economic and financial system or decouple from it altogether. But a better solution would be to establish a tripod IMS supported by the renminbi, the euro, and the US dollar, that matches the structure of the global economic fundamentals.

Chapter 8: Fundamental Misalignment in the World Order

The second component of the global superstructure is the global governance system, or the world order. Chapter 8 explains the fundamental misalignment between the structure of the global economic fundamentals and the global governance system. While the structure of the GVC is now a tripod with Asia, Europe, and North America as the three legs, the global governance system is still led by the United States alone. The United States has been dominating the world order since the end of World War II, as evidenced by its de jure and de facto power in international governance organizations such as the International Monetary Fund and the World Trade Organization.

As globalization enters the era of global innovation, the core public goods that the world needs have changed, and so should the nature of global governance. Hegemonic succession should come to an end, to be replaced by competitive coexistence of great powers. The new world order can have two layers: a global layer, comprising global governance institutions to handle multilateral issues; and a tripod regional layer, comprising regional governance institutions to handle regional issues such as trade and investment rules. This two-layer tripod global governance system will better align with the tripod GVC and the putative tripod IMS.

Chapter 9: What Determines the Future of US-China Great Power Competition?

Success or failure in great power competition can be measured by long-term GDP growth: the winner achieves higher growth along the optimal path, while loser suffers stagnation or even negative growth along the crisis path. Chapter 9 develops the Growth-Crisis Model to analyze possible paths and outcomes of the great power competition between China (the rising power) and the United States (the ruling power). There are four possible outcomes: the win–win equilibrium where both countries realize their optimal GDP growth rates; the win-lose equilibrium, where the United States achieves its optimal growth rate while China falls into a crisis; the lose-win equilibrium, where China realizes its optimal growth rate and the United States falls into a crisis; and the lose-lose equilibrium, where both countries fall into a crisis.

As the rising power, China may face various types of crises, including Japan-type, Soviet-type, public policy, financial, social, or regional security crisis. As the ruling power, the United States may also face various types of crises, including social crisis, cultural crisis, financial crisis, constitutional crisis, public policy crisis, and regional security crisis. The US-China trade war can be seen as the US attempt to instigate a Japan-type crisis in China. If China successfully avoids such a crisis, there is still a possibility that the United States would provoke a regional security crisis in China. For China and the United States to avoid a large-scale military conflict and achieve a peacefully transition to the new world order, China needs to maintain healthy economic growth, establish the convertibility of the renminbi and promote its use as an international currency, and build up its military power to rival that of the United States.

According to these three conditions, a probability of war between US and China in their great power competition is calculated at the end of this chapter.

Chapter 10: Technological Competition: The Leader's Dilemma and the Chaser's Trap

Chapter 10 discusses US-China competition in the field of technology. There are two types of technological innovation: incremental innovation, achieved through iterative updates of existing technologies; and disruptive innovation, where the new technology supplants the old technology. Competition in incremental innovation is an R&D investment race, where the lagger is at a disadvantage and may fall into the chaser's trap. Competition in disruptive innovation is a choice between the new technology and the old one, where the leader in the old technology faces a greater opportunity cost of switching to the new technology (the leader's dilemma) while the lagger has the opportunity to leapfrog ahead.

Artificial intelligence and non-fossil energy are two major areas of technological competition between the United States and China. The former is characterized by incremental innovation, while the latter is characterized by disruptive innovation. The United States is currently ahead in the field of artificial intelligence, but faces the leader's dilemma in the field of non-fossil energy; China is currently ahead in the field of non-fossil energy, but may fall into the chaser's trap in the field of artificial intelligence or be pushed into it by US policies to contain its technological progress at every stage of the innovation-market cycle. The key to escaping the chaser's trap is government intervention to stimulate the development of indigenous core technologies and to create market demands for them.

Chapter 11: International Financial Competition

Chapter 11 discusses US-China competition in the field of international finance. Because of the dominant position of the dollar internationally, US monetary policy can create negative spillovers on the rest of the world in the form of global inflation and capital flow surges, and US foreign policy can exploit the advantage to impose crippling financial sanctions on other countries. China's objective is to protect itself from the risks of a financial crisis and a financial blockade by the United States.

To protect itself from financial sanctions, China needs to accelerate the internationalization of the renminbi and the opening of its capital account. To forestall a financial crisis, China needs to manage cross-border capital flows. We propose two policies to get around this dilemma. The first is to construct a firewall for capital flows in the form of a progressive tax with a rate that starts at zero and increases with the size of the transaction—this would allow free cross-border capital flows under normal circumstances, but would effectively suppress cross-border capital flows under abnormal circumstances, thus preventing capital flight from triggering a financial crisis. The second is to promote the adoption of the central bank digital currency (CBDC), the e-yuan, and the development of a CBDC cross-border payment platform. As CBDCs become more widespread around the world, this disruptive financial innovation could weaken the US dollar's grip on the IMS and the power of US financial sanctions.

Chapter 12: Competition in the Global Governance System

Chapter 12 discusses US-China competition in the field of global governance, specifically, global trade governance. The international organization that maintains the global rules of trade is the World Trade Organization (WTO). But the WTO's fundamental principles of non-discrimination, fair competition, trade liberalization, and transparency are being eroded and the organization is failing to perform some of its key functions.

Existing in parallel with the WTO are regional trade arrangements (RTAs) like the European Union and the United States-Mexico-Canada Agreement (USMCA), which define the rules of trade for Europe and North America, respectively. But trade governance in Asia is currently fragmented. Key RTAs encompassing Asia–Pacific countries are the Regional Comprehensive Economic Partnership (RCEP), of which China is a member, and the Comprehensive and Progressive Agreement for Trans-Pacific Partnership (CPTPP), of which China is not (yet) a member.

In its competition with China for global trade governance, the United States could form strategic alliances through RTAs to isolate China. The best response for China is to build an Asian Community of economies in East and Southeast Asia and around the world with which it has close economic links, based on the WTO principles of trade. The Asian Community would first focus on technology market liberalization, gradually develop into a common market, and ultimately establish the trade governance system for Asia, becoming the third leg (along with the European Union and the USMCA) in the tripod global governance system.

The construction principle of the "Asian" community is "market for rules", unilateral liberalization of the Chinese market in exchange for compliance with WTO rules by the community members. The construction path is unilateral liberalization, bilateral negotiation, easy before difficult, and orderly entry.

Chapter 13: The Innovative World

A new millennium marks the beginning of a new world. What essentially distinguishes the driving forces of the development in the old and new worlds is the difference in the dominant factors of production. Over the past 10,000 years of human history, it was physical capital, land, machines, and plants that determined social development and distribution. However, since the 1990s, human capital, knowledge and technology have gradually replaced physical capital as the dominant forces in social development and distribution.

Chapter 13 introduces the Innovative World Model, which describes the process of innovation as four stages: generating ideas; transforming ideas into knowledge and technology; using technology to improve productivity; and realizing value from the innovation.

The innovation process consists of two cycles: the first one is the cycle between the innovator and the idea cloud, and the second one is the cycle between the innovator, the R&D organization and the market. Within the first cycle, the innovator randomly draws ideas from the idea cloud, and new ideas generated by the innovator are fed back to the idea cloud and become part of it. For the second cycle, when the innovator obtains new ideas of a certain quality, they combine labor, capital, and other intermediate inputs to engage in R&D activities, innovate and produce new technologies. The higher the quality of the new idea, the better the new technology created. The new technology realizes profits in the market, a part of which is reinvested into R&D to continue the next stage of innovation.

The accumulative set of all ideas from all people since the dawn of mankind forms part of the idea cloud. An idea cloud is characterized in this chapter by five hypotheses: the quality of ideas obeys a Pareto distribution; the quality distribution of ideas is regionalized; the quality distribution of ideas has historical dependence; ideas have the property of public goods, and the evolution of ideas is objective and subjective.

There are three conundrums in the innovative world. The first is whether innovation should be centralized (government-led) or decentralized (market-led). The second is whether innovations should be publicly or privately owned. The third is whether innovations should be created independently (building core technologies from scratch) or by imitation (building on existing core technologies). A good innovation system strikes a balance in each of these three conundrums, with varying emphases at different times.

The emergence of so-called Big Tech monopolies is one characteristic of the innovative world. While this is inevitable given the increasing returns to scale in key industries, it could be dangerous for state or market monopolies to control data, technology, and potentially even ideas.

Guaranteeing equality for all people before the "idea cloud" lies at the heart of the new world's challenge. A tripod structure, two layers system of world governance provides a foundation for addressing this key challenge.

Chapter 14: China's Competition Strategy for the Next Ten Years (2025–2035)

Chapter 14 synthesizes all the preceding chapters and presents China's competition strategy for the next ten years. The goal for China is to achieve average GDP growth of 5% per year over the next ten years in order to catch up with US GDP by 2035. Such a goal is both challenging and realistic. On the one hand, China's GDP has reached 18% of the world's GDP. The competition among the great powers has entered a stalemate, so that it has become more and more difficult to increase China's share in the world market, which is called "total volume effect". On the other hand, China's GDP per capita is only 1/6 of that of the United States, which still has a huge space for development, which is called the "level effect". The former represents the challenge of the strategic goal; the latter represents the realizability. China's strategic approach is to minimize and avoid the negative effects of the "total volume effect," and promote the positive effects of the "level effect".

In the US-China great power competition, China's approach can be summarized as: "Not Seeking Hegemony; Anchoring Asian Market; Sharing for All."

China will not attempt to replace the United States as the world hegemon, nor does it want to help the United States to manage the world. Instead, China should anchor a regional market—an Asian Community of 2–2.5 billion people—and establish the regional economic order based on WTO principles, ensure regional technological security, and safeguard regional capital market stability. Within the Asian Community, it is envisioned that all will participate in and benefit from the creation and sharing of knowledge and technology.

Kolibri 360 GmbH
Ferdinand-Jühlke-Straße 7
99095 Erfurt, Deutschland
produktsicherheit@kolibri360.de